THE GILCREASE-HARGRETT CATALOGUE OF IMPRINTS

UNIVERSITY OF OKLAHOMA PRESS : NORMAN

In cooperation with
Thomas Gilcrease Institute of American History and Art : Tulsa

The

GILCREASE-HARGRETT CATALOGUE *of* IMPRINTS

COMPILED BY

Lester Hargrett

PREPARED FOR PUBLICATION
AND WITH AN INTRODUCTION BY

G. P. Edwards

FOREWORD BY

John C. Ewers

ALSO BY LESTER HARGRETT

A Bibliography of the Constitutions and Laws of the American Indians (Cambridge, Mass., 1947)
Oklahoma Imprints, 1835–1890 (New York, 1951)

LIBRARY OF CONGRESS CATALOGING IN PUBLICATION DATA

Thomas Gilcrease Institute of American History and Art, Tulsa, Okla. Library
The Gilcrease-Hargrett catalogue of imprints.

1. Indians of North America—Bibliography. 2. Five Civilized Tribes—Bibliography. 3. The West—History—Bibliography. I. Hargrett, Lester, 1902–1962, comp. II. Title.

Z1209.2.U5T48 016.9703 72–859

ISBN 0–8061–1020–1

 Composed and printed at Norman, Oklahoma, U.S.A., by the University of Oklahoma Press. First edition.

The Library of the Gilcrease Institute
expresses its gratitude
to
the late HOPE HOLWAY
and to
CLARE KERR
for their devoted services

FOREWORD

Since World War II the study of American Indian history has attracted a growing number of able scholars. There has emerged a new and challenging field of ethnohistory, to which both historians and anthropologists are making contributions. This same period has witnessed the passing of Indians who possessed lively memories of tribal life before the early decades of the present century. Consequently, anthropologists, traditionally committed to fieldwork among living Indians, have become increasingly dependent upon the examination and interpretation of documents for their understanding of Indian life as it was lived as recently as the last quarter of the nineteenth century.

Locating rare or unique copies of printed sources which throw light upon the history of the tribe or tribes he wishes to study, and upon those Indians' varied relations with other Indians and with non-Indians, has posed problems for the ethnohistorian. The late Thomas Gilcrease, of Tulsa, Oklahoma, rendered an invaluable service to scholars by assembling in one large collection thousands of rare published documents relating to more than forty-five Indian tribes of North America. These items range from broadsides to first editions of early books about Indians. They include contemporary accounts of Indian trade, missions, hostilities, and removals. Many items concern federal or state negotiations with Indians, treaties, and laws relating to Indians and their lands. Equally significant, although less well known, are the many legal documents pertaining to tribal governments and claims. Some of the rarest items are early examples of printing in the various Indian languages.

Thomas Gilcrease was himself of Creek Indian descent, and so it is not surprising that this collection is especially rich in documents relating to the Five Civilized Tribes—the Cherokees, Chickasaws, Choctaws, Creeks, and Seminoles. More than one thousand items concern these tribes—their early residence in the Southeast, their removal and resettlement in the West, their participation in the Civil War, and aspects of their more recent history.

This catalogue of published documents in the Gilcrease Collection, preserved in the institution that bears his name, should provide further encouragement for studies in Indian history. It should also help bring about a better and more accurate understanding of American Indians among all literate peoples.

Arlington, Virginia
January 26, 1972

John C. Ewers

INTRODUCTION

The Thomas Gilcrease Institute of American History and Art Library contains a notable collection of materials about the country west of the Mississippi, recording the historical events of the region in great detail, as well as the broader picture. The collection contains about sixty thousand books, manuscripts, maps, pamphlets, and broadsides describing the exploration and settlement of the trans-Mississippi West and the indigenous American Indian tribes and the papers of well-known Indian leaders, such as John Ross and Peter Pitchlynn.

Thomas Gilcrease was a remarkable man. His interests were diversified: he not only collected an extraordinary library but also gathered an equally fascinating art and archaeology collection. He was born in Robeline, Louisiana, in 1890. His father was Scotch-Irish, and his mother was one-fourth Creek Indian. When he was only a few months old, the family moved to what was then Indian Territory to take advantage of Mrs. Gilcrease's rights as a Creek citizen. In 1899 each member of the family received an allotment of 160 acres of land in the Creek Nation. Thomas Gilcrease, registered on the final roll of Creek citizens by blood, received a tract lying near the heart of what was soon to become the first major oil-producing field in Indian Territory, Glenn Pool, southwest of Tulsa.

With his early oil earnings Gilcrease attended Bacone Indian College, near Muskogee, Oklahoma, and then briefly attended a state college in Emporia, Kansas. Soon, however, he was busy trading in oil leases, drilling wells, and accumulating the fortune that provided him the means to pursue his interest in American history. Beginning in 1925, he made many trips to Europe to educate himself in art, architecture, and history. While in Europe he observed in museums, art galleries, and libraries rich showcases of history and reconstructions of earlier cultures. He realized that Oklahoma had no museum or library—nothing to show of the civilizations of the Americas before Columbus, the development of the Southwest, or the story of the Indians. Gilcrease began to form his collection. In his efforts his business acumen and reticence served him well.

The purpose of *The Gilcrease-Hargrett Catalogue of Imprints* is to make known to historians and to the general public some of the resources of the Gilcrease Institute of American History and Art Library. The catalogue is an annotated bibliography of printed materials pertaining to the American Indian. Most of the items deal with the Five Civilized Tribes of Oklahoma, but there is also a broad range of western Americana, both Indian and white, most of it published in the nineteenth century. There are also listings of maps, newspapers, and government documents. Some of the entries in the catalogue are well known and available in other collections, but others, such as *The President's Proclamation of Pardon and Amnesty in the Cherokee Language,* printed in 1863, is the only known copy. A goodly number of items are listed for the first time in this book, and many others are excessively rare. This catalogue is by no means a complete list of the holdings of printed matter in the Institute's library. It does, however, give the reader a very good idea of the main thrust of the Gilcrease Library collection.

The Gilcrease Library has published two earlier books dealing with the library's other holdings. In 1962, Clevy Strout, of the University of Tulsa, compiled the *Catalog of Hispanic Documents*, a listing of the extensive collection of Hispanic manuscripts. *A Guidebook to Manuscripts*, prepared for publication by Mrs. H. H. Keene, of the library staff, was published in 1969. For the first time it made available to the scholar a complete record of the manuscripts at Gilcrease. This, the third publication, concerns the materials that Thomas Gilcrease purchased from Lester Hargrett in 1946.

Lester Hargrett was born in Tifton, Georgia, on May 30, 1902, and received his degree from the University of Georgia, where he was elected to Phi Beta Kappa. He had a deep and lasting interest in the history of the American Indians, especially the Indians of the Southeast and the Southwest. To the subject he brought scholarship of a high order and exceptional skill in bibliographical work. For many years he was the only scholar in his field of study. From 1935 to 1947 he resided in Washington, D.C., where he carried on his historical and bibliographical work, and during those years he carefully collected printed and manuscript materials relating to the American Indian. In time his collection became the largest and most valuable in the country.

Besides this catalogue Hargrett compiled two other bibliographies: *A Bibliography of the Constitutions and Laws of the American Indians* (Harvard University Press, 1947), and *Oklahoma Imprints, 1835–1890* (Bibliographical Society of America, 1951). Both of these books were significant contributions to American historical scholarship and are generally regarded as models of this kind of literature. In 1946, Hargrett's outstanding collection of printed Indian materials was purchased by Gilcrease, and it became the nucleus of the Gilcrease Library. From 1947 to 1949, Hargrett served as the second director of the Institute. After leaving the Institute, he moved to Tallahassee, Florida. He died there in February, 1962.

The arrangement of this catalogue is in Hargrett's original form, a chronological listing of items by subject. Because of the overlapping of subjects, it is suggested that the reader consult the table of contents to gain an understanding of the format. The index provides a detailed guide to the contents.

In 1955 the Gilcrease collections were placed under the control of the city of Tulsa and successive curators, with the result that there has been a certain amount of dislocation in the library. The transition from private library to institutional one has made it impossible to locate all the items, though Gilcrease personally saw every one of them. I found it desirable to include all the entries because of their value as bibliographical notes. An asterisk at the end of the entry indicates that the item has not been located.

The comments by Hargrett at the end of each entry were accurate in 1946, when he compiled the catalogue; but with the passing of time many private collections have been broken up, and the holdings of public institutions have increased. Some of

Hargrett's comments are undoubtedly out of date, but I think it important that we not lose sight of the value of the bibliographical information he provided.

In forming his collection, Thomas Gilcrease set very high standards, which will become apparent as the reader uses the catalogue. It was his desire that the results of his collecting would benefit the interested general reader, as well as the professional researcher.

Tulsa, Oklahoma
January 1, 1972

G. P. Edwards
Curator of History
Library of the Gilcrease Institute

CONTENTS

ILLUSTRATIONS

THE GILCREASE-HARGRETT CATALOGUE OF IMPRINTS

ABENAKI INDIANS

1866

MAURAULT, J. A.

Histoire des Abenakis, depuis 1605 jusqu'a nos jours. Par l'Abbe J. A. Maurault. Imprime a l'Atelier Typographique de la "Gazette de Sorel." 1866.*

[1], iii, x, [1], 631, [9] p. 20 cm.

ARAPAHOE INDIANS

1883

COLBY, L. W.

Juan Jose Herrera vs. The United States and Arapahoe Indians. Defendants' Request for Findings of Fact. Objections to Findings of Fact requested by Claimant. Brief and Argument of Counsel for the Defense. [Washington, 1883.]*

17 p. 23 cm. Wrapper title.

An interesting claim for the value of mules, horses, and oxen stolen from Herrera by Arapahoe Indians in Wyoming in 1870.

1899

SANFORD, D. A., tr.

Tune: Missionary Hymn. [Bridgeport, Okla. 1899?]

Broadside. 19.5 cm.

A hymn translated into the Arapahoe language. Excessively rare.

ARIZONA INDIANS

1863

CARLETON, JAMES H.

Head Quarters Department of New Mexico, Santa Fe, N.M., October 23, 1863. General Orders No. 27. [Santa Fe, 1863.]

Broadsheet. 20 cm.

Establishment of the Military District of Northern Arizona, and provision for protection from Indians of the hordes of miners flocking to the gold fields recently discovered near the San Francisco Mountains. Unrecorded, and the only known copy.

1865

Acts, Resolutions and Memorials adopted by the First Legislative Assembly of the Territory of Arizona. Prescott: Office of the Arizona Miner, 1865.

79 p. 21.5 cm.

This and subsequent entries comprise an unbroken run of the rare and important acts and resolutions of the first ten sessions of the Arizona Legislative Assembly, or, in other words, for the first fourteen years of Arizona territorial history, a period marked by constant Indian hostilities, raids, and depredations. The set, together with the journals of the first four sessions, here present, constitutes an incomparable source of authoritative historical information.

Head-Qrs. Dist. of the Upper Arkansas, Fort Riley, Kansas, July 25th, 1865. General Orders No. 31. [Fort Riley, 1865.]

Broadside. 20 cm.

An order prohibiting "all trade, intercourse and interviews" with the Apaches, Arapahoes, Cheyennes, Comanches, and Kiowas.

Head-Qrs. Dist. of the Upper Arkansas, Fort Riley, Kansas, August 18th, 1865. [Fort Riley, 1865.]

[3] p. 20 cm. Caption title.

Articles of agreement entered into with the chiefs and headmen of the Apache, Comanche, and Kiowa tribes. Highly important and excessively rare.

Journals of the First Legislative Assembly of the Territory of Arizona. Prescott: Office of the Arizona Miner, 1865.

250, xviii p. 22.5 cm.

1866

Acts, Resolutions and Memorials adopted by the Second Legislative Assembly of the Territory of Arizona. Prescott: Office of the Arizona Miner, 1866.

98 p. 21.5 cm.

Journals of the Second Legislative Assembly of the Territory of Arizona. Prescott: Office of the Arizona Miner, 1866.

258 p. 22.5 cm.

1867

Acts, Resolutions and Memorials adopted by the Third Legislative Assembly of the Territory of Arizona. Prescott: Office of the Arizona Miner, 1867.

72 p. 21.5 cm.

Journals of the Third Legislative Assembly of the Territory of Arizona. Prescott: Office of the Arizona Miner, 1867.

267, [2] p. 22.5 cm.

1868

Acts, Resolutions and Memorials adopted by the Fourth Legislative Assembly of the Territory of Arizona. Prescott: Office of the Arizona Miner, 1868.

74 p. 22.5 cm.

Journals of the Fourth Legislative Assembly of the Territory of Arizona. Prescott: Office of the Arizona Miner, 1868.

261, [2] p. 22 cm.

1869

Acts, Resolutions and Memorials adopted by the Fifth Legislative Assembly of the Territory of Arizona. Tucson: Tucson Publishing Co., 1869.

71 p. 22 cm.

1871

Acts, Resolutions and Memorials adopted by the Sixth Legislative Assembly of the Territory of Arizona. Tucson: Office of the Arizona Citizen, 1871.

144 p. 22.5 cm.

1873

Acts, Resolutions and Memorials adopted by the Seventh Legislative Assembly of the Territory of Arizona. Tucson: Office of the Arizona Citizen, 1873.

177 p. 22.5 cm.

1875

Acts, Resolutions and Memorials adopted by the Eighth Legislative Assembly of the Territory of Arizona. Tucson: Office of the Arizona Citizen, 1875.

238 p. 22 cm.

1877

Acts, Resolutions and Memorials of the Ninth Legislative Assembly of the Territory of Arizona. Tucson: Office of the Arizona Citizen, 1877.

xiii, 132 p. 22.5 cm.

1879

Acts, Resolutions and Memorials of the Tenth Legislative Assembly of the Territory of Arizona. Prescott: Office of the Arizona Miner, 1879.

xiv, 160 p. 20.5 cm. Errata slip.

1879

Willcox, O. B.

Annual Report of Colonel O. B. Willcox, Twelfth Infantry, Brevet Major General (assigned), commanding Department of Arizona, for 1878–79. Whipple Barracks, Prescott, 1879.

9 p. 20 cm.

Important notices of Indian hostilities. The volume is rare.

1882

Willcox, O. B.

Annual Report of Bvt. Maj.-Gen. O. B. Willcox, commanding the Department of Arizona. For the year 1881–82. Office of the Assistant Adjutant General. Whipple Barracks, Prescott, A.T., 1882.*

17 p. 20 cm.

Rare and important.

WILLCOX, O. B.

[Report. Prescott, 1882.]

10 p. 21 cm. Blueprint map.

With Appendix C [14 p.], and Appendix D [10 p.]

The report is devoted to a narrative by Major J. W. Mason of a visit to the Hualpai Indians and to correspondence about their disposition. Appendix C consists of lively and important narratives of operations against the Chiricahuas. Appendix D is devoted to a narrative by Major A. W. Evans of his pursuit of and skirmishes with the San Carlos renegades.

1883

CROOK, GEORGE

Annual Report of Brigadier General George Crook, U.S. Army, commanding Department of Arizona. 1883. [Prescott, 1883.]

43 p. 19.5 cm. Wrapper title.

Rare and important.

1886

CLEVELAND, GROVER

Message of the President of the United States communicated to the Two Houses of Congress at the Beginning of the Second Session of the Forty-ninth Congress. Washington, 1886.*

39 p. Folio. Printed wrappers.

With the signature on the wrapper of E. Pitchlynn, the Choctaw.

The message touches upon the growing Indian problem, the Apache prisoners at St. Augustine, and the intrusions upon Indian lands.

CROOK, GEORGE

[Report of his operations against the hostile Chiricahuas. Fort Bowie, A.T., 1886.]*

82 p. 20 cm. Printed without title page or caption.

Excessively rare.

CROOK, GEORGE

Resume of Operations against Apache Indians, 1882 to 1886. By Brigadier Gen'l. George Crook, U.S. Army. 1886. [Omaha, 1886.]

25 p. 20 cm. Wrapper title.

A very rare volume.

1887

Letter from the Secretary of War transmitting Correspondence with General Miles relative to the Surrender of Geronimo. [Washington, 1887.]

77 p. 23 cm. Caption title.

1890

Letter from the Secretary of War transmitting Correspondence regarding the Apache Indians. [Washington, 1890.]

18 p. 23 cm. Caption title.

Letter from the Secretary of War transmitting Reports relative to the Treatment of certain Apache Indians. [Washington, 1890.]

53 p. 23 cm. Caption title.

1894

MESERVE, CHARLES F.

A Tour of Observation among Indians and Indian Schools in Arizona, New Mexico, Oklahoma, and Kansas. By Charles F. Meserve. Philadelphia, 1894.

43 p. 23 cm. Printed wrappers.

1905

WIGGLESWORTH, A. M.

Hospital of the Good Shepherd. A Hospital and Christian Mission for the Navajo Indians. [Chilocco, Okla.: Indian Print Shop, 1905.]

[8] p. 13 cm. Photographs.

1914

ALLIOT, HECTOR

Bibliography of Arizona, being the Record of Literature collected by Joseph Amasa Munk, and donated by him to the Southwest Museum of Los Angeles, California. Los Angeles, 1914.

431 p. 23.5 cm.
An indispensable bibliography.

WEBER, ANSELM

The Navajo Indians. A Statement of Facts. By Rev. Anselm Weber, O.F.M., St. Michaels, Arizona. [N.p., 1914.]*

29 p. 23 cm.

1931

HAURY, EMIL W., and LYNDON L. HARGRAVE

Recently dated Pueblo Ruins in Arizona. Washington, 1931.*

120 p. 24.5 cm. Printed wrappers. Plates.

1934

Report of Southern Arizona Indian Conference held at Phoenix, Arizona, March 15–16, 1934, for the Purpose of Explaining the Howard-Wheeler Bill to the Assembled Indians. Phoenix, Arizona: Phoenix Indian School Print Shop, [1934].*

33 p. 23.5 cm.

ARKANSAS

1800

TATHAM, WILLIAM

Communications concerning the Agriculture and Commerce of America: containing Observations on the Commerce of Spain with her American Colonies in Time of War. Written by a Spanish Gentleman in Philadelphia, this present year, 1800.

With sundry other papers concerning the Spanish Interests. Edited in London by William Tatham. London: J. Ridgway, 1800.

120 p. 21 cm.

Contains a highly interesting "Account of the Country of Ouachita." Excessively rare.

1821

NUTTALL, THOMAS

A Journal of Travels into the Arkansas Territory during the year 1819. With Occasional Observations on the Manners of the Aborigines. Philadelphia: Thos. H. Palmer, 1821.

xii, 9–296 p. 21.5 cm. Map, plates.
Field 1145.

1830

Acts passed at the Sixth Session of the General Assembly of the Territory of Arkansas. Little Rock: William E. Woodruff, 1830.

137, [4] p. 19.5 cm. Uncut and unopened.

1834

Acts passed at the eighth session of the General Assembly of the Territory of Arkansas. Little Rock: William E. Woodruff, 1834.

119, iii p. 19.5 cm.

1842

Report in relation to Depots established in Arkansas, by C. A. Harris, for Emigrating Indians. [Washington, 1842.]*

10 p. 24 cm. Caption title.

1851

Charter of the Arkansas Central Rail Road Company. [Little Rock, 1851.]

4 p. 32.5 cm. Caption title.

The development of a railroad system in Arkansas exercised a profound influence upon Indian Territory. No other copy seems to be recorded.

1855

CONWAY, ELIAS N.

Governor's Message. [Little Rock, 1855.]

16 p. 21 cm. Caption title.

1861

Convention Act, passed both Houses of the General Assembly on the 14th day of January, 1861. [Little Rock, 1861.]

Broadside. Folio.

Preparations for secession. Two issues. Of the highest rarity.

An Ordinance and Resolutions recommended by a Conference Committee and passed by the State Convention on Wednesday March 20th, 1861. [Little Rock, 1861.]

Broadside. Folio.

Call for an election on the question of secession. Excessively rare.

Resolutions passed by the Convention of the People of Arkansas on the 20th day of March, 1861. [Little Rock, 1861.]*

Broadside. Folio.

Resolutions urging secession. Excessively rare.

True Democrat Bulletin. Telegraphs by the Memphis & Little Rock Line. Little Rock, September 20, 1861. [Little Rock, 1861.]*

Broadside. 29 cm.

Contains a proclamation by General Ben McCulloch, deeply affecting the war course of the Indian Territory tribes. The only known copy.

1867

Du Val, E. R.

Cholera as it appeared in Fort Smith, Arkansas, in the Fall of 1866: with a Few Thoughts upon the Nature of the Disease, and its Treatment. By E. R. Duval, M.D. Fort Smith, Ark.: Herald Printing Establishment, John F. Wheeler, Printer, 1867. [See page 10.]

7 p. 21 cm. Wrapper title.

The epidemic struck Indian Territory as well; apparently it followed the course of the Arkansas River. One of only two known copies.

1868

Hot Springs Case. William H. Gaines, et al., vs. John C. Hale; and Henry M. Rector vs. John C. Hale. Cross-appeals from Hot Spring Circuit Court in Chancery. Little Rock: Gazette Office, Woodruff & Blocher, [1868].

58 p. 22.5 cm.

The mass of evidence presented in the trial of this case, and found in this and the following two volumes, comprises an important source of information about the Quapaws, who once occupied and hunted over the Hot Springs vicinity, and about other early Indian visitors to Hot Springs. The only known copy.

1870

Pike, Albert, and Robert W. Johnson

Henry M. Rector vs. The United States. Claim of Title to the Hot Springs of the Ouachita. Washington: Cunningham & McIntosh, [1870].*

117, 46 p. 24 cm. Uncut.

1871

William H. Gaines et al. vs. John C. Hale and Henry M. Rector. Transcript of Record. [Washington, 1871.]*

v, 671 p. 22.5 cm. Wrapper title.

1874

Parker, I. C.

Indian Appropriations. Speech of Hon. Isaac C. Parker, of Missouri, in the House of Representatives, April 29, 1874. Washington, 1874.*

21 p. 21.5 cm.

Parker later attained celebrity as the Fort Smith "hanging judge."

CHOLERA

AS IT APPEARED IN

FORT SMITH, ARKANSAS,

IN THE FALL OF

1866;

WITH

A few thoughts upon the Nature of the Disease, and its Treatment.

BY

E. R. DUVAL, M. D.

FORT SMITH, ARK.

HERALD PRINTING ESTABLISHMENT, GARRISON AVENUE,

JOHN F. WHEELER, BOOK AND JOB PRINTER.

1867.

1885

Du Val, Ben. T.

Address of Ben. T. Du Val, at the Opening of the Sixth Annual Fair of Western Arkansas, October 13, 1885, at Fair Ground near Fort Smith, Arkansas. Fort Smith: Weekly Elevator Office Print, 1885.

16 p. 23 cm. Wrapper title.

With incidental notice of Fort Smith's Indian neighbors. Very scarce.

1886

Dawes, Anna L.

A United States Prison. [Philadelphia, 1886.]*

4 p. 23.5 cm. Caption title.

A sorry picture of the horrors to which Indian Territory prisoners were subjected in the federal prison at Fort Smith.

1889

History of Benton, Washington, Carroll, Madison, Crawford, Franklin, and Sebastian Counties, Arkansas. From the Earliest Time to the Present, including a Department devoted to the Preservation of Sundry Personal, Business, Professional and Private Records; besides a Valuable Fund of Notes, Original Observations, etc. etc. Illustrated. Chicago: Goodspeed Publishing Co., 1889.

1382 p. 25 cm.

Contains much incidental Indian history. The volume is scarce.

1890

Letter from the Attorney-General in response to a Resolution of the 2d instant, with reference to the Practice of the United States Courts at Fort Smith, Ark., and Paris, Texas, in the Appointment of Commissioners for the Investigation of Offenses committed in the Indian Territory. [Washington, 1890.]*

5 p. 23 cm. Caption title.

Parker, I. C.

Memorial Address of Judge I. C. Parker. Delivered at the Decoration of the Graves of the Dead Union Soldiers at the National Cemetery, Fort Smith, Ark. May 30, 1890. Fort Smith: J. H. Mayers & Co., [1890].

23 p. 26 cm. Wrapper title.

An address by the terror of Indian and frontier evildoers.

1895

Pope, William F.

Early Days in Arkansas. Being for the most part the Personal Recollections of an Old Settler. By Judge William F. Pope. Arranged and edited by his Son, Dunbar H. Pope. With an Introduction by Hon. Sam W. Williams, of the Little Rock bar. Little Rock: Allsopp, 1895.

330 p. 19.5 cm. Frontisp. port. and plates.

Interesting references to Indian emigrants journeying across the territory.

1898

HARMAN, S. W., and C. P. STERNS

Hell on the Border; He Hanged Eighty-Eight Men. A History of the Great United States Criminal Court at Fort Smith, Arkansas, and of Crime and Criminals in the Indian Territory, and the Trial and Punishment thereof before His Honor Judge Isaac C. Parker, "The Terror of the Law-Breakers." Fort Smith: Phoenix Publishing Company, [1898].

xiii, 720 p. 22 cm. Printed wrappers. Photographs.

A fine copy of this classic, in a protective case.

1921

LANGFORD, ELLA MOLLOY

Johnson County, Arkansas. The First Hundred Years. Clarksville, Arkansas: Sallis, Threadgill & Sallis, Printers, 1921.

210 p. 22.5 cm. Photographs.

Early Cherokee emigrants from the South settled in what became Johnson County before 1820.

1940

ENO, CLARA B.

Historic Places in Arkansas. Compiled by Miss Clara B. Eno. [Van Buren, 1940.]

111, [2] p. 23 cm. Printed wrappers.

CADDO INDIANS

1841

Caddo Indian Treaty. Testimony taken under a commission from the Committee on Indian Affairs. [Washington, 1841.]

48 p. 25.5 cm. Caption title.

Important testimony on the treaty's negotiation.

1852

Seventh Annual Report of the Missionary Society of the Methodist Episcopal Church, South. Louisville, Ky.: Morton & Griswold, 1852.*

175 p. 20.5 cm.

The reports on Indian Territory missions include a hitherto entirely overlooked narrative of a journey by J. E. Robinson to the Caddo village on the Washita River. The narrative possesses high historical and ethnological value.

CALIFORNIA INDIANS

1850

The Statutes of California, passed at the First Session of the Legislature. Begun the 15th Day of Dec. 1849, and ended the 22d Day of April, 1850, at the City of Pueblo de San Jose. With an Appendix and Index. San Jose: J. Winchester, 1850.

ix, 482 p. 25 cm.

Contains the important laws "for the Government and Protection of Indians." A rare volume.

1853

Letter from the Secretary of the Interior communicating the Report of Edward F. Beale, Superintendent of Indian Affairs in California respecting the Condition of Indian Affairs in that State. [Washington, 1853.]
18 p. 25 cm. Caption title. Uncut and unopened.

1873

Ames, John G.

Report of Special Agent John G. Ames, in regard to the Condition of the Mission Indians of California. With Recommendations. [Washington, 1873.]
15 p. 23 cm. Printed wrappers.

1875

Wetmore, Charles A.

Report of Chas. A. Wetmore, Special U.S. Commissioner of Mission Indians of Southern California. Washington, 1875.
17 p. 23 cm. Wrapper title.

1876

Vandever, William

Mission Indians of California. Report of William Vandever, United States Indian Inspector. [San Francisco? 1876.]
8 p. 23 cm. Printed wrappers.

1886

Painter, C. C.

A Visit to the Mission Indians of Southern California, and other Western Tribes. Philadelphia, 1886.
29 p. 23 cm. Printed wrappers.

1902

Holmes, William Henry

Anthropological Studies in California. Washington, 1902.*
Pp. 155–84. 24.5 cm. Printed wrappers. Many plates.

1934

Harrington, John P.

A New Original Version of Boscana's Historical Account of the San Juan Capistrano Indians of Southern California. Washington, 1934.*
62 p. 24.5 cm. Printed wrappers. Plates.
A presentation copy, inscribed by Dr. Harrington.

CATAWBA INDIANS

1803

Minutes of the Charleston Baptist Association, convened at Ebenezer, Jeffer's Creek, November 5th, 1803. [Charleston, 1803.]
10 p. 21 cm. Caption title.
Contains a notice of the mission to the Catawba Indians. There is very little contemporary material on this obscure tribe. The pamphlet is excessively rare.

THE BIG FOUR

Brand Book

CONTAINING

Nearly all the Brands West of the 100th Meridian to the Foot Hills on all Four Rivers: Arkansas, Cimarron, Beaver, and Canadian Rivers and their Tributaries, Covering the Parts of Five States: Kansas, Colorado, Oklahoma Territory, Texas and New Mexico.

FOR THE SPRING WORK OF

1897.

These Brands were all Gathered New in the Year 1896.

EAR-MARK.

Left  Right

---

Published by C. V. SHEPLER, 614 Charlotte St.,
KANSAS CITY, MO.

Press of HUDSON-KIMBERLY PUB. CO.

CATTLE BRANDS

1883

Southwestern Brand Book! containing the Marks and Brands! of the Cattle and Horse Raisers of Southwestern Kansas, the Indian Territory and the Panhandle of Texas. For the Round-up of 1883. Published by Medicine Lodge Cresset: Barbour County Index: 1883.

84 p. 16 cm.

Not recorded in the Union Catalog, and no other copy traced.

1897

The Big Four Brand Book, containing nearly All the Brands West of the 100th Meridian to the Foot Hills of the Four Rivers: Arkansas, Cimarron, Beaver, and Canadian Rivers and their Tributaries; covering the Parts of Five States: Kansas, Colorado, Oklahoma Territory, Texas and New Mexico. For the Spring Work of 1897. These Brands were all Gathered New in the Year 1896. Published by C. V. Shepler, 614 Charles St., Kansas City, Mo. Press of Hudson-Kimberly Pub. Co. [See page 14.]

iv, 117, [1] p. 16 cm.

Not recorded in the Union Catalog.

CAYUGA INDIANS

1876

Hawley, Charles

Jesuit Missions among the Cayugas, from 1656 to 1684. Auburn, N.Y., 1876.

42 p. 23 cm. Printed wrappers.

CHEROKEE INDIANS

1698

The Two Charters granted by King Charles IId. to the Proprietors of Carolina. With the First and Last Fundamental Constitutions of that Colony. London: Richard Parker, [1698.] [See page 16.]

60 p. 20 cm.

The earliest extension of English law over the Cherokee and other southern tribes. The volume is excessively rare.

1765

Timberlake, Henry

The Memoirs of Lieut. Henry Timberlake (who accompanied the Three Cherokee Indians to England in the year 1762) containing whatever he observed Remarkable, or worthy of Public Notice, during his Travels to and from that Nation; wherein the Country, Government, Genius, and Customs of the Inhabitants are Authentically Described. Also, the Principal Occurrences during their Residence in London. Illustrated with an Accurate Map of their Over-hill Settlement, and a Curious Secret Journal, taken by the Indians out of the Pocket of a Frenchman they had killed. London: Printed for the Author, 1765.

viii, 160 p. 20 cm. Map.

A very fine copy.

THE TWO

CHARTERS

Granted by

King *CHARLES* IId.

TO THE

PROPRIETORS

OF

CAROLINA.

With the First and Last

FUNDAMENTAL CONSTITUTIONS

OF THAT

COLONY.

LONDON:

Printed, and are to be Sold by *Richard Parker*, at the *Unicorn*, under the *Piazza* of the *Royal Exchange*.

1813

Aldridge, J.

An Interesting Narrative of the Life of John Marrant (a Man of Colour), containing an Account of his Birth, Extraordinary Conversion, and Remarkable Success among the Cherokee Indians, his Arrival in England, and Departure as a Missionary to America. Compiled originally by the Rev. J. Aldridge, late Minister of Jewry-street Meeting, London. A New Edition. Brighton: T. Sharp, 1813.

27, [1] p. 17 cm.

Rare.

1814

North Carolina General Assembly

[Memorial asking the construction of a road "from Waynesville in Haywood County, through the lands of the Cherokee Indians to the United Road leading from Tennessee to Augusta in Georgia." Raleigh, 1815.]

Broadside. Folio.

Unrecorded, and no other copy known.

1815

Aldridge, J.

A Narrative of the Life of John Marrant, of New York, in North America: giving an Account of his Conversion when only fourteen years of age; his leaving his Mother's House from Religious Motives, wandering several days in the Desert without Food, and being at last taken by an Indian Hunter among the Cherokees, where he was Condemned to Die. Leeds: Davies & Co., 1815.*

24 p. 20 cm.

Perhaps rarer than the 1813 edition.

1816

North Carolina House of Commons

[Memorial for the purchase of Cherokee lands in North Carolina. Raleigh, 1816.]

Broadside. 25 cm.

Unrecorded, and the only known copy.

Worcester, Samuel

Salem, December 21, 1816. To Mr. Elias Cornelius, Very Dear Sir. [Salem, Massachusetts, 1816.]

Broadside. 25 cm.

A letter enlisting the support of Elias Cornelius in raising funds for the American Board's mission to the Cherokees. The only known copy.

1818

Reflections on the Institutions of the Cherokee Indians, from Observations made during a recent Visit to that Tribe: In a Letter from a Gentleman of Virginia to Robert Walsh, Jun. June 1st, 1817. [In The Analectic Magazine, Philadelphia, No. 67, Vol. 12, July 1818.]*

The account runs to twenty pages. It has been uniformly overlooked by investigators.

1819

Catharine Brown, the Converted Cherokee: a Missionary Drama, founded on Fact. Written by a Lady. New Haven: S. Converse, 1819.

27 p. 19 cm.

Rare.

Memoirs of Henry Obookiah, a Native of Owhyee, and a Member of the Foreign Mission School; who died at Cornwall, Conn. Feb. 17, 1818, aged 26 years. New Haven: Nathan Whiting, 1819. [See page 18.]

129, 40, 32, 8, 6 p. 14 cm.

Considerable historical information on the famous mission school which trained, among others, the Cherokee leaders Elias Boudinot and John Ridge.

1821

Cornelius, Elias

The Little Osage Captive, an Authentic Narrative. To which are added some Interesting Letters written by Indians. York, 1821.

184 p. 14 cm. Plates.

Field 368; Newberry-Ayer 53.

The little Osage captive was rescued by missionaries from the Cherokees and given the name of Lydia Carter.

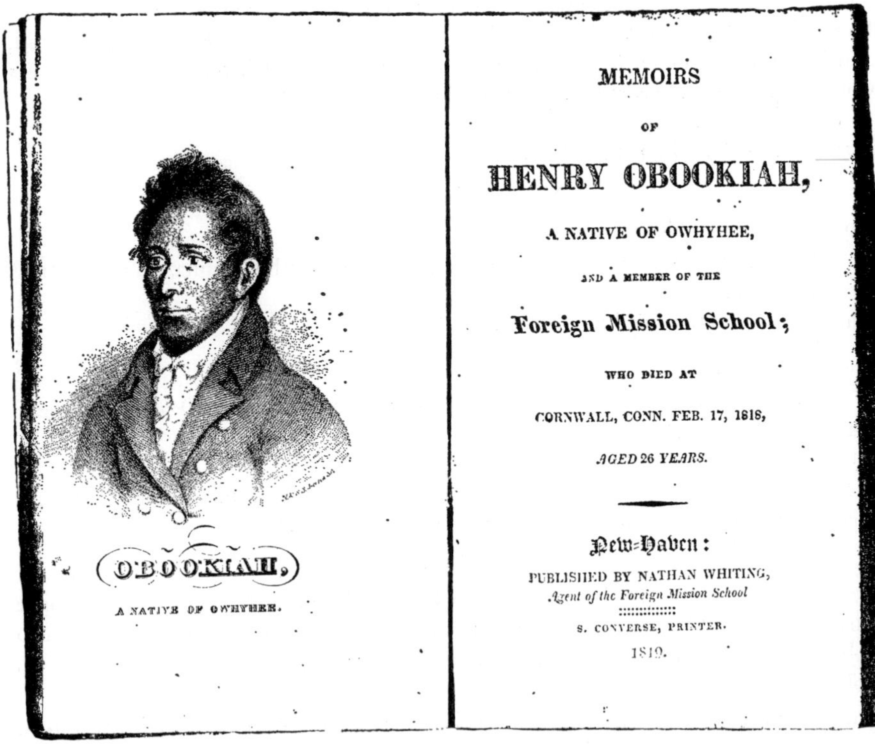
OBOOKIAH,
A NATIVE OF OWHYHEE.
MEMOIRS
OF
HENRY OBOOKIAH,
A NATIVE OF OWHYHEE,
AND A MEMBER OF THE
Foreign Mission School;
WHO DIED AT
CORNWALL, CONN. FEB. 17, 1818,
AGED 26 YEARS.
New-Haven:
PUBLISHED BY NATHAN WHITING,
Agent of the Foreign Mission School
S. CONVERSE, PRINTER.
1819.

1822

Cornelius, Elias

The Little Osage Captive, an Authentic Narrative. Boston: Armstrong and Crocker & Brewster, 1822.

108 p. 14 cm. 2 engraved plates, one a view of Brainerd Mission.

Message from the President of the United States transmitting a Report of the Secretary of War of the Measures hitherto devised and pursued for the Civilization of the several Indian Tribes within the United States. Washington: Gales & Seaton, 1822.

23 p. 24 cm. Folded table.
The earliest available printing of the laws of the Cherokee Nation from 1808 to 1820.

1824

Message from the President of the United States, transmitting a Copy of Instructions under which the Articles of a Treaty with the Cherokee Indians were formed by Daniel Smith and R. J. Meigs, Acting Commissioners of the United States, at Tellico, on the 24th October, 1804; with Copies of all other Correspondence, or other Documents relating to that Instrument. Washington: Gales & Seaton, 1824.

17 p. 22 cm.

Wofford, J. D.

Sunalei akvlvgi no'gwisi alikalvvsga zvlvgi gesvi. The American Sunday School Spelling Book; translated into the Cherokee Language. By J. D. Wofford, one of the Students at the Valley Towns' School. New York: published for the benefit of those who cannot acquire the English Language. Gray & Bunce, printers, 1824.

52 p. 18 cm. Text in Cherokee in the Roman alphabet.
The second book in the Cherokee language. Excessively rare, only two other copies being known.

1825

Anderson, Rufus

Memoir of Catharine Brown, a Christian Indian of the Cherokee Nation. Boston: Armstrong and Crocker & Brewster, 1825.

180 p. 14.5 cm. Eng. Frontisp.

Anderson, Rufus

Memoir of Catharine Brown, a Christian Indian of the Cherokee Nation. Second edition. Boston: Crocker & Brewster, 1825.

144 p. 14 cm.
Field 32.

Letter from the Secretary of War, transmitting Copies of Letters from Joseph McMinn, deceased, late Agent of Indian Affairs, in the Cherokee Nation; together with a Copy of the Plan proposed by the direction of the Secretary of War, for the Extinguishment of the Cherokee Claim to Lands then occupied by them in Georgia, Tennessee, and Alabama. Washington: Gales & Seaton, 1825.

12 p. 22.5 cm.

The Lord's Prayer in Cherokee. [Boston? 1825?].
Broadside. 20 cm. Text in Cherokee in the Roman alphabet.

WORCESTER, LEONARD

A Sermon delivered in Park Street Church, August 25, 1825, at the Ordination of Rev. Messrs. Elnathan Gridley and Samuel Austin Worcester as Missionaries to the Heathen. By Leonard Worcester, Pastor of a Church in Peacham, Vt. Boston: Crocker & Brewster, 1825.

40 p. 24 cm. Printed wrappers.
This ordination sermon launched Samuel Austin Worcester upon his highly important career among the Cherokees.

1826

DARNEILLE, J.

Discourse or Lecture on the subject of Civilizing the Indians, in which is exhibited a New Plan to Effect their Civilization and to Meliorate their Condition. By the Rev. J. Darneille, formerly Rector of Amherst Parish, Virginia. Washington: F. S. Myer, 1826.

36 p. 21 cm.
Darneille proposed to establish a missionary school and a farm among the Arkansas Cherokees. The pamphlet is very scarce.

Lights of Education, or, Mr. Hope and his Family. By a Lady. Baltimore: E. J. Coale, 1826.

165 p. 14 cm.
Contains an account of a year and a half's residence with the Cherokees. One of only three known copies.

SEQUOYAH, or GEORGE GUESS

[The Cherokee syllabary. Washington, 1826.]
Broadside. 8 cm. high × 11 cm. wide.
The first printing of the Sequoyan syllabary. A proof struck from the plate used in illustrating Document 102 [Washington, 1826], which has hitherto, until discovery of this proof, been considered the earliest printing of the syllabary. The only known copy. [See page 21.]

1827

Acts of the General Assembly of the State of Georgia, passed in Milledgeville at an Annual Session in November and December, 1827. Published by authority. Milledgeville: Camak & Ragland, 1827.*

296 p. 21 cm.
Besides documents on the extension of Georgia's laws over the Indians, there is an important report [pp. 236–50] on Cherokee lands.

MACKENTOSH, JOHN

Receipts for the Cure of most Diseases incident to the Human Family. By the celebrated Indian doctor, John Mackentosh, of the Cherokee Nation; none of which have ever before been communicated to the world. New York: Printed for the Publisher, 1827.

12 p. 20.5 cm.

Rare.

1828

BLACK Fox and others

Communication from a Deputation of the Cherokee Indians West of the Mississippi, to the Honorable James Barbour, Secretary of War. February 1828. Washington: Gales & Seaton, 1828.

28 p. 23 cm.

A fine copy of a privately printed document signed by Black Fox, Thomas Graves, George Guess (Sequoyah), and other prominent Arkansas Cherokees or old settlers. The communication and its accompanying documents relate to Lovely's purchase and to Osage hostilities. Rare.

Cherokee Council to Col. H. Montgomery. Message from the President of the United States transmitting a Copy of the Letter from the Cherokee Council to Col. Hugh Montgomery, &c. [Washington, 1828.]

13 p. 23.5 cm. Caption title.

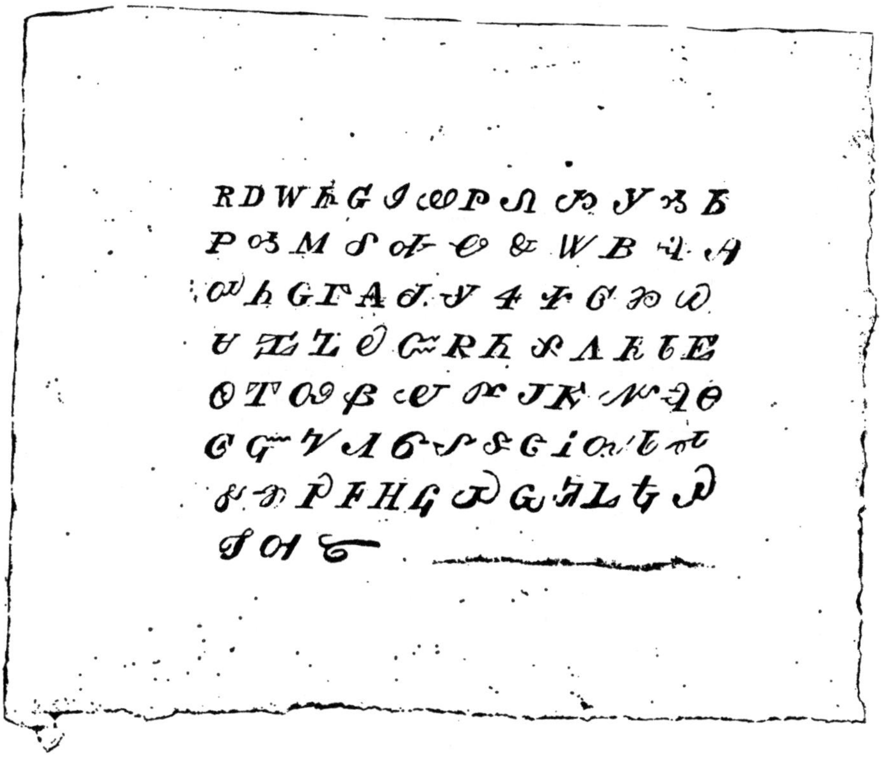

Cherokee Government. Message from the President of the United States transmitting the Information required by a Resolution of the House of Representatives, of the 3d instant, in relation to the Formation of a New Government by the Cherokee Tribe of Indians within the States of North Carolina, Georgia, Tennessee, and Alabama, &c. Washington: Gales & Seaton, 1828.

19 p. 25 cm. Uncut.

Conversations principally on the Aborigines of North America. Salem, Mass.: W. & S. B. Ives, 1828.

179 p. 14.5 cm. Printed wrappers.

Considerable material, compiled from missionary narratives and reports, on the Cherokees and others.

Georgia Lands Occupied by the Cherokee Indians. Report of a Committee and Resolutions of the Legislature of the State of Georgia in relation to Certain Lands occupied by the Cherokee Indians, belonging to the said State. Washington: Gales & Seaton, 1828.

13 p. 22 cm.

Negotiation for Cherokee Lands. Letter from the Secretary of War transmitting the Report of the Commissioners appointed to negotiate with the Cherokee Indians for a certain portion of their country. Washington: Gales & Seaton, 1828.

40 p. 22 cm.

Contains, besides other important documents, the full text of the Cherokee constitution of 1827. A fine copy, uncut and unopened.

Resolutions of the Legislature of Georgia, requesting the Senators and Representatives from that State, in Congress, to Use their Best Exertions to Obtain the Extinguishment of the Title of the Cherokee Indians to Land in the State of Georgia. Washington: Duff Green, 1828.*

13 p. 20.5 cm.

1829

Articles of Cession between the United States and Georgia, and Treaty with the Cherokee Indians. Message from the President of the United States, transmitting Information in relation to Measures taken in Execution of the Act of 9th May last, making an appropriation for carrying into effect the Articles of Agreement and Cession of 24th April, 1802, between the State of Georgia and the United States. [Washington, 1829.]

14 p. 25 cm. Caption title. Uncut and unopened.

Boudinot, Elias, and S. A. Worcester

Cherokee Hymns compiled from Several Authors and revised. By E. Boudinot and S. A. Worcester. Printed for the American Board of Commissioners for Foreign Missions. New Echota: Jno. F. Wheeler, Printer, 1829.

50, [2] p. 12 cm. Printed wrappers. Title page in English and Cherokee. Text in Cherokee.

The first book in the Sequoyan syllabary, and a very great rarity.

CAMPBELL, ROBERT

To the Honourable the President and Members of the Senate of the State of Georgia. [Savannah, 1829.]

20 p. 21 cm. Caption title, with a preliminary note printed without caption. This rare document possesses extraordinary interest as being one of the very few voices raised in Georgia at this period against the spoliation of the Cherokees.

EVARTS, JEREMIAH

Essays on the Present Crisis in the Condition of the American Indians; first published in the National Intelligencer, under the signature of William Penn. Boston: Perkins & Marvin, 1829.

112 p. 23.5 cm. Printed wrappers.
A fine exposition of the wrongs against the Cherokees.

Examination of the Relations between the Cherokees and the Government of the United States. New York, June, 1829.

16 p. 14 cm.
Rare.

Memorial of the Cherokees. [New Echota, 1829.]

Broadside. 30.5 cm. Text in Cherokee and English.
A highly important statement of the Cherokee case. "Our Neighbor, the State of Georgia, is pressing hard upon us." Unrecorded, and the only known copy.

ROSS, JOHN

Cherokee Indians. Memorial of John Ross and others, Representatives of the Cherokee Nation of Indians. [Washington, 1829.]

3 p. 22.5 cm. Caption title.

1830

Cherokee Alphabet. [New Echota? 1830?].

Broadside. 19 cm.
With a manuscript note at the bottom in the hand of Rev. Samuel A. Worcester, and signed with his initials. No other copy of this edition can be traced.

Cherokee Indians. Memorial of a Delegation of the Cherokee Nation of Indians. [Washington, 1830.]

4 p. 22 cm. Caption title.

HUMPHREY, HEMAN

Indian Rights and Our Duties. An Address delivered at Amherst, Hartford, etc. December, 1829. By Heman Humphrey, D.D. President of Amherst College. Amherst: J. S. & C. Adams & Co., 1830.

24 p. 18 cm. Printed wrappers.
A strong protest against the spoliation of the Cherokees. The first edition.

HUMPHREY, HEMAN

Indian Rights and Our Duties. An Address delivered at Amherst, Hartford, etc.

December, 1829. By Heman Humphrey, D.D., President of Amherst College. Second edition. Amherst: J. S. & C. Adams & Co., 1830.
24 p. 18 cm. Printed wrappers.

Indian Matters. [Little Rock, 1830.]
Broadsheet. 51.5 cm.
Headed: Supplement to the Arkansas Gazette. Little Rock, A.T., December 8, 1830.
An unsigned letter to the editor on affairs of the Western Cherokees, then living in Arkansas. The letter is in answer to one addressed by Tekatoka to "Standing Bear, alias Gen. Sam Houston." Of the greatest importance and rarity. No other copy can be traced.

Intrusions on Cherokee Lands. [Washington, 1830.]*
49 p. 21.5 cm. Caption title.

Memorials of the Cherokee Indians, signed by their Representatives, and by 3,085 Individuals of the Nation. [Washington, 1830.]
9 p. 22.5 cm. Caption title.
A strong protest against removal.

New York Citizens

To the Senate and House of Representatives of the United States in Congress assembled, the undersigned would respectfully represent. [New York, 1830.]*
8 p. 22.5 cm. Caption title.
A protest against the violation of Cherokee treaty rights. No other copy traced.

Pittsburgh Citizens

Memorial of the Inhabitants of Pittsburgh relative to Protecting Indians in Georgia. [Washington, 1830.]
7 p. 22.5 cm. Caption title.

Red Jacket

First Impressions on Reading the Message of the Governor of Georgia, 1830, relative to the Indians. [N.p., 1830.]
4 p. 22 cm. Caption title.
Excessively rare.

The Removal of the Indians. An Article from the American Monthly Magazine: an Examination of an Article in the North American Review; and an Exhibition of the Advancement of the Southern Tribes in Civilization and Christianity. Boston: Peirce and Williams, 1830.
[2], 72 p. 22 cm.

Report and Remonstrance of the Legislature of Georgia, in relation to the Indian Tribes within that State, and Acts of Certain States, Extending Jurisdiction over the Indian Tribes within their Limits. [Washington, 1830.]
13 p. 22 cm. Caption title.

Ross, John

Message of the Principal Chief to the General Council of the Cherokee Nation. [New Echota, 1830.]

Broadside. 24 cm.

A valuable report on the state of tribal affairs at a critical period of Cherokee history. Unrecorded, and no other copy known.

Tekatoka

To "Standing Bear," alias Gen. Samuel Houston. [Little Rock, 1830.]

Broadsheet. 45 cm.

Headed: Supplement to the Arkansas Gazette. Little Rock, October 20, 1830.

The Tekatoka letter is prefaced by a Letter to the Public [on a private quarrel] by the editor, Wm. E. Woodruff.

A rare and invaluable discussion of the affairs of the Western or Arkansas Cherokees. Unrecorded, and the only known copy.

Tuttle, Sarah

Letters and Conversations on the Cherokee Mission. Boston: T. R. Marvin, 1830.

116 p. 14.5 cm.

Vol. 2 only.

A vindication of the Cherokee Claims, addressed to the Town Meeting in Philadelphia, on the 11th of January, 1830. [Philadelphia, 1830.]

8 p. 23 cm.

Wirt, William

An Opinion on the Claims for Improvements by the State of Georgia on the Cherokee Nation, under the Treaties of 1817 & 1828. New Echota: Printed for the Cherokee Nation at the Office of the Cherokee Phoenix and Indians' Advocate. John F. Wheeler, Printer, 1830.

22, 6 p. 21 cm.

In a protective case. A very great rarity.

Wirt, William

Opinion on the Right of the State of Georgia to Extend her Laws over the Cherokee Nation. By William Wirt, Esq. Baltimore: F. Lucas, 1830.

29 p. 21 cm.

Inscribed: For Mr. Chase from his friend Wm. Wirt.

1831

Anderson, Rufus

Memoir of Catharine Brown, a Christian Indian, of the Cherokee Nation. Philadelphia, [1831?].

138 p. 14 cm.

Everett, Edward

Speech of Mr. Everett, of Massachusetts, in the House of Representatives, on the

14th and 21st of February, 1831, on the Execution of the Laws and Treaties in Favor of the Indian Tribes. [Washington, 1831.]*

23 p. 21.5 cm. Caption title.

A highly important review of Cherokee history and of treaty rights.

HUMPHREY, HEMAN

Indian Rights and Our Duties. An Address delivered at Amherst, Hartford, etc. December, 1829. By Heman Humphrey, D.D., President of Amherst College. [Boston, 1831.]*

24 p. 17.5 cm. Printed wrappers.

Wrapper title: The Indian Advocate. No. 1. February, 1832.

HARTFORD CITIZENS

Plea for the Indians. [Hartford, 1831.]*

8 p. 22.5 cm. Caption title.

"The following document was written as a Memorial to be signed by citizens of Hartford, Connecticut. The form, which was actually forwarded, however, was not so long; but as the argument is here conducted with great spirit and propriety, it is printed for general circulation, with a few immaterial variations from the original draft."

LUMPKIN, WILSON

Communication of the Governor of Georgia, in compliance with the request of the House of Representatives, communicating Information in the possession of the Executive, together with his views in relation to the Cherokee Nation and the Immediate Survey and Occupancy of the Cherokee Lands. Milledgeville: Office of the Federal Union, 1831.

8 p. 21 cm.

An official statement of the greatest moment to the Cherokees. Unrecorded, and no other copy located.

PETERS, RICHARD

The case of the Cherokee Nation against the State of Georgia; argued and determined at the Supreme Court of the United States, January term 1831. With an Appendix. By Richard Peters, counsellor at law. Philadelphia: John Grigg, 1831.

[8] 286 p. 23 cm.

Field 1206.

The authoritative report of the case.

TAYLOR, RICHARD, and others

Memorial of a Delegation from the Cherokee Indians. Presented to Congress January 18, 1831. [Washington, 1831.]

8 p. 21.5 cm. Caption title.

The memorial is signed by R. Taylor, John Ridge, and W. S. Coodey. Appended is an address by Henry Dearborn, Secretary of War, "To the beloved Chief of the Cherokee Nation, the Little Turkey."

1832

Blunt, Joseph

Brief Examination of the Relations between the Cherokees and the Government of the United States. By Joseph Blunt. New York: Clayton & Van Norden, 1832.

15 p. 22 cm. Printed wrappers.

Only two other copies are recorded.

Cherokee Indians. Memorial of a Delegation of the Cherokee Tribe of Indians. [Washington, 1832.]

5 p. 22.5 cm. Caption title.

Cumming, William

Georgia and the Supreme Court. An Examination of the opinion of the Supreme Court of the United States, at January Term, 1832, delivered by Mr. Chief Justice Marshall, in the case of Samuel A. Worcester, Plaintiff in Error, versus The State of Georgia. Augusta, 1832.

22 p. 22.5 cm.

Signed: Ogelthorpe.

Excessively rare, only the Yale University copy being located by the Union Catalog.

Marshall, John

Opinion of the Supreme Court of the United States at January Term, 1832, delivered by Mr. Chief Justice Marshall, in the case of Samuel A. Worcester, Plaintiff in Error, versus The State of Georgia. Washington: Gales & Seaton, 1832.

20 p. 21.5 cm.

Marshall, John

Opinion of the Supreme Court of the United States, at January Term, 1832, delivered by Mr. Chief Justice Marshall, together with the Opinion of Mr. Justice McLean, in the case of Samuel A. Worcester, Plaintiff in Error, versus The State of Georgia. With a statement of the case, extracted from the Records of the Supreme Court of the United States. Printed from authenticated copies. Washington: Gales & Seaton. 1832.

39 p. 23.5 cm.

This edition is considerably scarcer than the twenty page edition above.

Pendleton, Edmund Henry

Remarks of Mr. Pendleton, of New York, in the House of Representatives, on the 28th of May, upon a Petition from Dutchess County, New York, relative to the Missionaries, Worcester & Butler, imprisoned under a Judgment of a State Court in Georgia. Washington: Printed at the office of Jonathan Elliot, Penn. Ave. 1832.

19 p. 21 cm.

Not noted by Field.

Rations to Emigrating Indians. Report of the Select Committee appointed by a Resolution of the House of Representatives "to Inquire whether an Attempt was made by the late Secretary of War, John H. Eaton, fraudulently to give to Samuel Houston, or any other Person or Persons concerned with Samuel Houston, a Contract for

Supplying Rations to such Indians as might Emigrate to their Lands West of Arkansas and Missouri; and whether the said Houston made a Fraudulent Attempt to Obtain said Contract." [Washington, 1832.]

75 p. 22.5 cm. Caption title.

An important and little known chapter in Indian history.

Report of the Committee to whom was referred so much of the Governor's Message as relates to the Enforcement of the Law making it penal, under certain restrictions, for white persons to reside within the limits of the Cherokee Nation. Milledgeville: The Federal Union Office, 1832.

10 p. 24 cm.

A document of the highest importance and rarity.

1833

Acts of the General Assembly of the State of Georgia, passed in Milledgeville at an annual session in November and December 1832. Published by authority. Milledgeville: Prince & Ragland. 1833.*

358 p. 20.5 cm.

Important acts on Georgia's seizure of the Cherokee country.

Boudinot, Elias

Poor Sarah; or, The Indian Woman, translated by E. Boudinot. New Echota: Published by the United Bretheren's Missionary Society at the expense of the American Tract Society. J. F. Wheeler and J. Candy, Printers, 1833.

12 p. 16.5 cm. Joint Cherokee and English title. Text in Cherokee.

Accompanying this volume are two different contemporary pamphlet issues of the English version. Excessively rare. [See page 29.]

Journal of the Times and Recorder of the Gold and Land Lotteries. Drawn at Milledgeville from the 22nd of October 1832 to the last of May 1833. Milledgeville: Printed at the Georgia Times Office. 1833.

822 p. 21 cm.

Upon discovery of gold in the Cherokee country, Georgia lost no time in seizing the Indian lands and dividing them among her citizens. Unrecorded, and the only known copy.

Prizes drawn in the Cherokee Gold Lottery, of the 1st, 2nd and 3rd quality, with their improvements, and the drawer's name and residence. Compiled from the numerical books, after a careful examination of them by the commissioners. Milledgeville: Times Office, M. D. J. Slade, 1833.

327 p. 24.5 cm.

The Union Catalog locates only the De Renne copy.

Prizes drawn in the Cherokee Land Lottery, of the 1st and 2nd quality, and of the 3rd having improvements; with the drawer's name and residence. Compiled from the numerical books, after a careful examination of them by the Commissioners. Milledgeville: Printed at the Times Office, by M. D. J. Slade. 1833.

205 p. 14 cm. Pp. 103–106 are lacking.

Unrecorded, and the only known copy.

POOR SARAH;

OR,

THE INDIAN WOMAN.

TRANSLATED BY E. BOUDINOT.

ᎤᏂ ᎢᏳᏍᏏᏕᎩ ᏎᎵ ᏴᎾᏪ ᎠᎨᏴ.

ᏧᏴᎵ ᎡᎯ ᎤᏓᏅᏗ ᎠᎨᏴ ᎤᏬᏪᎳᏅᎯ ᏕᏔᎩᎾᏃ ᎤᏁᎵᏔᏅᎯ.

ᏩᏍᎩ ᏅᏓᏕᎨᏍᏁᏗᏍᎬ ᎤᏜᏳᏍ ᏗᏂᏂᎵ ᎬᏩᏆᏳᎯᏳ ᏂᏕᎨᏍᏗᏍᎬᎩ—Ꮪ.

NEW ECHOTA:

PUBLISHED BY THE UNITED BRETHREN'S MISSIONARY SOCIETY AT THE EXPENSE OF THE AMERICAN TRACT SOCIETY.

J. F. WHEELER AND J. CANDY, PRINTERS.

ᏆᏦᏗ: ᎪᏧᏩ ᏩᏮᏑᏩᏃ ᏗᏂᎣᏴᏔᏅᎯ.

1833.

Tuttle, Sarah

Conversations on the mission to the Arkansas Cherokees. Boston: Massachusetts Sabbath School Society, 1833.

[6], 74 p. 14 cm.

A very rare volume.

Worcester, Samuel A., and Elias Boudinot

The Acts of the Apostles translated into the Cherokee Language. By S. A. Worcester and E. Boudinot. Printed for the American Board of Commissioners for Foreign Missions. New Echota: John F. Wheeler and John Candy, Printers. 1833.

127 p. 12 cm. Title page in English and Cherokee. Text in Cherokee.

Excessively rare.

Worcester, Samuel Austin, tr.

Cherokee hymns compiled from several authors and revised. By S. A. Worcester & E. Boudinot. Fourth edition. New Echota: J. F. Wheeler and J. Candy, printers. 1833.

46, [2] p. 12 cm.

Excessively rare.

Worcester, S. A., tr.

Select passages from the Holy Scriptures. [New Echota, 1833?].

24 p. 12 cm. Caption title, in English and Cherokee. Text in Cherokee.

Excessively rare.

1834

Acts of the General Assembly of the State of Georgia, passed in Milledgeville, at an Annual Session in November and December, 1833. Published by authority. Milledgeville: Polhill & Fort, 1834.

456, 43 p. 20.5 cm.

Laws relating to the Cherokees.

Edwards, B. B.

Memoir of the Rev. Elias Cornelius. Second edition. Boston: Perkins, Marvin & Co., 1834.*

360 p. 18.5 cm.

Contains much information about the missions established by Cornelius among the Cherokees and Choctaws.

Georgia Legislature

A Bill to amend an Act entitled an "Act more effectually to Provide for the Government and Protection of the Cherokee Indians residing within the Limits of Georgia, and to Prescribe the Bounds of their Occupant Claims." [Milledgeville, 1834.]

4 p. 23 cm. Caption title.

Headed: In House of Representatives, read first time 13th Dec. 1334 [sic]: 300 copies ordered to be printed.

Of the greatest importance. Unrecorded, and no other copy known.

Memorial of the President and Trustees of the University of Nashville to the Congress of the United States. Nashville: Republican and Gazette Office, 1834.*

12 p. 19.5 cm.

Includes a review of the title to lands yielded by the Cherokees and in dispute between Tennessee and North Carolina.

1835

Benton County [Alabama] Citizens

Public Meeting. [Huntsville, 1835.]

Broadside. Folio.

Resolutions of protest against a proposal to allow individual Cherokees to take reservations of land, remain in the state, and become United States citizens. Unrecorded, and the only known copy.

Charges against Hon. John W. Hooper, Judge of the Superior Courts of the Cherokee Circuit; referred to the Committee of the House of Representatives for Investigation. Milledgeville, Georgia: Printed at the Office of the Federal Union, 1835.*

140 p. 24 cm. The last leaf, of two pages, in photostat. Not listed in the Union Catalog.

Cherokee Almanac for the year of our Lord, 1836. Union: Mission Press: John F. Wheeler, printer. 1835.

16 p. 16.5 cm.

A very rare volume. The first Cherokee almanac and one of the excessively rare issues of the Oklahoma press in the first year of its existence.

Documents relative to the Judicial Administration of the Hon. John W. Hooper. Published by order of the Committee of Investigation of the House of Representatives. Milledgeville, Georgia: Printed at the Office of the Federal Union, 1835.

41 p. 24 cm. Title page in photostat.

This and the following volume are two of the rarest and most important documents on relations between the Cherokees and the State of Georgia after extension of state laws over the Indians and before their final removal. Hooper was presiding judge of the circuit which embraced the Cherokee country and the investigations centered upon his conduct of cases in which Cherokee Indians were involved. Not listed in the Union Catalog.

Hicks, Elijah, and others

At a Meeting of the Undersigned Citizens of Coosoowatee District, convened at Rabbit Trap, to consider the Expediency of changing the Representation from this District to the National Committee, the undersigned have unanimously adopted the following Considerations and Resolutions. [New Echota, 1835.]

Broadside. Folio. Text in English and in Cherokee.

Signed by Elijah Hicks, Katihee, Kullonoohaskee, Bear Meat, and fifteen other prominent members of the Ross or anti-Treaty faction.

The resolutions demanded the resignation of John Ridge from the National Committee on the ground that he had ceased to show patriotism and firmness to the Cherokee cause. A document of the highest importance and one of the earliest steps toward the assassinations of 1839 and the tribal civil war that followed. Unrecorded, and the only known copy.

Indians—Cherokee. Memorial of a Council at Running Waters, in the Cherokee Nation, in Georgia, November 28, 1834, on behalf of those Members of the Cherokee Tribe of Indians who are desirous of removing West of the Mississippi. [Washington, 1835.]

19 p. 25.5 cm. Caption title.
Proceedings of a meeting of the Ridge or treaty faction.

Opinions of the Judges of the Supreme Court of the State of Tennessee. The State vs. James Foreman. Printed by order of the Senate. Nashville: W. Hasell Hunt & Co., Printers to the Senate: Banner & Whig Office, 1835.

142 p. 21 cm.
A highly important case. James Foreman, a Cherokee, killed a fellow tribesman in that part of the Cherokee Nation which lay in Tennessee. The question before the court was one of jurisdiction, counsel for Foreman holding that such a crime was punishable only by Cherokee national authorities. It is interesting to note that James Foreman himself was killed a few years later in Arkansas by Stand Watie, who was acquitted of the charge of murder when brought to trial at Van Buren. Unrecorded, and the only known copy.

Ross, John, and others

Memorial of John Ross and others, on behalf of the Cherokee Nation of Indians, praying Protection from the United States, and Protesting against certain Articles of Agreement between the Agent of the United States and a certain part of said Cherokee Nation of Indians. [Washington, 1835.]

51 p. 26 cm. Caption title.
A fine copy, uncut and unopened.

Schermerhorn, John F.

Notice. [New Echota, 1835.]

Broadside. 17.5 cm. Text in Cherokee.
The call for the treaty council of the Cherokees at New Echota on the third Monday in December, 1835, which resulted in the signing by the Ridge party of the momentous New Echota treaty of removal. Abel, Indian Consolidation, p. 404: "He [Schermerhorn, U.S. treaty commissioner] called another meeting for the third Monday in December, at New Echota, and in excess of his instructions, submitted an entirely new treaty to the Indians. Accepted conditionally by them, it went to the Senate. . . . John Ross protested, but in vain. The treaty was ratified and the Cherokees were doomed." Unrecorded, and the only known copy. With a translation into English by Reverend Richard Glory.

1836

Articles of a Treaty concluded at New Echota, in the State of Georgia, on the 29th day of December, 1835, by General William Carroll and John F. Schermerhorn, Commissioners on the part of the United States, and the Chiefs, Head Men, and People of the Cherokee Tribe of Indians. [Washington:] Gales & Seaton, [1836].

192 p. 24 cm. Caption title.
Headed: Confidential.

"The following Treaty was read, referred to the Committee on Indian Affairs, and ordered to be printed, in confidence, for the use of the Senate." A secret document of the highest importance and vitality; it contains every pertinent document on the momentous New Echota treaty of removal and on the questionable means used by the United States commissioners in negotiating it. Excessively rare.

Memorial of the Cherokee Representatives, submitting the Protest of the Cherokee Nation against the Ratification, Execution, and Enforcement of the Treaty negotiated at New Echota, in December, 1835. [Washington, 1836.]
167 p. 22.5 cm. Caption title.

Message transmitting a Letter of Major Davis, relative to the Cherokee Treaty, and the Accompanying Documents. [Washington, 1836.]
Paged 147–67. 22 cm. Caption title.

PAYNE, JOHN HOWARD

The Captivity of John Howard Payne by the Georgia Guard. [In The North American Quarterly Magazine, Vol. 7, No. 33, January, 1836. Philadelphia, 1836.]
Pp. 107–24.

An extremely interesting and valuable narrative by Payne of his arrest and detention by the Georgia Guard on a charge of encouraging Cherokee resistance to that state's authority.

ROSS, JOHN

Letter from John Ross, Principal Chief of the Cherokee Nation of Indians, in answer to Inquiries from a Friend regarding the Cherokee Affairs with the United States. Followed by a Copy of the Protest of the Cherokee Delegation laid before the Senate and House of Representatives at the City of Washington, June 21, 1836. [Philadelphia, 1836.]
31 p. 23 cm.

A masterful exposition of Cherokee grievances against the state and national governments.

TYSON, JOB R.

Discourse on the Surviving Remnant of the Indian Race in the United States. Philadelphia: A. Waldie, 1836.
38 p. 21 cm.

The address deals largely with the Cherokee Indians and their relations with the State of Georgia.

WORCESTER, SAMUEL A., tr.

Select Passages from the Holy Scriptures. [Park Hill: Mission Press, 1836?].*
24 p. 13 cm. Caption title, in English and Cherokee. Text in Cherokee.
Pilling, Iroquoian Bibliography, p. 152.

1837

Boudinot, Elias

Letters and other Papers relating to Cherokee Affairs: being in Reply to Sundry Publications authorized by John Ross. By E. Boudinot, formerly Editor of the Cherokee Phoenix. Athens, Georgia: Printed at the Office of "The Southern Banner." 1837.

66 p. 19.5 cm.

One of the most important publications on the New Echota treaty of 1835 and the internal difficulties and divisions which preceded the final removal of the tribe. A volume of the utmost rarity.

Brigadier General Wool. Message from the President of the United States, transmitting the Proceedings of the Court of Inquiry in the case of Brevet Brigadier General Wool. [Washington:] Thomas Allen, [1837].

85 p. 24.5 cm. Caption title.

Contains valuable information on Cherokee removal.

Cherokee Almanac for the year of our Lord 1838. Park Hill: Mission Press. John F. Wheeler, printer. 1837.

24 p. 16.5 cm. Joint Cherokee and English title. Text in Cherokee and English.

Kennedy, John

To the Chiefs, Head-Men, and People of the Cherokee Nation. [Athens, Tennessee, 1837.]

Broadside. Folio.

A stern warning to the Cherokees that they must delay no longer in removing to the West. Unrecorded, and the only known copy.

Long, Stephen H.

Report of a Reconnoissance & Survey of the Western & Atlantic Rail Road of the State of Georgia. By S. H. Long, Lieut. Colonel, Chief Engineer. Milledgeville: Printed at the Federal Union Office, by Park & Rogers. 1837.

51 p. 21 cm.

Georgia's plan and survey for a railroad through the Cherokee country even before the final removal of the tribe had been accomplished. The terrain is described in valuable detail. The volume is a top rarity, only one other copy, that at the Boston Athenaeum, being recorded.

Ross, John

Letter from John Ross, the Principal Chief of the Cherokee Nation, to a Gentleman of Philadelphia. [Philadelphia, 1837.]

40 p. 22.5 cm. Printed wrappers.

Stuart, John

A Sketch of the Cherokee and Choctaw Indians. By John Stuart, Capt. United States Army, Choctaw Nation. Little Rock: Printed by Woodruff & Pew. 1837.

42 p. 24.5 cm.

One of the earliest, rarest, and most highly desirable descriptions of Indian Territory.

Only two other copies are known, and of the three this is easily the finest, being entirely untrimmed. This copy originally belonged to the prominent Choctaw, Daniel Folsom, of Eagletown, the editor in 1848 of the first Choctaw newspaper, and it has his signature on the title page.

Wool, John E.

Head Quarters, Army. Cherokee Nation, New Echota, Ga., March 22nd, 1837. Cherokees: [New Echota, 1837.]

Broadside. 24.5 cm.

A highly interesting and significant address to the Cherokees, urging them to cease resistance and to accept the inevitability of removal. Signed in autograph by General Wool. Excessively rare.

1838

Boudinot, Elias

Documents in relation to the Validity of the Cherokee Treaty of 1835. Letters and other Papers relating to Cherokee Affairs: being a Reply to Sundry Publications authorized by John Ross. By E. Boudinot, formerly Editor of the Cherokee Phoenix. [Washington:] Blair & Rives, [1838].

43 p. 22.5 cm. Caption title.

An able and highly important statement of the position of the anti-Ross or treaty faction of the tribe.

Cherokee Almanac for the year of our Lord 1839. Park Hill: Mission Press. John F. Wheeler, printer. [1838].

36 p. 16.5 cm. Joint Cherokee and English title. Text in Cherokee and English.

Cherokee Delegation. Memorial of the Cherokee Delegation, submitting the Memorial and Protest of the Cherokee People to Congress. [Washington, 1838.]

7 p. 23 cm. Caption title.

Cherokee Indians. Letter from the Secretary of War transmitting the Information required by a Resolution of the House of Representatives of the 2d instant, in relation to the Cherokee Indians East of the Mississippi. [Washington:] Thomas Allen, print. [1838].

13 p. 25.5 cm. Caption title. Uncut and unopened.

Dawson, William C.

Speech of William C. Dawson, of Georgia, on the Bill making Appropriation for the Suppression and Prevention of Indian Hostilities, for the year 1838, and to Carry into Execution the Treaty made with the Cherokee Indians in 1835; and to Provide for their Removal, &c; and in Vindication of the Policy of Georgia towards the Cherokees. Delivered in the House of Representatives, in Committee of the Whole, May 31, 1838. Washington: Printed by Gales and Seaton. 1838.

31 p. 22.5 cm.

Kennedy, John

Opinion of Commissioner Kennedy, in the Case of Looney Riley, an Applicant for the Value of a Reservation, under the Treaty of the 29th Dec. 1835, and the Supplement thereto. [Washington, 1838.]

Broadside. Folio.

An important review of Cherokee treaty rights. The only known copy.

LOWREY, GEORGE

The Evil of Intoxicating Liquor, and the Remedy. Park Hill: Mission Press. John F. Wheeler, printer, 1838.

12 p. 16.5 cm. Text in Cherokee.

The author was assistant principal chief.

MCKINNEY, JOHN

An Opinion in John Bean's case. [Athens, Tennessee? 1838?].

12 p. 23.5 cm. Caption title.

John Bean was a Cherokee Indian. Unrecorded, and the only known copy.

Memorial of a Delegation of the Cherokee Nation, remonstrating against the Instrument of Writing (Treaty) of December, 1835. [Washington:] Thomas Allen, print. [1838].

49 p. 22.5 cm. Caption title.

Report from the Secretary of War in relation to the Cherokee Treaty of 1835. [Washington, 1838.]

1090 p. 23 cm. Folded Map.

SCOTT, WINFIELD

Major General Scott, of the United States Army, sent to the Cherokee People remaining in North Carolina, Georgia, Tennessee, and Alabama, this Address. [Cherokee Agency, Tennessee, 1838.]

Broadside. 25 cm.

A final and plain warning to the Cherokees that unless they remove willingly they will be forcibly removed. Excessively rare.

SCOTT, WINFIELD

Orders No. (25). Head Quarters, Eastern Division. Cherokee Agency, Ten. May 17, 1838. [Cherokee Agency, 1838.]

Broadside. Folio.

Minute instructions to his command for rounding up, disarming, and transporting the Cherokees to the West. The order, which is signed in autograph by General Scott, possesses the very highest degree of importance and interest. Very rare, and a fine copy.

SCOTT, WINFIELD

Removal of the Cherokees. Letter from the Secretary of War, transmitting Copies of the Correspondence between the War Department and Major General Scott, in relation to the Removal of the Cherokees. [Washington:] Thomas Allen, [1838].

26 p. 25 cm. Caption title. Uncut and unopened.

SMITH, JAMES F.

The Cherokee Land Lottery, containing a Numerical List of the Names of the

Fortunate Drawers in said Lottery, with an Engraved Map of each District. By James F. Smith, of Milledgeville, Geo. New York: Harper & Bros., 1838.

413, [1] p. 22.5 cm. 59 maps.

The volume is very scarce.

WORCESTER, SAMUEL A., and ELIAS BOUDINOT

The Gospel of Jesus Christ according to John. Translated into the Cherokee Language by S. A. Worcester and E. Boudinot. Park Hill: Mission Press. John F. Wheeler, Printer. 1838.

101 p. 13 cm. Title page in English and Cherokee. Text in Cherokee.

1839

Cherokee Almanac for the year of our Lord 1840. Park Hill: Mission Press, John Candy, printer, [1839].

24 p. 16.5 cm.

EVERETT, HORACE

Speech of Horace Everett in the House of Representatives, May 31, 1838, on the Cherokee Treaty. Washington: Gales & Seaton, 1839.

47 p. 21 cm.

KENNEDY, JOHN

The Opinion of Commissioner Kennedy, in the Case of the Widow and Heirs of Daniel McNair, Applicants for the Value of a Reservation upon the Lands ceded by the Treaty of the 29th December, 1835. Athens, Ten., Friday, February 22, 1839.

Broadside. Folio.

Headed: Athens Courier.

The only known copy.

TAWSE, JOHN, and GEORGE LYON

Report to the Society in Scotland for Propagating Christian Knowledge, of a Visit to America, by their appointment, in reference to the fund under their charge for the Education of Native Indians. Edinburgh: William White, 1839.

xv. 68 p. 22 cm.

Important observations on the Cherokees and Choctaws. The volume has been generally overlooked. The Union Catalog locates only one copy.

1840

Cherokee Indians. Letter from the Secretary of War respecting the Interference of any Officer or Agent of the Government with the Cherokee Indians in the Formation of a Government for the Regulation of their own Internal Affairs, &c. [Washington, 1840.]

64 p. 22.5 cm. Caption title.

The Constitution and Laws of the Cherokee Nation: Passed at Tah-le-quah, Cherokee Nation, 1839. Washington: Printed by Gales & Seaton, 1840.

36 p. 19.5 cm. Printed wrappers.

The first official printing of the Act of Union, the Constitution, and the laws of 1839—the first adopted after the reunion of the tribe in the West.

Harden, Edward

Documents in support of the Claims of Edward Harden for Legal Services rendered to the Cherokees. [Athens, Georgia, 1840.]*

Broadsheet. Folio.

General Harden rendered valuable legal services to the Cherokees in the period just before their removal from Georgia. No other copy can be traced.

Indians, Cherokee Nation, West. Memorial of the Delegates and Representatives of the Cherokee Nation West. [Washington:] Blair & Rives, [1840].

15 p. 23 cm. Caption title.

Memorial—Indians—Cherokee Delegation. Memorial of the Delegation of the Cherokee Indians. [Washington, 1840.]

117 p. 25 cm. Caption title.

Valuable documents on the re-establishment of Cherokee government in the West and on the civil disorders which disturbed the tribe during the early years of its reunion.

Report of the Secretary of War exhibiting the Present State of the Difficulties which have existed, and the Arrangements made, or attempted to be made, between the Government and the Cherokee People. [Washington:] Blair & Rives, [1840].

62 p. 22 cm. Caption title.

Worcester, Samuel A.

Cherokee Primer. Park Hill, 1840.

24, 4 p. 13 cm. Plain wrappers. Joint English and Cherokee title. Text in Cherokee.

Very rare.

Worcester, Samuel A., tr.

The Gospel according to Matthew. Translated into the Cherokee Language. Third edition revised. Park Hill: Mission Press. J. Candy, Printer. 1840.

120 p. 13 cm. Title page in English and Cherokee. Text in Cherokee.

1841

Boudinot, Elias, and S. A. Worcester

Cherokee Hymns, compiled from several Authors and revised. Sixth edition, with the addition of many New Hymns. Park Hill: Mission Press: John Candy, Printer. 1841.

65, [2] p. 13 cm. Title page in English and Cherokee. Text in Cherokee.

Butler, Pierce Mason

Notice. [Park Hill, 1841.]

Broadside. 24 cm.

Terms upon which white men will be allowed to live in the Cherokee Nation. Butler was the Cherokee Agent. Unrecorded, and the only known copy.

Cherokee Almanac for the year of Our Lord 1842. Park Hill: Mission Press: John Candy, Printer, [1841].

36 p. 17.5 cm. Printed wrappers. Joint Cherokee and English title. Text in Cherokee and English.

WORCESTER, SAMUEL A., tr.

The Gospel of Jesus Christ according to John. Translated into the Cherokee Language. Second edition. Park Hill: Mission Press: John Candy, Printer. 1841.

101 p. 13 cm. Title page in English and Cherokee. Text in Cherokee.

WRIGHT, JOS. J. B.

Army Medical Reports. By Jos. J. B. Wright, M.D., Assistant Surgeon U.S. Army. [An extract from The American Medical Intelligencer, December, 1841, Vol. 1, No. 6, pp. 113–20.]*

A valuable report on the diseases observed among the soldiers stationed at Fort Gibson and among the neighboring Indians.

1842

Cherokee Almanac for the year of our Lord 1843. Park Hill: Mission Press. John Candy, printer. [1842].

36 p. 17 cm. Joint Cherokee and English title. Text in Cherokee and English.

HITCHCOCK, ETHAN ALLEN

Colonel Hitchcock—Cherokee Indians. [Washington, 1842.]

5 p. 24 cm. Caption title.

A copy from the Hitchcock papers, with penciled notes throughout in Colonel Hitchcock's hand.

LOWREY, GEORGE

[Temperance tract, entirely in Cherokee. Park Hill: Mission Press, 1842.]

11 p. 13 cm.

The author was assistant principal chief. The little volume is rare.

Removal of the Cherokees West of the Mississippi. [Washington, 1842.]

100 p. 23 cm. Caption title.

Contains the constitution of the Cherokee Nation, the act of union, and the acts and resolutions of 1839, the earliest adopted after the reunion of the tribe in the West.

ROGERS, JOHN, and others

Memorial. [Park Hill?, 1842.]

7 p. 24.5 cm. Caption title.

Dated: Cherokee Nation, near Fort Gibson, April 16, 1842.

Signed by John Rogers, Thomas Wilson, and five other prominent members of the Western Cherokees.

One of two known copies.

Supreme Court of the United States. No. 74. Robert Porterfield, Compl't and Appl't, vs. Merriwether L. Clarke, and Martha L., William P., George R. and Thomas J. Clarke, Heirs and Devisees of William Clark, dec., et al, Resp's. On Appeal from the Circuit Court U.S. for the District of Kentucky. [N.p., 1842.]*

257 p. 23.5 cm.

A claim for a grant of land in the old Cherokee Overhill country. Title is traced back to eighteenth century Cherokee treaties and deeds, which, together with scores of valuable related documents, are quoted in full. A source volume of the highest importance. Unrecorded, and no other copy traced.

WORCESTER, SAMUEL A., tr.

The Acts of the Apostles, translated into the Cherokee Language. Second edition. Park Hill: Mission Press: John Candy, Printer. 1842.

124 p. 13 cm. Title page in English and Cherokee. Text in Cherokee.

1843

Bank United States, Assignee of Williamson Smith. Report of the Committee on the Judiciary. [Washington, 1843.]

11 p. 25 cm. Caption title.

The claim grew out of Smith's transactions as contractor for removal of Cherokee Indians.

BOUDINOT, ELIAS, tr.

Poor Sarah. [Park Hill: Mission Press], 1843.

18 p. 13 cm. Title page in English and Cherokee. Text in Cherokee.

The Union Catalog locates only the copy at the Library of Congress. Very rare.

Cherokee Alphabet. [Park Hill, 1843?].*

Broadside. 24.5 cm.

No other copy of this edition can be traced.

HITCHCOCK, ETHAN ALLEN

Frauds upon Indians—Right of the President to Withhold Papers. Report of the Committee on Indian Affairs, to whom was referred the Message of the President of the United States, accompanying Sundry Reports made by Lieutenant Colonel Hitchcock to the Department of War, relative to the Affairs of the Cherokee Indians, and certain Frauds alleged to have been committed upon them and the Government. [Washington, 1843.]

229 p. 25.5 cm. Caption title. Uncut and unopened.

PASCHAL, GEORGE WASHINGTON

A Report of the Trial of Stand Watie, charged with the Murder of James Foreman. By George W. Paschal, one of the Judges of the Supreme Court of Arkansas. Van Buren: Thomas Sterne, 1843.*

44 p. 21 cm.

Included is a speech of A. W. Arrington, defense counsel. Paschal was married to Watie's sister. Of the very greatest interest, rarity, and importance. Only one other copy is known, and that is in private hands.

Removal of the Cherokees, &c. [Washington, 1843.]

70 p. 22.5 cm. Caption title.

Considerable detail on the removal.

WORCESTER, SAMUEL A., tr.

The Epistles of John translated into the Cherokee Language. Second edition. Park Hill: Mission Press: John Candy, Printer. 1843.

20 p. 13 cm. Title page in English and Cherokee. Text in Cherokee.

WORCESTER, SAMUEL A., tr.

Treatise on Marriage. [Park Hill: Mission Press, 1843?].

20 p. 13 cm. Caption title, in English and Cherokee. Text in Cherokee. Pilling, Iroquoian Bibliography, p. 161.

Two copies.

1844

Cherokee Almanac for the year of our Lord 1845. Park Hill: Mission Press: John Candy and John F. Wheeler, printers. [1844].

36 p. 17 cm. Joint Cherokee and English title. Text in Cherokee and English. [See page 42.]

The Constitution and Laws of the Cherokee Nation: Passed at Tah-le-quah, Cherokee Nation, 1839. Washington: Gales and Seaton, 1840.

107 p. 19 cm.

Pages 36–107 were printed at the Baptist Mission Press, in the Cherokee Nation, in 1844. They contain the laws passed by the Council from 1840 to 1844. One of only two known copies.

JONES, EVAN

The Cherokee Messenger. [Baptist Mission Press, 1844–1846.]

192 p. 22.5 cm.

Nos. 1–12, a complete file, of Oklahoma's earliest periodical publication. Excessively rare.

LOWREY, GEORGE

The Evil of Intoxicating Liquor, and the Remedy. Second edition. Park Hill: Mission Press: John Candy, Printer. 1844.

24, [4] p. 13 cm. Title page in Cherokee and English. Text in Cherokee.

WORCESTER, SAMUEL A., tr.

The Gospel according to Matthew. Translated into the Cherokee Language. Fourth edition. Park Hill: Mission Press: John Candy, Printer. 1844.

120 p. 13 cm. Title page in English and Cherokee. Text in Cherokee.

WORCESTER, SAMUEL A., tr.

Miscellaneous Pieces. [Park Hill: Mission Press, 1844.]*

24 p. 13 cm. Caption title, in English and Cherokee. Text in Cherokee.

1845

BUTLER, P. M.

Cherokee Agency, Dec. 20th, 1845. Lt. Col. R. B. Mason, 1st Dragoons. Sir: . . . . [Tahlequah, 1845.]

3 p. 25 cm.

ᏅᏙ ᏗᏎᏍᏗ

ᎤᏕᏘᏴᏌᏗᏒ

1845.

CHEROKEE ALMANAC

For the year of our Lord

1845.

ᏂᎪᎯᎸ ᎡᎶᎯ ᎨᏒᎢ ᎢᏝ ᎤᎵᏍᏆᏗᏍᏗ ᏱᎩ ᎠᏓᏄᏟᏴᏏᏒ ᎠᎾᏯᏗᏍ ᎨᏒᎢ, ᎠᎴ ᎦᏟᎰᏗᏍ ᎤᎦᎹᎾᏨᎯ, ᎤᏴᏢᏃ ᎠᎴ ᎤᏗᎴᎩ, ᎪᎩᏃ ᎠᎴ ᎪᎳ, ᎢᎦᏃ ᎠᎴ ᏒᏃᏱ.—ᏥᏂᏏ 8: 22.

Reading Room of the Seminary

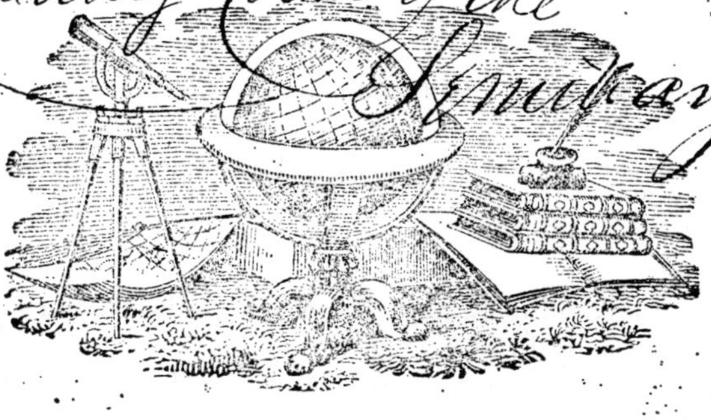

While the earth remaineth, seed time and harvest, and cold and heat, and summer and winter, and day and night shall not cease.—*Gen.* 8: 22.

PARK HILL:

Mission Press: John Candy and John F. Wheeler, Printers.

ᎠᎾ ᎤᏓᏴᏍᏗᏍ: ᏣᏩᏥᏍᏣ ᏙᏧᏣᏃ ᏧᏂᏍᏴᏩᏅᎯ.

The final printed document in this violent controversy. Excessively rare, only one other copy having been traced.

BUTLER, P. M.

Extracts from Reports made by P. M. Butler, United States Agent for the Cherokee Indians. [Tahlequah, 1845.]

38 p. 19 cm. Caption title.

Governor Butler's criticism of Colonel R. B. Mason, the commanding officer at Fort Gibson, for the latter's high-handed treatment of civilian officials, traders, and the Indians themselves. An extremely valuable picture of conditions at this frontier post. Of the very greatest rarity, the only other known copy being that in the British Museum.

Laws of the Cherokee Nation, passed at Tahlequah, Cherokee Nation, 1844–5. Tahlequah: Printed at the Office of the Cherokee Advocate, 1845.

26 p. 20 cm.

One of but three known copies, none of them in Oklahoma.

MASON, R. B.

Fort Gibson, May 28, 1845. Sir: I herewith transmit you a printed pamphlet put in circulation by Governor Butler, the Cherokee Agent . . . . [Tahlequah, 1845.]

32 p. 21.5 cm. Printed without title page or caption.

Colonel Mason's spirited reply to Governor Butler's strictures. The only known copy.

Report of the Secretary of War communicating the Report and Correspondence of the Board of Inquiry to prosecute an Examination into the Causes and Extent of the Discontents and Difficulties among the Cherokee Indians. [Washington, 1845.]

143 p. 22.5 cm. Caption title.

A mine of valuable information on the Old Settler Cherokees.

TRACY, E. C.

Memoir of the Life of Jeremiah Evarts, Esq., late Corresponding Secretary of the American Board of Commissioners for Foreign Missions. Boston: Crocker & Brewster, 1845.

448 p. 24 cm. Frontisp. port.

Contains considerable matter on the southern Indians, especially the Cherokees.

VANN, DAVID, and others

To the Cherokee People. [Tahlequah, 1845.]

Broadside. 24.5 cm. Text in English and Cherokee.

Signed: David Vann, W. S. Coodey, D. R. Coodey, William P. Ross, J. D. Wofford, Moses Daniel, George W. Adair.

A call by leading citizens of the tribe for a mass meeting at Tahlequah to discuss the wisdom of demanding, in view of recent outrages upon Cherokee citizens by soldiers stationed at Fort Gibson, the removal of all United States troops from the Cherokee Nation. Unrecorded, and the only known copy.

WORCESTER, SAMUEL A., tr.

Catechism. [Park Hill: Mission Press, 1845.]*

4 p. Caption title, in English and Cherokee. Text in Cherokee.

Pilling, Iroquoian Bibliography, p. 30.

1846

The Cherokee Singing Book. Printed for the American Board of Commissioners for Foreign Missions, by Alonzo P. Kenrick, Boston, 1846.

86, [2] p. 16 cm. high × 24 cm. wide.

Hymns in Cherokee, with music. A fine copy, with General E. A. Hitchcock's bookplate. The volume is quite rare; the Union Catalog locates only the Newberry Library copy.

Documents in relation to Difficulties in the Cherokee Nation of Indians. [Washington, 1846.]

9 p. 23 cm. Caption title.

[Laws of the Cherokee Nation, Annual Session of the Council 1846.]

A fragment, of one leaf (pp. 3/4). No copy of the volume itself is known.

Message of the President of the United States relative to the Internal Feuds among the Cherokees. [Washington, 1846.]*

224 p. 22.5 cm. Caption title.

Report of the Secretary of War communicating a Report of the Commissioner of Indian Affairs, in relation to Claims against the Cherokees, under the Treaty of August 6, 1846. [Washington, 1846.]*

189 p. 22.5 cm. Caption title.

ROSS, JOHN, and others

Memorial of John Ross and others, representatives of the Cherokee Nation of Indians, on the subject of the Existing Difficulties in that Nation, and their Relations with the United States. [Washington:] Ritchie & Heiss, [1846].

59 p. 22.5 cm. Caption title.

STAMBAUGH, S. C., and AMOS KENDALL

A Faithful History of the Cherokee Tribe of Indians, from the Period of Our First Intercourse with them, down to the Present Time. The Reasons and Considerations which produced a Separation of the Tribe, at an Early Period; Organizing a Nation East and a Nation West of the Mississippi River. With a Full Exposition of the Causes which Led to their Subsequent Division into Three Parties, and Involving them in their Present Deplorable Condition, and of the Nature and Extent of their Present Claims. In a Condensed and Readable Form. Washington: Jesse E. Dow, 1846.

40 p. 22.5 cm.

Excessively rare. The only copy recorded is that in the Library of Congress.

1847

Report of the Committee on Indian Affairs (on the Memorial of David Vann and William P. Ross, Cherokee Delegates). [Washington, 1847.]

5 p. 22.5 cm. Caption title.

RICHMOND, LEGH, and G. C. SMITH

The Dairyman's Daughter: By Rev. Legh Richmond. Bob the Sailor Boy, by Rev. G. C. Smith, Penzance. Park Hill: Mission Press: J. Candy & E. Archer, Printers. 1847.

67 p. 13 cm. Title page in English and Cherokee. Text in Cherokee.
Two copies, accompanied by an undated New York edition, in English, of thirty-six pages.

STAMBAUGH, S. C., and AMOS KENDALL

Western Cherokees. Statement and Argument on their Claims arising under Treaties of 1835–'46. [Washington, 1847.]

10 p. 21.5 cm. Caption title.
A rare and privately printed pamphlet. It contains an excellent review of treaty relations between the Western Cherokees and the United States.

WORCESTER, SAMUEL A., tr.

Gospel of Jesus Christ according to John. Translated into the Cherokee Language. Third edition. Park Hill: Mission Press: J. Candy & E. Archer, Printers. 1847.

101 p. 13 cm. Title page in English and Cherokee. Text in Cherokee.

1848

CHEROKEE COUNCIL

Whereas, a Communication has been received by the National Committee from the Acting Chief, enclosing Communications from the Cherokee Agent, to him, dated September 16th, 1848, etc. [Tahlequah, 1848.]

Broadside. 25 cm.
A resolution of the Council calling for complete statistical information on the Catawba Indians before entertaining the proposal of the government to remove the remnant of that tribe from Carolina and settle it in the Cherokee Nation. Unrecorded, and the only known copy.

Cherokee Indians. Memorial of the Heirs of Families of the Cherokee Nation of Indians, and the Children of their Heirs and Representatives, praying Redress for the Wrongs and Injuries they have suffered by the Officers of the United States in relation to certain Reservations and Pre-emptions of Lands, and Indemnities for Improvements and Spoliations. [Washington, 1848.]

71 p. 25 cm. Caption title.

JONES, EVAN, and JOHN B. JONES

The Epistle of Paul, the Apostle, to the Ephesians. Translated into Cherokee, for the Am. Baptist Missionary Union, by Evan Jones and John B. Jones. Cherokee: Baptist Mission Press: H. Upham, Printer. 1848.

24 p. 13.5 cm. Title page in English and Cherokee. Text in Cherokee.
One of only two known copies.

JONES, EVAN, and JOHN B. JONES

The Epistle of Paul, the Apostle, to the Galatians, and the 1st. and 2nd. Epistles General of Peter, translated into Cherokee, for the Am. Baptist Missionary Union, by Evan Jones, and John B. Jones. Baptist Mission Press: H. Upham, Printer. 1848.

48 p. 13.5 cm. Title page in English and Cherokee. Text in Cherokee.
One of only three known copies.

JONES, EVAN, and JOHN B. JONES

The Epistle of Paul, the Apostle, to the Philippians. [Baptist Mission Press, Cherokee Nation. 1848.]

24 p. 13.5 cm. Caption title, in English and Cherokee. Text in Cherokee. Imprint and date appear at the end.
One of only two known copies.

MALAN, CESAR

The Swiss Peasant. By Rev. Cesar Malan, of Geneva. The One Thing Needful. Park Hill: Mission Press: Edwin Archer, Printer. 1848.

24 p. 13 cm. Title page in English and Cherokee. Text in Cherokee.
Two copies.

WORCESTER, SAMUEL A.

Confession of Faith and Covenant of the Church at Park Hill, adopted June 4, 1837. Park Hill: Mission Press: Edwin Archer, printer. 1848.

12 p. 13 cm. Plain wrappers. Joint English and Cherokee title. Text in English and in Cherokee. At the end is a Pastoral letter signed by S. A. Worcester.
The little volume is excessively rare.

1849

JONES, EVAN, and JOHN B. JONES

The First and Second Epistle of Paul, the Apostle, to the Corinthians, and the Revelation of John. Translated into Cherokee, for the American Baptist Missionary Union, by Evan Jones, and John B. Jones. Baptist Mission Press: Cherokee Nation. 1849.

150 p. 13.5 cm. Title page in English and Cherokee. Text in Cherokee.
One of but three known copies.

MAHONEY, JAMES W.

The Cherokee Physician, or Indian Guide to Health, as given by Richard Foreman, a Cherokee Doctor; comprising a Brief View of Anatomy, with General Rules for Preserving Health without the Use of Medicines. The Diseases of the U. States, with their Symptoms, Causes, and Means of Prevention, are treated in a satisfactory manner. It also contains a Description of a Variety of Herbs and Roots, many of which are not explained in any other book, and their Medical Virtues have hitherto been unknown to the Whites; to which is added a Short Dispensatory. By Jas. W. Mahoney. Asheville, N.C.: Edney & Dedman, 1849.

308, 5 p. 19.5 cm.

The Union Catalog lists only the 3rd edition, New York 1857. Unrecorded, and the only known copy.

Report: The Select Committee "appointed to inquire into and fully investigate the Course pursued by the Commissioner of Indian Affairs in the Administration of his Official Duties, and especially into the Charges made and preferred in debate in this body on the 9th day of August, 1848, by the Hon. T. L. Clingman, a member of the House," and to which said committee the resolution adopted on the 12th August, 1848, was referred, respectfully report: . . . . [Washington, 1849.]
71 p. 25 cm. Caption title.
Relates to Cherokee affairs.

Ross, William P., and others
Memorial of Will. P. Ross, W. S. Coodey, and John Drew, in behalf of the Old Settler, or Western Cherokees, complaining that they have been deprived of Certain Rights accruing under Treaty Stipulations. [Washington, 1849.]
5 p. 22.5 cm. Caption title.

Worcester, Samuel A., tr.
The Epistles of Paul to Timothy. [Park Hill: Mission Press, 1849.]
24 p. 13 cm. Caption title, in English and Cherokee. Text in Cherokee.
Pilling, Iroquoian Bibliography, p. 63, errs in place and date of printing.

Worcester, Samuel A., tr.
Isaiah. I–VII, XI, LII–LV. [Park Hill: Mission Press, 1849.]
32 p. 13 cm. Caption title, in English and Cherokee. Text in Cherokee.
Pilling, Iroquoian Bibliography, p. 174, errs in place and date of printing.

Worcester, Samuel A., tr.
Psalms. [Park Hill: Mission Press, 1849.]
34 p. 13 cm. Caption title, in English and Cherokee. Text in Cherokee.
Pilling, Iroquoian Bibliography, p. 174, errs in place and date of printing.

1850

Worcester, Samuel A., tr.
[The Epistles of John. Park Hill: Mission Press, 1850.]
16 p. 13 cm. Caption title and text in Cherokee.
Pilling, Iroquoian Bibliography, p. 63, errs in place and date of printing.

Worcester, Samuel A., tr.
The Epistles of Peter. [Park Hill: Mission Press, 1850.]
24 p. 13 cm. Caption title, in English and Cherokee. Text in Cherokee.
At end: Second edition.
Pilling, Iroquoian Bibliography, p. 63, errs in place and date of printing.
Two copies.

Worcester, Samuel A., tr.
The General Epistle of James. Translated into the Cherokee Language. Second edition. Park Hill: Mission Press: Edwin Archer, Printer. 1850.

16 p. 13 cm. Title page in English and Cherokee. Text in Cherokee. Two copies.

WORCESTER, SAMUEL A., tr.

The Gospel according to Luke. Translated into the Cherokee Language. Park Hill: Mission Press: Edwin Archer, Printer. 1850.

134 p. 13 cm. Title page in English and Cherokee. Text in Cherokee. Two copies.

WORCESTER, SAMUEL A., tr.

The Gospel According to Matthew. Translated into the Cherokee Language. Fifth edition. Park Hill: Mission Press: Edwin Archer, Printer. 1850.

120 p. 13 cm. Title page in English and Cherokee. Text in Cherokee.

WORCESTER, SAMUEL A., tr.

The Revelation of John. Chapters I–V and XX–XXII. Translated into the Cherokee Language. Park Hill: Mission Press: Edwin Archer, Printer. 1850.

28 p. 13 cm. Title page in English and Cherokee. Text in Cherokee.

1851

DRENNEN, JOHN

Notice! To Old Settler or Western Cherokees. [Tahlequah, 1851.]

Broadside. 23.5 cm.

A call for a convention of the Old Settlers to meet at Tah-lon-tus-kee. Unrecorded, and the only known copy.

1852

KENDALL, AMOS

A Letter to the Hon. George E. Badger, in relation to the Claim of A. & J. E. Kendall against the United States, for Certain Wrongs done them, with an Appendix. By Amos Kendall. Washington: Buell & Blanchard, 1852.

27 p. 21 cm.

An exposition of the claim of the Kendalls for services rendered the Western Cherokees.

KENDALL, AMOS

Report of the Secretary of the Interior communicating the Correspondence with Persons Claiming to be Creditors of the Western Cherokees. [Washington, 1852.]

90 p. 22 cm. Caption title.

A review of the Kendall claim, with important documents.

Laws of the Cherokee Nation: Adopted by the Council at Various Periods. Printed for the Benefit of the Nation. Tahlequah: Cherokee Advocate Office, 1852.

179, 248 p. 17.5 cm.

An indispensable compilation, which contains all the laws and constitutions of the Cherokee Nation from 1808 to 1851.

[Laws of the Cherokee Nation: Adopted by the Council at Various Periods. Printed for the Benefit of the Nation. Tahlequah: Cherokee Advocate Office, 1852.]

148, 31, 276 p. 17.5 cm.
The Cherokee version of the preceding volume. One of three known complete copies.

1853

Cherokee Almanac 1854. Calculated for the Cherokee Nation, Lat. 35° 50′ N. Lon. 95° 7′ W. Park Hill: Mission Press: Edwin Archer, Printer. [1853].
36 p. 17.5 cm.

Laws of the Cherokee Nation; passed at the Annual Sessions of the National Council of 1852–3. Published by Authority. Tahlequah, C.N.: Cherokee Advocate Print, 1853.
33 p. 19.5 cm.
A fine, uncut copy. The only known copy, with the signature on the title page of George Butler, a prominent Cherokee of the period.

WORCESTER, SAMUEL A., tr.

The Epistles of Paul to Timothy. [Park Hill: Mission Press, 1853.]
24 p. 13 cm. Caption title, in English and Cherokee. Text in Cherokee.
Pilling, Iroquoian Bibliography, p. 63, errs in place and date of printing.

WORCESTER, SAMUEL A., tr.

Exodus; of the Second Book of Moses. Translated into the Cherokee Language. Park Hill: Mission Press: Edwin Archer, Printer. 1853.
13 cm. 152 p. Title page in English and in Cherokee. Text in Cherokee.

1854

BOUDINOT, ELIAS, and SAMUEL A. WORCESTER

Cherokee Hymns. Compiled from several Authors and revised. Ninth edition. Park Hill: Mission Press: Edwin Archer, Printer. 1854.
69, [2] p. 13.5 cm. Plain wrappers. Joint English and Cherokee title. Text in Cherokee.
Two copies.

Cherokee Almanac 1855. Calculated by Benjamin Greenleaf, A.M., author of "National Arithmetic," "Practical Algebra," &c., for the Latitude and Longitude of Tahlequah, Cherokee Nation. Park Hill: Mission Press: Edwin Archer, Printer. [1854].
36 p. 17.5 cm.

Cherokee Rosebuds. Tahlequah: Female Seminary, August 2, 1854. Vol. 1. No. 2. [Tahlequah: Advocate Office, 1854.]
8 p. 29 cm. Caption title.
Apparently the only known issue. Two Cherokee girls, Catharine Gunter and Nancy E. Hicks, were the editors.

[Laws of the Cherokee Nation; passed at the Annual Sessions of the National Council of 1852–53. Published by Authority. Tahlequah, C.N.: Cherokee Advocate Print, 1854.]
34 p. 17 cm. Title and text in Cherokee.
One of only two known copies; the other is at the New York Public Library.

WORCESTER, SAMUEL A.

Cherokee Primer. Park Hill: Mission Press: Edwin Archer, printer, 1854.

24 p. 12.5 cm. Joint Cherokee and English title. Text in Cherokee.

WORCESTER, SAMUEL A., tr.

The Gospel of Jesus Christ according to John. Translated into the Cherokee Language. Fourth edition. Park Hill: Mission Press: Edwin Archer, Printer. 1854.

93 p. 13 cm. Title page in English and Cherokee. Text in Cherokee. Two copies.

1855

GILMER, GEORGE R.

Sketches of Some of the First Settlers of Upper Georgia, of the Cherokees, and the Author. New York: Appleton, 1855.

587, [4] p. 22.5 cm. Frontisp. port.
A noteworthy book of remarkable frankness; it contains biographical and genealogical sketches of the Gilmers and the neighboring families, an account of the settlement of upper Georgia, and an autobiography, including important documents on the Cherokees.

Laws of the Cherokee Nation; passed at the Annual Sessions of the National Council of 1854–'55. Published by Authority. Tahlequah, C.N.: Cherokee Advocate Print, 1855.

29 p. 17 cm.
The only known copy.

Opinion of Judge Scarburgh. J. K. Rogers vs. the United States. [N.p., 1855.]

The claim here analyzed and reviewed was denied on the grounds that Rogers, although admittedly a Cherokee by birth, had ceased to be a citizen of the Cherokee Nation and had become a citizen of Georgia.

1856

Cherokee Almanac 1857. Calculated by Benjamin Greenleaf, A.M., Author of "National Arithmetic," "Practical Algebra," &c., for the Latitude and Longitude of Tahlequah, Cherokee Nation. Park Hill: Mission Press: Edwin Archer, Printer. [1855].

36 p. 17.5 cm.

[Laws of the Cherokee Nation; passed at the Annual Sessions of the National Council of 1854–'55. Tahlequah: Cherokee Advocate Print, 1856.]

30 p. 17 cm. Title page and text in Cherokee.
The only known copy.

SUMMERS, THOMAS O.

Joseph Brown; or, The Young Tennessean whose Life was Saved by the Power of Prayer. An Indian Tale. Nashville, Tenn.: Stevenson & Evans, 1856.

126 p. 14 cm.

Newberry-Ayer 286.

Brown was captured by the Cherokee Indians. Very rare; the Union Catalog locates but two copies.

WORCESTER, SAMUEL A., tr.

Genesis, or the First Book of Moses. Park Hill: Mission Press: Edwin Archer, Printer, 1856.

173 p. 13 cm. Title page in English and Cherokee. Text in Cherokee.

1857

WORCESTER, SAMUEL A., tr.

The Negro Servant. [Park Hill: Mission Press, 1857.]*

40 p. 12.5 cm. Caption title, in English and Cherokee. Text in Cherokee. Pilling, Iroquoian Bibliography, p. 128, errs in place and date of printing.

1858

Cherokee Almanac 1859. Calculated by Benjamin Greenleaf, A.M., Author of "National Arithmetic," "Practical Algebra," &c., for the Latitude and Longitude of Tahlequah, Cherokee Nation. Park Hill: Mission Press: Edwin Archer, Printer. [1858].

36 p. 17.5 cm.

KENDALL, AMOS

Petition. [Washington, 1858.]

23 p. 23 cm. Caption title.

A statement of the Kendall claim for services rendered the Old Settler Cherokees.

WORCESTER, SAMUEL A., tr.

The Epistle of Paul to the Philippians. [Park Hill: Mission Press, 1858.]

43 p. 13 cm. Caption title, in English and Cherokee. Text in Cherokee. Pilling, Iroquoian Bibliography, p. 62, errs in place and date of printing.

WORCESTER, SAMUEL A., tr.

The Epistle of Paul to Titus. [Park Hill: Mission Press, 1858.]*

49 p. 13 cm. Caption title, in English and Cherokee. Text in Cherokee. Pilling, Iroquoian Bibliography, p. 62, errs in place and date of printing.

WORCESTER, SAMUEL A., tr.

The Epistles of Paul to the Corinthians. Park Hill: Mission Press: Edwin Archer, Printer. 1858.*

125 p. 13 cm. Title in English and Cherokee. Text in Cherokee.

WORCESTER, SAMUEL A., tr.

The General Epistle of Jude. [Park Hill: Mission Press, 1858.]*

66 p. Caption title, in English and Cherokee. Text in Cherokee.

Pilling, Iroquoian Bibliography, p. 69, errs in place and date of printing.

1859

Cherokee Almanac 1860. Calculated by Benjamin Greenleaf, A.M., Author of "National Arithmetic," "Practical Algebra," &c., for the Latitude and Longitude of

Tahlequah, Cherokee Nation. Park Hill: Edwin Archer, Printer. [1859].
34, [2] p. 17.5 cm. Printed on green, blue and white paper.

Ross, John
Message of the Principal Chief of the Cherokee Nation. Printed at the "Cherokee Messenger" Office. Baptist Mission, C.N., 1859.
8 p. 21.5 cm.
Excessively rare.

1860

Rocky Mountain Gold Mines. Idaho (Gem of the Mountains) Gold & Silver Mining Company, Quartz Hill, Nevada District, Pike's Peak. Baltimore: John W. Woods, [1860].
15 p. 23 cm. Printed wrappers.
Contains an account of the accidental discovery of gold by a party of Cherokee hunters in 1849 on the banks of the Cache a la Poudre and of the subsequent prospecting by the Russel party of Georgia and a party of Cherokees. The only known copy.

Worcester, Samuel A., tr.
The Acts of the Apostles. [Park Hill: Mission Press, 1860?].*
114 p. 13 cm. Caption title, in English and Cherokee. Text in Cherokee.
Pilling, Iroquoian Bibliography, p. 173, errs in the place of printing.

Worcester, Samuel A.
The Epistle of Paul to the Romans. [Park Hill: Mission Press, 1860?].*
55 p. 13 cm. Caption title, in English and Cherokee. Text in Cherokee.
Pilling, Iroquoian Bibliography, p. 62.

Worcester, Samuel A., tr.
[The Gospel according to Mark. Park Hill: Mission Press, 1860?].*
70 p. Caption title and text in Cherokee.
Pilling, Iroquoian Bibliography, p. 70, errs in the place of printing.

1861

Ross, John
Correspondence. [Tahlequah, 1861.]
Broadsheet. 28 cm.
Correspondence between Principal Chief John Ross, General Ben McCulloch, and Confederate Indian Commissioner David Hubbard regarding Cherokee neutrality. The only known copy of a document of prime importance.

Ross, John
Proclamation to the Cherokee People. [Tahlequah, 1861.]
Broadsheet. Folio.
The momentous proclamation of Cherokee neutrality. Appended is correspondence between Principal Chief Ross and Arkansas, Texas, and Confederate officials regarding the neutral stand taken by the Cherokees. The only known copy.

Treaty with the Cherokees. [N.p., 1861.]
26 p. 22.5 cm. Caption title.
The momentous treaty of alliance negotiated by Albert Pike on behalf of the Confederate States of America.

TURNER, JESSE

Correspondence. Hon. Jesse Turner's Position. [Van Buren, Arkansas, 1861.]
Broadside. 31 cm.
The attitude toward secession in this frontier town was strongly reflected in the neighboring Cherokee country. No other copy recorded.

1863

Amos Kendall and John E. Kendall vs. the United States. Washington: McGill & Witherow, [1863].
15 p. 23 cm. Caption title. The imprint is at the foot of the first page.
The claim grew out of services rendered by the Kendalls to the Western Cherokees.

DAVIS, JEFFERSON

Message of the President. [Richmond, 1863.]
16 p. 24.5 cm. Caption title.
A review of the fortunes of the Confederacy, with some attention to the Cherokee alliance.

LINCOLN, ABRAHAM

The President's Proclamation of Pardon and Amnesty in the Cherokee Language. Translated and printed at Fort Gibson, C.N. by Order of Colonel Wm. A. Phillips, commanding First Brigade, Army of the Frontier. [1863].
4 p. 19.5 cm.
The only known copy, and perhaps the only state paper of Lincoln's translated into the Cherokee language. [See page 54.]

1864

SCOTT, WINFIELD

Memoirs of Lieut.-General Scott, LL.D. Written by himself. New York: Sheldon & Company, 1864.
2 vols. Portraits.
Contains valuable material on the Cherokee removal and the Black Hawk War.

1865

MISSOURI CITIZENS

A Memorial to the President and Congress of the United States and the Secretary of War, asking for a Fort or Garrison to be established near the Southwest Corner of the State. [Neosho, Missouri, 1865.]
Broadside. Folio.
Ostensibly a plea for protection against "bands of marauders, who infest the country, robbing, murdering and leaving their mark of death and desolation wherever they go." Actually, however, the memorial reflects the desire of the people of southwestern Missouri to gain control of the salt springs in the Cherokee Nation and to exploit them under military protection. Unrecorded, and no other copy known.

THE

PRESIDENT'S PROCLAMATION

OF PARDON AND AMNESTY

IN THE CHEROKEE LANGUAGE.

TRANSLATED AND PRINTED AT FORT GIBSON, C. N.

BY ORDER OF COLONEL WM. A. PHILLIPS,

COMMANDING FIRST BRIGADE, ARMY OF THE FRONTIER.

1866

BOUDINOT, ELIAS CORNELIUS

Reply of the Southern Cherokees to the Memorial of certain Delegates from the Cherokee Nation, together with the Message of John Ross, ex-Chief of the Cherokees, and Proceedings of the Council of the "loyal Cherokees," relative to the Alliance with the so-called Confederate States. Washington: McGill & Witherow, 1866.

19 p. 22.5 cm. Printed wrappers.

Cherokee Hymn Book. Compiled from several authors, and revised. Philadelphia, 1866.

96 p. 12.5 cm. Joint English and Cherokee title. Text in Cherokee. Hymn titles in English.

The Cherokee Question. Report of the Commissioner of Indian Affairs to the President of the United States, June 15, 1866. Being Supplementary to the Report of the Commissioners appointed by the President to Treat with the Indians South of Kansas, and which assembled at Fort Smith, Ark., in September, 1865. Washington, 1866.

58 p. 23 cm. Printed wrappers.

Very rare, and a fine copy. The volume was issued apparently in an effort to discredit John Ross and the northern or loyal faction of the Cherokees. John Ross died a few weeks after its publication and it is thought that the edition was then largely destroyed. The volume contains highly important letters and documents and casts much light on Cherokee diplomatic and military history of the Confederate period.

Communication of the Delegation of the Cherokee Nation to the President of the United States, submitting the Memorial of their National Council, with the Correspondence between John Ross, Principal Chief, and Certain Officers of the Rebellious States. Washington: Gibson Bros., 1866.

48 p. 22.5 cm. Printed wrappers.

Letters and documents of great importance in the history of negotiation of the Confederate alliance with the principal tribes of Indian Territory.

Memorial of the Delegates of the Cherokee Nation to the President of the United States, and the Senate and House of Representatives in Congress. Washington: Chronicle Print, 1866.

12 p. 23 cm.

Contains important acts of the Loyal Cherokee government passed during the war. One of only four known copies.

Reply of the Delegates of the Cherokee Nation to the Demands of the Commissioners of Indian Affairs. May, 1866. Washington: Gibson Bros., 1866.

14 p. 23 cm. Printed wrappers.

Statement of the position and views of the Loyal Cherokees.

Reply of the Delegates of the Cherokee Nation to the Pamphlet of the Commissioner of Indian Affairs. Washington, D.C., 1866.

16 p. 21 cm.

Reply of the Loyal Cherokee delegation to *The Cherokee Question.* The pamphlet is rare.

Ridge, John R., and others

Comments on the Objections of certain Cherokee Delegates to the Proposition of the Government to Separate Hostile Parties of the Cherokee Nation. Washington: Intelligencer Printing House, 1866.*

16 p. 21.5 cm. Wrapper title.

Signed: John R. Ridge, Richard Fields, Wm. P. Adair, Saladin Watie, E. C. Boudinot, Cherokee Delegates.

1867

Articles of Agreement made this 8th day of April, A.D. 1867, between the Cherokee Nation, represented by William P. Ross, Principal Chief, Riley Keyes and Jesse Bushyhead, Delegates duly authorized, parties of the first part, and the Delaware Tribe of Indians, represented by John Connor, Principal Chief; Charles Journeycake, Assistant Chief; Isaac Journeycake, and John Sarcoxie, Delegates for and on behalf of said Delaware Tribe, duly authorized. [Washington, 1867.]

3 p. 23 cm. Caption title.

Two copies.

Amendments to the Constitution of the Cherokee Nation, adopted Nov. 26, 1866. Washington, 1867.

7 p. 13.5 cm. Wrapper title.

The only known copy. The amendments were dictated by the recent Union defeat of Confederate arms.

1868

Laws of the Cherokee Nation, passed during the years 1839–1867, compiled by Authority of the National Council. St. Louis: Missouri Democrat Print, 1868.

208 p. 23 cm.

Ridge, John Rollin

Poems. By John R. Ridge. San Francisco: Henry Payot & Company, publishers. 1868.

137 p. 17.5 cm.

The first edition. A fine copy, complete with portrait.

Walker, R. J.

Opinion relating to the Western Boundary of the Cherokee Country. [N.p., 1868.]

8 p. 22 cm. Caption title.

1869

Doolittle, James R.

Argument of the Hon. James R. Doolittle, submitted by him as of Counsel for the Cherokee Nation to the Senate Committee on Indian Affairs. Washington, D.C., April, 1869. Washington: Intelligencer Printing House, 1869.

7 p. 23 cm. Wrapper title.

Report of the Cherokee Delegation of their Mission to Washington, in 1868 and 1869. [N.p., 1869].

5, clxiv p. Wrapper title.

Rare and important.

SCHINDELL, J. P.

Department of the Missouri. Fort Gibson, Indian Territory. [N.p., 1869.]*

Broadside. 25.5 cm.

A minute description of Fort Gibson and its location and of the neighboring country.

WASHBURN, CEPHAS

Reminiscences of the Indians. By the Rev. Cephas Washburn, A.M., many years Superintendent of the Dwight Mission among the Cherokees of the Arkansas. With a Biography of the author. By Rev. J. W. Moore, of Arkansas, and an Introduction by Rev. J. L. Wilson, D.D., Secretary of Foreign Missions. Richmond: Presbyterian Committee of Publication. [1869].

236 p. 18.5 cm.

Field 1622.

WRIGHT, JOHN W.

Reply of John W. Wright, Attorney for the Cherokee and Creek Indians, to Certain Libelous Statements published in the New York Tribune and in a Certain Pamphlet signed by James G. Blunt. Washington: H. Polkinhorn & Co., 1869.

15 p. 21.5 cm.

1870

The Act of Union between the Eastern and Western Cherokees, the Constitution and Amendments, and the Laws of the Cherokee Nation, passed during the Session of 1868 and Subsequent Sessions. Tah-le-quah: National Press, Edwin Archer, printer, 1870.

100 p. 18.5 cm.

ADAIR, W. P.

Protest of W. P. Adair, Chairman Cherokee Delegation, against the Right claimed by the United States Government to Exact Licenses from Adopted Cherokees, under the Intercourse Act of 1834, to Trade in the Indian Country, and for other purposes. Washington: Pearson, 1870.

16 p. 23 cm. Wrapper title.

BOUDINOT, ELIAS C.

Memorial of Elias C. Boudinot, a Cherokee Indian, to the Senate and House of Representatives of the United States. Can a Bureau or Department Annul the Stipulations of a Treaty? What is the Money Value of the Honor of a Nation Solemnly Pledged? [N.p., 1870.]

10 p. 25 cm.

Boudinot, in partnership with his uncle, Stand Watie, built and operated a tobacco factory in the Cherokee Nation. Under treaty stipulations, their product was free from Federal tax. Arkansas and Kansas manufacturers and merchants succeeded, however, in persuading the government to circumvent the treaty and tax their Indian competitors. The case dragged on for several years, as subsequent entries in this list will show, and Boudinot finally lost the case and his factory.

CHEROKEE BAPTIST ASSOCIATION

[Minutes of the Annual Meeting held with Tsu-wo-sto-yi Church, September 14–17, 1870. National Printing Office: Tahlequah, Cherokee Nation. 1870.]

10, [1] p. 18 cm. Title page and text wholly in Cherokee.

Not in Foreman, and no other copy known.

CHEROKEE BAPTIST ASSOCIATION

Minutes of the Cherokee Baptist Association held with the Tsu-wo-sto-yi Church, September 14–17, 1870. National Printing Office: Tahlequah, Cherokee Nation. 1870.

11, [1] p. 18 cm.

Not in Foreman, and no other copy known.

DOWNING, LEWIS

Cherokee Nation. Letter from Lewis Downing, Principal Chief of the Cherokee Nation, inclosing Petitions of Numbers of Various Tribes against a Proposed Territorial Government over them. [Washington, 1870.]

15 p. 23 cm. Caption title.

DOWNING, LEWIS, and others

Memorial of the Principal Chief and Delegates of the Cherokee Nation of Indians, remonstrating against a Territorial Form of Government, Legislative Jurisdiction of Congress, the Abrogation of Existing Treaties and the Burden of Government Taxation without Representation, and in favor of the Payment by the United States of all Just Obligations to said Nation. [Washington, 1870.]

7 p. 23 cm. Caption title.

DOWNING, LEWIS, and others

To the Honorable Judiciary Committee, House of Representatives. [Washington, 1870.]

4 p. 23 cm. Caption title.

An address signed by the principal chief and the Cherokee delegation, on the issues of the Boudinot Tobacco Case.

GOULDING, F. R.

Sal-o-quah; or, Boy-life among the Cherokees. By F. R. Goulding, author of "Young Marooners," "Marooner's Island," "Frank Gordon," etc. Philadelphia, 1870.

265 p. 16.5 cm. Frontisp.

An excellent and little known picture of Cherokee life in Georgia. The volume is rare, the Union Catalog locating only the copy in the De Renne Library.

JONES, JOHN B.

Elementary Arithmetic, in Cherokee and English, designed for Beginners. By John B. Jones. Prepared by Authority of the Cherokee National Council. Cherokee National Press: Tahlequah, Cherokee Nation. 1870.

60 p. in double. 16.5 cm. Joint English and Cherokee title. Text in Cherokee and in English. A rare volume.

MORRIS, ISAAC N.

Argument of the Hon. Isaac N. Morris, of Illinois, Attorney for the Cherokee Nation, in answer to the Argument of Judge Thomas W. Bartley, of Ohio, Attorney for the Government in the Boudinot Case, involving the Question of the Power of the Government to Collect Taxes in the Indian Territory, and whether the Indian is a Citizen by virtue of the Fourteenth Amendment, showing the Truth of the Negative of each, and the Right to make Treaties with Indians. Washington, 1870.

18 p. 23 cm.

Relates to the Boudinot Tobacco Case.

MORRIS, ISAAC N.

Argument of Hon. Isaac N. Morris, of Illinois, of Counsel for the Cherokee Indians, before the House Committee on Indian Affairs, against the Bill Proposing to Establish a Territorial Government over the Indians. Submitted Feb. 2, 1870. Washington: Chronicle Print, 1870.

15 p. 22 cm. Printed wrappers.

Some Reasons Why the Pending Cherokee Treaty Should be Ratified. We Ask to be Heard. Washington: Joseph L. Pearson, 1870.*

20 p. 23 cm. Wrapper title.

An address by the Cherokee delegation.

Treaties between the United States of America and the Cherokee Nation, from 1785. National Printing Office: Tahlequah, Cherokee Nation. 1870.

144, [1] p. 16.5 cm.

Presentation copy, inscribed, from Charles Thompson, Principal Chief, and William Rasmus, Executive Secretary.

1871

BOUDINOT, ELIAS CORNELIUS

Speech of Col. E. C. Boudinot, of the Cherokee Nation, on the Indian Question, delivered at Vinita, Cherokee Nation, the Junction of the Atlantic and Pacific and the Missouri, Kansas and Texas Railroads, on Thursday, September 21. Terre-Haute, [1871].*

11 p. 21.5 cm.

The printing date on the title page has been trimmed off in binding.

Boudinot urged the opening of Indian Territory to railroads and white settlers. The volume is very rare.

BUTLER, BENJAMIN F.

Argument (in Brief) on the Exemptions of the Cherokee Nation from Internal Taxation. By Benj. F. Butler. Washington: McGill & Witherow, 1871.*

14 p. 23 cm. Wrapper title.

An important argument, delivered in the Boudinot Tobacco Case.

[Compiled laws, in Cherokee. Tahlequah, 1871.]

310 p. 20 cm. Title page and text entirely in Cherokee.
A translation of the 1868 and 1870 compilations, in English.

DOWNING, LEWIS, and others

Protest of the Cherokee Nation against a Territorial Government. Washington: Cunningham & McIntosh, 1871.

13 p. 22 cm.

1872

BOUDINOT, ELIAS C.

Speech of Elias C. Boudinot, a Cherokee Indian, delivered before the House Committee on Territories, February 7, 1872, in behalf of a Territorial Government for the Indian Territory, in reply to Wm. P. Ross, a Cherokee Delegate, in his Argument against any Congressional Action upon the subject. Washington: McGill & Witherow, 1872.

30 p. 21.5 cm. Printed wrappers.

BOUDINOT, ELIAS C.

Speech of Elias C. Boudinot, of the Cherokee Nation, delivered before the House Committee on Territories, March 5, 1872, on the Question of a Territorial Government for the Indian Territory, in Reply to the Second Argument of the Indian Delegations in Opposition to such Proposed Government. Washington: McGill & Witherow, 1872.

16 p. 23 cm. Printed wrappers.

BOUDINOT, ELIAS C.

Speech of Elias C. Boudinot, a Cherokee Indian, on the Indian Question, delivered at Vinita, Cherokee Nation, the Junction of the Atlantic and Pacific, and the Missouri, Kansas and Texas Railroads, September 21, 1871. Washington: McGill & Witherow, 1872.*

18 p. 21.5 cm.

HOLABIRD, S. B.

Proposals for Regular Sup'lies. Chief Quartermaster's Office, San Antonio, Texas, August 1, 1872. Sealed Proposals will be received at this office and also at the office of the U.S. Quartermaster at Fort Gibson, Indian Ter., for furnishing and delivering at said Fort such Quantities of Regular Supplies as may be required at the Post, etc. [San Antonio, 1872.]

Broadside. 30.5 cm.
The only known copy.

Laws and Joint Resolutions of the National Council. Passed and adopted at the Regular and Extra Sessions of 1871. Tahlequah: Frank J. Dubois, 1872.

42 p. 16.5 cm.
One of only seven known copies, none of which is in Oklahoma.

Message from the President of the United States communicating Information relative to the Recent Affray at the Courthouse in Going Snake, Indian Territory, [Washington, 1872.]*

10 p. 23 cm. Caption title.

Message from the President of the United States, communicating Information relative to the Recent Affray at the Court House in Going Snake, Indian Territory, and recommending the Erection of a Judicial District in the Indian Territory. [Washington, 1872.]

20 p. 23 cm. Caption title.

1873

BRYAN, J. M.

To the Members Elect of the National Council. The Following Copy of Protest is submitted for your Consideration. [Tahlequah, 1873.]

Broadside. Folio.

A claim for the value of improvements at Chouteau Station seized in the public interest. The only known copy.

Laws and Joint Resolutions of the National Council, passed and adopted at the Extra and Regular Sessions of 1872. Tahlequah: John Doubletooth, Printer, 1873.*

61 p. 17 cm.

1874

E. C. Boudinot, the Indian Orator and Lecturer. [N.p., 1874?].

[16] p. 15.5 cm.

A sketch of his life, with a portrait; press notices of his lectures and readings, and letters of commendation. Bound with others.

Statement of the Cherokee Funds from July, 1866, to July, 1874. Washington: Gibson Bros., [1874].

8 p. Folio. Wrapper title.

1875

BELL, JAMES M., and SUT BECK

Address to the Citizens of the Cherokee Nation by James M. Bell and Sut Beck. [N.p., 1875?].*

3 p. 27 cm.

An argument by prominent Cherokees in favor of territorial status for the tribes of Indian Territory and the allotment of their lands in severalty.

Cherokee Alphabet. [Tahlequah? 1875?].

Broadside. 25.5 cm.

No other copy has been traced.

Constitution and Laws of the Cherokee Nation. Published by Authority of the National Council. St. Louis: R. & T. A. Ennis, 1875.

284, [7] p. 22 cm.

[Constitution and Laws of the Cherokee Nation. Published by Authority of the National Council. St. Louis: R. & T. A. Ennis, 1875.]

284, [vii] p. 22 cm.
A translation into Cherokee of the 1875 compilation. A fine copy.

Memorial of the Old Settlers or Western Cherokees. [N.p., 1875.]
29 p. 23 cm. Caption title.

Paschal, George W.
The Constitution of the United States. [N.p., 1875?].*
24 p. 26 cm. Caption title.
The proof sheets of Paschal's well-known annotations to the Constitution, with his autograph signature and numerous notes and corrections in his hand. Paschal married into the prominent Cherokee family, the Ridges, and while practicing law at the border town of Van Buren, Arkansas, played a prominent hand in Cherokee affairs in the 1840's.

Protest of the Cherokees against the Establishment by Congress of a Territorial Government of the United States over them. [N.p., 1875.]*
23 p. 12.5 cm. Caption title.
The protest is signed by several thousand Cherokees—a valuable list of names.

Ross, D. H., and W. P. Adair
Letter of Cherokee Delegation to Commissioner of Indian Affairs respecting the Claims of the "Old Settler Cherokees." [Washington, 1875.]
13 p. 23 cm. Caption title.

1876

Answer of the Legally Authorized Delegates of the Cherokee, Creek, Choctaw, and Seminole Nations of Indians of the Indian Territory, to the Argument of Gardner G. Hubbard, Attorney for the Foreign Bondholders of the M. K. & T. R. R. Co. and others, made before the Committee on Territories of the House of Representatives, February 11, 1876. Washington: Gibson Bros., 1876.*
15 p. 23 cm. Wrapper title.

Claim of the Old Settlers or Western Cherokees against the United States. Statement of the Case and Argument for Claimants, before the Committees on Indian Affairs of the 46th Congress. Washington: John L. Ginck, [1876].
40 p. 22.5 cm. Wrapper title.

Elias C. Boudinot vs. The United States. Findings of Fact. [Washington, 1876.]
8 p. 23 cm. Caption title.
A succinct review by the Court of Claims of the Boudinot Tobacco Case.

[A letter, printed without title page or caption, to the Chairman of the Committee on Indian Affairs. Washington, 1876.]
9 p. 22.5 cm.
Unfulfilled treaty obligations to the Old Settlers.

[A letter, printed without title page or caption, from the Cherokee Delegation in relation to the claims of the Western Cherokees. Washington, 1876.]
12 p. 21 cm.

To the Hon. Chairman of the Committee on Territories of the House of Representatives. [N.p., 1876.]

6 p. 22.5 cm. Caption title.

A protest by Old Settler Cherokee Commissioners against the granting of Indian lands to railroads.

To the Honorable Committee of the House of Representatives on Indian Affairs. Washington, D.C., February, 1876. [Washington, 1876.]*

5 p. 22.5 cm. Caption title.

An appeal for justice, signed: Old Settler Cherokee Commission.

To the Honorable Committee on Indian Affairs of the House of Representatives. [N.p., 1876.]

8 p. 22.5 cm. Caption title.

An appeal for the settlement of the Old Settler claim.

WILSON, WILLIAM

To Old Settler Cherokees. [Tahlequah, 1876.]

Broadside. 21 cm. high × 29 cm. wide.

A call for meetings of Old Settlers for the purpose of signing a memorial. Unrecorded, and the only known copy.

1877

BOUDINOT, ELIAS C.

The Memorial of Elias C. Boudinot to the Congress of the United States. [Fayetteville, Ark., 1877.]

42 p. 23 cm. Caption title.

On the subject of the Boudinot Tobacco Case.

BOUDINOT, ELIAS C.

To the Congress of the United States. Elias C. Boudinot, who has heretofore submitted his Memorial for your consideration, now respectfully submits the following Brief in support of that Memorial. [Fayetteville, Ark., 1877.]

24 p. 23 cm. Caption title.

Relates to the Boudinot Tobacco Case.

BOUDINOT, ELIAS, and S. A. WORCESTER

Cherokee Hymn Book. Compiled from several authors and revised. Philadelphia, 1877.*

96 p. 12 cm.

CHEROKEE BAPTIST ASSOCIATION

Minutes of the Eighth Annual Meeting of the Cherokee Baptist Association held with the Round Spring Baptist Church, Delaware District, Cherokee Nation, Indian Territory, commencing on Wednesday, October 12, 1876. Tahlequah: National Book and Job Printing Office, 1877.

11 p. 20 cm.

Not in Foreman, and no other copy known.

CHEROKEE BAPTIST ASSOCIATION

[Minutes of the Eighth Annual Meeting of the Cherokee Baptist Association held with the Round Spring Baptist Church, Delaware District, Cherokee Nation, Indian Territory, commencing on Wednesday, October 12, 1876. Tahlequah: National Book and Job Printing Office, 1877.]

9, [1] p. 20 cm. Title page and text in Cherokee.
Not in Foreman, and no other copy known.

CHEROKEE BAPTIST ASSOCIATION

Minutes of the Ninth Annual Meeting of the Cherokee Baptist Association, held with the Long Prairie Baptist Church, Going Snake District, Cherokee Nation, Indian Territory, commencing on Friday, October 19th, 1877. Chicago [1877].

10, [1] p. 22 cm. Printed wrappers.

In the Matter of the Claim of the "Old Settler" Cherokee Indians against the United States. [N.p., 1877.]

16 p. 22.5 cm. Caption title.

Laws and Joint Resolutions of the National Council. Passed and adopted at the Regular Session of 1876. Tahlequah: Cherokee Advocate, Geo. W. McFarlin, printer, 1877.

[2], 52, 4 p. 23 cm. Printed wrappers. Errata slip.
One of but five known copies.

Statement of the Case of the "Old Settler" Cherokees. [N.p., 1877.]

4 p. 22 cm. Caption title.

1878

CHEROKEE BAPTIST ASSOCIATION

Minutes of the Tenth Annual Meeting of the Cherokee Baptist Association, held with the Antioch Baptist Church, Going Snake District, Cherokee Nation, Indian Territory, commencing on Thursday, October 3d, 1878. Chicago: American Baptist Publication Society, [1878].

12 p. 21 cm.

Objections of the Delegation of the Cherokee Nation to Senate Bill No. 107, 45th Congress. [N.p., 1878.]

4 p. 23.5 cm. Caption title.
A protest against an Indian citizenship bill.

Official Statement of the Cherokee Delegation in regard to the Expenditure of Cherokee Funds and the Financial Condition of the Cherokee Nation, and in relation to the Educational Situation of said Nation. [N.p., 1878.]

18 p. 22.5 cm. Caption title.

Penal Law. [Tahlequah, 1878.]

Broadside. Folio.

Headed: Weekly Advocate.
An extra number of the paper. Unrecorded, and the only known copy.

1879

Brief on behalf of the Cherokee Nation on the Question touching her Jurisdiction. [N.p., 1879.]

16 p. 23 cm. Caption title.

An able review by the Cherokee Delegation of the historical and legal aspects of Cherokee sovereignty.

BUSHYHEAD, D. W.

Cherokee Nation. By D. W. Bushyhead, Principal Chief. Thanksgiving Proclamation. [Tahlequah, 1879.]

Broadside. Folio.

One of only two known copies.

BUSHYHEAD, D. W.

First Annual Message of Hon. D. W. Bushyhead, Principal Chief of the Cherokee Nation, delivered at Tahlequah, C.N., November 10, 1879. [Tahlequah, 1879.]

9 p. 21.5 cm. Caption title.

BUSHYHEAD, D. W.

Memorial of the Principal Chief, and Cherokee Delegation, to the Commissioner of Indian Affairs, praying for the Removal of Intruders from the Cherokee Nation. [N.p., 1879.]

20 p. 23 cm. Caption title.

CHEROKEE BAPTIST ASSOCIATION

Minutes of the Eleventh Annual Meeting of the Cherokee Baptist Association, held with the Fourteen Mile Creek Baptist Church, Tahlequah District, Cherokee Nation, Indian Territory, commencing on Thursday, Oct. 9, 1879.

12 p. 20.5 cm.

Memorial of the "Old Settler" or "Western" Cherokee Indians, praying for a Settlement and Payment of the Balance claimed to be due them from the United States under the Treaties of 1835–36 and 1846. [Washington, 1879.]

4 p. 24 cm. Caption title.

1880

[Articles of Faith, in Cherokee. Tahlequah: Cherokee Advocate, 1880.]*

[2], 39, [1] p. 14.5 cm. Plain wrapper. Title and text in Cherokee.

Unrecorded, and the only known copy.

BUSHYHEAD, DENNIS W.

Second Annual Message of Hon. D. W. Bushyhead, Principal Chief of the Cherokee Nation, delivered at Tahlequah, Cherokee Nation, on the 3rd day of November, 1880. [Tahlequah, 1880.]

Broadside. 66 cm. 4 columns.

A rare broadside.

VOORHEES, D. W.

The Boudinot Tobacco Case. How an Indian Treaty was Respected. Speech of

Hon. D. W. Voorhees, of Indiana, in the Senate of the United States, April 22, 1880. Washington, 1880.

21 p. 22.5 cm. Printed wrappers.

1881

[An address, printed without title page or caption, from the Cherokee Delegation to Congress. Washington, 1881.]

7 p. 22 cm.

A request for payment of moneys still due the Cherokees from "lands west of the Arkansas River."

CHEROKEE BAPTIST ASSOCIATION

[Minutes of the Cherokee Baptist Association, held at Long Prairie Church, Going Snake District, September 4–6, 1881. Tahlequah: Cherokee Advocate Office, 1881.]*

[12] p. 21.5 cm. Plain wrappers. Title and text in Cherokee.

Unrecorded, and the only known copy.

Compiled Laws of the Cherokee Nation published by Authority of the National Council. Tahlequah: National Advocate Print, 1881.

348, [6] p. 23 cm.

[Compiled Laws of the Cherokee Nation published by Authority of the National Council. Tahlequah: National Advocate Print, 1881.]

335, vii p. 22.5 cm. Title page and text in Cherokee.

The 1881 compilation translated into Cherokee.

Summary of the Census of the Cherokee Nation, taken by the Authority of the National Council, and in Conformity to the Constitution, in the year 1880. Prepared for and submitted to the National Council in compliance with an Act approved by D. W. Bushyhead, Principal Chief, C.N., on the 3d day of December, A.D. 1879. Washington: Gibson Bros., 1881.

15 p. 23 cm.

A valuable census.

1882

CHEROKEE BAPTIST ASSOCIATION

Minutes of the Fourteenth Annual Meeting of the Cherokee Baptist Association, held with the Antioch Baptist Church (Going Snake District), Cherokee Nation, Indian Territory. Commencing on Thursday, Oct. 12th, 1882. Ottawa, Kansas: Kessler & M'Allister, 1882.

10, [1] p. 21 cm.

Mineral Law. [Tahlequah, 1884.]*

Broadsheet. Folio.

The form for a mineral license is printed on the reverse. The act was approved Dec. 12, 1882. One of only two known copies.

STEVENS, SPENCER S.

The Indian Question discussed by Spencer S. Stevens, of the Cherokee Nation. Titusville, Pa.: Morning Herald Print, 1882.*

33 p. 21.5 cm.

Unrecorded, and the only known copy. The author was a prominent Cherokee.

1883

BUSHYHEAD, DENNIS W.

First Annual Message (Second Term) of Hon. D. W. Bushyhead, Principal Chief Cherokee Nation. Delivered at Tahlequah, C.N. Nov. 7th, 1883. [Tahlequah, 1883.]

23, 9 p. 21.5 cm. Caption title. Two folded tables.

BUSHYHEAD, D. W.

Thanksgiving Proclamation to the Cherokee People. [Tahlequah, 1883.]

Broadside. Folio.

Gilt paper seal of the Cherokee Nation pasted down in lower left corner. Unrecorded, and the only copy located.

CHEROKEE BAPTIST ASSOCIATION

Minutes of the Fifteenth Annual Meeting of the Cherokee Baptist Association, held with the Fourteen Mile Creek Baptist Church (Tahlequah District), Cherokee Nation, Indian Territory, commencing on Thursday, October 18th, 1883. Ottawa, Kansas: Kessler & M'Allister, 1883.

10 p. 22.5 cm. Printed wrappers.

Cherokee Indian Lands in Indian Territory. Message from the President of the United States transmitting a Communication from the Secretary of the Interior relative to the Claim of the Cherokee Indians for Certain Lands in the Indian Territory. [Washington, 1883.]

39 p. 23 cm. Caption title.

Message from the President of the United States, transmitting a Communication of the 12th instant from the Secretary of the Interior, submitting Report of Commissioner of Indian Affairs of December 8, 1883, on the subject of the "Old Settler" or "Western Cherokees." [Washington, 1883.]

10 p. 23 cm. Caption title.

Senate Bill No. 2. Extra Session 1883. [Tahlequah, 1883.]*

Broadside. 21.5 cm.

A bill authorizing Cherokee officials to convey certain tribal lands to the Pawnees, Poncas, Nez Percés, Otoes, Missourias, and Osages. The only known copy.

Whereas, the Cherokee Nation are the Owners of the Lands in fee simple, patented by the United States, and Whereas, the Cherokee Nation through their Council are the Proper and Only Authority that can legally grant a Right of Way through the Cherokee lands . . . . [Tahlequah, 1883.]*

12 p.

A bill introduced in the Cherokee Council for the incorporation of the Cherokee National Railway.

Wolfe, Richard M., and Robert B. Ross

[Report of the Cherokee Delegation to the Principal Chief on its activities at Washington in protesting the encroachments of Kansas cattle men upon the Cherokee Strip. Tahlequah, 1883.]

Broadside. 22 cm. Entirely in Cherokee.

Unrecorded, and the only known copy.

1884

Bryan, Joel M., and others

Joel M. Bryan, William Wilson and William H. Hendricks, for themselves, and as Commissioners of the "Old Settlers" or "Western Cherokee" Indians, Plaintiffs, vs. The United States, Defendant. [Washington, 1884.]*

5 p. 23 cm. Caption title.

Bushyhead, Dennis W.

Second Annual Message, Second Term of Hon. D. W. Bushyhead, Principal Chief, Cherokee Nation. Tahlequah: Advocate Print, 1884.

31 p. 21.5 cm.

The only known copy.

Buttrick, Daniel Sabin

Antiquities of the Cherokee Indians. Compiled from the Collection of Rev. Daniel Sabin Buttrick, their Missionary from 1817 to 1847; as presented in the Indian Chieftain, published at Vinita, Ind. Ter., during the year 1884. Vinita: Indian Chieftain, 1884.

[6], 20 p. 23.5 cm. Printed wrappers.

A valuable contribution to ethnology.

Couch, Nevada

Pages from Cherokee Indian History, as identified with Samuel Austin Worcester. St. Louis: R. P. Studley & Co., [1884].

25, [1] p. 20 cm. Printed wrappers.

Couch, Nevada

Pages from Cherokee Indian History, as Identified with Samuel Austin Worcester, D.D., for 34 Years a Missionary of the A. B. C. F. M. among the Cherokees. A Paper read at the Commencement of Worcester Academy, at Vinita, Ind. Ter., June 18, 1884, by Miss Nevada Couch, a Member of the Academy. Published for the Institution. Third Edition, revised. St. Louis: R. P. Studley & Co., Printers, [1884].

27 p. 19.5 cm. Printed wrappers.

Laws and Joint Resolutions of the Cherokee Nation, enacted during the Regular and Special Sessions of the years 1881–2–3. Published by Authority of an Act of the National Council. Tahlequah, Cherokee Nation: E. C. Boudinot, Jr., Printer, 1884.*

176 p. 23 cm.

Letter from the Secretary of the Interior, transmitting Report of Commissioner of Indian Affairs relative to the Amount appropriated March 3, 1883, for Cherokee

Nation, and Legislation to Protect the Rights of Adopted Citizens of said Nation. [Washington, 1884.]
25 p. 22.5 cm. Caption title.

The Lord's Prayer (in Cherokee). [Vinita? 1884?].*
Broadside. 15 cm.
Text in Sequoyan characters, in Cherokee in Roman characters, and in a literal English translation from the Cherokee. Not in Foreman, and no other copy traced.

Reply of the Cherokee Delegation to Ex. Doc. No. 86. [N.p., 1884.]
7 p. 22 cm. Caption title.
Protest against the participation by Negro freedmen in Cherokee tribal payments.

1885

BUSHYHEAD, DENNIS W.

Sixth Annual Message of Hon. D. W. Bushyhead, to the Senate and Council of the Cherokee Nation. [Tahlequah, 1885.]
20 p. 21 cm. Wrapper title.
The only copy known in wrappers.

BUSHYHEAD, D. W.

To the Cherokees and other Indians. [Tahlequah, 1885.]
Broadside. Folio. Mourning border.
Proclamation of a day of mourning for the death of former President U. S. Grant. Unrecorded, and no other copy traced.

CHEROKEE BAPTIST ASSOCIATION

Minutes of the Seventeenth Annual Session of the Cherokee Baptist Association, held with the Tahlequah Baptist Church, Tahlequah District, Cherokee Nation, Indian Territory, commencing Thursday, October 15, 1885. Muskogee: Indian Journal, 1885.
19 p. 21 cm. Printed wrappers.
Not in Foreman, and no other copy known.

1886

BUSHYHEAD, DENNIS W.

Fourth Annual Message (Second Term) of Hon. D. W. Bushyhead, Principal Chief of the Cherokee Nation, I.T. Delivered at Tahlequah, Cherokee Nation, November 2nd, 1886. Tahlequah: Advance Job Office, [1886].*
20 p. 21 cm. Wrapper title.

BUSHYHEAD, DENNIS W.

Thanksgiving Proclamation. Executive Department, Cherokee Nation, I.T., [Tahlequah, 1886.]
Broadside. 27.5 cm.
One of only two known copies.

WALLACE, J. G.

Argument of J. G. Wallace in the Case of Concho Cattle Company et al. vs.

G. T. Thompson et al., in behalf of Defense. August 23, 1886. Nashville, Tenn.: Marshall & Bruce, 1886.

47 p. 26 cm.

The litigation arose from a stock-raising agreement made by Thompson, a Cherokee Indian, with the Concho Cattle Company.

1887

Council Bill No. 1. An Act authorizing the Principal Chief in the name, stead, and behalf of the National Council to Dissent from Allowance per mile for Right of Way through the Cherokee Domain of the Kansas and Arkansas Valley Railway. [Tahlequah, 1887.]*

Broadsheet. 18 cm.

The only known copy.

Laws and Joint Resolutions of the Cherokee Nation, enacted by the National Council during the Regular and Extra Sessions of 1884–5–6. Published by Authority of the National Council. Tahlequah, C.N.: E. C. Boudinot, Jr., 1887.*

99, iii p. 23 cm. Printed wrappers.

Less than ten copies are known.

[Laws and Joint Resolutions of the Cherokee Nation, enacted by the National Council during the Regular and Extra Sessions of 1884–5–6. Published by Authority of the National Council. Tahlequah, C.N.: E. C. Boudinot, Jr., 1887.]

87 p. 23 cm. Plain wrappers.

A translation into Cherokee of the preceding compilation.

Sanders, George, and others

Resolution of the National Party and Honorable Samuel Smith's Answer. [Tahlequah, 1887.]

Broadside. 24.5 cm.

Resolutions urging conciliation in the settlement of party conflict and the principal chief's reply. Unrecorded, and the only known copy.

1888

Chamberlin, A. N.

Cherokee Pictorial Book. With Catechism and Hymns compiled and translated by Rev. A. N. Chamberlin. 1888. T. W. Foreman, printer. Tahlequah, I.T. Copyright secured.

143, [2] p. 14.5 cm. Joint English and Cherokee title. Text in Cherokee.

Fitzgerald, O. P.

John B. McFerrin. A Biography. By O. P. Fitzgerald, D.D., editor of the Christian Advocate. Nashville, Tenn., 1888.

448 p. 19.5 cm. Frontisp. port.

The volume contains an interesting account of McFerrin's experiences as a missionary to the Cherokees before their removal.

Mayes, Joel B.

[Annual Message of Principal Chief Joel B. Mayes. Tahlequah, 1888.]*

23 p. 21 cm. Wrapper title. Title and text in Cherokee.
One of but two known copies.

A Tale of Home and War. By E. P. H. Portland, Maine: Brown Thurston & Co., 1888.

200 p. 18.5 cm.

Running title: Addie and I among the Cherokees.
A missionary's reminiscences of life in the Cherokee Nation during the Civil War.

1889

Annual Report of the Board of Education of the Cherokee Nation, Indian Territory, for the school year ending September 30, 1887, for the school year ending September 30, 1888; also a Comparative Table showing the Number, Attendance, and Branches taught in the Schools in the year 1845. Tahlequah, Cherokee Nation, Indian Territory, 1889. St. Louis: Robt. D. Patterson Stationery Co., [1889].

31 p. 22 cm. Printed wrappers.

Arrow Extra. Five O'clock Edition. Wednesday Morning. Bold! A Stunning Letter by Chief Mayes to the U.S. Commission creates a Flurry of Excitement and a World of Wonder. Does it Sound like a Declaration of War? [Tahlequah, 1889.]

Broadside. Folio.
Unrecorded, and the only known copy.

CHEROKEE BAPTIST ASSOCIATION

Proceedings of the 19th Annual Session of the Cherokee Baptist Association, held with Lee's Creek Church, October 18th, 19th, and 20th, 1889. Siloam Springs, Arkansas: Herald Job Print, [1889].

22 p. 19.5 cm. Wrapper title. Two folded tables.
In the title 19th annual session has been changed with pen to read 20th and 21st annual sessions.

FOSTER, GEORGE E.

Literature of the Cherokees, also Bibliography and the Story of their Genesis. Ithaca, N.Y., 1889.*

[2], 2, 69, [1], 28, 12, [7] p. 17.5 cm.

Letter from the Secretary of the Interior, transmitting Papers relative to an Appropriation for the Benefit of the Cherokee Freedmen. [Washington, 1889.]

6 p. 23 cm. Caption title.

List of Illegal Votes. [Tahlequah, 1889.]

Broadside. 30 cm.
List of illegal votes cast in Cooweescoowee District at the general election of August, 1887. The only known copy.

1890

Elias Cornelius Boudinot. Born August 1, 1835. Died September 27, 1890. [Chicago, 1890.]

78, [1] p. 20 cm. Frontisp. Portrait.

A memorial volume, with a biographical sketch. Boudinot long played a prominent role in Cherokee affairs.

EUBANKS, WILLIAM

[A system of shorthand representation of the Sequoyan characters. Tahlequah, 1890.]

Broadside. 22.5 cm.

The Sequoyan characters, each with its appropriate shorthand character, arranged in six columns. Unrecorded, and no other copy located.

Law Instructing the Several Revenue Officers of the Cherokee Nation. [Tahlequah, 1890.]

Broadside. Folio.

Unrecorded, and the only known copy.

Laws of Cherokee Nation. [Tahlequah, 1890.]*

3 p. on 3 leaves broadside. 33.5 cm. Caption title.

Acts of 1888 and 1889. One of three known copies.

MAYES, JOEL B.

Fourth Annual Message of Hon. J. B. Mayes, Principal Chief of the Cherokee Nation. Delivered at Tahlequah, I.T., November 4th, 1890. [Tahlequah, 1890.]

19 p. 20 cm. Wrapper title.

THOMAS, CYRUS

The Cherokees in pre-Columbian times. New York: N. D. C. Hodges, 1890.*

[6], 97 p. 18.5 cm.

1891

The Case of the Western Cherokees. Opinion. [Washington, 1891.]

24 p. 22.5 cm. Wrapper title.

The opinion, delivered by Judge Nott of the Court of Claims, constitutes a history of the Old Settler Cherokees in their relations with the United States.

MAYES, JOEL B.

Executive Department, Cherokee Nation, Ind. Ter. Tahlequah, July 14, 1891. Hon. Alex. McCoy, Illinois Dist., C.N. [Tahlequah, 1891.]

Broadside. 24.5 cm.

A Downing party political circular. Unrecorded in Foreman, and the only known copy.

MAYES, JOEL B.

[Annual Message, Nov. 4, 1891, wholly in Cherokee. Tahlequah, 1891.]

16 p. 22 cm. Caption title.

MAYES, JOEL B.

First Annual Message (Second Term) of Hon. Joel B. Mayes, Principal Chief, C.N. Delivered at Tahlequah, I.T. November 4, 1891. [Tahlequah, 1891.]

28 p. 21.5 cm. Caption title.

[A pamphlet entirely in Cherokee characters. Tahlequah, 1891.]*
8 p. 25 cm. Caption title.

1892

Constitution and Laws of the Cherokee Nation. Published by an Act of the National Council, 1892. [Parsons, Kansas, 1892.]
426 vii p. 21.5 cm.

New Jury Law. [Tahlequah, 1892.]
Broadside. Folio.
Unrecorded, and the only known copy.

The United States, Appellant, vs. The "Old Settlers," or Western Cherokee Indians, by Joel M. Bryan, William Wilson, and William H. Hendricks, Commissioners, and Joel M. Bryan, Treasurer, etc. The "Old Settlers," or Western Cherokee Indians, by Joel M. Bryan, William Wilson, and William H. Hendricks, Commissioners, and Joel M. Bryan, Treasurer, etc., Appellants, vs. The United States. Appeals from the Court of Claims.
305 p. 23.5 cm. Wrapper title.
The record, which contains scores of important documents illustrating the history of the Old Settlers from the 1830's.

1893

CHEROKEE CITIZENSHIP ASSOCIATION

Memorial of the Cherokee Citizenship Association, in the Cherokee Nation, Indian Territory. Afton: The News Print, [1893.]
[6] p. 22.5 cm. Printed wrappers.

[Constitution and Laws of the Cherokee Nation. Published by an Act of the National Council. 1892. Parsons, Kansas, 1893.]
340, vii p. 22 cm.
The 1892 compilation translated into Cherokee.

GATSCHET, ALBERT S.

The Indian Tribes settled in the Cherokee Nation. Vinita, 1893.
Broadside. Folio.
Apparently a supplement to the Indian Chieftain. A highly interesting account of the smaller tribes living in the northwestern corner of the Cherokee Nation. Unrecorded, and the only known copy.

Identification and Description of the Lands covered by selections and allotments under the Act of March 3, 1893, and the Agreements with the Cherokee Nation and Tonkawa and Pawnee Tribes of Indians ratified thereby. Washington, 1893.
38 p. 23 cm. Printed wrappers.

Memorial and Joint Resolutions to the President and Congress of the United States on Statehood with Oklahoma Territory. [Tahlequah, 1893.]*
5 p. on 5 leaves broadside. 30.5 cm. Caption title.
A protest by the Cherokee council and principal chief. Excessively rare. Not in Foreman.

ROSS, MRS. WILLIAM P.

The Life and Times of Hon. William P. Ross. Fort Smith: Weldon & Williams, 1893.

[23], 272 p. 20.5 cm. Port.

STEPHENS, WILLIAM

Petition of William Stephens to the Cherokee Council for Admission to Citizenship in the Cherokee Nation, Ind. Ter. Fort Smith: Elevator Job Print, [1893].

20 p. 22 cm. Wrapper title.

1894

BELL, LUCIEN B., and E. C. BOUDINOT

To the President and Congress of the United States. [Checotah, 1894.]*

Broadsheet. 28.5 cm.

The protest against the allotment of Indian lands in severalty includes a review of Cherokee progress. Signed in autograph by Bell and Boudinot, who were prominent Cherokees. Not in Foreman, and no other copy traced.

The Memorial of the Cherokee Nation opposing McRae Bill in the House of Representatives and Senate. Washington: Gibson Bros., 1894.

9 p. 23.5 cm. Wrapper title.

Old Settler Cherokee Cases. [Washington, 1894.]

27 p. 23 cm. Caption title.

Reply of the Cherokee National Council to the Propositions of the Dawes Commission in regard to Change of Government for the Cherokee Nation. Washington: Gibson Bros., 1894.

16 p. 22 cm. Printed wrappers.

1895

WATTS, W. J.

Cherokee Citizenship and a Brief History of the Internal Affairs of the Cherokee Nation, with Records and Acts of the National Council from 1871 to date. By W. J. Watts, President of the Cherokee Citizenship Association. Muldrow, Indian Territory: Register Print, 1895.

[2], 143, [1] p. 20 cm. Wrapper title.

The volume is quite rare.

1896

An Act to Appropriate and Pay Certain Monies out of Monies arising from the Sale of the Cherokee Outlet to the Freedmen of the Cherokee Nation. Cherokee Nation, Indian Territory. 1896. [Tahlequah, 1896.]

7 p. 19 cm. Wrapper title.

The only known copy.

Communication to the United States Commissioners in relation to a Conference on Propositions of the Government, by Commission on part of the Cherokee Nation. St. Louis: R. & T. A. Ennis Stationery Co., 1896.

36 p. 23 cm. Printed wrappers.

HARRIS, C. J., and others

Letter of the Cherokee Delegation to the President of the United States relating to Intruders in the Cherokee Nation. Washington: Gibson Bros., 1896.

28 p. 23 cm. Wrapper title.

MAYES, SAMUEL H.

Letter of the Principal Chief and Delegation of the Cherokee Nation to the Congress of the United States with reference to Conditions in the Cherokee Nation. Washington: Gibson Bros., 1896.

27 p. 23.5 cm. Wrapper title.

MAYES, SAMUEL H.

Second Annual Message of Chief Samuel H. Mayes. Delivered at Tahlequah, November 3rd, 1896. [Tahlequah, 1896.]

8 p. 22 cm. Wrapper title.

Report of Board of Appraisers on Improvements of Intruders in the Cherokee Nation. [Washington, 1896.]

46 p. 23 cm. Caption title.

1897

Acts of the National Council Authorizing and Directing the Sale of Intruder Improvements. Tahlequah: Sentinel Print, 1897.*

11 p. 21 cm. Wrapper title.

One of only three known copies.

MAYES, SAMUEL H.

To the Citizens of the Several Districts (of the Cherokee Nation.) [Tahlequah, 1897.]

Broadside. 15 cm. Text in English and Cherokee.

The proclamation relates to registration of citizens for a tribal roll. The only known copy.

1898

GARLAND, A. H., and R. C. GARLAND

William Stephens et al. vs. Cherokee Nation. Appeal (to the U.S. Supreme Court) from the Indian Territorial United States Court. Washington: McGill & Wallace. [1898].

8 p. 23.5 cm. Wrapper title.

Laws of Cherokee Nation, Compilation of 1892. Freedmen claiming Residence in Cooweescoowee District and placed on Doubtful and Rejected Lists by the Dawes Commission. [Tahlequah, 1898.]*

Broadsheet. 21.5 cm.

MAYES, SAMUEL H.

[Fourth Annual Message of Principal Chief Samuel H. Mayes. Tahlequah, 1898.]*

8 p. 21.5 cm. Caption title, in Cherokee. Text in Cherokee.

MAYES, SAMUEL H.

Fourth Annual Message of S. H. Mayes, Principal Chief of the Cherokee Nation, delivered at Tahlequah, I.T., November 8, 1898. [Tahlequah, 1898.]*
10 p. 21 cm. Printed wrappers.

Memorial of the Cherokee Nation asking for the Removal of Intruders. February 1st, 1897. Washington: Advertising Co. Print, 1898.
12 p. 21.5 cm. Wrapper title.

Penal Laws of the Cherokee Nation passed by the National Council and approved for the years 1893-4-5-6. Tahlequah, I.T.: Sentinel Print, 1898.*
14 p. 21.5 cm. Wrapper title.
One of only four known copies.

1899

Agreement concluded with the Commission (to the Five Civilized Tribes) upon the part of the Cherokee Nation at Muscogee, Indian Territory, January 14, 1899. [N.p., 1899.]
16 p. 23.5 cm. Caption title.

Cherokee Gospel Tidings. [Various places, various dates, as below.] A large portion of each issue is in the Cherokee language.

II,	10	Siloam Springs, Ark.	Oct. 1899	8 p.
IV,	5	Marble, Ind. Ter.	May 1901	8 p.
IV,	6	Dwight Mission, Marble, I.T.	June 1901	8 p.
IV,	7	" " "	July 1901	6 p.
IV,	8	" " "	Aug. 1901	6 p.
IV,	11	" " "	Nov. 1901	6 p.
IV,	12	" " "	Dec. 1901	8 p.
V,	4	" " "	Apr. 1902	6 p.
V,	5	" " "	May 1902	8 p.
V,	6	" " "	June 1902	8 p.
V,	7	" " "	July 1902	8 p.
V,	8	" " "	Aug. 1902	8 p.
V,	9	" " "	Sept. 1902	8 p.
V,	10	" " "	Oct. 1902	4 p.
VI,	5 & 6	" " "	May & June 1903	8 p.
VI,	9	" " "	Sept. 1903	4 p.

Commission to the Five Civilized Tribes. Agreement concluded with the Commission upon the part of the Cherokee Nation at Muscogee, Indian Territory, January 14, 1899. [Tahlequah, 1899.]
16 p. 23.5 cm.

FOSTER, GEORGE E.

Story of the Cherokee Bible. An Address, with Additional Explanatory Notes. Second edition enlarged. Ithaca, N.Y.: Democrat Press, 1899.*
x, 89 p. 17 cm. Printed wrappers.

Contains, with separate title page and pagination, Foster's Reminiscences of Travel in Cherokee Lands, q.v.

FOSTER, GEORGE E.

Reminiscences of Travel in Cherokee Lands. An Address. Ithaca, N.Y.: Democrat Press, 1899.*

viii, 76 p. 17 cm. Printed wrappers.

Bound with Foster's Story of the Cherokee Bible, q.v.

STARR, EMMET

Gazetteer of the Cherokee Nation, Indian Territory. Containing Full Lists of Municipal, Church and Lodge Officials of each Town in the Cherokee Nation, together with Full Notes on Dates of Incorporation and Elections, Officers of Grand Lodges, Medical, Legal and other Organizations. Contains Correct Time Table at Every Railroad Station throughout the Cherokee Nation. Also Time of Meetings of all Lodges and Churches. General and Useful Information. By Emmet Starr. [Tahlequah, 1899.]

27, [2] p. 20.5 cm.

The prospectus, autographed by the author, of a work never published. Even the prospectus, however, contains information of value. The rarest of all this Cherokee historian's writings.

THOMPSON, WILLIAM P., and WILLIAM W. HASTINGS

In the United States Court of Appeals for the Indian Territory. January Term, 1899. Belle Rush et al., vs. Johnson Thompson et al. Appeal from the United States Court for the Northern District in the Indian Territory. Brief for Appellees. Muskogee: Phoenix Printing Co., [1899].*

5 p. 25 cm. Wrapper title.

A contest over a Tahlequah town lot and its improvements. Not recorded in Foreman.

1900

Acts of the National Council Authorizing and Directing the Sale of Intruder Improvements. [Tahlequah, 1900.]*

6 p. 23 cm. Wrapper title.

One of only three known copies.

Cherokee Hymns. [Dwight Mission Press, 1900.]*

Broadsheet. 21 cm. Text entirely in Cherokee.

A leaflet issued probably as a supplement to the Cherokee Gospel Tidings. Not in Foreman.

KEETOOWAH SOCIETY

To Honorable Thomas M. Buffington, Principal Chief of the Cherokee Nation. A Brief Statement of the Organization of the Emigrant Cherokees. [Tahlequah, 1900.]

[4] p. 24.5 cm.

KEETOOWAH SOCIETY

Whereas, the U.S. Commission to the Five Civilized Tribes, known as the "Dawes

Commission," is preparing a Roll of Citizens of the Cherokee Nation for the purpose, as it seems, of Allotting the Lands of the Cherokee Nation . . . . [Tahlequah, 1900.]
4 leaves, broadside. Bound like a law brief. 35 cm.

Memorial of the Cherokee Indians for Moneys due them from the United States. [Washington, 1900.]
37 p. 23 cm. Caption title.
James Mooney's copy, with his signature on the first page.

Mooney, James
The Cherokee River Cult. [N.p., 1900.]
10 p. 24 cm. Wrapper title.

Resolutions of the Freedmen Convention held at Fort Gibson, I.T., December 18, 1900. [Fort Gibson, 1900.]
Broadside. 30.5 cm.
Unrecorded, and the only known copy.

1901

Kern, R. H.
In re Cherokee Freedmen's Roll. Statement of R. H. Kern. [St. Louis, 1901.]
13 p. 26 cm. Wrapper title.

Springer, William M.
In the Matter of the Application of the Cherokee Oil and Gas Company. Brief and Argument of the Cherokee Nation in reply to the Brief and Argument of the Applicant. William M. Springer, Attorney for the Cherokee Nation. [Washington, 1901.]
9 p. 23.5 cm. Wrapper title.

Starr, Emmet
To All Cherokee Voters. [Claremore, 1901.]
Broadside. 21.5 cm.
The Cherokee historian in the role of candidate for the National Council. Unrecorded.

Stephens, Spencer S.
To the Cherokee People. [Wagoner, 1901.]
Broadside. 20 cm.
A demand that the National Council make a final settlement of the landed and financial interests of the Cherokee people. Unrecorded, and the only known copy.

1902

The Cherokee Nation et al., appellants vs. Ethan A. Hitchcock, Secretary of the Interior. Appeal from the Court of Appeals of the District of Columbia. Brief for Appellee. [Washington, 1902.]
56 p. 23 cm. Wrapper title.

Hutchings, William T., and William W. Hastings
Before the Honorable Commission to the Five Civilized Tribes. In the Matter of

the Application for Enrollment as Citizens of the Cherokee Nation of Francis M. Dawson, et al. Brief on part of the Cherokee Nation. Vinita: Leader Printing Co., [1902].

43 p. 22.5 cm. Wrapper title.

The testimony elicited in the case throws interesting light upon the operation of the Cherokee Citizenship Commission in the early 1880's.

1903

STREET, O. D.

Marshall County One Hundred Years Ago. Guntersville, Ala.: Guntersville Democrat Print, [1903].*

[46] p. 21 cm. Printed wrappers.

A very scarce Alabama county history which contains considerable information about the Cherokee Indians before removal.

1904

ROGERS, WILLIAM C.

Second Annual Message of Hon. William C. Rogers, Principal Chief of the Cherokee Nation. Delivered at Tahlequah, I.T., November 9th, 1904. [Tahlequah, 1904.]

10 p. 23 cm. Wrapper title.

1905

Bartlesville, Ind. Ter. The Metropolis of the Cherokee Nation and the Supply Center of the Oil Field. [Bartlesville, 1905.]

72 p. 21.5 cm. Printed wrappers. Photographs. Folded map.

The map is entitled Kansas, Indian Territory and Oklahoma Oil Fields. Not in Foreman.

1906

Charles O. Frye. As an Official of the Cherokee Nation, as appears from the Official Records of the Noted Flippin Case, Anna Flippin et al. vs. Cherokee Nation. [Tahlequah, 1906.]*

Broadside. Folio.

A campaign attack upon a political candidate. Not in Foreman, and no other copy traced.

1907

[To Emigrant Cherokees. Notice. Tahlequah, 1907.]

Broadside. 27 cm. Text in Cherokee.

Advice from the acting commissioner of Indian Affairs on registration for a special tribal roll. Unrecorded, and the only known copy.

PARKER, THOMAS VALENTINE

The Cherokee Indians, with Special Reference to their Relations with the United States Government. New York, [1907].

116 p. 19 cm. Plates.

1909

Cherokee Hymns. Marble City, Okla.: Dwight Mission Press, 1909.

64, [6] p. 13 cm. Printed wrappers.

Revised Ordinances of the Town of Westville, Oklahoma. In effect and force September 1st, 1908. Revised by O. E. Hamblen, Towns Attorney. Published by authority of the Board of Trustees. Westville: New Era Printing House, [1908].

[57] p. 22.5 cm. Printed wrappers.

1909–1910

William Brown and Levi B. Gritts vs. The United States. [Washington, 1909–1910.]*

Briefs, records, etc.

6 vols., aggregating about 330 pages.

A suit in the Court of Claims and appealed to the Supreme Court of the United States to compel the removal of restrictions from the leasing of Cherokee allotments. Judge Peele, in delivering the Court of Claims opinion, said: "The importance of the case can hardly be overestimated."

1910

David Muskrat and J. Henry Dick, on their own behalf and on behalf of all Cherokee Citizens enrolled as such for Allotment as of September 1, 1902, Appellants, vs. The United States. [Washington, 1910.]

Briefs, records, etc.

3 vols., aggregating 120 pages.

The case before the Supreme Court turned upon the power of Congress in 1906 to increase the number of persons entitled to share in the final distribution of lands and funds of the Cherokees beyond those enrolled for allotment as of September 1, 1902.

[Starr, Emmet]

Cherokees "West" 1794–1839. Claremore, Oklahoma, 1910.

164 p. 23 cm.

1914

Keetoowah Organization Start Recovery of Money. [Tahlequah, 1914.]

[7] p. 23 cm. Caption title.

1915

Anderson, Mabel W.

Life of General Stand Watie, the only Indian Brigadier General of the Confederate Army and the Last General to Surrender. [Pryor, Okla.: Mayes County Republican, 1915.]

58 p. 22 cm. Printed wrappers.

1917

Copeland, J. Riley, and others

Cherokees Take Notice. [Jay, Oklahoma, 1917.]

An Address to the Old Settler party.

1923

Schwarze, Edmund

History of the Moravian Missions among the Southern Indian Tribes of the

United States. By the Rev. Edmund Schwarze, Pastor of the Cavalry Moravian Church, Winston-Salem, N.C. Bethlehem, Penna.: Times Publishing Company, 1923.
xvii, 331 p. Plates.
A valuable treatise, with information, not to be found elsewhere, on the earliest missions to the Cherokees.

1934

PAYNE, JOHN HOWARD

Indian Justice. A Cherokee Murder Trial at Tahlequah in 1840. As reported by John Howard Payne. Edited with Introduction and Footnotes by Grant Foreman. Oklahoma City: Harlow, 1934.
[4], xii, [1], 112 p. 22 cm. Map plates.
A fine copy.

Undated

DUNCAN, W. A.

[A letter to the Chairman of the Senate Judiciary Committee. [N.p., n.d.]*
7 p. 23 cm. Printed without title page or caption.
A protest against curtailment of the jurisdiction of Cherokee courts.

FREY, D.

Konduir, das Cherokesenmadchen. Eine Erzahlung aus den Zeiten der Grundung Tennessees von D. Frey. Mulheim a. d. Ruhr. Verlag von Julius Bagel. [N.d.].
62 p. 14.5 cm. Pictorial wrappers.
A tale of Indians and pioneers in Tennessee in 1793.

CHEROKEE INDIANS OF NORTH CAROLINA

1827

NORTH CAROLINA LEGISLATURE

Report of the Joint Select Committee, appointed by the Legislature of N. Carolina to Memorialize Congress upon the Subject of the Cherokee Lands. 1827. Raleigh, N.C.: Lawrence & Lemay, 1827.
8 p. 22.5 cm.
No other copy can be traced.

1828

Cherokee Lands—North Carolina. [Washington, 1828.]
8 p. 24.5 cm. Caption title. Uncut and unopened.

SAUNDERS, R. M.

Report of General R. M. Saunders on the subject of Cherokee Lands. Raleigh, N.C.: Lawrence & Lemay, Printers to the State, 1828.
8 p. 22.5 cm.
No other copy can be traced.

1833

Report of the Joint Select Committee (of the North Carolina Legislature) relative to the Cherokee Indians. [Raleigh, 1833.]

4 p. 21 cm. Caption title.
No other copy can be traced.

1846

THOMAS, WILLIAM H.

Argument of William H. Thomas, in support of the Rights of the Cherokee Indians remaining in the State of North Carolina to the Lands granted to them in fee simple by that State in 1783; and showing that those Lands were not conveyed to the United States under the Treaty of 1835. Containing, also, a Proposition to relinquish, for the benefit of the States of North Carolina and Tennessee, all their Interest in those Lands, on condition that an Equitable Portion of the Moneys stipulated to be paid by the United States to the Cherokee People be paid to them. Washington: Ritchie & Heiss, 1846.

16, 2 p. 22 cm.
Rare.

THOMAS, WILLIAM H.

Memorial and Argument in the Claim of James Raper, for the Value of a Preemption Right under the Cherokee Treaty of 1835. [Murphy, N.C.? 1846.]

6 p. 22.5 cm. Wrapper title.

THOMAS, WILLIAM H.

Memorial and argument submitted to the Cherokee Commissioners in the claim of Nancy Reed and Children, Cherokee Indians of North Carolina, for the Value of a Reservation of Six Hundred and Forty Acres of Land, granted them under the Eighth Article of the Cherokee Treaty of 1817, as modified and continued by the Second Article of the Treaty of 1819. Also, a Memorial of the Eastern Cherokees, and a Report of the Committee of the Senate, in relation to the Claims of the Cherokee Indians against the United States. Washington, D.C.: Kennedy & Brown, 1846.

16, 2, 5 p. 22 cm. Wrapper title.
Also an issue of only sixteen pages.

THOMAS, WILLIAM H.

Memorial and Argument submitted to the Cherokee Commissioners in the Claim of Tickoneeska, a Cherokee Indian of North Carolina. Also, an Explanation of the Circumstances under which he and other Cherokees became Citizens of that State, with a Brief History of the North Carolina Cherokees from the year 1809. Washington, D.C.: Kennedy & Brown, 1846.

24 p. 23 cm. Wrapper title.
Very rare.

1850

LEA, LUKE

Cherokee Census. To the Cherokee Indians now remaining in the State of North Carolina. [Washington, 1850.]

Broadside. 25 cm.
Notice that an official roll of the tribe will be compiled. No other copy is known.

1851

THOMAS, WILLIAM H.

Explanations of the Rights and Claims of the Cherokee Indians. [Washington? 1851.]

16 p. 21 cm. Caption title.

THOMAS, WILLIAM H.

Explanations of the Rights of the North Carolina Cherokee Indians, submitted to the Attorney General of the United States. By William H. Thomas. Washington City, 1851.

18 p. 19.5 cm. Wrapper title.

1852

FLEMING, ROBERT

Sketch of the Life of Elder Humphrey Posey, First Baptist Missionary to the Cherokee Indians, and Founder of Valley Town School, North Carolina. By Robert Fleming, of Newnan, Georgia. Published by the Western Baptist Association of Georgia. 1852. [Philadelphia: King & Baird, 1852].

103 p. 15 cm.

1853

THOMAS, WILLIAM H.

A Letter to the Commissioner of Indian Affairs upon the Claims of the Indians Remaining in the States East. By Wm. H. Thomas. Washington: Buell & Blanchard, 1853.

46 p. 23 cm. Wrapper title.

1854

Cherokee Indians. Report of the Committee on Indian Affairs to whom was referred the Memorial of Cherokee Indians residing in States East of the Mississippi River praying the Payment of Money which they claim to be due them per capita under the Treaty of 1835–'36 and 1846. [Washington, 1854.]

13 p. 25 cm. Caption title.

1858

THOMAS, WILLIAM H.

Explanation of the Fund held in Trust by the United States for the North Carolina Cherokees. By Wm. H. Thomas. Washington: Lemuel Towers, 1858.

16 p. 22 cm. Printed wrappers.

1868

Claim of the Cherokees of North Carolina to an Equal Participation, in Proportion to their Numbers, in All the Moneys and Property of the Cherokee Nation. James G. Blunt, Attorney. Washington: Turner, Printer, 1868.

18 p. 23 cm. Wrapper title.

1869

The Claim of the North Carolina Indians to a Participation in Proportion to

Numbers in all the Lands and Moneys of the Cherokee Nation. Washington, February, 1869.
16 p. 22 cm.

DOWNING, LEWIS, and others
Reply to the Claims of the Cherokees of North Carolina to an equal participation, in proportion to their numbers, in all the moneys and property of the Cherokee Nation. Washington: Intelligencer Printing House, 1869.
18 p. 23 cm. Wrapper title.

1871

Ho! For the West. [Loudon, Tennessee, 1871.]*
Broadside. 21.5 cm.
A notice that the Memphis & Charleston Railroad will furnish transportation to the eastern band of Cherokee Indians from eastern Tennessee to Indian Territory. The only known copy.

1874

SMITH, EDWARD P.
[Statement relative to the Eastern Cherokee Indians in North Carolina. Washington, 1874.]
8 p. 25 cm.

1875

Claim of W. W. Rollins and O. F. Presbrey, under Contract of May 15th, 1874, with Eastern Band of Cherokee Indians, for Services in Recovery of Eighty-five Thousand Acres of Land in Courts of North Carolina. Washington: Jos. L. Pearson, [1875].
78 p. 23.5 cm. Wrapper title.

Letter of the Commissioner of Indian Affairs to the Hon. Secretary of the Interior, December 10, 1875, relative to Claims of the North Carolina Cherokees. Washington, 1875.
9 p. 23 cm. Printed wrappers.

1876

TRAMPER, ROBERT
Petition of Robert Tramper, Chairman of Council of the Eastern Band of the Cherokee Indians, and Bill asking for Completion of Land Titles and Final Settlement of all their Accounts. Reply of the Secretary of the Interior. Washington City: Beardsley & Snodgrass, 1876.
28 p. 24 cm.

1877

TAYLOR, JAMES
An Open Letter to the President and People of the United States, setting forth the Treatment of the Cherokee Nation and its Bands. [Washington, 1877.]
Broadside. Folio.

1878

Objections of the Cherokee Delegation to Bill S. No. 230 and Bill H. R. No. 228 and Similar Measures pending before the 1st Session, 45th Congress, Authorizing the so-called "Eastern Band" of the Cherokees (Citizens of North Carolina) to Sue the Cherokee Nation, &c. [N.p., 1878.]

8 p. 23.5 cm. Caption title.

WELCH, LOYD R.

Statement of the Case of the Eastern Band of Cherokee Indians referred to in Senate Bill 230 and House Bill 228. [Washington, 1878.]

9 p. 23 cm. Caption title.

Welch was principal chief of the Eastern Cherokees.

1879

ROSS, JOHN

Address of John Ross, Chief of the Eastern Band of North Carolina Cherokees, at Cheoah Council Ground, near Robbinsville, Graham County, North Carolina. October 6th, 1879. Asheville, N.C.: Journal Job Print, 1879.

8 p. 19.5 cm. Printed wrappers.

The only known copy.

1880

Memorial of the Cherokee Delegation objecting to the Passage by Congress of any Act, allowing Certain Citizens of the State of North Carolina, of Cherokee Descent, commonly called "North Carolina Cherokees," an interest in the Lands and Funds of the Cherokee Nation. Washington: John L. Ginck, [1880].

13 p. 23 cm. Wrapper title.

Memorial of Cherokee Delegation protesting against Senate Bill No. 505. [N.p., 1880?].*

7 p. 21.5 cm. Caption title.

A protest against the proposed participation of the Eastern, or North Carolina, Cherokees in Cherokee national funds.

1882

In the Matter of the Claim of the Eastern Band of Cherokee Indians against the Cherokee Nation West and the United States. Washington: W. H. Moore, 1882.

34 p. 23 cm. Wrapper title.

1883

SMITH, N. J.

Inaugural Address of Honorable N. J. Smith, Principal Chief of the Eastern Band of Cherokees, delivered before the Annual Council at Cherokee Council House, Cherokee, Swain County, North Carolina, October 4, 1883. Washington: W. H. Moore, 1883.

5 p. 22 cm. Wrapper title.

The only known copy.

1884

Bushyhead, George, and James Taylor

Petition of Hon. George Bushyhead, Ex-Chief, and James Taylor, Esq., with Twelve Hundred or more North Carolina Cherokee Indians before the Congress of the United States, for a Final Settlement of all Matters pending between the Government of the United States and said Indians, pertaining to Monies due them under the Treaties of 1835 and 1836. Washington: W. H. Moore, 1884.

64 p. 24 cm. Wrapper title.

Wallace W. Rollins and Otis F. Presbrey vs. The United States. Petition. Washington: R. Beresford, 1884.*

52 p. 23.5 cm. Wrapper title.

1888

Circular Issued by North Carolina Yearly Meeting of Friends, held at High Point, in Guilford County, from the 8th to the 14th of 8th month, 1888, in the Interest of the Eastern Cherokee Indians. [High Point, N.C., 1888.]

[2] p. 21.5 cm. Caption title.

James Mooney's copy, with his signature.

Painter, C. C.

The Eastern Cherokees. A Report. Philadelphia, [1888].

16 p. 23 cm.

1889

Garland, A. H.

[An opinion by the Attorney General on points of North Carolina Cherokee Indian citizenship. Washington, 1889.]

Broadsheet. 24 cm.

1892

Donaldson, Thomas

Extra Census Bulletin. Indians. Eastern Band of Cherokees of North Carolina. Washington: United States Census Printing Office, 1892.

24 p. 31 cm. Folded maps. Photographs.

A valuable survey.

1907

Miller, Guion

Eastern Cherokees! Notice! [Washington, 1907.]

Broadside. Folio.

Notice that applications must be filed for inclusion in the official roll of the tribe. The resulting roll, which is known as the Guion Miller Roll, is one of the most important ever made of the Cherokees.

CHEROKEE NEUTRAL LANDS

1866

Ex-Secretary Harlan's Letter, etc. [Washington, 1866.]

Broadside. Folio.

Harlan's defense of his course in the sale of the Cherokee Neutral Lands. No other copy is known.

1867

COX, JOHN T., and W. A. PHILLIPS

Notice to Settlers. [N.p., 1867.]

Broadside. Folio.

A notice to settlers on the Cherokee Neutral Lands that they must register their claims and that all lands and improvements will be officially appraised. Unrecorded, and no other copy known.

Rules for the Appraisement of the Cherokee Neutral Lands, &c., in Kansas, under the provisions of 17th article (as amended by the Senate) and the 19th article of the Treaty concluded with the Cherokee Nation of Indians July 19, 1877, approved by the Secretary of the Interior August 10, 1867. [Washington, 1867.]

3 p. 25.5 cm. Caption title.

1869

COATES, KERSEY

[An address, printed without title page or caption. Kansas City, 1869.]

14 p. 22 cm.

The pamphlet contains important information on the sale of the Cherokee Neutral Lands. The author was president of the M. R., F. S. & Gulf R. R. Co.

1870

CRAIG, JAMES

Argument of Gen. James Craig, attorney for the Fort Scott and Gulf Railroad Co. relative to their title to the Neutral Lands. Washington: Gibson Bros., 1870.

38 p. 22 cm.

Report of the House Committee appointed to Visit the Cherokee Neutral Lands. 1870. Topeka, Kansas: S. S. Prouty, Public Printer: "Commonwealth" State Printing House. 1870.

164 p. 22 cm. Printed wrappers.

A Vindication of Senator Harlan, of Iowa, from the Attacks of the Correspondent of the Cincinnati Gazette. [N.p., 1870.]*

56 p. 22 cm. Caption title.

Harlan was involved in the sale of the Delaware lands, the sale of the Cherokee Neutral Lands, and in the mismanagement of supplies for starving Indians.

1871

Cherokee Neutral Lands in Kansas. [Washington, 1871.]

49, [1] p. 22 cm.

Report on a bill to dispose of the lands to actual settlers only.

Peter F. Holden vs. James F. Joy. And William H. Warner vs. James F. Joy. Appeals (to the Supreme Court) from the Circuit Court of the United States for the District of Kansas. Opinion of the Court. [Washington, 1871.]*

10 p. on 10 leaves broadside. 34 cm. Caption title.

A lengthy examination of the title to the Cherokee Neutral Lands.

1872

Circular. Disposal of the Cherokee Strip. [Washington, 1872.]
3 p. 26.5 cm. Caption title.
Provisions for the sale of the Cherokee Neutral Lands.

Report of the Committee on Public Lands, to whom was referred Senate Bill No. 1213 "For the Relief of Settlers on the Cherokee Neutral Lands in Kansas." [Washington, 1872.]
12 p. 22 cm. Caption title.

CHEROKEE STRIP

1878

Letter from the Secretary of the Interior to the Chairman of the Committee on Indian Affairs, transmitting a Copy of a Report of a Commission appointed in pursuance of law to Appraise certain Lands in the Indian Territory lying West of the 96th degree of West Longitude. [Washington, 1878.]*
21 p. 23 cm. Caption title.

1883

Brief and Argument in the Matter of Application of Peter Hollenbeck, et al., to Secure Rights to Stock Ranges on Cherokee Strip. [N.p., 1883.]
4 p. 23 cm. Caption title.

Cherokee Strip Live Stock Association, the Charter and By-Laws of Association, adopted at Cherokee Strip Meeting, held at Caldwell, Kan., March 6, 7 & 8, 1883. [Caldwell, 1883.]
16 p. 23.5 cm. Caption title.
A fine copy and the only one known.

HOLLENBECK, PETER

In the matter of Application of Peter Hollenbeck et al. to Secure Prior Rights to Stock Ranges on Cherokee Strip. Petition and Abstract of Testimony. [Washington, 1883.]
7 p. on 7 leaves broadside. 36 cm. Caption title.
The affidavits presented offer detail of considerable value.

1885

Senate Bill No. 19. Introduced by Robert B. Ross. An Act in relation to the Cherokee Domain West of 96°. [Tahlequah, 1885?].*
[4] p. 22.5 cm. Caption title.

WILLIAMS, R. N.

Notice. To All who are Interested in Acquiring a Right in the Cherokee Nation, Indian Territory, the following will be interesting. [Columbus, Kansas? 1885?].
Broadside. 19.5 cm.
A circular promoting settlement on the Cherokee Outlet. The only known copy.

1887

Headquarters of the Army, Adjutant General's Office, Washington, March 8, 1887. General Orders No. 20. [Washington, 1887.]

4 p. 20 cm.
Publication of two opinions of the Attorney General bearing upon the prosecution of intruders upon the Cherokee Strip.

PARKER, I. C.

Title of Cherokee Nation to its Lands West of Arkansas River. [Tahlequah, 1887.]

Broadside. Folio.
Unrecorded, and the only known copy.

1889

FAIRCHILD, LUCIUS, and WILSON, A. M.

To the Cherokee National Council, Tahlequah, Indian Territory. [Tahlequah, 1889.]

12 p. 21 cm. Caption title.
A letter from the Cherokee Commission presenting arguments in favor of the sale by the Indians of the Cherokee Outlet. The only known copy.

Letter from the Secretary of the Treasury transmitting Information relative to the Alleged Bribery of the Cherokee Council. [Washington, 1889.]*

6 p. 22.5 cm. Caption title.
An investigation of the charge of bribery by agents of the Cherokee Strip Live Stock Association.

MERRITT, WESLEY

Headquarters Department of the Missouri (In the Field), April 27, 1889. [Oklahoma City, 1889.]

Broadside. 14 cm.
A warning to those passing through the Cherokee Strip not to leave the public highways or attempt any settlement there. The third known example of Oklahoma City printing. Unrecorded, and the only known copy.

[An Opinion, by the Assistant Attorney General on the question, "whether relinquishment of title to the Cherokee Outlet by the Cherokee Council violates the Cherokee Constitution." Tahlequah, 1889.]*

11 p. 22 cm. Without title or caption.
Printed for distribution by the Cherokee Commission to members of the National Council.

1890

The Correspondence of 1889 between the United States Commission and Cherokee National Authorities, and a Cherokee Memorial, as to a Cession of Cherokee Country West of 96th Meridian of Longitude, in the Indian Territory. Washington, D.C. Gibson Bros., 1890.

127 p. 21 cm. Wrapper title.
A valuable discussion.

Harrison, Benjamin

Intrusions on Cherokee Strip, February 17, 1890. By the President of the United States of America. A Proclamation. [Washington, 1890.]

Broadside. 25.5 cm.

An order for the removal of all cattle and live stock from the Strip. Two issues.

Harrison, Benjamin

Proclamation. [Washington, 1890.]

Broadside. 25.5 cm.

Relates to removal of cattle herded on the Cherokee Strip. No other copy can be traced.

Memorial of the Chief and Delegates of the Cherokee Nation, remonstrating against the Amendments of the House of Representatives to Bill (S. 895) proposing to Organize a Territorial Government for Oklahoma which includes within the Boundaries of said Territory a Portion of the Cherokee Strip. [Washington, 1890.]

4 p. 24.5 cm. Caption title.

Notice concerning Alleged Cattle Leases on Indian Lands in the Indian Territory and the Territory of Oklahoma. [Washington, 1890.]

Broadside. Folio.

A warning, aimed apparently at the Cherokee Strip Live Stock Association, that all cattle or other live stock must be removed from Indian lands.

1891

McAtee, John L.

Brief for the Cherokee Strip Live Stock Association. The Cherokee Strip Live Stock Association vs. The McClellan Cattle Co., Cass Land and Cattle Co., Head & Lawrence, Jot Gunter, Tom Green Cattle Co., Hall Bros., Smith, Tuttle & Holcraft, Winfield Cattle Co., Geo. W. Miller, J. R. Stoller, Constable & Fuelling, J. V. Andrews, Eli Titus, the Kansas and New Mexico Land and Cattle Co., Limited, and others. Statement, Points and Authorities for Plaintiff. Jno. L. McAtee, Attorney for Plaintiff. Kansas City: Lawton & Burnap, [1891].

78 p. 23.5 cm. Wrapper title.

Notice. [Washington, 1891.]

Broadside. 24 cm.

An order forbidding illegal or premature entry upon the Cherokee Strip. No other copy has been traced.

Owen, Robert L.

A Plan for Saving to the Cherokee People Millions of Dollars. [Muskogee? 1891.]

14 p. 22 cm. Wrapper title.

Relates to the sale of the Cherokee Strip. Unrecorded, and no other copy located.

Public Notice. [Washington, 1891.]

Broadside. Folio.

A warning to cattlemen to remove all stock from the Cherokee Strip.

[Report on the Cherokee Outlet. Washington, 1891.]

9 p. 23 cm.

Struble, Isaac S.

[Report on the Cherokee Outlet. Washington, 1891.]

27 p. 23 cm.

1893

Articles of Agreement concerning the Cession of the Cherokee Outlet, together with the Provisions to carry the same into effect. Washington, 1893.

8 p. 23 cm.

Cherokee Outlet. By the President of the United States of America. A Proclamation. [Washington, 1893.]

22 p. Folio. Caption title.

The proclamation opening the Cherokee Outlet, defining its boundaries, and laying down regulations governing its settlement.

Cherokee Outlet. By the President of the United States of America: A Proclamation. [Washington, 1893.]

25 p. 22.5 cm. Caption title.

The President's proclamation opening the Cherokee Strip, and forms to be executed by settlers.

Constitution and By Laws of the Primitive Baptist Colonial Organization. [Valley Center, Kansas, 1893.]*

[7] p. on one leaf, folded. 14 cm. Caption title.

The object of the association was the establishment of a settlement on the Cherokee Strip. The leaf contains a glowing description of the Strip. The only known copy.

Hardie, F. H.

The Signal. People having Certificates to enter the Strip will please line up by 11 o'clock tomorrow morning, Saturday, September 16th, 1893, in a Space Two Miles East of the City Limits and One Mile West of same. The Signal to Enter Strip will be Fired Precisely at 12 M., tomorrow, Santa Fe Time, by Capt. Hardie, 3rd Cavalry, etc. [Alva, 1893.]

Broadside. 20 cm.

The following is an extract from an official report of events at Alva: "On September 16 troopers were posted out in front with orders to keep back the crowd, numbering about 5,000, until the proper time, and promptly repeat the signal for starting. The people were eager and excited. At about four minutes before 12 o'clock some person, either accidentally or on purpose, discharged a pistol in the crowd of horsemen near the railroad bridge. This started the crowd, and Capt. Hardie, seeing quickly that it was impossible to stop the people, fired his pistol, which was answered along the line promptly, and made the start practically simultaneous." Unrecorded, and the only known copy.

Opening of the Cherokee Strip. Letter from the Secretary of War transmitting Information relative to the Opening of the Cherokee Strip. [Washington, 1893.]

86 p. 23 cm. Caption title. Large folded map.

A rare and important document, with many first-person accounts, in the form of depositions and affidavits, of events during the rush.

RENFROW, W. C.

Oklahoma and the Cherokee Strip, with Map. Prepared under the direction of Hon. W. C. Renfrow, Governor of Oklahoma. Chicago: Poole Bros., 1893.

16 p. 18 cm. Folded map.

Statistics and Information concerning the Indian Territory, Oklahoma, and the Cherokee Strip, with its Millions of Acres of Unoccupied Lands, for the Farmer and Stock-raiser. [St. Louis: Woodward & Tiernan Printing Co., 1893.]

85, [3] p. 19 cm. Printed wrappers. Folded map.
The wrapper states that this is the first edition.

1898

Statistics and Information concerning the Indian Territory, Oklahoma, and the Cherokee Strip, with its Millions of Acres of Unoccupied Lands, for the Farmer and Stock-raiser. [St. Louis: Woodward & Tiernan Printing Co., 1898.]*

85, [3] p. 19.5 cm. Printed wrappers. Map.

1925

RAINEY, GEORGE

The Cherokee Strip: its History. By Geo. Rainey. [N.p., 1925.]

[30] p. 17 cm. Printed wrappers.

CHEYENNE INDIANS

1867

HANCOCK, W. S.

Reports of Major General W. S. Hancock upon Indian Affairs, with Accompanying Exhibits. Washington: McGill & Witherow, [1867].

133 p. 23 cm. Printed wrappers.
An extremely rare and valuable detailed report on Cheyenne, Sioux, Kiowa, Comanche and Arapahoe hostilities.

Reports of the Secretaries of War and Interior, in answer to resolutions of the Senate and House of Representatives in relation to the Massacre at Fort Phil. Kearney, on December 21, 1866; with the View of Commissioner Lewis V. Bogy, in relation to the Future Policy to be pursued by the Government for the Settlement of the Indian Question; also Reports of Gen. Pope and Col. Eli S. Parker, on same subject. Washington, 1867.*

63 p. 22.5 cm. Printed wrappers.

1879

POPE, JOHN

[Report of affairs in the Department of the Missouri. Fort Leavenworth, 1879.]

4, [2] p. Folio.
A highly important report in detail on the troubles with the Northern Cheyenne Indians, the Payne Invasion of Indian Territory, the hostilities on the part of the Utes in Colorado and the Apaches in New Mexico and Arizona, and the incursions into Texas of hostile Indians from Mexico. A very scarce volume.

1880

MILES, JOHN D.

Notice. [Darlington, 1880.]

Broadside. 20.5 cm.

A warning to legal residents of the Cheyenne and Arapahoe Reservation not to harbor returning intruders recently expelled. Unrecorded, and the only known copy.

Report of the Select Committee to Examine into the Circumstances connected with the Removal of the Northern Cheyennes from the Sioux Reservation to the Indian Territory. [Washington, 1880.]

327 p. 23 cm. Caption title.

1882

Immediate Action. The citizens of this Part of the Territory owe it to their Own Safety and the Respect due their Murdered Fellow Citizen, Robert Poisal, that the Murderer be Brought to Justice. [Darlington, 1882.]

Broadside. 20.5 cm.

Unrecorded, and the only known copy.

MILES, JOHN D.

Notice to Stockmen! [Darlington, 1882.]

Broadside. 25 cm.

Notice by the Cheyenne and Arapahoe agent that intruders upon the Indian lands will be ejected. Unrecorded, and the only known copy.

MILES, JOHN D.

$600.00 Reward!! will be paid by the undersigned for the Arrest of Johnson Foster, Dead or Alive, the Murderer of Robert Poisal, who was Shot Down in Cold Blood on Monday, Sept. 18, 1882, while driving along the Road in the Shawnee Country, near Widow Deer's Ranch, by a Young Creek Indian, 18 or 20 years old, sharp featured and very dark complexioned. When last seen had on Black Slouch Hat, Common Slicker Coat, Jeans Pants and Hickory Shirt. The above Money has been subscribed by the Citizens of this Country for the Apprehension of the Murderer, Dead or Alive, and is in my hands. [Darlington:] "Cheyenne Transporter" Print, [1882].

Broadside. 20.5 cm.

Unrecorded, and the only known copy.

1883

Message from the President of the United States transmitting a Communication from the Secretary of the Interior of the 4th instant submitting Draft of Bill "to confirm the Title to Certain Land in the Indian Territory to the Cheyennes and Arapahoes, and the Wichitas and Affiliated Bands, to provide for the Issuance of Patents therefor." [Washington, 1883.]

82 p. 23 cm. Caption title. 2 folded maps.

The maps are exceptionally interesting and valuable.

1885

Indian Depredations. Claim of Wm. H. Moore, surviving partner of Wm. H.

Moore & Co., against the Tribe of Cheyenne Indians. Statement of Claim and Brief. Washington: Beresford, [1885].*

17 p. 23.5 cm.

[Proclamation of President Cleveland ordering cattlemen off the Cheyenne and Arapahoe Reservation. Washington, 1885.]*

2 p. 34 cm. Printed in script.

1890

Before the Honorable Lucius Fairchild, Alfred M. Wilson, Warren D. Sayre, United States Commissioners, authorized to Negotiate with Certain Indians by Act of Congress approved March 2, 1889. Brief and Argument, Samuel J. Crawford, Attorney for the Cheyenne and Arapahoe Tribes. Washington: Wm. H. Moore, [1890].

22 p. 23 cm. Wrapper title.

Message from the President of the United States transmitting a Letter of the Secretary of the Interior and Documents relative to the Condition of the Northern Cheyenne Indians. [Washington, 1890.]

18 p. 23 cm. Caption title. Folded map.

Message from the President of the United States, transmitting a Letter of the Secretary of the Interior with an Agreement by the Cherokee Commission with the Cheyenne and Arapahoe Indians for the Cession of Certain Lands. [Washington, 1890.]

24 p. 23 cm. Caption title.

1891

Agreement with Cheyenne and Arapahoe Indians. [Washington, 1891.]*

5 p. 22.5 cm. Caption title.

1895

PETTER, RODOLPHE

Zistxuisto, or Cheyenne Reading Book. Quakertown, Pa.: U.S. Stauffer, Printer, 1895.

36 p. 19.5 cm. Printed wrappers.

The first printing in the Cheyenne language, and one of only two known copies.

1896

SHELLABARGER & WILSON

West Reno City vs. Persie Snowden and Rosa Goenawein. [Washington, 1896.]*

25 p. 24 cm. Caption title.

An interesting land dispute which grew out of the Cheyenne and Arapahoe Run of April 19, 1892.

1898

EVERTS, HATTIE A.

Cheyenne and Arapahoe Work at the Watonga Mission. [Watonga, 1898.]

[8] p. 14.5 cm. Caption title. Plain wrappers.

A crudely printed narrative of missionary labors among the Cheyennes and Arapahoes. Apparently the only known copy.

1899

SANFORD, D. A., tr.

The Lord's Prayer. [Bridgeport, Okla., 1899?].*

Broadside. 11.5 cm.

A translation into the Cheyenne language. Unrecorded.

1900

Christmas with the Cheyennes and Arapahoes. [Watonga, 1900?].

Broadside. 28 cm.

A highly interesting account by an anonymous missionary of a Cheyenne and Arapahoe Christmas celebration. Unrecorded, and the only known copy.

1901

The Case of Dull Knife's Band. Washington, 1901.

14 p. 23 cm. Printed wrappers.

1904

PETTER, RODOLPHE

Assetosemeheo heamoxovistavatoz ("The Pilgrim's Progress") na hosz maheoneeszistotoz (and some Bible portions). Printed for the interest of the Mennonite Mission among the Cheyenne Indians. Berne, Indiana: Witness Print, [1904].

[4], 264 p. 19 cm. Printed wrappers.

A scarce volume.

1905

SEGER, JOHN H.

Tradition of the Cheyenne Indians. Arapaho Bee Print. [1905].

12 p. 22.5 cm. Wrapper title.

The rare original edition.

1907

MOONEY, JAMES

The Cheyenne Indians. By James Mooney. Sketch of the Cheyenne Grammar, by Rodolphe Petter. Lancaster, Pa.: New Era Printing Co., 1907.*

361, 495 p. 25 cm. Printed wrappers.

Two highly authoritative works.

1909

PETTER, RODOLPHE

Zesse-nemeortoz (Cheyenne Songs.) Printed in the Interest of the Mennonite Mission. Berne, Ind.: Witness Print, 1909.

38 p. 18 cm. Printed wrappers. Text in Cheyenne.

Very scarce.

1930

SEGER, JOHN H.

Tradition of the Cheyenne Indians. [Geary, Okla.: Seger Publishing Co., 1930.]*

[28] p. 20.5 cm. Wrapper title.

A reprint, with some new plates, or the rare original printed in 1905 at Arapahoe.

SEGER, NEATHA H.

Cheyennes and Arapahoes in Oklahoma. Indian News Items (in Indian English). [Geary, 1930.]*

Broadside. 28 cm. 3 columns.

Headed: Enough for 4 installments. Use 1–4 each week.

1932

MICHELSON, TRUMAN

The Narrative of a Southern Cheyenne Woman. Washington, 1932.

13 p. 24.5 cm. Printed wrappers.

Undated

PETTER, RODOLPHE

Key to the Cheyenne Alphabet. [N.p., n.d.].*

3 p. on 3 leaves broadside. 27.5 cm. Caption title.

Accompanied by four sample leaves from his English-Cheyenne Dictionary.

CHICKASAW INDIANS

1807

Accompanying a Bill making Appropriations for carrying into effect a Treaty between the United States and Chickasaw Tribe of Indians, presented the 27th of January, 1807. Washington City: A. & G. Way, 1807.

6 p. 21 cm.

1813

TENNESSEE GENERAL ASSEMBLY

[Memorial for the extinguishment of the Chickasaw and Cherokee titles to lands in Tennessee. Nashville, 1813.]*

Broadside. 26 cm.

Unrecorded, and the only known copy.

1828

MCKENNEY, THOMAS L.

Reports and Proceedings of Col. McKenney on the subject of his Recent Tour among the Southern Indians. Washington: Gales & Seaton, 1828.

37 p. 23 cm.

A fine copy of a rare and privately printed narrative. McKenney journeyed to the Chickasaw and Choctaw tribes with the purpose of persuading those Indians to exchange their lands in Mississippi for a new country in the West. The highly important reports include McKenney's talks to the Indians and their replies.

SHELBY, JAMES

Chickasaw Treaty. An Attempt to Obtain the Testimony of James Jackson, Esq. to Prove the Connexion of Gen Andrew Jackson with a Company of Land Speculators, while acting as United States' Commissioner; and to sustain the statement on that subject of the late Governor Shelby, by his son James Shelby. October, 1828. [Lexington, Kentucky, 1828.]

8 p. 23.5 cm.
Headed: Kentucky Reporter Extra.
Excessively rare.

1830

Public Dinner given in honor of the Chickasaw and Choctaw Treaties, at Mr. Parker's Hotel, in the City of Natchez, on the 10th day of October, 1830. [Natchez, 1830.]
16 p. 23.5 cm. Caption title.
Very rare.

1831

EATON, J. H., and COFFEE, JOHN
Brothers of the Chickasaw Nation. Franklin, Ten., Dec. 30, 1831.
12 p. 22 cm. Caption title.
An address, in English, distributed among the Indians at the treaty council. This copy was found in the papers of Peter P. Pitchlynn, later Choctaw principal chief, who was present at the council. No other copy is recorded.

1832

Instructions to Deputy Surveyors. [Natchez? 1833?].
13, [3] p. 21 cm.
Dated: Surveyor's Office, Chickasaw Cession, Mi.
Instructions for surveying the lands recently ceded by the Chickasaws. The only known copy.

Lease of Indian Reservation—Chickasaws. Report of the Committee on Public Lands. [Washington, 1832.]
49 p. 22.5 cm. Caption title.
Contains important information on the negotiation and execution of the treaty signed with the Chickasaws at Franklin, Tennessee, August 31, 1830.

1833

Specimen Field Notes for the Use of Deputy Surveyors in the Chickasaw Cession. 1833. [Natchez? 1833.]
[4], 11, [1] p. 15.5 cm.
The only known copy.

TUTTLE, SARAH
Letters on the Chickasaw and Osage missions. Second edition. Boston, 1833.
169 p. 14.5 cm.
Compiled from missionary reports.

1834

Regulations prescribing the Mode of Executing Certain Duties required by the Treaties with the Chickasaws of Pontitoc, entered into the 22d of October, 1832; and of Washington, entered into the 24th day of May, 1834. [Washington, 1834.]
4 p. 32.5 cm. Caption title.

1837

Van Buren, Martin

[A proclamation opening to settlement the lands in Mississippi acquired by the 1832 treaty with the Chickasaw Indians. Washington, 1837.]

Broadside. Folio.

1840

Land within the Chickasaw Cession. Message from the President of the United States in relation to Lands sold which lie within the Chickasaw Cession, &c. [Washington, 1840.]

9 p. 22.5 cm. Caption title.

Watson, J. C.

To the Honorable the Senate and House of Representatives of the United States, in Congress assembled. [Columbus, Ga., 1840.]*

6 p. 21.5 cm. Caption title.

Dated at end: Columbus, Georgia, November, 1840.

No other copy is known.

1845

Chickasaw Fund. Letter from the Secretary of War transmitting a Report of the Investigation into the Investment of the Chickasaw Fund. [Washington, 1845.]

97 p. 25 cm. Caption title.

A fine copy, uncut and unopened.

1848

Land Sale. Pontotoc, Miss. [Pontotoc, 1848.]

Broadside. 25 cm.

Sale of lands acquired by treaty from the Chickasaws. The only known copy.

1849

An Act Establishing a Committee of Vigilance, and for other purposes. The better to Watch the Interest of our Nation and the more securely to Protect the Rights of Our People. [Paris, Texas, 1849.]

Broadside. Folio.

Imprint at end: Printed at the Western Star Office.

The first printed laws of the Chickasaws, who formed at the time a district of the Choctaw Nation. Unrecorded, and the only known copy.

1859

Journal de la guerre du Micissippi contre les Chicachas, en 1739 et finie en 1740, le ler d'Avril. Par un Officier de l'Armee de M. de Nouaille. Nouvelle York, Isle de Manate, de la Presse Cramoisy de Jean-Marie Shea. M.DCCC.LIX.

92 p. 20 cm.

Field 807.

1860

Constitution, Laws, and Treaties of the Chickasaws, by Authority. Tishomingo City: E. J. Foster, 1860.

232 p. 23.5 cm.

A valuable compilation.

1866

LATROBE, JOHN H. B.

Argument (in the Overton Love case). [Baltimore, 1866.]*

11 p. 22.5 cm. Caption title. Plain wrappers.

1869

The Chickasaw "Orphans" and "Incompetents," under Articles 4 of the Treaties of 1834 and 1852, vs. The United States. Claimant's Brief, with Evidence attached. Washington: Thomas McGill & Co., [1869].

54 p. 22.5 cm. Wrapper title.

COLBERT, HOLMES

Exceptions to the Account stated, under the direction of the Secretary of the Interior, exhibiting in detail all the moneys which from time to time had been placed in the Treasury to the credit of the Chickasaw Nation, resulting from the Treaties of 1832 and 1834, and all the disbursements made therefrom. Filed by Holmes Colbert, Chickasaw Commissioner. Washington; Thomas McGill & Co., 1869.

11 p. 22.5 cm. Wrapper title.

COLBERT, HOLMES

Objections to Payments made by the United States out of Funds held in trust for the Benefit of Orphan and Incompetent Chickasaws. March 25, 1869. Filed by Holmes Colbert, Chickasaw Commissioner. Washington: Thomas McGill & Co., [1869].

7 p. 22.5 cm. Wrapper title.

LATROBE, JOHN H. B.

Chickasaw Claim to Four Miles Square on the Big Sandy under the Treaty of June 22d, 1852. [Baltimore, 1869.]

27 p. 23 cm. Wrapper title.
Very scarce.

Testimony relating to Disbursements made by the United States from the General Fund of the Chickasaws. Washington: Thomas McGill & Co., [1869].

7 p. 23 cm. Wrapper title.

Testimony relating to Payments made by the United States out of Trust Funds held for the Benefit of Orphan and Incompetent Chickasaws. Taken before Martin Chollar, Indian Agent, in the Indian Territory and at Washington, D.C., in November and December, 1868, and February and March, 1869. Washington: Thomas McGill & Co., [1869.]

27 p. 22.5 cm. Wrapper title.

1870

The Chickasaw Nation of Indians, under Article 4 of the Treaty of 1852, vs. The United States. Claimant's Brief, with Evidence attached. Washington: Thomas McGill & Co., [1870].

31 p. 23 cm. Wrapper title.

COLBERT, HOLMES

Letter from Hon. Holmes Colbert, Chickasaw Commissioner, and other Indian Delegates, to Hon. J. D. Cox, Secretary of the Interior, in relation to the Attempt of the Commissioner of Internal Revenue to Levy and Collect Taxes on the Interest due Chickasaws and other Indian Nations, on Bonds held in trust by the U.S. Washington: J. L. Pearson, [1870].

7 p. 23 cm. Wrapper title.

LATROBE, JOHN H. B.

Argument by J. H. B. Latrobe, of Baltimore, Md., for the Chickasaw Nation, in the Matter of the Orphan and Incompetent Chickasaws, under Article 4th of the Treaty between the United States and the Chickasaws, concluded June 22, 1852. Washington: Joseph L. Pearson, 1870.

20 p. 22.5 cm. Wrapper title.

1871

General Laws passed by the Legislature of the Chickasaw Nation, during the years 1867, 1868, 1869 and 1870. By Authority. Sherman, Texas: Printed at "The Courier Job Printing Office," 1871.

70 p. 22 cm. Printed wrappers.

This is the only copy known in wrappers, and hence the only known complete copy, since the full title with imprint appears only on the front wrapper. The inside title is practically a half title. A magnificent copy.

1873

Chikasha Okla i Kunstitushun micha i Nan Ulhpisa. Chikasha i Nan Apesa yut Apesa tok mak oke. [New York, 1873.]

350 p. 22.5 cm.

Compiled laws, in Choctaw. The Reverend Allen Wright was the translator. One of six known copies.

1874

JAMES, GEORGE D.

Memorial of George D. James, a Delegate representing the Chickasaw Nation, remonstrating against the passage of Senate Bill 680, giving Persons of African Descent, formerly Slaves of the Chickasaw and Choctaw Indians, an Individual Interest in all Lands and Moneys of the Respective Nations, contrary to Treaty Stipulations, and asking for the passage of Senate Bill 812, which proposes to give said Freedmen what the Treaty provided, to wit: Forty Acres of Land, with the privilege of becoming Citizens of the Nation. [N.p., 1874.]

8 p. 23 cm.

1875

To the Congress of the United States. [N.p., 1875.]

3 p. 23 cm. Caption title.

A protest against territorial government signed by the senators, representatives, governor, and national officers of the Chickasaws.

1877

Permit Law of the Chickasaw Nation. [Tishomingo City, 1877.]
Broadside. 26 cm.
Unrecorded, and the only known copy.

1878

Constitution, Laws and Treaties of the Chickasaws. By Authority. Sedalia: Sedalia Democrat Co., 1878.
231 p. 22.5 cm.
The volume is rare.

HARRIS, GEORGE E., and RICHARD MCALLISTER

Abstract, Brief and Argument in support of the Petition of Eli Ayres, to quiet Land Titles growing out of the Treaty between the United States and the Chickasaw Indians, concluded May 24, 1834, to which a careful and candid consideration is respectfully invited. By George E. Harris and Richard McAllister, Counsel for Ayres. [N.p., 1878.]
32, 3 p. 23 cm. Wrapper title.

OVERTON, B. F.

Permit Law of the Chickasaw Nation. [Washington, 1878.]
21 p. 23 cm. Wrapper title.
Overton was governor of the Chickasaw Nation.

1879

OVERTON, B. F.

Petition of B. F. Overton, Delegate from the Chickasaw Nation of Indians. [Washington, 1879.]
4 p. 24 cm. Caption title.

1880

OVERTON, B. F.

Annual Message of Gov. B. F. Overton, to the Chickasaw Council, at Tishomingo City, September 7th. Muskogee: Indian Journal Office Print, 1880.
15 p. 22 cm. Wrapper title.
The only known copy.

1881

Laws of the Chickasaw Nation from 1878–1881. Published by Authority. [Chickasaw Male Academy, 1881.]
18 p. 24.5 cm. Wrapper title.
One of only three known copies, the others being at the Harvard Law School and the New York Bar Association.

1882

Memorial of the Chickasaw Nation. [N.p., 1882.]
3 p. 25.5 cm. Caption title.
This presentation of Chickasaw grievances bears at the end the signatures of the two members of the delegation and of B. F. Overton, Governor.

1883

The Chickasaw Nation vs. The United States. Brief for the Chickasaw Nation. Washington: Thomas McGill & Co., [1883].

46 p. 22.5 cm. Wrapper title.

1884

General and Special Laws of the Chickasaw Nation. Passed during the Sessions of the Legislature for the years from 1878 to 1884, inclusive. By Authority. Muskogee: Indian Journal Steam Job Office, 1884.

64, [2] p. 22 cm. Printed wrappers.
The only copy known in wrappers. Also a copy in the usual sheep.

Reply to Objections. Statement of the Case. In the Matter of the House Bill "To Quiet Certain Land Titles in the State of Mississippi," under the Chickasaw Treaty of 1834. [Washington, 1884.]

19 p. 21.5 cm. Caption title.

1885

ENON BAPTIST ASSOCIATION

Minutes of the First Session of the Enon Baptist Association, held with the Wilson Creek and New Hope Churches, August 29, and October 16 and 17, 1885. Gainesville, Texas: Register Pub. Co., [1885].

10, [1] p. 20.5 cm. Printed wrappers.
The Enon Baptist Association was in the Chickasaw Nation.

1888

Letter from the Secretary of the Interior, transmitting a Letter from the Commissioner of Indian Affairs relative to the Freedmen in the Chickasaw Nation. [Washington, 1888.]

18 p. 23 cm. Caption title.

1890

Chikasha Okla i Kunstitushun micha i Nan Ulhpisa micha United States a Nan Itimapehinsa Tok Mak Oke. Chikasha Okla i Nan Apesa yut apesa tok mak oke. Atoka: Indian Citizen Print, 1890.

394, vii p. 22.5 cm.
The preceding volume translated into Choctaw. One of only six known copies.

Constitution, Treaties and Laws of the Chickasaw Nation. Made and Enacted by the Chickasaw Legislature. Atoka: Indian Citizen Print, 1890.

343, vii p. 22.5 cm.

PAINE, HALBERT E.

Interest on Chickasaw Trust Fund. Argument before the House Committee on Indian Affairs, by Halbert E. Paine, Attorney of the Chickasaw Nation. Washington: Gibson Bros., 1890.

27 p. 23 cm. Wrapper title.

1894

Statement of the Chickasaw Freedmen Setting Forth their Wrongs, Grievances, Claims and Needs. 1894. Fort Smith: J. H. Mayers & Co., [1894].

50 p. 23.5 cm. Wrapper title.

1896

Enon Baptist Association

Minutes of the Twelfth Annual Session of the Enon Baptist Association. Held with New Hope Baptist Church, near Marsden, I.T., September 8–11, 1896. Ardmore, I.T.: Baptist Beacon Print, 1896.

16 p. 21 cm. Printed wrappers. Folded table.

Not in Foreman.

Laws of the Chickasaw Nation, I.T., relating to Intermarried and Adopted Citizens and the Rights of Freedmen. Ardmore: Press of the Chronicle, [1896].

48 p. 23 cm.

One of only five known copies.

Zion Baptist Association, Chickasaw Nation

Minutes of the Third Annual Session of Zion Association held with Cippio Church August 14, 15 and 16, 1896. South Canadian, I.T.: J. D. Tignor, [1896].*

11, [1] p. 23 cm. Plain wrappers.

Not in Foreman.

1899

Chikasha Okla i Kunstitushun micha i Nan Ulhpisa micha Yonaitet Estets Nan Ittim Apehinsa tok 1832 micha 1834, 1837, 1852, 1855 micha 1866 kvt afoyukka hoke. Mikma holisso illappat toba chi ka Nov. 2, 1897, ash o Chikasha okla I nan apesa yut apesa tok makoke. Davis A. Homer, akosh snumpa toshole ho. Parsons, Kansas: Foley Railway Printing Co., 1899.

531, [1], xi p. 21 cm.

The preceding volume translated into Choctaw. The volume is rare.

Constitution and Laws of the Chickasaw Nation together with the Treaties of 1832, 1833, 1834, 1837, 1852 and 1866. Published by Authority of the Chickasaw Legislature by Davis A. Homer. Parsons, Kansas: Foley Railway Printing Co., 1899.

549, [1], x p. 21 cm.

Decisions of United States Courts in Indian Territory on Citizenship Cases and Chickasaw Mining Laws. Washington, 1899.

Title and pp. [458]–536. 23 cm.

1902

Regulations (June 3, 1902) governing the Introduction by Non-Citizens of Live Stock in the Chickasaw Nation, Indian Territory. [Washington, 1902.]

[6] p. 23.5 cm. Wrapper title.

1904

Report of the Superintendent of Public Instruction of the Chickasaw Nation, to the National Legislature. Tishomingo, I.T.: Chickasaw Capital Office, 1904.

[11] p. 21.5 cm. Wrapper title.
Unrecorded, and no other copy known.

TAFF, JOSEPH A.

Description of the Unleased Segregated Asphalt Lands in the Chickasaw Nation, Indian Territory. Washington, 1904.

14 p. 23 cm. Printed wrappers.

1906

MURROW, J. S.

Rich Yet Poor. [Atoka, 1906.]*

Broadside. 27 cm.
A reprint from the Indian Citizen of June 7, 1906, of an account by the missionary J. S. Murrow of the mistreatment of a Chickasaw child.

THOMPSON, JOHN Q.

John T. Ayres, Executor of the Estate of Eli Ayres, deceased, vs. The United States. Defendant's Objections to Claimant's Requests for Findings of Fact; Defendant's Requests to Amend Findings; and Defendant's Brief. [Washington, 1906.]

33 p. 23 cm. Wrapper title.
A Chickasaw citizenship contest.

1907

RUSSELL, CHARLES W.

United States Circuit Court of Appeals, Eighth Circuit. Bettie Ligon et al., vs. Douglas H. Johnston et al. Appeal from the United States Court of Appeals in the Indian Territory. Brief for Appellees. St. Louis: Buxton & Skinner, [1907].*

18 p. 23 cm. Wrapper title.
An important case arising from the purchase of land from Chickasaws of disputed blood and citizenship.

1910

JOHNSTON, DOUGLAS H.

Argument on behalf of the Chickasaw Nation against the Reopening of the Choctaw and Chickasaw Citizenship Rolls. Washington, 1910.

47 p. 23 cm. Printed wrappers.
Contains also Governor Johnston's Annual Message of September 1900 and various acts of the Chickasaw Legislature.

1911

WALLACE, W. H., compiler

Ordinances of the City of Pauls Valley. Compiled and revised by W. H. Wallace, City Attorney. Pauls Valley: Enterprise Print, 1911.

247 p. 22.5 cm. Wrapper title.

1919

MALONE, JAMES H.

The Chickasaw Nation. A Short Sketch of a Noble People. Souvenir of Memphis Centenary Celebration May 19–24, 1919. [Memphis, 1919.]

175 p. 25 cm. Printed wrappers.

CHINOOK INDIANS

1899

Dictionary of the Chinook Jargon, Indian Trade Language of the North Pacific Coast. Victoria, B.C.: T. N. Hibben & Co., 1899.

35, [1] p. 21.5 cm. Printed wrappers.

CHIPPEWA INDIANS

1835

The Ten Commandments. [N.p., 1835?].

Broadside. Folio. Text in Chippewa.

No other copy seems to be recorded.

1860

[Questions in Ojibway, answers in English. N.p., 1860?].

62 p. 15.5 cm.

Caption on p. 1: For Questioning, affirming, denying, going, coming, etc. An early volume, not recorded by Pilling.

1873

Petition of the Catholic Clergy for the Agency of the Chippewas of Lake Superior. Washington: H. Polkinhorn & Co., 1873.

24 p. 22 cm.

1874

WILSON, EDWARD F.

The Ojebway Language: a Manual for Missionaries and others employed among the Ojebway Indians. In three parts: Part I, The Grammar. Part II, Dialogue and Exercises. Part III, The Dictionary. By the Rev. Edward F. Wilson. Toronto: Roswell & Hutchinson, 1874.

412 p. 12.5 cm.

1878

BOTTINEAU, JOHN B.

Chippewa Indians of Northern Dakota Territory. Jno. B. Bottineau, Member of the Tribe, before the Hon. Secretary of the Interior, February 16, 1878. Will the Government Recognize their Claim and Provide for them? The Pembina Band of Chippewa Indians who are now roving around the Frontier Settlements of Northern Minnesota and Dacota Territory in a Destitute Condition, ask Assistance at the hands of the Government, and in consideration therefor are willing to relinquish their unceded Territory on which the White Man is yearly trespassing, and which he has long since ruined by driving all the Game out of the Country, that being the Sole Dependence of these Indians. Washington: Thos. J. Brashears, 1878.*

15 p. 22 cm.

1917

MEANS, PHILIP AINSWORTH

Preliminary Survey of the Remains of the Chippewa Settlements on La Pointe Island, Wisconsin. Washington, 1917.*

15 p. 24.5 cm. Printed wrappers.

CHOCTAW INDIANS

1779

Manifiesto de los motivos en que se ha fundado la conducta del Rey Christianisimo respecto a la Inglaterra, con la Exposicion de los que han guiado al Rey nuestro Senor para su modo de proceder con la misma Potencia. Madrid, 1779.

[2] 41 p. 21 cm.

Important notes on the British alienation of the Choctaws, Chickasaws, and Cherokees from the Spanish interest. Excessively rare.

1810

MADISON, JAMES

By the President of the United States. A Proclamation. [Washington, 1810.] The proclamation authorized C. C. Claiborne, Governor of Orleans Territory, to seize in the name of the United States the lands south of Mississippi Territory and east of the Mississippi River to the Perdido River, in short, West Florida, which was held at the time by Spain and claimed, and to some extent occupied, by the Choctaw Indians. A highly important document of which no other copy is known.

1814

Report of the Committee of Claims on the Petition of John Pitchlynn. Washington: A. & G. Way, 1814.

[3] p. 21 cm.

A claim for compensation for services as United States interpreter for the Choctaws from 1786 to 1792. John Pitchlynn was the father of Choctaw Principal Chief Peter P. Pitchlynn.

1824

Memorial of the Legislature of the State of Mississippi, relative to the Purchase of Certain Indian Territory, &c. Washington: Gales & Seaton, 1824.*

3 p. 24.5 cm.

1825

MOOSHULATUBBE, and others

Address from the Choctaw Delegation of Indians in Washington relative to their Condition in common with other Tribes and praying that the same may be Improved. Washington: Gales & Seaton, 1825.

7 p. 22 cm.

WRIGHT, ALFRED, and CYRUS BYINGTON

Spelling Book written in the Chahta Language, with an English Translation; prepared and published under the Direction of the Missionaries in the Chahta Nation, with the Aid of Captain David Folsom, Interpreter. Cincinnati: Published by Morgan, Lodge and Fisher for the Missionary Society.

84 p. 16 cm.

The first book in the Choctaw language, and an excessively rare volume.

1827

Encroachments on Choctaw Lands. Letter from the Secretary of War, transmitting Information in relation to Encroachments by White Men upon Lands ceded to the Choctaw Indians in the Territory of Arkansas. [Washington, 1827.]

8 p. 22 cm.

Letter from the Secretary of War transmitting a Report of the Commissioners appointed in pursuance of an Act of the last Session of Congress to hold Treaties with the Choctaw and Chickasaw Tribes of Indians for the purpose of Extinguishing their Claims to Lands within the State of Mississippi. Washington: Gales & Seaton, 1827.

51 p. 22 cm.

1828

Laws of the State of Mississippi passed at the Eleventh Session of the General Assembly held in the Town of Jackson. Jackson: Peter Isler, 1828.

147, viii, [10] p. 20 cm.

Important information on deplorable conditions among the Choctaws and Chickasaws and recommendations for the expulsion of vicious and disorderly whites.

1829

Laws of the State of Mississippi, passed at the Twelfth Session of the General Assembly, held in the Town of Jackson. Published by Authority. Jackson: Peter Isler, 1829.

123, vi, [10] p. 19.5 cm.

Contains the highly important act extending the laws of Mississippi over the Choctaw and Chickasaw Indians and memorials relating to Indian lands.

Wright, Alfred, and Cyrus Byington

Chahta uba isht taloa. Boston: Crocker & Brewster, 1829.

84 p. 15 cm.

The Choctaw hymn book. Pilling could not find a copy.

1830

LeFlore, Greenwood, and others

[Documents, transmitted by President Jackson, on Choctaw removal. Washington, 1830.]

10 p. 24.5 cm.

Headed: Confidential.

Highly important letters, transmitted to the Senate in confidence, from Greenwood LeFlore, Peter P. Pitchlynn, Israel Folsom, and other tribal leaders, regarding the true feeling of the Choctaws towards the recent Treaty of Dancing Rabbit Creek.

Mississippi Legislature

A Bill to be entitled an Act to Extend the Laws of the State of Mississippi over the Persons and Property of the Indians resident within its limits. [Jackson, 1829.]*

Broadside. Folio.

Unrecorded, and the only known copy. One of the foundation documents on Choctaw and Chickasaw removal.

Tuttle, Sarah

Conversations on the Choctaw Mission. Boston: T. R. Marvin, 1830.

2 volumes in one.

Compiled from missionary reports.

1831

Dukes, Joseph, tr.

The History of Joseph and His Bretheren. In the Choctaw Language. Utica, N.Y.: Press of William Williams, 1831.

48 p. 14 cm.

With a short introductory note by John Pitchlynn. Joseph Dukes, the translator, was a native Choctaw.

Laws of the State of Mississippi, passed at the Fifteenth Session of the General Assembly, held in the Town of Jackson. Published by Authority. Jackson: Peter Isler, 1831.

172, xviii p. 19.5 cm.

Laws affecting the Choctaws and Chickasaws, now about to be removed to the West.

Martin, George W.

To those who Claim Reservations under the Treaty of Dancing Rabbit Creek. [Natchez? 1831.]

Broadsheet. 28 cm.

An address to those Choctaws electing to remain in Mississippi and become citizens of that state. Unrecorded, and the only known copy.

Wright, Alfred, tr.

Holisso Holitopa, Chitokaka Chisus im Anumpeshi Luk, Chani Itatuklo kut Holissochi tok mak o. A kashapa kut Chahta im Anumpa isht Holisso hoke. Utica, N.Y.: Press of William Williams, 1831.

151, [3] p. 17 cm.

The rare first edition.

1832

Extent of Country and Number and Origin of the Choctaws. [Boston, 1832.]

[4] p. 24 cm.

Headed: Monthly paper of the American Board of Commissioners for Foreign Missions. No. III. June, 1832.

An important survey. The first page is devoted to a map of the Choctaw and Chickasaw Nations in Mississippi.

Fulton, John T.

Rations for Indians. Proposals, in writing, and sealed, for furnishing and delivering to the Emigrating Choctaw Indians, Complete Rations, together with Forage for Teams and Pack-horses, while travelling to their New Country, West of the Mississippi River, on the following Routes, will be received at this office, etc. Little Rock: Ark. Ter.: Wm. E. Woodruff, Printer, 1832.

Broadside. Folio.

Highly important. Itineraries are given in detail. The only known copy.

Laws of the Colonial and State Governments, relating to Indians and Indian Affairs, from 1633 to 1831, inclusive: with an Appendix containing the Proceedings of the Congress of the Confederation. And the Laws of Congress, from 1800 to 1830, on the same subject. Washington City: Thompson & Homans, 1832.

xvi, [9]–250, 72 p. 22.5 cm.

Choctaw Principal Chief Peter P. Pitchlynn's copy, with his penciled signature on the title page and inside the front cover.

1833

BROWN, J.

Public Sale of U.S. Wagons and Teams. Little Rock, Arkansas Territory: Wm. E. Woodruff, Printer, 1833.

Broadside. Folio.

"The above Wagons and Teams are superior to any in the Territory for the service of Indian Emigration, etc." The only known copy.

1834

Message from the President of the United States, with certain Documents relating to the Sales of Public Lands acquired from the Choctaw Indians. [Washington, 1834.]

6 p. 22 cm. Caption title.

1835

BOGY, JOSEPH

Petition of Joseph Bogy, praying Compensation for Spoliations on his Property by a Numerous Party of Choctaw Indians, then at Peace with the United States, whilst on a Trading Expedition on the Arkansas River, under Authority of a License derived from the United States. [Washington:] Gales & Seaton, [1835].

14 p. 22.5 cm. Caption title.

While on a trading expedition on the Arkansas River in 1807, Bogy was robbed of property to the value of nine thousand dollars by a war party of Choctaw Indians led by Pushmataha. The Choctaws were at the time at war with the Osages.

WILLIAMS, LORING S.

Family Education and Government: a Discourse in the Choctaw Language. By L. S. Williams. Boston: Crocker & Brewster, 1835.

48 p. 18.5 cm.

WILLIAMS, LORING S., tr.

Religious Tracts in the Choctaw Language. Second Edition, Revised. Boston: Crocker & Brewster, 1835.

39 p. 17 cm.

WRIGHT, ALFRED

Chahta Na-holhtina: or Choctaw Arithmetic. Boston: Crocker & Brewster, 1835.

72 p. 18.5 cm.

WRIGHT, ALFRED, tr.

Ulla I Katikisma: or Child's Catechism in Choctaw: being a Translation of Dr. Watts' Second Catechism for Children. Boston: Crocker & Brewster, 1835.

16 p. 17 cm.

Wright, Alfred, and Cyrus Byington

Chahta Holisso. Ai isht ia ummona. Third edition, revised. Boston: Crocker & Brewster, 1835.

72 p. 17.5 cm.

Wright, Alfred, and Cyrus Byington

Triumphant Deaths of Pious Children. In the Choctaw Language. By Missionaries of the American Board of Commissioners for Foreign Missions. Boston: Crocker & Brewster, 1835.

54 p. 14.5 cm.

1836

Treaties of the United States, with the Choctaw and Chickasaw Indians. Printed by Order of the Senate. Jackson, Mi.: G. R. & J. S. Falls, 1836.

35 p. 22 cm.
Very rare.

Wright, Alfred, and Cyrus Byington

Chahta Holisso it im Anumpuli. Or the Choctaw Reader. For the Use of Native Schools. Union: John F. Wheeler, printer, 1836.

123, [3] p. 16.5 cm.
Excessively rare. Pilling recorded only two copies.

1839

Byington, Cyrus, tr.

The Acts of the Apostles, translated into the Choctaw language. Chisus Kilaist im anumpeshi uhliha ummona kut nana akaniohmi tok puta isht annoa, Chahta anumpa isht atashoa hoke. Boston: Crocker & Brewster, 1839.

165 p. 18 cm.

1840

The Constitution and Laws of the Choctaw Nation. Park Hill, Cherokee Nation: John Candy, Printer, 1840.

34, [2] p. 17.5 cm.
One, and perhaps the finest, of four known copies. This is the first printing of Choctaw laws and the first law book of any kind printed in present Oklahoma.

1841

Choctaw Treaty—Dancing Rabbit Creek. Letter from the Secretary of War transmitting a Communication from the Commissioner of Indian Affairs, in respect to the Manner in which certain Stipulations in the Choctaw Treaty of Dancing Rabbit Creek have been Fulfilled. [Washington, 1841.]

179 p. 26 cm. Caption title.
A fine, untrimmed copy of this matchless source of information on the Choctaw Academy.

Indians—Choctaw Citizens of Mississippi. Memorial of the Choctaw Citizens of the State of Mississippi to the Congress of the United States. [Washington, 1841.]

5 p. 24.5 cm. Caption title.

1842

Letter from the Secretary of War in relation to the Adjustment of Claims arising under the 14th and 19th Articles of the Treaty of Dancing Rabbit Creek with the Choctaw Indians. [Washington, 1842.]

13 p. 24.5 cm. Caption title. Uncut and unopened.

1843

Proceedings of the Board of Choctaw Commissioners. [Natchez, 1843.]

17 p. 21.5 cm. Caption title.

A rare and important document.

1844

FISHER, CHARLES L., and HENRY L. MARTIN

Choctaw Claims. [Jackson, Miss., 1844.]

40 p. 23.5 cm. Caption title.

Very rare.

Message from the President of the United States transmitting the Correspondence in relation to the Proceedings and Conduct of the Choctaw Commission under the Treaty of Dancing Rabbit Creek. [Washington, 1844.]

224 p. 22.5 cm. Caption title.

WRIGHT, ALFRED, and CYRUS BYINGTON

Chahta uba isht taloa holisso, or Choctaw Hymn Book. Third edition revised. Boston: Press of T. R. Marvin, 1844.

175 p. 13.5 cm.

Presentation copy from Cyrus Byington.

1845

Choctaw Academy in Kentucky. Report of the Committee on Indian Affairs to whom was referred a Resolution instructing the said Committee to Inquire into the Manner in which the Choctaw Academy, in Kentucky, is conducted; "whether the Indian Youth sent there for Instruction are properly attended to in respect to their Clothing, Boarding, Morals, and General Education." [Washington, 1845.]

13 p. 22.5 cm. Caption title.

Report of the Secretary of War communicating Information in relation to the Contracts made for the Removal and Subsistence of the Choctaw Indians. [Washington, 1845.]

53 p. 22.5 cm. Caption title.

1846

Choctaw Treaty. Message from the President of the United States, transmitting a Report of the Secretary of War relative to the Claims arising under the Choctaw Treaty. [Washington, 1846.]

9 p. 22.5 cm. Caption title.

Notice respecting the Re-opening, for Private Entry, of Lands in that portion of

the Choctaw Cession of 1830, included in the Grenada District, in the State of Mississippi. [Washington, 1846.]
Broadside. Folio.
Also entered, erroneously, under Creek Indians of 1846.

1847

Circular to the United States' Registers and Receivers in Mississippi, Louisiana, Alabama, and Arkansas. [Washington, 1847.]*
Broadside. 25.5 cm.
Relates to Choctaw land claims. Also entered, erroneously, under Creek Indians of 1847.

1848

ALLEN, L. L.
A Thrilling Sketch of the Life of the Distinguished Chief Okah Tubbee, alias Wm. Chubbee, son of the Head Chief, Mosholeh Tubbee, of the Choctaw Nation of Indians. New York, 1848.
43 p. 19.5 cm. Printed wrappers.

FOLSOM, DANIEL
Prospectus for the "Choctaw Telegraph;" a Weekly Newspaper to be published in Doaksville, Choctaw Nation. [Doaksville, 1848.]
Broadside. 27 cm.
The earliest printing known to have been executed in that large section of southeastern Oklahoma originally embraced within the old Choctaw Nation. The short-lived Choctaw Telegraph was the first Choctaw newspaper. Unrecorded, and the only known copy.

Legal Representatives of William Armstrong. Report of the Committee on Indian Affairs on the Memorial asking Compensation for certain Services rendered by the late William Armstrong, as an Officer of the Indian Department. [Washington, 1848.]
29 p. 22.5 cm. Caption title.
Contains a review of Choctaw Agent Armstrong's services to the government and to the Indians.

1850

The Shorter Catechism of the Westminster Assembly of Divines, translated into the Choctaw Language. Ubanumpa isht utta uhleha hut Westminsta ya ai itunahut aiashut Katikisma ik falaio ikbu tok. Chahta anumpa isht a toshowa hoke. Richmond: Presbyterian Committee of Publication. [1850].
48 p. 11.5 cm. Plain wrappers.
P. P. Pitchlynn's copy, with his dated signature on the front wrapper. Pilling recorded but one copy.

1851

WRIGHT, H. B., and JOSEPH DUKES, tr.
Scripture Biography from Adam to Noah. By T. H. Gallaudet. Abridged, and translated into the Choctaw Language. Alam atok a isht ia hosh Noah atok a ont

uhli isht anumpa. Rev. T. H. Gallaudet ut Holissochi tok ut, ik falaiot toshowit Chahta anumpa toba hoke. [New York, 1851.]

68, 88, 42 p. 15 cm. Text in Choctaw.

Each of the three series of pagination, which contain additional biographies, has a separate title page. Joseph Dukes was a native Choctaw.

1852

BYINGTON, CYRUS

Holisso anumpa tosholi. An English and Choctaw Definer; for the Choctaw Academies and Schools. By Cyrus Byington. New York: S. W. Benedict, 1852.

252 p. 16 cm.

The first edition.

The Constitution and Laws of the Choctaw Nation. Printed at Doaksville, 1852.

110 p. 17.5 cm. Caption title.

One of only three known copies. There is evidence that the edition was largely destroyed in a fire at Doaksville.

WRIGHT, ALFRED

Uba anumpa mak a na ponaklo holisso. A Book of Questions on the Gospel of Mark, in the Choctaw Language; for the Use of Bible Classes and Sabbath Schools. By Rev. Alfred Wright, Missionary to the Choctaws. New York: S. W. Benedict, 1852.

75 p. 15 cm.

The first edition.

WRIGHT, ALFRED, tr.

The Books of Joshua, Judges, and Ruth, translated into the Choctaw Language. Chochua, nan apesa uhleha holisso, micha lulh holisso aiena kvt toshowvt Chahta anumpa toba hoke. New York, 1852.

151 p. 17.5 cm.

WRIGHT, ALFRED, tr.

The First and Second Books of Samuel, and the First Book of Kings, translated into the Choctaw Language. Samuel i holisso ummona, atukla itatuklo, micha miko uhleha, isht anumpa ummona aiena kvt toshowvt Chahta anumpa toba hoke. New York, 1852.*

256 p. 17.5 cm.

1853

Correspondence on Slavery. [Boston, 1853.]

An exchange by officials of the American Board of letters on Negro slavery in the Choctaw Nation. Important information nowhere else available on social and economic conditions in that tribe.

1855

COINCON, F. X.

To George W. Manypenny, Commissioner of Indian Affairs. [Fort Smith, 1855.]

Broadsheet. 25.5 cm.

The French trader protests against the action of Choctaw Agent Douglas H. Cooper in closing his store in the Choctaw Nation, confiscating his stock of goods, and driving him from the country. No other copy can be traced.

Papers relating to the Claims of the Choctaw Nation against the United States, arising under the Treaty of 1830. Washington: A. O. P. Nicholson, 1855.

53 p. 25 cm. Uncut.

Presentation copy from Peter P. Pitchlynn to Col. Peter Force, with inscription. Contains important documents on the violation of the treaty of 1820 and the non-execution of the treaty of 1830.

Papers respecting the Rights and Interests of the Choctaw Nation, and their Relations with the United States, the Chickasaws and other Indian Tribes. Washington: Geo. S. Gideon, 1855.

88 p. 22 cm. Printed wrappers.

1856

Memorandum of Particulars in which the Choctaw Nation and Individuals are entitled to Relief and Compensation in case they are not paid the Nett Proceeds of their Lands ceded by the Treaty of Sept. 27, 1840. Washington: Gideon, printer, [1856].

43 p. 22.5 cm. Caption title. The imprint is at the foot of the first page.

Notes Upon the Choctaw Question. [N.p., 1856.]

13 p. 22.5 cm. Caption title.

A review of Choctaw land titles and treaty rights.

Pitchlynn, Peter P.

Report of the Choctaw Delegation. Washington: G. S. Gideon, [1856].

8 p. 22.5 cm. Caption title. The imprint is at the foot of the first page. The report is signed by Peter P. Pitchlynn and is addressed to Geo. Harkins, N. Cochanauer, and Peter Folsom, chiefs of the Choctaw Nation.

1857

The Constitution of the Choctaw Nation, adopted January, 1857. Fort Smith: Wheeler & Sparks, Herald Office, 1857.

19 p. 20.5 cm.

The only known copy.

Smedes, William C.

Letter to the Hon. Jacob Thompson, Secretary of the Interior, in relation to the Right of the State of Mississippi to Five Per Cent. on Lands located in her Limits with Choctaw Scrip, under the Act of Congress of August 23, 1842. By Wm. C. Smedes, Esq., Agent of the State. Vicksburg: Printed at the Vicksburg Whig Steam Book and Job Office, 1857.

8 p. 20.5 cm.

Wright, Alfred, and Cyrus Byington, tr.

The New Testament of Our Lord and Saviour Jesus Christ, translated into the

Choctaw Language. Fin chitokaka pi okchalinchi Chisus Klaist in Testament himona, Chahta anumpa atoshowa hoke. New York, 1857.

818 p. 17 cm.

P. P. Pitchlynn's copy, with his autograph and manuscript notes.

1858

Acts and Resolutions of the General Council of the Choctaw Nation, from 1852 to 1857, both inclusive. Published by Authority of the General Council. Fort Smith, Ark.: Josephus Dotson, Printer for the Nation, 1858.

240 p. 21 cm.

An extremely important compilation.

Harkins, George W.

To the Choctaw People. Bretheren and Friends. [Clarksville, Texas, 1858.]

Broadside. 60.5 cm.

A full and important statement by a highly intelligent Choctaw of the position and views of the conservative element of the tribe with regard to the serious constitutional divisions which threatened at this time to bring about a complete breakdown in Choctaw governmental functions. Unrecorded.

Wright, Alfred, and Cyrus Byington

Chahta uba isht taloa holisso. Choctaw Hymn Book. Sixth edition. Boston: T. R. Marvin, 1858.

[3], 252 p. 14 cm.

1859

Acts and Resolutions of the General Council of the Choctaw Nation, at the Called Sessions thereof, held in April and June 1858, and the Regular Session held in October, 1858. Published by Authority of the General Council. Fort Smith, Ark.: Josephus Dotson, Printer for the Nation, 1859.*

80 p. 21 cm.

P. P. Pitchlynn's copy, with his signature on the title page.

Discontinuance of the Mission to the Choctaws. [Boston, 1859.]

7 p. 23.5 cm. Caption title.

Important for its authoritative account, based upon missionary reports, of Negro slavery in the Choctaw Nation.

Iki Chinto

Choctaw Matters. [Fort Smith, 1859.]

Broadside. Folio.

An important discussion of Choctaw constitutional and political matters. Unrecorded, and the only known copy.

Iki Chinto

To the Choctaw People. Fort Smith: Fort Smith Herald, 1859.

Broadside. Folio.

An important discussion of Choctaw constitutional and political dissensions. The only known copy.

1860

Acts and Resolutions of the General Council of the Choctaw Nation, for the year 1859. Published by Authority of the General Council. Fort Smith, Ark.: Printed at the Times Office for Campbell Le Flore, Printer for the Choctaw Nation. 1860.*

53 [2] p. 22.5 cm.

The volume is rare.

BENSON, HENRY C.

Life among the Choctaw Indians, and Sketches of the Southwest. By Henry C. Benson, with an Introduction by Rev. T. A. Morris. Cincinnati: L. Swormstedt & A. Poe, 1860.

314 p. 18.5 cm.

Field 113.

CREECY, JAMES R.

Scenes in the South, and other Miscellaneous Pieces, by the late Col. James R. Creecy. Washington: Thomas McGill, 1860.*

294 p. 18.5 cm.

The volume contains chapters on the Choctaws.

Missionary Convention for the Purpose of Raising Funds for the Support of the Choctaw Mission. New York: Edward O. Jenkins, 1860.

14 p. 22 cm.

PITCHLYNN, P. P.

Memorandum in regard to the Amount found due the Choctaws under the Award of the Senate, made March 9th, 1859, pursuant to the Eleventh Article of the Treaty of 1855 with the Choctaws and Chickasaws. Washington: G. S. Gideon, [1860].

5 p. 22 cm. Caption title.

Report of the Committee on Indian Affairs. [Washington, 1860.]

8 p. 24 cm. Caption title.

A report on Choctaw claims under the Treaty of 1855.

1861

Constitution and Laws of the Choctaw Nation. Boggy Depot, Choctaw Nation, 1861. Printed by J. Hort. Smith, Proprietor of the National Register.*

137 p. 21 cm. Plain wrapper.

The only known complete copy of the only volume of Indian laws printed within the jurisdiction of the Confederate States of America. [See page 117.]

Resolutions passed by the Convention of the Choctaws and Chickasaws, held at Boggy Depot, March 11th, 1861. [Boggy Depot, Choctaw Nation, 1861.]

Broadside. Folio.

The resolutions touch upon the imminence of war, authorize the raising of troops of Minute Men, and approve the allotment of communally owned lands. Unrecorded, and the only known copy.

Page - 93

CONSTITUTION AND LAWS

OF THE

Choctaw Nation.

BOGGY DEPOT, CHOCTAW NATION:
1861.

PRINTED BY
J. HORT. SMITH,
PROPRIETOR OF THE NATIONAL REGISTER.

1863

Goode, William H.

Outposts of Zion, with Limnings of Mission Life. By Rev. William H. Goode, Ten Years a Member of Frontier Conferences. Cincinnati: Poe & Hitchcock, 1863.

464 p. 19 cm. Frontisp. port.

Wagner-Camp 390. The first edition.

A presentation copy from Choctaw Principal Chief Allen Wright to Sophia C. Pitchlynn, the daughter of Principal Chief P. P. Pitchlynn. Goode's narrative of his life among the Choctaws possesses great interest and value.

1864

Head Quarters, Dist. Ind. Ter'y. Fort Towson, C.N., Oct. 31st, 1864. The following Act of the General Council of the Choctaw Nation is published for information. [Fort Towson, 1864.]

Broadside. 20 cm. Caption title.

Promulgation of "An Act entitled An Act requiring the District Chiefs of this Nation to Employ or Make Arrangements with Citizens to Hire Wagons to Haul Supplies for the Indigent and Choctaw Refugees." The only known copy.

1865

Pitchlynn, P. P.

Message of P. P. Pitchlynn, Principal Chief of the Choctaw Nation, delivered before the Choctaw Council in Extra Session, held at Goodwater Seminary, C.N., on the Second Monday in January, 1865. Government Printing Office, Fort Towson, C.N.

8 p. 20 cm.

The only known copy of a message of the highest interest and importance. The fortunes of the Confederate states and their allies were at very low ebb at the time.

1866

Pitchlynn, Peter P., and Winchester Colbert

Address by P. P. Pitchlynne, Principal Chief of the Choctaw Nation, and Winchester Colbert, Governor of the Chickasaw Nation, to the Choctaws and Chickasaws: Explanatory of the Circumstances under which the Treaty with the United States, concluded April 28, 1866, was Negotiated, and of the more Important Stipulations contained therein, with Suggestions as to the Policy proper to be pursued hereafter by the two Nations. Washington: Joseph L. Pearson, 1866.

8 p. 23 cm. Wrapper title.

Inscribed "With respects of P. P. Pitchlynn To Col. T. B. Turnbull, District Chief of Pushmattaha, C.N."

A Treaty between the United States and the Choctaws and Chickasaws. [Washington, 1866.]

56 p. 22 cm. English and Choctaw texts in parallel columns.

The treaty of 1866.

A Treaty between the United States and the Choctaws and Chickasaws. [Washington, 1866.]

56 p. 22 cm. Text in English and in Choctaw.
The only treaty, so far as is known, officially printed at Washington in one of the Indian languages. This copy belonged to former Principal Chief Peter P. Pitchlynn, one of the witnesses for the Choctaws, and has his signature on the title page.

1867

BLUNT, JAMES G.

Argument of James G. Blunt, Counsel for Loyal Choctaw and Chickasaw Claimants, in Reply to John H. B. Latrobe, Counsel for the Nations. Washington: McGill & Witherow, 1867.
29 p. 23 cm. Wrapper title.

JOHNSON, S. M.

Argument of S. M. Johnson, in the Matter of the Report of the Commissioners appointed under the 49th Article of the Treaty of July 10, 1866, between the United States and the Choctaw and Chickasaw Nations. Washington: Joseph L. Pearson, [1867].
8 p. 23 cm. Printed wrappers.

LATROBE, JOHN H. B.

Letter of John H. B. Latrobe of Baltimore, Counsel for Choctaw and Chickasaw Nations, to Honorable N. G. Taylor, Commissioner of Indian Affairs, touching the Award reported by Messrs. Rice & Jackson, Commissioners, under Article 49 of the Treaty of 10th July, 1866, between the United States, the Choctaw and Chickasaw Nations. May 22nd, 1867. Washington: J. L. Pearson, 1867.
9 p. 22.5 cm. Wrapper title.

LATROBE, JOHN H. B.

Papers submitted by John H. B. Latrobe, Counsel for Choctaw and Chickasaw Nations, at different times, in their behalf, touching the Report and Awards of Messrs. Rice and Jackson, Commissioners, appointed by the President under the 49th Article of the Treaty between the United States, the Choctaw and Chickasaw Nations, proclaimed July 10, 1866; with the Instructions of Hon. D. N. Cooley, Commissioner of Indian Affairs to said Commissioners. Also, a Letter from J. H. B. Latrobe, Counsel, &c., to Hon. N. G. Taylor, Commissioner of Indian Affairs, relative to the Licenses to Trade under Article 39 of said Treaty. Washington: Intelligencer Printing House, 1867.
64 p. 22 cm. Wrapper title.

LATROBE, JOHN H. B.

Reply of John H. B. Latrobe, Counsel for Choctaw & Chickasaw Nations, to the Supplemental Statement of Messrs. Rice and Jackson, late Commissioners, appointed under Article 49 of the Treaty of July 10, 1866, between the United States, the Choctaw and the Chickasaw Nations. [Washington:] J. L. Pearson, [1867].
26 p. 22.5 cm. Wrapper title.

LATROBE, JOHN H. B.

To the Honorable the Secretary of the Interior. [Washington, 1867.]

Objections to the findings of the commission appointed to examine the claims of loyal Choctaws and Chickasaws.

1868

The Choctaws, and their Debts due Joseph G. Heald and Reuben Wright. Washington: McGill & Witherow, [1868].
20 p. 23 cm. Wrapper title.

PITCHLYNN, P. P.
Memorial of P. P. Pitchlynn, Choctaw Delegate. [N.p., 1868.]
8 p. 22.5 cm. Caption title.
With a presentation inscription by the author.

PITCHLYNN, P. P.
Statement, Supplemental to Memorial of P. P. Pitchlynn, Choctaw Delegate. [Washington, 1868.]
4 p. 24 cm. Caption title.
With the author's autograph at the end.

PITCHLYNN, P. P.
To His Excellency the Principal Chief and General Council of the Choctaw Nation. Washington: McGill & Witherow, [1868.]
12 p. 22.5 cm. Wrapper title.
A report of activities at Washington.

PITCHLYNN, P. P.
To His Excellency the Principal Chief and General Council of the Choctaw Na-Nation. Washington: McGill & Witherow, [1868].
12 p. 26 cm. Printed wrappers.
The rare large paper issue of the report.

1869

Constitution and Laws of the Choctaw Nation. Together with the Treaties of 1855, 1865, and 1866. Published by Authority and Direction of the General Council by Joseph Folsom, commissioner for the purpose. Chahta Tamaha, 1869. New York: Wm. P. Lyon & Son, [1869].
508 p. 22 cm.
An important compilation.

DOOLITTLE, JAMES R.
Argument of Hon. James R. Doolittle, upon the validity of the Choctaw Claim, submitted by him as Counsel for the Choctaw Nation, to the Senate Committee on Indian Affairs, April, 1869. [Washington, 1869.]
9 p. 22.5 cm. Wrapper title.

LATROBE, JOHN H. B.
Opinion of John H. B. Latrobe on the Effect of the Tenth Article of the Choctaw and Chickasaw Treaty of 1866. Washington: J. L. Pearson, [1869.]
8 p. 23 cm. Wrapper title.

Pitchlynn, Peter P.

Report of Peter P. Pitchlynn (for himself and his Co-Delegates) to the Principal Chief and General Council of the Choctaw Nation, respecting the Claim of said Nation to the Net Proceeds resulting from the Treaty of 1830. [Washington:] J. L. Pearson, [1869].

13 p. 22 cm. Wrapper title.

1870

Byington, Cyrus

Grammar of the Choctaw Language, by the Rev. Cyrus Byington. Edited from the Original Mss. in the Library of the American Philosophical Society, by D. G. Brinton, M.D. Philadelphia: McCalla & Stavely, 1870.

56 p. 23 cm. Printed wrappers.
With an inscription on the title page by P. P. Pitchlynn.

Charter of the Choctaw and Chickasaw Thirty-fifth Parallel Railroad Company. Published by the Company, for the Information of the Choctaw and Chickasaw Peoples. Chahta Chikasha itatuklo chata palelil pokole tuchena akocha tulhape bachaya ka tuli hina kumpeni oke. Chahta mikmut Chikasha okla nana akostanecha chi pulla kuk o kumpeni illuput holisso ha ikbe tok oke. Little Rock, Ark.: Woodruff & Blocher, Printers, 1870.

24 p. in double. 26.5 cm. Printed wrappers. Title and text in English and in Choctaw.
An act passed by the Choctaw Council April 8, 1870. The only known copy.

Pitchlynn, P. P.

Argument submitted by P. P. Pitchlynn, Choctaw Delegate, to the Judiciary Committee of the U.S. Senate, upon the Question whether the People of the Choctaw Nation have become citizens of the United States by virtue of the Fourteenth Amendment to the Constitution. Washington: Cunningham & McIntosh, 1870.

8 p. 23 cm. Printed wrappers.

Pitchlynn, P. P.

Letter of P. P. Pitchlynne, Choctaw Delegate, for himself and Co-Delegates, to the Senate Committee on the Judiciary. February, 1870. [Washington, 1870.]

19 p. 22.5 cm. Wrapper title.
Presentation copy, with inscription on front wrapper, from P. P. Pitchlynn to Honorable James B. Beck.

Pitchlynn, P. P.

Letter of P. P. Pitchlynn to the People of the Choctaw and Chickasaw Nations upon the Question of Sectionizing and Dividing their Lands in Severalty. 1870. [Washington, 1870.]

15 p. 22 cm. Wrapper title.

Pitchlynn, P. P.

[A Memorial to the Senate and House of Representatives. Washington, 1870.]

4 p. 23.5 cm. Printed without title page or caption title.

PITCHLYNN, P. P.

Report of P. P. Pitchlynn, Choctaw Delegate, to His Excellency the Principal Chief and General Council of the Choctaw Nation, with Appendix containing Correspondence on the Survey of the Chickasaw District, and Letter addressed to the Secretary of the Interior requesting a Survey of the Eastern Boundary Line of the Choctaw Nation. Washington: Cunningham & McIntosh, 1870.

34 p. 22 cm. Wrapper title.

Remonstrance, Appeal and Solemn Protest of the Choctaw Nation addressed to the Congress of the United States. [Washington, 1870.]

21 p. 23 cm. Wrapper title.

Survey of Choctaw and Chickasaw Lands. Protest of Choctaw Nation, and Correspondence. August and September, 1870. Washington, D.C.: Cunningham & McIntosh, 1870.*

16 p. 24.5 cm.

1871

PITCHLYNN, P. P., and PETER FOLSOM

Special Report of P. P. Pitchlynn and Peter Folsom, Choctaw Delegates, to His Excellency the Principal Chief and the General Council of the Choctaw Nation, with Appendix, containing Opinion of the Attorney General, and Papers received by the Delegates from John H. Latrobe, as well as Papers filed by said Latrobe and Douglas H. Cooper with the Secretary of the Treasury. Washington: Powell, Ginck & Co., 1871.

33 p. 22 cm. Wrapper title.

WEED, JOHN J., and GEORGE W. WRIGHT

Arguments submitted to the Secretary of the Treasury by John J. Weed and George W. Wright upon the Question of the Right of the Delegates of the Choctaw Nation to Receive the Bonds authorized to be delivered to said Nation by the Acts of Congress approved March 2, 1861, and March 3, 1871. Washington: Jos. L. Pearson, 1871.*

30 p. 23 cm. Wrapper title.

WRIGHT, ALFRED, tr.

The Books of Joshua, Judges, and Ruth, translated into the Choctaw Language. Choshua, nan apesa uleha holisso, micha lulh holisso aiena kvt toshowvt Chahta anumpa toba hoke. New York, 1871.

151 p. 17 cm.

WRIGHT, ALFRED, tr.

The First and Second Books of Samuel, and the First Book of Kings, translated into the Choctaw Language. Samuel i holisso ummona, atukla itatuklo, micho miko uleha, isht anumpa ummona aiena kvt toshowvt Chahta anumpa toba hoke. New York, 1871.*

339 p. 17 cm.

1872

Cooper, D. H.

Letter to Hon. William Bryant, Principal Chief of the Choctaw Nation, from D. H. Cooper, Remonstrating against Injustice done Hon. J. H. B. Latrobe and others. Washington: Joseph L. Pearson, 1872.*
24 p. 23.5 cm. Printed wrappers.

Letter of the Solicitor of the Treasury to the Secretary of the Treasury in relation to the Choctaw Claim. November 14, 1872. Washington, 1872.*
46 p. 22.5 cm. Printed wrappers.

Memorial of the Choctaw Nation of Indians remonstrating against the Establishment of a Territorial Government over their Country. [Washington, 1872.]
6 p. 23 cm. Caption title.

Pitchlynn, P. P.

Letter of Peter P. Pitchlynn, Delegate of the Choctaw Nation, to Hon. George S. Boutwell, Secretary of the Treasury, in relation to the Issue of Bonds to said Nation. Washington: Powell & Ginck, 1872.
17 p. 23 cm.

Pitchlynn, P. P.

The Principal Chief and General Council of the Choctaw Nation: [N.p., 1872?].*
Galley proofs, 2 leaves.
A report on his activities as delegate to Washington.

Wright, Alfred, and Cyrus Byington

Chahta Holisso. Ai isht ia ummona. The Choctaw Spelling Book. Eighth edition. Richmond, [1872].
107 p. 14 cm.

Wright, Alfred, and Cyrus Byington

Chahta uba isht taloa holisso. Choctaw Hymn Book. Sixth Edition. Richmond, 1872.
252 p. 13 cm.
P. P. Pitchlynn's copy, presented to him in 1873 by T. J. Bond, a leading Choctaw physician of that day.

Wright, Allen

Letter from Ex-Gov. Wright, in Answer to one Written by P. P. Pitchlynn. [Boggy Depot, 1872.]*
Broadside. 20.5 cm.
Beginning in a blank space at the foot of the last column and running over and filling the reverse side of the leaf is a manuscript letter by Wright to Nicholas Cochnauer extending his printed attack upon Pitchlynn. Excessively rare.

1873

Bond, T. J., and others

To All Lovers of Truth. [Atoka, 1873.]

Broadside. 14 cm. high × 18.5 cm. wide.
An appeal by prominent Choctaws and missionaries for assistance in the distribution of religious literature among the Choctaws. Unrecorded, and the only known copy.

CHOCTAW and CHICKASAW BAPTIST ASSOCIATION

Minutes of the Choctaw and Chickasaw Baptist Association convened with the Rehoboth Church at A-to-ka, Choctaw Nation, Indian Territory, July 5th, 6th, and 8th, 1872. St. Louis. Barns & Beynon, 1873.
16 p. 21 cm.
Minutes of the first annual meeting. Excessively rare.

CHOCTAW AND CHICKASAW BAPTIST ASSOCIATION

Minutes of the Second Annual Meeting of the Choctaw and Chickasaw Baptist Association, held at Perryville, Choctaw Nation, Indian Territory. July 18th and 19th, 1873. St. Louis: Barns & Beynon, 1873.
14 p. 21 cm.

Choctaw Claims. Letter from the Secretary of the Treasury, relative to the Claim against the Government known as the Choctaw Claim. [Washington, 1873.]
23 p. 23 cm. Caption title.

Choctaw Claims. Memorial of the Choctaw Nation, in answer to the Letter of the Honorable Secretary of the Treasury, transmitting a Letter of the Solicitor of the Treasury in relation to the Choctaw Claims. [Washington, 1873.]
31 p. 23 cm. Caption title.

COOPER, DOUGLAS H.

Address and Memorial by Douglas H. Cooper to the General Council of the Choctaw Nation assembled. Boggy Depot, C.N.: Vindicator Print, October, 1873.
[22] p. 23 cm.
A very rare pamphlet, no other copy having been traced.

COOPER, DOUGLAS H.

Reply to Charges made by J. P. C. Shanks, late Chairman of the Committee on Indian Affairs, in regard to Matters connected with Choctaw and Chickasaw Affairs, by Douglas H. Cooper. Washington: Jos. L. Pearson, 1873.
46, 2 p. 23 cm. Wrapper title.

HEISTON, T. B.

The Defalcation Charges against Gen. Cooper. Boggy Depot, Choctaw Nation, October 4, 1873.
Broadside. Folio.
Headed: Vindicator Extra.
A defense of General Cooper's transactions in Choctaw funds in 1861. The only known copy.

JONES, R. M.

A Reverend Libeler. [New Boggy? 1873.]
4 p. 23 cm. Caption title.

A vitriolic attack upon former Choctaw Principal Chief Allen Wright. Jones was one of the leading Choctaws and the wealthiest member of the tribe. His blast throws interesting light upon Choctaw internal affairs.

LATROBE, JOHN H. B.

An Address to the Choctaw and Chickasaw Nations, in regard to matters connected with the Treaty of 1866, by John H. B. Latrobe. [Baltimore, 1873.]
16 p. 23 cm. Wrapper title.

PITCHLYNN, P. P.

Hon. Columbus Delano, Secretary of the Interior of the United States. [N.p., 1873.]
6 p. 22 cm. Caption title.
A statement of the Choctaw claims.

PITCHLYNN, P. P.

Reply of Peter P. Pitchlynn, Choctaw Delegate, to a Libelous Pamphlet published by Douglas H. Cooper. Washington, D.C., 1873.
41 p. 22.5 cm. Printed wrappers.

PITCHLYNN, PETER P.

Report of Peter P. Pitchlynn to the Principal Chief and General Council of the Choctaw Nation. October, 1873. [N.p., 1873.]
7 p. 22.5 cm. Wrapper title.

PITCHLYNN, P. P.

To the Senate and House of Representatives of the United States of America. [Washington, 1873.]
2 p. 24.5 cm. Caption title.

The Solicitor of the Treasury and the Choctaw Claims. [N.p., 1873.]
54 p. 23 cm. Caption title.
An important review.

Treaty Stipulations with Choctaw Nation. [Washington, 1873.]
29 p. 22.5 cm. Caption title.

1874

CHOCTAW and CHICKASAW BAPTIST ASSOCIATION

Minutes of the Third Annual Meeting of the Choctaw and Chickasaw Baptist Association, held at Atoka, Choctaw Nation, Indian Territory, July 17th, 18th and 19th, 1874. St. Louis: Barns & Beynon, 1874.
22 p. 23 cm. Printed wrappers.

Choctaw Award. [Washington, 1874.]
17 p. 23 cm. Caption title.
The report was submitted by Isaac C. Parker, who later attained fame at Fort Smith.

Choctaw Award. Report of the Committee on Indian Affairs to whom was referred the Memorial of P. P. Pitchlynn. [Washington, 1874.]
12 p. 23 cm. Caption title.

PITCHLYNN, P. P.

Memorial of P. P. Pitchlynn, Delegate of Choctaw Nation of Indians, upon the Right of that Nation to be paid the Money awarded to it by the United States Senate on the 9th day of March, A.D. 1859. [Washington, 1874.]

46 p. 23 cm. Caption title.

PITCHLYNN, P. P., and others

Report of the Delegates of the Choctaw Nation upon the "Net Proceeds" Claim, made to the Principal Chief & National Council, at the October Session, 1874. Washington: Powell & Ginck, 1874.

22 p. 22.5 cm. Wrapper title.

Remonstrance of the Choctaw Delegates. [Washington, 1874.]

11 p. 23 cm. Caption title.

A protest against the extension of citizenship and annuity privileges to Negro freedmen.

WESTERN BAPTIST ASSOCIATION

Minutes of the Forty-sixth Annual Session of the Western Baptist Association, held with the Church at Senoia, Coweta County, Ga. September 19, 20 and 21, 1874. West Point, Ga.: Office of the State Line Press, 1874.*

10, [2] p. 21 cm. Printed wrappers.

Contains references to the work in Indian Territory of the Reverend J. S. Murrow, the missionary of the Rehoboth Association, and to the Reverend Peter Folsom, the native Choctaw missionary supported by the Western Baptist Association. The back wrapper is devoted to a portrait of Folsom.

1875

BOND, T. J., and others

To the Friends of the Indians in the States. [Atoka? 1875.]

Broadsheet. 22 cm.

An appeal for funds to help pay for the Baptist chapel at Atoka. At the end is a short manuscript letter from T. J. Bond, a prominent Choctaw physician and one of the authors of the appeal, to former Choctaw Principal Chief P. P. Pitchlynn.

CHOCTAW and CHICKASAW BAPTIST ASSOCIATION

[Minutes of the Fourth Annual Session of the Choctaw and Chickasaw Baptist Association at Sardis Church, Jacks Fork County, Choctaw Nation, November 21, 1875. Atoka? 1875.]

10, [1] p. 17.5 cm. Wrappers, probably printed, are lacking.

PITCHLYNN, P. P.

The Claim of the Choctaw Nation for the Net Proceeds of the Land Ceded by the Treaty concluded at Dancing Rabbit Creek, September 27, 1830. [N.p., 1875?].

57 p. 22.5 cm. Caption title.

A full review of the claim.

PITCHLYNN, P. P.

Memorial of P. P. Pitchlynn, Choctaw Delegate, accompanying a Memorial of

the Choctaw Council, asking payment of the award made to the Choctaw Nation March 9, 1859. [Washington, 1875.]
4 p. 24.5 cm. Caption title.

PITCHLYNN, P. P.
Memorial to the Congress of the United States. [Washington, 1875.]
6 p. on 6 leaves broadside. 32 cm. Caption title.
Presentation of Choctaw grievances.

WESTERN BAPTIST ASSOCIATION
Minutes of the Forty-seventh Annual Session of the Western Baptist Association, held with the Church at Greenville, Meriwether County, Georgia, September 18th, 19th and 20th, 1875. West Point, Georgia: Office of the State Line Press, 1875.*
10, [3] p. 22 cm. Printed wrappers.
Contains some information on the Association's mission to the Choctaws.

1876

CHOCTAW and CHICKASAW BAPTIST ASSOCIATION
Minutes of the Fifth Annual Meeting of the Choctaw and Chickasaw Baptist Association, held with the Nun-ny Cha-ha Church, Toboxy County, Choctaw Nation, Indian Territory, commencing on Friday, August 11th, 1876. Chicago, [1876].
16 p. 21 cm.

Choctaw Indians. Report of the Committee on Indian Affairs, to whom was referred the Memorial of the Choctaw Nation, asking for the Settlement of their Claims for Lands ceded to the United States under the Treaty of 1830. [Washington, 1876.]
23 p. 23 cm. Caption title.

Claims of the Choctaw Nation. Memorial of the Choctaw Nation, asking for the Settlement of their Claims. [Washington, 1876.]
95 p. 22.5 cm. Caption title.

Memorial of the Choctaw Nation praying the Settlement of its Claim arising under the Treaty of 1855. [Washington, 1876.]
Broadsheet. 24 cm.

PITCHLYNN, P. P.
To the Choctaw People. [N.p., 1876.]*
8 p. 23 cm. Caption title.
Differences between himself and Principal Chief Coleman Cole.

1877

CHOCTAW and CHICKASAW BAPTIST ASSOCIATION
Minutes of the Sixth Annual Meeting of the Choctaw and Chickasaw Baptist Association, held with the Philadelphia Church, Blue County, Choctaw Nation, Indian Territory, commencing on Friday, August 10, 1877. St. Louis: Wright & Fleming, 1877.
13, [1] p. 22 cm. Printed wrappers.

Choctaw Claims. Memorial of the Choctaw Nation asking for the Settlement of its Claim arising under the Treaty of 1855. [Washington, 1877.]*

4 p. 23.5 cm. Caption title.

COLE, COLEMAN

Proclamation, by Coleman Cole, Prin. Chief, Choctaw Nation. To the People of the Choctaw Nation, and all concerned. Eufaula, I.T.: Indian Journal Print, [1877].

Broadside. Folio.

The proclamation and its accompanying correspondence relate to Principal Chief Cole's demand for the removal of Choctaw Agent Marston. Unrecorded, and the only known copy.

Memorial of Delegates and Agents of the Choctaw and Chickasaw Nations of Indians, remonstrating against the Passage of Senate Bill No. 107 to enable Indians to become Citizens. [Washington, 1877.]

3 p. 24 cm. Caption title.

PARKER, I. C.

Ex parte James E. Reynolds. Application for Habeas Corpus before Hon. I. C. Parker, Judge of the District Court of the Western District of Arkansas. [Fort Smith, 1877.]

12 p. 23 cm. Caption title.

An important document. Reynolds, a white man and a Choctaw citizen by marriage, demanded his release from Federal custody on a charge of murder, on the grounds that both he and his victim, one Puryear, also a white man, were citizens of the Choctaw Nation and that the United States Court was therefore without jurisdiction in the case. Judge Parker ruled that Puryear's wife was not a bona fide member of the Choctaw tribe, that Puryear was himself therefore a citizen of the United States, and that the United States Court consequently had jurisdiction in the case.

PITCHLYNN, PETER P.

"Nearer My God to Thee." Translated into Choctaw. By Peter P. Pitchlynn, in 1877. [Atoka, 1877.]*

Broadside. 24 cm.

Unrecorded, and the only known copy.

1878

Akinsa Ulhti Anukaka ya Yakni Tullaya ho Chahta Okla Hat Pit Halalli imma ka Holisso Ilupput Haiyakechi hoke. [Atoka? 1878.]

[5] p. 24 cm. Text in Choctaw.

Correspondence regarding a tract in Arkansas claimed by the Choctaws.

Chahta Okla i Nanalhpisa, Nanapisa affami 1876 micha 1877. Aiena Nanalhpisa tok oke. Atoka, Chahta Yakni: W. J. Hemby, Holisso ai ikbe. 1878.

61 p. 22 cm. Printed wrappers. Text in Choctaw.

One, and perhaps the finest, of only five known copies. A translation into Choctaw of the preceding volume.

Choctaw and Chickasaw Baptist Association

Minutes of the Seventh Annual Meeting of the Choctaw and Chickasaw Baptist Association, held with the Stonewall Church, Pontotoc County, Chickasaw Nation, Indian Territory, commencing on Friday, August 9th, 1878.*

13, [1] p. 21 cm.

The Choctaw Nation of Indians. [Washington, 1878.]

39 p. 23 cm. Caption title.

Pasted down on the first page is a long pencilled note in the hand of Peter P. Pitchlynn. The report relates to the Net Proceeds Claim.

Laws of the Choctaw Nation passed at the Choctaw Councils of 1876 and 1877. Atoka, Choctaw Nation: W. J. Hemby, Printer, 1878.

71 p. 22 cm. Printed wrappers.

Undoubtedly the finest copy known.

Letter to the President of the United States from Delegates representing the Indian Territory, protesting against the Decision of the District Court for the Western District of Arkansas in the case of Ex parte James E. Reynolds. [N.p., 1878.]*

6 p. 23 cm. Caption title.

A discussion of the greatest importance in the matter of United States or Indian jurisdiction over certain crimes committed in Indian Territory.

Memorial of the Choctaw Nation asking for a Settlement of their Claims arising under the Treaty of 1855. [Washington, 1878.]

4 p. 24 cm. Caption title.

Western Baptist Association

Minutes of the Fiftieth Annual Session of the Western Baptist Association, held with the Church at Newnan, Coweta County, Georgia, Sept. 14, 15 and 16, 1878. Atlanta, Ga.: James P. Harrison & Co., [1878].

14, [2] p. 21 cm. Wrapper title.

Contains a report on the Association's mission to the Choctaws.

1879

Amount due Choctaw Nation. [Washington, 1879.]

4 p. 23.5 cm. Caption title.

Choctaw and Chickasaw Baptist Association

Minutes of the Eighth Annual Meeting of the Choctaw and Chickasaw Baptist Association held with the Church at Hebron, Choctaw Nation, Indian Territory, commencing on Friday, September 19th, 1879. Denison, Texas: M. F. Dearing, 1879.

11, [1] p. 21 cm.

Garvin, Isaac L.

Proclamation. [Wheelock, Choctaw Nation, 1879.]

Broadside. 13 cm. high × 17 cm. wide.

The proclamation forbids the cutting of timber in the Choctaw Nation. Unrecorded, and the only known copy.

Report of the Committee on Public Lands . . . (on) the late Survey of the Western Boundary of Arkansas. [Washington, 1879.]*

5 p. 24 cm. Caption title.

1880

Acts and Resolutions passed at the Regular Term of the General Council of the Choctaw Nation, October, 1880. From Nos. 1 to 41 inclusive. Denison, Texas: M. F. Dearing, Lessee Herald Job Office, 1880.*

29 p. 21 cm. Wrapper title.
One of only five known copies.

Choctaw and Chickasaw Baptist Association

Minutes of the Ninth Annual Meeting of the Choctaw and Chickasaw Baptist Association held with the Church at Nun-ny Cha-ha, Choctaw Nation, Ind. Terr., commencing on Friday, Sept. 20th, 1880. Muskogee, I.T.: Indian Journal Office, 1880.

12, [1] p. 22.5 cm. Printed wrappers.

McCurtain, Jackson F.

Message of Chief McCurtain to the Senate and House of Representatives of the Choctaw Nation. [Atoka? 1880.]

Broadside. Folio.
The only known copy.

Wright, Allen

Chahta Leksikon. A Choctaw and English Definition. For the Choctaw Academies and Schools. By Allen Wright. St. Louis, [1880].

311, [7] p. 18.5 cm.
The first edition.

1881

Choctaw and Chickasaw Baptist Association

Minutes of the Tenth Annual Meeting of the Choctaw and Chickasaw Baptist Association, held with the Church at Ephesus, Blue County, Choctaw Nation, Indian Territory, commencing on Friday, August 26, 1881. Sedalia, Mo.: Democrat Steam Job Printing House, 1881.

13, [2] p. 22.5 cm. Printed wrappers.

Choctaw and Chickasaw Baptist Association

Minutes of the Tenth Annual Meeting of the Choctaw and Chickasaw Baptist Association held with the Church at Ephesus, Choctaw Nation, Ind. Ter., commencing on Friday, August 26th, 1881. St. Louis, Mo.: American Baptist Flag Office, 1881.

13 p., [1] p. 22.5 cm. Printed wrappers.

The Choctaw and Chickasaw Nations vs. The Missouri, Kansas and Texas Railway Co. [Washington, 1881.]*

Briefs, records, etc.

5 vols., aggregating 203 p.
A suit to recover the value of tribal property (timber, stone, and coal) used or de-

stroyed in construction of the railroad. The case throws interesting light on Indian Territory railroad history.

The Choctaw Nation vs. The United States. [Washington, 1881–85.]

Records, briefs, etc.

10 volumes, aggregating over 2600 pages.

The literature of the famous Net Proceeds case easily ranks as one of the very great sources of Choctaw history. The rare two volumes of evidence, running to something over 1700 pages and containing hundreds of depositions and affidavits on family relationships and on personal experiences in the removal from Mississippi, are an almost fabulous mine of tribal history.

General and Special Laws of the Choctaw Nation, passed at the Regular Session of the General Council, convened at Chahta Tamaha, October 3rd and adjourned November 12th, 1881. By Authority. Denison, Texas: News Job Printing House, Murray & Dearing, 1881.*

66 p. 21.5 cm. Printed wrappers.

One of only four known copies.

1882

Choctaw and Chickasaw Baptist Association

Minutes of the Eleventh Annual Meeting of the Choctaw and Chickasaw Baptist Association held with the Church at Richland, Red River County, Choctaw Nation, Ind. Ter., commencing on Friday, August 26, 1882. Sedalia, Mo.: Democrat Steam Printing House and Book Bindery, 1882.

11, [1] p. 21 cm. Printed wrappers.

1883

Choctaw and Chickasaw Baptist Association

Minutes of the Twelfth Annual Session of the Choctaw and Chickasaw Baptist Association, held with the Church at High Hill, Choctaw Nation, Indian Territory, commencing Friday, Aug. 24, 1883. Ottawa, Kansas: Kessler & M'Allister, 1883.

15, [1] p. 22 cm. Printed wrappers.

The Freedmen and Registration Bills, passed at a Special Session of the Choctaw Council, Indian Territory. May, 1883. Denison, Texas: Printed at Murray's Steam Printing House, 1883.

8 p. 22 cm. Wrapper title.

One of only two known copies; the other is at Harvard.

Laws of the Choctaw Nation, passed at the Choctaw Council at the Regular Session of 1883. Sedalia, Mo.: Democrat Steam Printing House and Book Bindery, 1883.

71, [1] p. 22.5 cm. Printed wrappers.

Less than ten copies are known, of which this is perhaps the finest.

Memorial of the Choctaw and Chickasaw Nations to the Secretary of the Interior of the United States, relating to their Jurisdiction of Persons and Property under the Treaty of June 22, 1855. Washington: W. H. Moore, 1883.

64 p. 23 cm. Wrapper title.
This refutation of the Ream claim throws important light upon early coal mining activities in the Choctaw Nation.

Wayland Baptist Missionary Association

Minutes of the First Annual Session of the Wayland Baptist Missionary Association, held with the Rehobeth Baptist Church, Atoka, Choctaw Nation, Thursday, Friday and Saturday, September 6, 7 and 8, 1883. Denison, Texas: Murray's Steam Printing House, 1883.
5, [1] p. 21 cm.

1884

General and Special Laws of the Choctaw Nation. Passed at the Regular Session of the General Council Convened at Tushka Homma, October 6 and adjourned November 7. By Authority. Muskogee: Indian Journal Steam Job Print, 1884.
47 p. 21 cm. Wrapper title.
One of only four known copies. The last leaf, printed on only one side and a small portion of the index, is lacking.

Short Mountain Baptist Association

Minutes of the First Session of the Short Mountain Baptist Association, and Proceedings of the Convention called for its Formation held with Short Mountain Baptist Church, Sans Bois County, Ind. Ter., Oct. 24th & 25th, 1884. Wincherville, Arkansas: Lee and Jennie Compere, [1884].
7 p. 18.5 cm. Wrapper title.
A Baptist association in the northern part of the Choctaw Nation.

1885

Koi Hommabii

One Hour of Solid Enjoyment. Koi Hommabii, a Choctaw Indian, who is without a Peer in his Art, will deliver one of his Unique and Popular Lectures . . . . Subject: A Description of the Territorial Tribes, both Savage and Civilized, Language spoken, Way of Singing, Customs and Costumes, Mode of Hunting and Fishing, and the Past and Present Form of Government, etc. [N.p., 1885?].
Broadside. Folio.
No other copy is known.

McCurtain, Edmund

Proclamation! Muskogee: Journal Steam Print, [1885].
Broadside. Folio.
The proclamation relates to the enrollment of Negro freedmen for Choctaw citizenship.

1886

Laws of the Choctaw Nation, passed at the Choctaw Council at the Regular Session of 1886. Sedalia, Mo.: Democrat Publishing Co., 1886.
53 p. 22 cm. Printed wrappers.
One of only four known copies.

LE FLORE, CAMPBELL

Appeal of the Choctaw Nation from the Decision of the Commissioner of Indian Affairs rendered January 23, 1886. Campbell LeFlore, Special Delegate, Choctaw Nation. Washington: R. O. Polkinhorn & Son, [1886].

24 p. 23.5 cm. Wrapper title.

LE FLORE, CAMPBELL

Statement of the Rights of Choctaw Citizens within the Chickasaw District, as Secured by the Agreement of January 17th, 1837, and the Treaties of June 22, 1855, and April 28, 1866; and the Request of the Choctaw Nation that the United States shall require the Chickasaws to admit and accord to the Choctaws their Rights under said Treaties in the Chickasaw District. Campbell LeFlore, Special Choctaw Delegate. [Washington, 1886.]

19 p. 23 cm. Wrapper title.

NEAL, C. B.

Before Hon. Robt. L. Owens, United States Indian Agent, Union Agency. Appeal of Harmon Mickle, W. T. Stephens, J. M. Bragg, J. M. Bynum. [Muskogee, 1886.]

5 p. 22.5 cm. Caption title.

Appeal of citizenship cases from the Choctaw Council. Unrecorded, and no other copy known.

WAYLAND MISSIONARY BAPTIST ASSOCIATION

Minutes of the Third Annual Session of the Wayland Missionary Baptist Association, held with the Centre Union Baptist Church, at Colbert, Ind. Ter., on Friday and Saturday, September 11th and 12th, 1885. Muskogee: Indian Journal Steam Print, 1886.

7, [1] p. 22 cm. Printed wrappers.

Not in Foreman.

1887

Articles of Faith. Choctaw and Chickasaw Baptist Association, Indian Territory. Tanisin Teksis: Murray, Holisso ai ikbe. [Denison, Texas: Murray, Printer, 1887.]*

8 p. 14 cm.

Chahta Okla i Nanulhpisa, Nanapesa afafmmi 1886 chiiya ka. Ahlopulli tok. Chahta anumpa atoshoa. Sedalia, Mo.: Democrat Publishing Co., 1887.*

49, iii p. 21.5 cm. Printed wrappers.

The acts of the regular session of 1886, translated into Choctaw. One of only four known copies.

Constitution, Treaties and Laws of the Choctaw Nation. Made and Enacted by the Choctaw Legislature. Sedalia, Mo.: Democrat Steam Press, 1887.

200, [iv] p. 22.6 cm.

JONES, JOHN G.

A Complete History of Methodism as connected with the Mississippi Conference of the Methodist Episcopal Church, South, written at the Unanimous Request of the

Conference. Volume 1. From 1799 to 1817. Nashville, Tenn. Printed for the author. 1887.*

461 p. 18.5 cm.

Vol. 2 was never published.

"An invaluable contribution."—Owen. The volume, which is now rare, contains important information not elsewhere available on the Choctaw and Chickasaw Indians before their removal to the West.

1888

The Memorial of the Choctaw Nation praying the Payment by the United States of the Judgment, and Interest thereon, rendered in its Favor, under a Mandate of the Supreme Court, by the Court of Claims on the 15th day of December, 1886. [N.p., 1888.]

4 p. 23 cm. Caption title.

Ward H. Lamon et al., Plaintiffs, vs. Henry E. McKee, et al., Defendants. [Washington, 1888–1894.]*

Briefs, records, etc.

4 vols., aggregating 665 pages.

The full record of this unsavory litigation over the large fees paid to attorneys representing the Choctaw Nation in Washington. Several reputations emerge a little less than untarnished.

1889

Choctaw and Chickasaw Baptist Association

Minutes of the Nineteenth Annual Meeting of the Choctaw and Chickasaw Baptist Association, held with Kulli Tooklo Baptist Church, Pontotoc County, Chickasaw Nation, I.T., commencing August 23, 1889. Atoka: Indian Citizen Print, 1889.

18, [1] p. 23 cm. Printed wrappers.

LeFlore, Campbell, and Edmund McCurtain

Disbursement of Delegate's 20 Per Cent of Net Proceeds Claim, by C. Leflore and E. McCurtain. [Atoka? 1889.]

8 p. 22 cm. Wrapper title.

Unrecorded.

1890

Choctaw and Chickasaw Baptist Association

Minutes of the Twentieth Annual Meeting of the Choctaw and Chickasaw Baptist Association, held with Choat's Prairie Baptist Church, Coal County, Choctaw Nation, I.T., commencing August 22, 1890. Atoka, I.T.: Indian Citizen Print, 1890.

19, [1] p. 22.5 cm. Printed wrappers.

The Choctaw and Chickasaw Nations vs. The United States and the Wichita and Affiliated Bands of Indians. [Washington, 1890–1900.]

Briefs, records, etc.

29 volumes, aggregating almost 3000 pages; with scores of maps and charts.

The finest and most complete set in existence of this rare and inexhaustible source of historical information about southwestern Oklahoma and its Indian inhabitants from the earliest times. Together with the two-volume record and other documents in the Greer County case (q.v.), this collection forms one of the cornerstones of Oklahoma history, since the portion of the state with which it deals in such abundant and authoritative detail was apparently the earliest to be settled by Indians within historic times.

Laws of the Choctaw Nation made and enacted by the General Council, from 1886 to 1890 inclusive. Atoka: Indian Citizen Print, 1890.
53, 62 p. 22.5 cm.

Laws of the Choctaw Nation passed at the Regular Session of the General Council convened at Tushka Humma, October 7th, 1889, and adjourned November 15, 1889. Atoka, Ind. Ter.: Indian Citizen Publishing Co., 1890.
60, [1] p. 22.5 cm. Printed wrappers.

Laws of the Choctaw Nation passed at the Regular Session of the General Council convened at Tushka Humma, October 6, 1890, adjourned November 14, 1890. [Paris, Texas: Marshall's Printing House, 1890.]
43 p. 22.5 cm.
One of only three known copies. None is in Oklahoma.

Letter from the Secretary of the Interior, transmitting a Report of the Commissioner of Indian Affairs respecting Intruders into the Choctaw and Chickasaw Nations. [Washington, 1890.]
119 p. 23 cm. Caption title.
Considerable information on intruding gamblers, whiskey runners, cattle thieves, and boomers.

Rules for the Government of the Circuit Courts of the Choctaw Nation. [Atoka? 1890.]
9 p. 18 cm. Wrapper title.
The only known copy. Portions of the last two leaves are lacking.

WAYLAND BAPTIST ASSOCIATION

Minutes of the Wayland Baptist Association, held with the Center Union Baptist Church, at Colbert Station, Chickasaw Nation, on Thursday, Friday and Saturday before the Second Lord's Day in September, 1889. Atoka: Indian Citizen Print, 1890.
13 p. 22 cm. Printed wrappers.
Not in Foreman.

1891

In the Matter of the Claim of John A. Rollings, and James Gilfillan, against the Choctaw Nation. [N.p., 1891.]*
20 p. 22 cm. Caption title.

Laws of the Choctaw Nation made and enacted by the General Council, from 1886 to 1890 inclusive. Atoka: Indian Citizen Print, 1891.
53, 62 p. 22.5 cm.
A later printing of the 1890 compilation.

1892

Laws of the Choctaw Nation passed at the Special Session of the General Council convened at Tushka Humma April 6, 1891, and adjourned April 11, 1891. [Paris, Texas: Marshall's Printing House, 1891.]

19 p. 22 cm. Wrapper title.

One of seven known copies.

Choctaw and Chickasaw Baptist Association

Minutes of the Twenty-second Annual Meeting of the Choctaw and Chickasaw Baptist Association. Held with Rock Creek Baptist Church, Choctaw Nation, I.T. commencing September 2, 1892. Oklahoma City, O.T.: Baptist Publishing Company Print, 1892.

20 p. 21.5 cm. Printed wrappers.

Laws of the Choctaw Nation passed at the Regular Session of the General Council convened at Tushka Humma, 1891. [Paris, Texas: Marshall's Printing House, 1892.]

47 p. 22.5 cm. Printed wrapper.

One of only four known copies.

Watkins, Ben

Complete Choctaw Definer. English with Choctaw Definition. By Ben Watkins. First edition. Van Buren, Ark.: J. W. Baldwin, 1892.

84, [9] p. 20 cm.

A fine copy of a very scarce volume.

1893

Bethel Baptist Association

Minutes of the First Annual Session of the Bethel Baptist Association of the Indian Territory, held at Durant, October 7, 1893. South McAlester: Baptist Watchman Print, 1893.

10 p. 19.5 cm. Printed wrappers.

Not in Foreman.

Jones, Wilson N.

Proclamation. [Tuskahoma? 1893.]

Broadside. 20.5 cm.

A call for an extra session of the Choctaw Council in order "to perfect legislation in reference to authorizing deed to a portion of the Leased District, recently occupied by the Cheyennes and Arapahoes." Unrecorded, and the only known copy.

Laws of the Choctaw Nation passed at the Regular Session of the General Council convened at Tushka Humma October 3rd, 1892 (for 1892), and adjourned November 4th, 1892. Atoka, Ind. Ter.: Indian Citizen Publishing Co., 1893.*

24, ii p. 21 cm. Printed wrappers.

One of only five known copies.

Old King Brady and the James Boys among the Choctaws; or, The Raid into

the Indian Nation in '81. By a New York Detective. New York: Detective Library, 1893.
30, [2] p. 32.5 cm.

1894

Baptist General Association

Minutes of the Nineteenth Annual Session of the Baptist General Association (Organized 1876) of Western Ark. and Ind. Territory; held with Duncan Prairie Church, Chickasaw Nat'n. September 8, 1894. Hackett, Ark.: Nickle Job Print, [1894].
14 p. 21 cm. Printed wrappers.

Bethel Baptist Association

Minutes of the Second Annual Session of the Bethel Baptist Association, held with Prairie Grove Church, beginning October 12, 1894. Waco, Texas: Baptist Standard Printing House, 1894.
8 p. 22 cm. Wrapper title.

Chahta Oklah i Nanvlhpisa Noshkobo micha Nanvlhpisa. Mikmut afammih 1837, 1855, 1865, 1866 kash Nanitimapisa tok (Treaties) aiena ho Chahta Oklah i Nanupusa chito ut upisa toko anotaka hosh A. R. Durant, ut ulhtuka yosh holisso achafa ilapa foki hoke. Davis Homer micha Ben Watkins, apiluchi. John F. Worley, holisso tulli isht ichuli micha holisso ikbi Tullis Teksis. 1894. [Dallas, Texas, 1894.]
428 p. 22 cm.
The following volume translated into Choctaw.

Constitution and Laws of the Choctaw Nation. Together with the Treaties of 1837, 1865 and 1866. Published by Authority of the General Council by A. R. Durant, commissioned for the purpose, and Davis A. Homer and Ben Watkins, assistant compilers. Dallas, Texas: John F. Worley, 1894.
352 p. 22 cm.

Statement of the Choctaw Freedmen, setting forth their Wrongs, Grievances, Claims and Wants. August, 1894. Fort Smith: J. H. Mayers & Co., [1894].
25 p. 23.5 cm. Wrapper title.
A publication of the Choctaw Colored Citizens' Association.

1895

Bethel Baptist Association

Minutes of the Third Annual Session of the Bethel Baptist Association, held with Philadelphia Church, Blue Co., Choctaw Nation, I.T., Friday before second Sunday in October, 1895. [N.p., 1895.]
8 p. 22 cm. Wrapper title. Folded table.
Not in Foreman.

Cantwell, Harry J.

Brief and Argument of Harry J. Cantwell (of Crews & Cantwell, Attorneys-at-law, St. Louis, Mo.) to the Committee on Indian Affairs of the House of Representatives and to the Committee on Indian Affairs of the Senate on the Rights of all

Persons (except the Former Slaves) to Transfer from the Roll of Limited Rights, called the "Freedmen Roll" of Choctaw-Chickasaw Tribes to the Rolls of Citizenship. [St. Louis, 1895?].*

91 p. 23.5 cm. Wrapper title.

A valuable review of the Choctaw and Chickasaw Negro problem.

The Choctaw Laws. Passed at the Special Sessions in January, 1894, and April, 1894, and the Regular Session, October, 1894. Antlers, I.T.: National Advocate Print, [1895].*

[1], 44 p. 22 cm. Printed wrappers.

One of only five known copies.

1896

Agreement between Five Civilized Tribes Commission and Choctaws. [N.p., 1896.]

8 p. 23 cm. Caption title.

Baptist General Association

Proceedings of Twentieth Annual Session of Baptist General Association of Western Arkansas and Indian Territory, held with South Canadian Baptist Church, at South Canadian, Choctaw Nation, Indian Territory, September 7th, 8th, 9th & 10th, 1895. Dallas, Ark.: Courier Print, 1896.

8 p. 23 cm.

Bethel Baptist Association

Minutes of the Fourth Annual Session of the Bethel Baptist Association, held with Yarnaby Church, Blue County, Choctaw Nation, I.T. Friday before Second Sunday in Oct. 1896. Atoka: Indian Citizen Pub. Co., 1896.

12 p. 13.5 cm. Wrapper title.

Not in Foreman.

Resolutions adopted by the Citizens of Grant, Kiamitia County, Choctaw Nation, I.T. [Grant? 1896.]

Broadside. Folio.

The resolutions touch upon the confusion resulting from the mixed jurisdiction of federal and local courts, and urge the speedy passage of the Dawes Bill. Unrecorded, and the only known copy.

1897

Acts and Resolutions of the General Council of the Choctaw Nation, passed at its Regular Session, October, 1897; and also All the School Laws of the Choctaw Nation. Fort Smith: Elevator Job Office, December, 1897.

66 p. 21.5 cm. Printed wrappers.

Acts of Council of the Choctaw Nation, passed at the Regular Sessions of October 1895 and 1896, and the Special Session of September, 1896. Talihina, I.T.: Choctaw News, [1897].

108, [2] p. 20.5 cm. Printed wrappers.

Agreement between the United States Commissioners to negotiate with the Five

Civilized Tribes, and the Commissioners on the part of the Choctaw and Chickasaw Indians. [Atoka? 1897.]

17 p. 23 cm. Wrapper title.

Agreement between the United States Commissioners to negotiate with the Five Civilized Tribes and the Commissioners on the part of the Choctaw and Chickasaw Indians. [Washington, 1897.]

11 p. 23 cm.

BAPTIST GENERAL ASSOCIATION

Minutes of the Twenty-Second Annual Session of the Baptist General Association (organized 1876) of Western Arkansas and Indian Territory, held with Salt Creek Church, Choctaw Nation, I.T., September 11 to 15, 1897. [Ardmore: Baptist Signal, 1897.]

24, 3 p. 20 cm. Wrapper title.

Not in Foreman.

FOSTER, T. N.

In the Choctaw and Chickasaw Citizenship Court at South McAlester. Glenn-Tucker et al. vs. The Choctaw and Chickasaw Nations. Plaintiff's Abstract, Brief and Argument. [South McAlester, 1897.]*

41 p. 22 cm. Wrapper title.

In interesting detail. Not recorded in Foreman.

WINTON, C. F.

Memorial and Petition on behalf of the Mississippi Choctaws. Nixon-Jones Printing Co., St. Louis, [1897].

22 p. 24.5 cm. Wrapper title.

1898

BETHEL BAPTIST ASSOCIATION

Minutes of the Fifth Annual Session of the Bethel Baptist Association, held with High Hill Church, Atoka County, Choctaw Nation, I.T. Friday before second Sunday in Aug., 1897. Atoka: Indian Citizen Pub. Co., 1898.*

17, [3] p. 23.5 cm. Wrapper title.

Not in Foreman.

LOGAN, W. A.

Emma Nabors et al., appellants, vs. The Choctaw Nation, appellee. Appeal from the United States Court in the Indian Territory, Central District. Brief on behalf of Appellants. By Walter A. Logan, William Hutchings. Muskogee: Phoenix Printing Co., [1898].*

26 p. 25.5 cm. Wrapper title.

STANDLEY, J. S.

Chahta micha Chikasha Okla ma. [Atoka, 1898.]

Broadside. 22 cm.

A translation into Choctaw of the following address. Unrecorded, and the only known copy.

STANDLEY, J. S.

A Letter to Choctaws and Chickasaws who Prefer the Curtis Bill. [Atoka, 1898.]
Broadside. 22.5 cm.
Unrecorded, and the only copy known.

1899

Acts and Resolutions of the General Council of the Choctaw Nation. Passed at its Regular Session, 1898, and its Special Session, 1899. Caddo, Ind. Ter.: Herald Press, 1899.
69 p. 20.5 cm. Printed wrappers.

CUSHMAN, H. B.

History of the Choctaw, Chickasaw and Natchez Indians. Greenville, Texas: Headlight Printing House, 1899.
607 p. 22 cm. Frontisp. port.
A mint copy, bright and sound, of an indispensable source volume which is usually found, because of its brittle paper, in very bad condition.

Instructions to Town-site Commissioners. Choctaw and Chickasaw Nations. Washington, 1899.
10 p. 23 cm. Printed wrappers.

1900

Acts and Resolutions of the General Council of the Choctaw Nation. Passed at its Regular Session 1899. South McAlester: News Press, 1900.
71, [2] p. 21.5 cm. Wrapper title.
One of only five known copies.

The Atoka Convention of Choctaw and Chickasaw Indians. [Atoka, 1900.]
17 p. 22.5 cm.
Very rare.

Platform of the Tuskahoma Party. [Tuskahoma? 1900.]
Broadside. 21 cm.
Unrecorded, and the only known copy.

THOMPSON, J. P.

Baptist Church. Mecha i nan uhl toka aiena nana ihst imai utta. Chahta anumpa toshowa hoke. J. P. Thompson, Holisso Tosholi. Atoka: Indian Citizen Printing Co., [1900?].
16 p. 15.5 cm. Printed wrappers.

1901

Acts and Resolutions of the General Council of the Choctaw Nation passed at its Regular Session, 1900, and Extra Session, 1901. Caddo: Herald Press, 1901.
57 p. 21.5 cm. Wrapper title.
One of only three known copies.

History of the First Baptist Church of Durant, I.T. Durant, Indian Territory: Times-Eagle Book Print, 1901.

12 p. 19.5 cm. Wrapper title.
Not in Foreman.

1902

Acts and Resolutions of the General Council of the Choctaw Nation passed at its Regular Session, 1901. Caddo: Herald Press, 1902.*
42, [2] p. 21 cm. Wrapper title.
One of only four known copies.

ADAMS, SPENCER B.

Choctaw and Chickasaw Nations or Tribes vs. J. T. Riddle, et als. Opinion of Court by Spencer B. Adams, Chief Judge, Walter L. Weaver, Henry S. Foote, Associate Judges concurring, together with the Rules of the Court. Greensboro, N.C.: Jos. J. Stone & Co., [1902].*
44, 9 p. 23 cm. Wrapper title.

The Choctaw-Chickasaw Treaty. Passed the House and Senate and approved July 1, 1902. [Muskogee, 1902.]
24 p. 22.5 cm. Caption title.

DICKERSON, PHILIP

Brief History and Directory of the Churches and Business and Professional Men of Wilburton (Choctaw Nation), "The Scranton" (Coal Mining Centre), Indian Territory. September, 1902. [Wilburton, 1902.]
20 p. 18.5 cm. Wrapper title.
Not in Foreman.

Nan Ittim Apesa Himona. [Muskogee? 1902.]
22 p. 22.5 cm. Caption title. Text in Choctaw.
The Choctaw-Chickasaw treaty of July 1, 1902, translated into the Choctaw language. Unrecorded, and no other copy known.

WOODS, J. H.

In the Supreme Court of the Territory of Oklahoma. January Term, 1902. The Choctaw Lumber Company vs. I. L. Gilmore. Brief of J. H. Woods, Attorney for the Defendant in Error. [Caddo:] Herald Print, [1902].*
7 p. 25 cm. Wrapper title.
Not recorded in Foreman.

1903

Acts and Resolutions of the General Council of the Choctaw Nation, passed at its Regular Session, 1902, and Extra Session, 1902. Hugo: Husonian Press, 1903.
85 p. 21.5 cm. Wrapper title.

[Memorial of the Choctaw Council against a territorial form of government or annexation to Oklahoma Territory. Atoka? 1903.]
[3] p. 22 cm.
No other copy can be traced.

Ordinances of the Town of Wilburton, Ind. Ter. Incorporated June 24, 1902. Wilburton: The News Print, 1903.
38 p. 20.5 cm. Wrapper title.
The only known copy.

Rules of Practice in Choctaw, Chickasaw and Cherokee Allotment Contest Cases before the Commission to the Five Civilized Tribes, the Commissioner of Indian Affairs, and the Secretary of the Interior. [Muskogee, 1905.]
8 p. 23.5 cm. Wrapper title.

1904

Acts and Resolutions of the General Council of the Choctaw Nation, passed at its Regular Session, 1903. Hugo: Husonian Job Print, [1904].
63 p. 21 cm. Wrapper title. Errata slip.

Rules and Regulations Governing the Sale of Unleased Coal and Asphalt Lands in the Choctaw and Chickasaw Nations. [Washington, 1904.]
6 p. 23 cm. Caption title.

TAFF, JOSEPH A.
Maps of Segregated Coal Lands in the Lehigh-Ardmore Districts, Choctaw and Chickasaw Nations, Indian Territory, with Descriptions of the Unleased Segregated Coal Lands. Washington, 1904.*
39 p. 23 cm. Printed wrappers. Folded maps.

TAFF, JOSEPH A.
Maps of Segregated Coal Lands in the McAlester District, Choctaw Nation, Indian Territory, with Descriptions of the Unleased Segregated Coal Lands. Washington, 1904.*
59 p. 23 cm. Printed wrappers. Maps.

TAFF, JOSEPH A.
Maps of Segregated Coal Lands in the McCurtain-Massey District, Choctaw Nation, Indian Territory, with Description of the Unleased Coal Lands, by Joseph A. Taff. Washington, 1904.*
54 p. 23 cm. Printed wrappers. 2 folded maps.

TAFF, JOSEPH A.
Maps of Segregated Coal Lands in the Wilburton-Stigler District, Choctaw Nation, Indian Territory, with Descriptions of the Unleased Segregated Coal Lands. Washington, 1904.
47 p. 23 cm. Printed wrappers. Maps.

WRIGHT, ALLEN
Chahta Leksikon. A Choctaw in English Definition. For the Choctaw Academies and Schools. By Allen Wright, D.D. Second edition. Revised by T. L. Mellen. Nashville, Tenn., 1904.
312 p. 18 cm. Printed wrappers.

1905

Acts and Resolutions of the General Council of the Choctaw Nation. Passed at its Regular Session 1904. Hugo: Hugo Husonian, [1905].

48 p. 21.5 cm. Wrapper title.

Choctaw Enrollment Case of Mary Elizabeth Martin. [Muskogee? 1905.]*

17 p. 22.5 cm. Caption title.

1906

Acts and Resolutions of the General Council of the Choctaw Nation. Passed at its Extraordinary and Regular Sessions, 1905. [Hugo? 1906.]

15. 56 p, [1]p. 20.5 cm. Wrapper title.

One, and the best, of only two known complete copies.

Bixby, Tams

Notice! Enrollment of Minor Children of Citizens of the Choctaw and Chickasaw Nations. [Muskogee, 1906.]

Broadside. Folio.

Not in Foreman, and the only copy traced.

The Estate of Charles F. Winton, deceased, and others, vs. Jack Amos and others, known as the "Mississippi Choctaws." [Washington, 1906.]*

28 p. 24 cm. Caption title.

Petition to the Court of Claims for adjudication of claims for services rendered the Mississippi Choctaws.

1908

McCurtain, Green

Annual Message of Governor Green McCurtain to the Choctaw Council. Assembled at Tuskahoma, Okla., Tuesday, Oct. 6, 1908. [Tuskahoma? 1908.]

19, [1] p. 23 cm. Wrapper title.

Proceedings of Choctaw and Chickasaw Citizenship Court in connection with Compensation of Attorneys. A Letter from the Attorney-General. [Washington, 1908.]

64 p. 23 cm. Caption title.

1910

Choctaw and Chickasaw Agreements. [Washington, 1910.]

66 p. 23 cm. Caption title.

An inquiry into Choctaw and Chickasaw coal leases.

Hamilton, Peter J.

Colonial Mobile. An Historical Study, largely from Original Sources, of the Alabama-Tombigbee Basin and the Old South West from the Discovery of the Spiritu Santo in 1519 until the Demolition of Fort Charlotte in 1821. Revised and enlarged edition. Boston: Houghton Mifflin Co., 1910.

xxix, 594 p. 22.5 cm.

A fine copy of the second (and far preferable) edition of this great source of information about the early history of the Choctaws, Chickasaws, and Creeks.

1911

Ordinances and Franchises of the Town of Madill, State of Oklahoma. Revised and compiled by authority of Board of Trustees. 1911. Madill: The Madill Times, [1911].

90 p. 23 cm. Printed wrappers.

1913

Elder, Mrs. S. B.

Life of the Abbe Adrien Roquette "Chahta-ima." Compiled and edited by Mrs. S. B. Elder from Material furnished by Friends. New Orleans: L. Graham Co., 1913.

187 p. 19.5 cm. Plates.

A very scarce volume. Father Roquette labored among the Mississippi Choctaws.

Memorial of the Choctaw and Chickasaw Nations relative to the Rights of the Mississippi Choctaws. Washington, 1913.

44 p. 23.5 cm.

1915

Code. City Ordinances of City of Lehigh, Oklahoma, effective April 1915. Lehigh: News Print, [1915].

[2], 111 p. 23 cm. Printed wrappers.

Contains the Lehigh charter of 1899 and pre-statehood ordinances of the town council.

1916

Ketcham, William H.

Kiahlik iksa nana-aiyimmika i katikisma Chahta anumpa isht a toshowa hoke. Washington, [1916].

200 p. 14.5 cm.

A catechism of the Catholic religion translated into the Choctaw language.

1917

The Estate of Charles F. Winton, deceased, and others, v. Jack Amos and others, known as the "Mississippi Choctaws." Opinion of the Court. [Washington, 1917.]*

31 p. 23.5 cm. Caption title.

Final disposition by the Court of Claims of a suit over services rendered the Mississippi Choctaws.

Hichushi-ililli [tuberculosis] ut hatak-upi-humma okla aiitintakla ya aiasha. Washington, 1917.

18 p. 23 cm.

A popular manual on the prevention and treatment of tuberculosis, translated into Choctaw.

1918

Swanton, John R.

An Early Account of the Choctaw Indians. [Lancaster, Pa., 1918.]*

Pp. 53–72. 25.5 cm. Wrapper title.

A "separate" of this valuable paper.

1921

Memorial Exercises at the Grave of Pushmataha, Congressional Cemetery, Washington, D.C. Decoration Day, May 29, 1921. Washington, 1921.

32 p. 24.5 cm.

1923

The Heirs of Samuel Garland, deceased, vs. The Choctaw Nation. [Washington and Kansas City, 1923–1926.]

Briefs, records, etc.

6 vols., aggregating about 335 pages.

A contest in the Court of Claims and in the Supreme Court over the accounting of funds paid to the heirs of the Choctaw Delegation of 1853. The documents yield a great deal of interest and value for the history of the tribe.

Sophia C. Pitchlynn and others, Heirs of Peter P. Pitchlynn, vs. The Choctaw Nation. [Washington, 1923–24.]

Briefs, records, etc.

7 vols., aggregating 275 pages.

The suit was brought in the Court of Claims to recover unpaid balances due Pitchlynn's estate for his long services to the Choctaw Nation. The documents presented throw considerable light on the financial history of the tribe.

1927

Harrison, William H.

An Address to the Choctaw People. By William H. Harrison, Principal Chief, Choctaw Nation, Poteau, Oklahoma, October 3, 1927. [Poteau, 1927.]*

8 p. 21.5 cm.

1928

Dillard, Anthony Winston

Dancing Rabbit Creek Treaty. Birmingham, 1928.*

31 p. 23 cm. Printed wrappers.

Contains a contemporary account, written by George S. Gaines and here first printed from the original manuscript, of the removal of the Choctaws from Alabama and Mississippi following the treaty of Dancing Rabbit Creek.

Harrison, William H.

An Address to the Choctaw People. William H. Harrison, Principal Chief, Choctaw Nation, Poteau, Oklahoma, October 1, 1928. [Poteau, 1928.]

11 p. 22 cm.

1931

Murray, William H.

Pocahontas and Pushmataha. Historical and Biographical Essays with Personal Sketches of other Famous Indians, and Notes on Oklahoma History. 2nd edition. Oklahoma City: Harlow Publishing Co., 1931.

106 p. 19 cm.

1940

Choctaw Indians of Mississippi. Hearing before the Subcommittee of the Committee on Indian Affairs, United States Senate. Washington, 1940.

18 p. 23 cm.

Natchez Trace Parkway. Letter of the Secretary of the Interior transmitting a Report of a Survey of the old Indian train, known as the Natchez Trace, with a view to Constructing a National Road on the Route to be known as the Natchez Trace Parkway. Washington, 1941.*

vi, 167 p. 23 cm. Printed wrappers. Photographs and maps.

An invaluable document, with considerable new information on the Choctaws and Chickasaws.

Undated

A Trip to the Farm. By the Editor of the Indian Citizen. [Atoka, n.d.]*

8 p. on 1 folded leaf. 16 cm.

A description of the Indian orphan farm nine miles north of Coalgate. The editor was accompanied on the trip by the Baptist missionary, J. S. Murrow.

Chuch im iksa ittibaiachuffa i naksish hiohli putta im anumpa noshkobo. [N.p., n.d.]*

4 p. 12.5 cm. Text in Choctaw.

CIVIL WAR (INDIAN TERRITORY)

1862

BLUNT, JAMES G.

General Order. Headquarters 1st Division, Army of the Frontier. Camp Bowen, 11th November, 1862. General Orders No. 14. [Camp Bowen, Arkansas: Army Press, 1862.]

4 p. 20 cm.

Unrecorded, and the only known copy of the only known Camp Bowen imprint. The order was issued on General Blunt's Indian Territory campaign.

BLUNT, JAMES G.

General Order. Headquarters 1st Division, Army of the Frontier. Camp Fort Wayne, C.N., Oct. 31, 1862. General Order No. 12. [Camp Fort Wayne, Cherokee Nation: Army Press, 1862.]

6 p. 20 cm.

Unrecorded, and the only known copy of the only known Fort Wayne imprint.

1863

BISHOP, A. W.

Loyalty on the Frontier, or Sketches of Union Men of the Southwest; with Incidents and Adventures in the Rebellion on the Border. By A. W. Bishop, Lieut. Col. First Arkansas Cavalry Volunteers. St. Louis: Studley & Co., 1863.

228 p. 19 cm.

Blunt, James G.

Headquarters, District of Kansas, Fort Leavenworth, March 3, 1863. Circular. [Fort Leavenworth: Military Press, 1863.]

Broadside. 13 cm.

Order for the Indian Regiments to proceed, via Fort Scott, to the Cherokee Country. Unrecorded, and the only known copy.

Blunt, James G.

Head Quarters District of the Frontier, Assistant Adjutant General's Office, Fort Scott, Kansas, August 22d, 1863. General Orders No. 11. [Fort Scott: Army Press, 1863.]*

Broadside. 19 cm.

An order establishing a military express between Fort Scott and Fort Blunt (Fort Gibson), Cherokee Nation. Unrecorded, and the only known copy.

District of the Frontier. General Orders June 13, 1863–Feb. 16, 1866. [Various places, as below.]

114 pieces.

The first order was issued at Fort Leavenworth, the next fourteen at Fort Scott, and the remainder at Fort Smith. This superb collection presents an unrivaled record of a phase of the Civil War profoundly affecting Indian Territory. No other file is known.

Head Quarters S. W. District, Mo. Springfield, January 1st, 1863. General Order No. 5. Fellow Soldiers. [Springfield, Mo., 1863.]

Broadside. 19 cm.

Congratulations by General Brown to his troops on successful campaigns which included the Battle of Prairie Grove and other frontier engagements.

Phillips, William A.

Head Quarters, 1st Brigade, Army of the Frontier, Fort Gibson, Cherokee Nation, Dec. 23d, 1863. General Orders No. 4. [Fort Gibson, 1863.]

Broadside. 18 cm. Mourning border.

Announcement of the death of Captain Oliver P. Willett from wounds received in the December 19 engagement with the forces of Stand Watie and William C. Quantrell. Unrecorded, and the only known copy.

1864

Phillips, William A.

Head Quarters, Indian Brigade, Fort Gibson, C.N., July 18th, 1864. General Orders No. 12. [Fort Gibson, 1864.]

Broadside. 10.5 cm.

Regulations governing the purchase from Indians of cattle of disputed ownership. Unrecorded, and the only known copy.

1865

Phillips, William A.

Circular. Headquarters 3d Brigade, 3d Division, 7th A. C., Fort Gibson, C.N., April 30, 1865. Circular. [Fort Gibson, 1865.]

Broadside. 16.5 cm.
Post hospital regulations. Unrecorded, and the only known copy.

PHILLIPS, WILLIAM A.

Head Quarters Indian Brigade, Fort Gibson, C.N., January 14, 1865. General Orders No. 4. Current Series. [Fort Gibson, 1865.]

[3] p. 20.5 cm. Caption title.
Measures ordered by Colonel William A. Phillips for protecting the Indian country from cattle thieves, whiskey runners, and jayhawkers. Unrecorded, and the only known copy.

1882

BRITTON, WILEY

Memoirs of the Rebellion on the Border, 1863, by Wiley Britton, late Sixth Kansas Cavalry. Chicago: Cushing, Thomas & Co., 1882.

458 p. 19 cm.
A large portion of the volume deals with the war in Indian Territory.

1907

MONKS, WILLIAM

A history of southern Missouri and northern Arkansas. Being an account of the early settlements, the Civil War, the Ku-Klux, and times of peace. By William Monks, West Plains, Mo. West Plains Journal Co. West Plains, Mo., 1907.*

247 p. 19 cm. Photographs.

1922

BRITTON, WILEY

The Union Indian Brigade in the Civil War. 1922. Kansas City: Franklin Hudson Publishing Co.

474 p. 19.5 cm.

COLORADO INDIANS

1861

General Laws, Joint Resolutions, Memorials, and Private Acts, passed at the First Session of the Legislative Assembly of the Territory of Colorado, begun and held at Denver, Colorado, Ter., Sept. 9th, 1861. Together with the Declaration of Independence, the Constitution of the United States, and the Organic Act of the Territory. Published by Authority. Denver: Thos. Gibson, Colorado Republican and Herald Office, 1861.

7, 578, [2] p. 22.5 cm.
Important provisions regarding the Indians. These are the earliest Colorado territorial laws.

1870

General Laws, Joint Resolutions, Memorials, and Private Acts passed at the Eighth Session of the General Assembly of the Territory of Colorado. Central City: David C. Collier, 1870.

180, [2] p. 23 cm. Printed wrappers.
Memorials and resolutions relating to Indian hostilities.

COMANCHE INDIANS

1830

HOFLAND, BARBARD (WREAKS) HOOLE

The Stolen Boy. A Story. Founded on Facts. By Mrs. Hofland. New-York: W. B. Gilley. 1830.

154 p. Eng. frontisp. and title. 14 cm.

The story of the captivity of Manuel Perez by the Comanche Indians in Texas.

1858

Head Quarters, Department of Texas, San Antonio, October 19, 1858. General Orders No. 25. [San Antonio, 1858.]*

3 p. 14 cm.

A report by General Twiggs of the famous massacre by troops under Major Earl Van Doren of the Comanche Indians at their camp near Wichita Village on October 1, 1858.

1863

General Orders No. 20. Head-Quarters, Department of New Mexico, Santa Fe, N.M., August 11, 1863. [Santa Fe, 1863.]

3 p. 18 cm. Caption title.

Measures for preventing "predatory incursions of the Comanche and Kiowa Indians."

1874

EASTMAN, EDWIN

Seven and Nine Years among the Comanches and Apaches. An Autobiography. Jersey City: Clark Johnson, 1874.*

308, [1] p. Frontisp. port. and 7 other plates.

Newberry-Ayer 90.

The first edition.

Headquarters Mil. Div. of the Missouri, Chicago, Illinois, July 10, 1874. General Orders No. 4. [Chicago, 1874.]

Broadside. 20 cm.

Hostilities with the Comanche, Kiowa, and Cheyenne Indians.

1886

DESHIELDS, JAMES T.

Cynthia Ann Parker. The Story of Her Capture at the Massacre of the Indians of Parker's Fort; of her Quarter of a Century Spent among the Comanches as the Wife of the War Chief, Peta Nocona; and of her Recapture at the Battle of Pease River by Captain L. S. Ross, of the Texan Rangers. "Truth is stranger than Fiction." St. Louis: Printed for the Author, 1886.

80 p. 18.5 cm. Plates.

1888

Lost and Found; or Three Months with the Wild Indians. A Brief Sketch of the Life of Ole T. Nystel, embracing his Experience while in Captivity to the Comanches, and Subsequent Liberation from them. Reflections and Religious Experience. Dallas, Texas: Wilmans Bros., 1888.

26 p. 20.5 cm. Printed wrappers.

A superb copy.

1902

John Moody vs. Louis Bentz. Comanche Indian Allotment. Argument of Counsel on behalf of contestee. Washington: McGill & Wallace, [1902].

31 p. 23.5 cm. Wrapper title.

1929

THOMAS, ALFRED B.

San Carlos, a Comanche Pueblo on the Arkansas River, 1787. A Study in Comanche History and Spanish Indian Policy. Denver, 1929.

13 p. 23 cm. Wrapper title.

Undated

Amalunga, die Tochter der Wildnis. Eine Erzahlung von B. Frey. Dritte Auflage. Mulheim a. d. Ruhr, verlag von Julius Bagel.

63 p. 16 cm. Pictorial wrappers.

Fights with the Comanches on the southwestern prairies in 1845.

CONFEDERATE STATES (INDIAN TERRITORY)

1862

DAVIS, JEFFERSON

Message of the President (transmitting to Congress the Report of the Acting Commissioner of Indian Affairs). [Richmond, Va., 1862.]

41 p. 21 cm.

Of superlative interest and importance. Excessively rare.

DAVIS, JEFFERSON

President's Message and Accompanying Documents. [Richmond, 1862.]

74, [3] p. 23 cm. Caption title.

Notice of Confederate Indian relations. Very rare.

Minutes of the Twenty-Fifth Annual Session of the Rehoboth Baptist Association, held with the Church at Forsyth, Monroe County, Georgia, on the 20th and 22nd of September, 1862. Forsyth, Georgia: Educational Journal Office, 1862.*

16 p. 22 cm. Printed wrappers.

Contains a short but important account of the difficulties encountered by the Baptist missionary, J. S. Murrow, in wartime Indian Territory. Rare.

SCOTT, S. S.

Address. Confederate States of America, War Department, Bureau of Indian Affairs, Richmond, December 26, 1862. To the Choctaws, Chickasaws, Cherokees, Creeks, Seminoles, and all other Indian Nations and Tribes Friendly to the Confederate States. [Richmond, 1862.]

3 p. 20.5 cm. Caption title.

The only known copy. Scott, who was Confederate states commissioner of Indian Affairs, wrote this important address shortly after his return from a tour of Indian Territory.

This Ticket for One Dollar, having been used in the Service of the Confederate States, will be redeemed by me with Confederate Notes at Fort McCulloch, C.N., when presented with others, making five, ten or twenty dollars. (Wm. Quesenberry) Maj. & Q. M., Dept. Ind. Ter. [Fort McCulloch: Confederate Military Press, 1862.]

Broadside, on marbled paper. 6 cm.

The only known copy of the only known issue of Confederate currency in Indian Territory. William Quesenberry, whose signature appears on the note, was the Arkansas artist and humorist who is perhaps better known as Bill Cush. Major Quesenberry was compelled to print and use these notes in official purchases because of the complete lack in Indian Territory in late 1862 of Confederate gold and currency.

1863

Cline, A. H.

Head Qrs., Dept. Ind. Ter., Camp Sabine, Oct. 15, 1863. [Camp Sabine: Confederate Military Press, 1863.]

Broadside. 23 cm.

Provision for subsisting the refugee Confederate Indians and for protecting them and the Confederate government against fraud. Unrecorded, and the only known copy. No other Camp Sabine imprint is known.

Moore, Mrs. M. B.

Geographical Reader for Dixie Children. Raleigh: Branson, Farrar & Co., 1863.

48 p. 19.5 cm. Colored maps.

Contains references to the southern Indians and their alliance with the Confederate States. Very rare.

Pitchlynn, Peter P.

Eagletown, Choctaw Nation, October 21, 1863. Col. Eakin, Editor Telegraph, Dear Sir: Inasmuch as reports are in circulation prejudicial to me as a Southern man and Choctaw, I solicit a place in your columns that I may place myself right before the public. [Washington, Arkansas, 1863.]

Broadside. 26.5 cm.

A defense of his course in the war. Unrecorded, and the only known copy.

To the People of Louisiana, Texas, Arkansas and Missouri, and the Allied Indian Nations. Shreveport: Printed at the office of the South-Western, [1863].*

Broadside. 30 cm.

An address by the governors of Texas, Louisiana, Arkansas, and Missouri on "the measures to be taken for the defence of our common cause." Unrecorded, and the only known copy.

1863–64

Smith, E. Kirby

8 General Orders issued from Head Quarters Trans-Mississippi Department,

Shreveport, Louisiana, relating to matters and events in Indian Territory. [Shreveport: Confederate Military Press, 1863–64.]
No other copies have been traced.

1864

DAVIS, JEFFERSON

Message of the President. [Richmond, 1864.]

3 p. 22.5 cm. Caption title.

The president transmits an estimate, submitted by S. S. Scott, Commissioner of Indian Affairs, "of funds required to meet our treaty obligations to the Indian Nations, for the period ending June 30th, 1865." Of the highest importance in the history of Confederate relations with the Indians.

MAXEY, SAMUEL B.

Head Quarters, Dis. Ind. Ter'y, Doaksville, Jan'y 14th, 1864. General Orders No. 7. [Doaksville: Confederate Military Press, 1864.]

Broadside. 17.5 cm.

Measures for the arrest and enrollment of evaders. Unrecorded, and the only known copy.

MAXEY, S. B.

Head Quarters Dist. Indian Territory, Doaksville, C.N., January 31st, 1864. Special Orders No. 25. [Doaksville: Confederate Military Press, 1864.]

Broadsheet. 19 cm.

Appointment of Superintendent of Issues to Indians, and publication or regulations governing rationing. Unrecorded, and the only known copy.

MAXEY, SAMUEL B.

"Extract." Head Quarters Dist. Ind. Ter'y. Fort Towson, C.N. March 15th, 1864. General Orders No. 30. [Fort Towson: Confederate Military Press, 1864.]

Broadside. 19 cm.

Measures for the apprehension of spies, deserters, evaders, horse thieves, renegades and traitors. Unrecorded, and the only known copy.

MAXEY, SAMUEL B.

Head Quarters Dist. Ind. Ter'y, Fort Towson, C.N. March—1864. General Orders No. 31. [Fort Towson: Confederate Military Press, 1864.]

3 p. 19.5 cm.

Review of court martial proceedings. Unrecorded, and the only known copy.

MAXEY, SAMUEL B.

Circular. Head Quarters District Ind. Ter., Fort Towson, C.N. May 14th, 1864. [Fort Towson: Confederate Military Press, 1864.]

3 p. 18 cm.

"The following Address of His Excellency Jefferson Davis, President of the Confederate States, is hereby published for the information of the people of the Six Confederate Indian Nations." Unrecorded, and the only known copy.

MAXEY, SAMUEL B.

Head Quarters, Dist. Ind. Ter'y, Fort Towson, C.N., May 20th, 1864. General Orders No. 41. [Fort Towson: Confederate Military Press, 1864.]

7 p. 19.5 cm.

Review of court martial proceedings. Unrecorded, and the only known copy.

MAXEY, SAMUEL B.

Circular. Head Quarters, Dist. Ind. Ter'y., Fort Towson, C.N., June 1st, 1864. [Fort Towson: Confederate Military Press, 1864.]

Broadsheet. 21 cm.

A requisition upon the Indian allies for enough men for three brigades, and an optimistic report on the fortunes of the Confederacy. Unrecorded, and the only known copy.

MAXEY, SAMUEL B.

Circular. Head Quarters, Dist. Ind. Ter'y. Fort Towson, C.N., June 15th, 1864. [Fort Towson: Confederate Military Press, 1864.]

Broadside. 19.5 cm.

"The Major General Commanding publishes with pleasure the subjoined Resolutions of the 5th Regiment Texas Partisan Rangers." Unrecorded, and the only known copy.

MAXEY, SAMUEL B.

Head Quarters, Dist. Ind. Territory, In the Field, C.N., June 25th, 1864. [Choctaw Nation: Confederate Military Press, 1864.]

Broadsheet. 20.5 cm.

"The subjoined Report and Resolutions of the First Choctaw Regiment are published for the information of all concerned." Unrecorded, and the only known copy.

MAXEY, SAMUEL B.

Circular. Head Quarters, Dist. Ind. Ter'y. Fort Towson, C.N., Sept. 29th, 1864. [Fort Towson: Confederate Military Press, 1864.]

Broadsheet. 26.5 cm.

Publication of a highly important address of S. S. Scott, Commissioner of Indian Affairs, to the Indian allies of the Confederate States, and two acts of the Confederate congress governing the election of Indian delegates to that body. Unrecorded, and the only known copy.

MAXEY, SAMUEL B.

Circular. Head Quarters, Dist. Ind. Ter'y. Fort Towson, C.N., Oct. 17th, 1864. [Fort Towson: Confederate Military Press, 1864.]*

4 p. 20 cm.

Publication of an order by Brigadier General D. H. Cooper commending the soldiers of the First Choctaw Battalion for their recent capture of a Union wagon train and for their successful operation against jayhawkers in the neighborhood of Fort Smith. Unrecorded, and the only known copy.

MAXEY, SAMUEL B.

Head Quarters, Dist. Ind. Ter'y. Fort Towson, C.N., Dec. 14th, 1864. General

Orders No. 71. [Fort Towson: Confederate Military Press, 1864.]
Broadside. 12.5 cm.
An order regarding foraging. Unrecorded.

PITCHLYNN, PETER P.
The Inaugural Address of Gov. Pitchlynn. [Fort Towson: Confederate Military Press, 1864.]*
3 p. 20 cm. Caption title.
One of two known copies, the other being at the Huntington Library. A corner of the first leaf of this copy is missing, with damage to the text. Accompanied by a photostat of the Huntington copy.

SMITH, E. KIRBY
General Orders No. 81. Head Quarters Trans-Miss. Department. Shreveport, La., October 12, 1864. [Shreveport: Confederate Military Press, 1864.]
Broadside. 12 cm.
Announcement by General E. Kirby Smith of the success of an expedition under Brigadier Generals Gano and Stand Watie; he calls it "one of the most brilliant raids of the war."

1865

COOPER, DOUGLAS H.
Head Quarters, Dist. Ind. Ter'y, Fort Towson, C.N., March 7th, 1865. Special Order No. 63. [Fort Towson: Confederate Military Press, 1865.]
Broadside. 16 cm.
Provision for army mechanics to repair tools and implements for impoverished Indian farmers.

1881

ROSE, VICTOR M.
Rose' Texas Brigade. Being a Narrative of Events connected with its Service in the late War Between the States. Louisville, Ky. Printed at the Courier-Journal Book and Job Rooms. 1881.*
185 p. 20 cm. Ports.
Considerable information on the war in Indian Territory.

1888

ROSE, VICTOR M.
The life and services of Gen. Ben McCulloch. Philadelphia: Pictorial Bureau of the Press. 1888.
260 p. 22.5 cm. 2 ports.
Highly important information on the war in the Indian Territory.

1898

NASH, CHARLES EDWARD
Biographical Sketches of Gen. Pat Cleburne and General T. C. Hindman together with Humorous Anecdotes and Reminiscences of the late Civil War. Little Rock: Tunnah & Pittard, 1898.*

300 p. 19 cm. Plates.
Hindman, it will be remembered, was Albert Pike's superior officer and the unhappy recipient of some of Pike's classically ironic letters.

CREE INDIANS

1876

Hunter, James, tr.

Oo meyo achimoowin St. John. The Gospel according to St. John; translated into the language of the Cree Indians, of the Diocese of Rupert's Land, Northwest America, by the Venerable James Hunter, D.D., late Archdeacon of Cumberland, Rupert's Land. London, 1876.

126 p. 17 cm.
Excessively rare. The Union Catalog locates only the copy at the Library of Congress.

CREEK INDIANS

1791

Authentic Memoirs of William Augustus Bowles, Esquire, Ambassador from the United Nations of Creeks and Cherokees, to the Court of London. London: Printed for R. Faulkner, New Bond-street. M.DCC.XCI.

[4], vi, 79 p. 15.5 cm.

Complete with the half title, which is lacking from the DeRenne copy.
"Ranked among the rarest works relating to American aborigines. Colonel Force once said that he had attempted for twenty years to procure a copy without success." Field 59. [See page 156.]

1800

Letter from the Secretary of War, accompanying his Report on the Petitions of William Milton and others exhibiting Claims for Militia Services in the State of Georgia. [Philadelphia, 1800.]

41 p. 23 cm.
The claims throw light upon the 1793 and 1794 expeditions against the Creeks and Cherokees.

1801

Hawkins, Benjamin

Letter from the Principal Agent for Indian Affairs, South of the Ohio. [Philadelphia, 1801.]

11 p. 22.5 cm.

Headed: No. 1 of Documents accompanying the President's Communications to Congress, the 8th day of December, 1801.
A very rare account of the Creek Indians, which possesses the highest interest and importance.

1802

Milfort, Le Clerc

Memoire ou coup-d'oeil rapide sur mes différens voyages et mon séjour dans la nation Crëck. Paris, 1802.

AUTHENTIC MEMOIRS

OF

WILLIAM AUGUSTUS BOWLES,

ESQUIRE,

AMBASSADOR

From the UNITED NATIONS of

CREEKS AND CHEROKEES,

TO THE

COURT OF LONDON.

LONDON:

Printed for R. FAULDER, New Bond-ſtreet.

M.DCC.XCI.

[4], 331, [1] p. 19.5 cm.
The verso of the title page bears the author's autograph. An important source. Milfort married a sister of Alexander McGillivray. [See page 158.]

1803

STEPHENS, ALEXANDER

The Life of General W. A. Bowles, a Native of America, born of English Parents in Frederic County, Maryland, in the year 1764. From "Public Characters, for 1802." London, printed: New York, reprinted by Robert Wilson, 1803.
31 p. 23 cm.
A fine copy, in a protective case. An excessively rare pamphlet.

1813

CLAIBORNE, C. C.

New Orleans, December 26, 1813. Sir. [New Orleans, 1813.]
Broadside. 24 cm.
"Whilst the brave Kentuckians are assisting to plant the American standard in Canada, and the gallant Tennesseans are avenging, in the Creek Nation, the massacre at Fort Sims, surely the Louisianians will not hesitate to turn out in defence of their homes . . . ."
Unrecorded, and the only known copy.

Journal of the Senate of the State of Georgia at an Annual Session of the Legislature, begun and held at Milledgeville, the Seat of Government, on Monday, the first day of November, 1813. Milledgeville: S. & F. Grantland, Printers to the State. [1813].*
96 p. 25 cm. Folded table.
A valuable source of information on Creek hostilities and depredations.

MADISON, JAMES

Message from the President of the United States to both Houses of Congress at the commencement of the Second Session of the Thirteenth Congress. Washington City: Roger C. Weightman, 1813.*
16 p. 20.5 cm.
Contains a review of the Creek War in the South.

TENNESSEE GENERAL ASSEMBLY

[Memorial for the opening of a public road through the Creek and Cherokee Nations. Nashville, 1813.]*
Broadside. 25 cm.
Unrecorded, and the only known copy.

1814

BUTLER, ROBERT

May Every Citizen be a Good Soldier, and Every Soldier a Good Citizen. [Nashville, Tennessee, 1814.]
Broadside. 25 cm.
"To determine how far the above lines are applicable to the people of Tennessee requires us only to take a retrospect of the last campaign against the hostile Creek Indians . . . ." Unrecorded, and the only known copy.

MÉMOIRE

OU

COUP-D'ŒIL RAPIDE

SUR mes différens voyages et mon séjour dans la nation Crëck.

PAR LE Gal. MILFORT,

Tastanégy ou grand Chef de guerre de la nation Crëck, et Général de brigade au service de la République française.

A PARIS,

DE L'IMPRIMERIE DE GIGUET ET MICHAUD,

RUE DES BONS-ENFANS, No. 6.

AN XI. — (1802.)

JACKSON, ANDREW, and JOHN COFFEE

Great Battle! [Nashville, Tennessee, 1814.]

Broadside. Folio.

Headed: Nashville Whig Extra.

Narratives by General Jackson and General Coffee of their victories over the Creek Indians. Unrecorded, and the only known copy.

1818

BENTON, THOMAS HART

Some Account of Some of the Bloody Deeds of General Jackson. [Franklin, Tennessee, 1818.]

Broadside. Folio.

Mourning border, and 18 cuts of coffins, representing Jackson's victims.

A violent attack upon General Jackson for his execution of the six militiamen, his "sanguinary massacre" at the bend of the Tallapoosa of over five hundred Indians, and his betrayal of the Creek leader, Francis the Prophet. The excessively rare original, and not the facsimile which has so often deceived the unwary.

Captain Cowan's Petition. [Washington, 1818.]

14 p. 24 cm. Caption title.

The claim arose from losses incurred in the Creek War.

Message from the President of the United States transmitting Copies of Correspondence between the Governor of Georgia, and Maj. Gen. Andrew Jackson, on the subject of the Arrest of Captain Obed Wright. Washington: E. De Krafft, 1818.*

21 p. 21.5 cm.

Captain Wright commanded troops of the Georgia militia in a cruel and unwarranted attack upon Chehaw Village, one of the Lower Creek towns.

1819

CLAIBORNE, NATHANIEL HERBERT

Notes on the War in the South; with Biographical Sketches of the Lives of Montgomery, Jackson, Sevier, the late Gov. Claiborne, and others. By Nathaniel Herbert Claiborne, of Franklin County, Va. A Member of the Executive of Virginia during the late War. Richmond: Published by William Ramsay, 1819.

112 p. 17 cm.

Field 320.

A fine copy.

CUMMINS, EBENEZER H.

A summary geography of Alabama, One of the United States. By Ebenezer H. Cummins, A.M. Philadelphia: Printed by William Brown, 1819. Price 25 cents.

24 p. 20 cm.

This excessively rare little volume, which was unknown even to Owen, contains important observations on the Creek and Cherokee Indians.

Letter from the Secretary of War transmitting Information respecting the Adjustment and Payment of the Claims of the Friendly Creek Indians, under the Treaty of the 9th August, 1814. Washington City: E. De Krafft, 1819.*

8 p. 23 cm.

1820

JACKSON, ANDREW

Memorial of Major General Andrew Jackson. Washington: Gales & Seaton, 1820.
61 p. 24 cm.

1822

CAPERS, WILLIAM

A Report made before the Bishops and South Carolina Conference of the Methodist Episcopal Church, at their Annual Meeting, held in Augusta, February 21, 1822. By William Capers, who had been appointed to Attempt a Mission among the Indians. Georgetown, S.C.: Printed at the Winyaw Intelligencer Office, 1822.*

31 p. 21.5 cm.

A detailed account of the first mission to the Creeks, and a volume of extraordinary importance and value. The only known copy.

1823

CAPERS, WILLIAM

Second Annual Report of the Missionary Committee of the South Carolina Conference, read before the Conference, and accepted, February 26, 1823. Milledgeville: Grantland & Orme, 1823.

20 cm. Plain wrappers.

The volume is devoted to a report by William Capers on the progress of the Methodist mission to the Creeks.

1824

Documents relating to the Claim of the State of Georgia for Militia Services. Washington: Gales & Seaton, 1824.*

41 p. 22 cm.

A claim for services rendered in suppressing Creek hostilities.

Report of the Committee of Ways and Means, to whom was referred a Resolution of the House of Representatives, of 27th February last, instructing said Committee to inquire into the Expediency of making an Appropriation to Compensate the Friendly Creek Indians for Property Lost and Destroyed during the late Creek War. [Washington, 1824.]

10 p. 22.5 cm. Caption title.

1825

Examination of the Controversy between Georgia and the Creeks. New York: Clayton & Van Norden, 1825.

31 p. 23 cm. Wrapper title.

Letter from the Secretary of War, transmitting Copies of the Report and Proceedings of the Commissioners appointed to Treat with the Creek Nation of Indians, for an Extinguishment of their Claim to Land, lying within the State of Georgia. Washington: Gales & Seaton, 1825.

41 p. 22 cm.

MURPHY, JOHN

Message. To the Speaker and Members of the House of Representatives (of the State of Alabama). [Cahawba, 1825.]

Broadside. Folio.

Official view of the Creek Indian problem and concern over the effects upon the people of Alabama of the late treaty between Georgia and the Creeks. Unrecorded, and the only known copy.

TROUP, GEORGE MCINTOSH

Governor's message to the General Assembly of the State of Georgia at the opening of the Extra Session, May 23, 1825, with a part of the Documents accompanying the same. Published by Order of the General Assembly. Milledgeville: Camak & Ragland, printers. 1825.*

128 p. 21 cm.

Highly important message and documents on the Creek troubles. The volume is very rare.

TROUP, GEORGE MCINTOSH

Governor's message to the General Assembly of the State of Georgia at the opening of the Annual Session, November 7, 1825. With the Documents accompanying the same. Published by Order of the General Assembly. Milledgeville: Camak & Ragland, State printers. 1825.*

265 p. 21 cm.

Message and documents on the Creek disturbances. The volume is excessively rare.

1826

Adjutant General's Office, Washington, April 28th, 1826. Orders No. 35. [Washington, 1835.]*

9 p. 17 cm. Caption title.

Review and approval of the court martial proceedings against Colonel Talbot Chambers, commanding officer of United States forces in the Creek country, who was cashiered from the army because of habitual drunkenness on duty. An illuminating commentary upon the type of men at that period representing the United States government among the Indian tribes.

BENTON, THOMAS H.

Mr. Benton, from the Committee of Conference, appointed by the Senate, on the Disagreeing Vote between the Senate and House of Representatives, on the Amendment adopted by the Senate, to the Bill appropriating Money to carry into effect the Treaty lately concluded with the Creek Indians, reports. [Washington, 1826.)

6 p. 25 cm. Caption title.

Georgia and the General government. Milledgeville: Camak & Ragland. 1826.*

79, [1] p. 21 cm.

Georgia's side of the disagreement with the federal government over the policy toward the Creeks and the acquisition of their lands. The volume is excessively rare.

Journal of the Senate of the State of Georgia at an Annual Session of the General Assembly, begun and held at Milledgeville, the Seat of Government, in Nov. and Dec. 1826. Milledgeville: Camak & Ragland, 1826.

359 p. 21 cm.

Contains highly important documents and reports on the Creeks and Cherokees.

Resolutions of the Legislature and Message of the Governor of the State of Alabama. Washington: Gales & Seaton, 1826.*

7 p. 22 cm.

On the subject of the 1825 Creek treaty.

Treaty with Creek Indians. Message from the President of the United States, transmitting a Copy of a Treaty with the Creek Nation of Indians, concluded 25th January last. Also, a Copy of a Treaty, superseded by the same, signed at the Indian Springs, on the 12th of January, 1825, &c. Washington: Gales & Seaton, 1826.*

15 p. 22 cm.

1827

Friendly Creek Indians. Letter from the Secretary of War on the Resolutions of the Legislature of the State of Georgia in relation to the Suffering Condition of the Friendly Creek Indians. Washington: Gales & Seaton, 1827.

4 p. 22 cm. Caption title.

Pennsylvania General Assembly

Appendix to the Senate Journal of the Session of 1826–27, containing Messages and Documents relative to the Controversy between Georgia and the Creek Indians. Harrisburg, Pennsylvania: Cameron & Kraus, 1827.*

399 p. 22.5 cm. Plain wrappers.

Hundreds of documents of incalculable value. The volume is very rare.

Report and Resolutions of the Legislature of Georgia, with accompanying Documents. Washington: Gales & Seaton, 1827.

404 p. 22 cm.

An encyclopedia of authoritative information on the Creek disturbances.

Report of the Select Committee of the House of Representatives to which were referred the Messages of the President U.S. of the 5th and 8th February, and 2d March, 1827, with accompanying Documents: and a Report and Resolutions of the Legislature of Georgia. Washington: Gales & Seaton, 1827.

xi, 846 p. 22 cm.

A great treasure house of authoritative information on the Creek disturbances.

The Survey of Creek Lands. Message from the President of the United States transmitting a Letter from the Governor of Georgia, with Accompanying Documents in relation to the Proceeding of Certain Indians in said State. Washington: Gales & Seaton, 1827.

7 p. 22.5 cm.

1828

Citizens of Georgia—Claims on Creek Indians. Memorial of the Legislature of Georgia on the subject of the Claims of the Citizens of that State against the Creek

Nation under the Treaty of the Indian Springs, of 1821. Washington: Gales & Seaton, 1828.

8 p. 22.5 cm.

Citizens of Georgia—Claims on Creek Indians. [Washington, 1828.]

23 p. 22.5 cm. Caption title.

Creek Indian Broke, &c. Letter from the Secretary of War, transmitting Information in relation to the Breaking of an Individual and Depriving him of his Authority among the Creeks; also, in relation to the Appointment of an Indian Chief in the Territory of Michigan, during the year 1827. Washington: Gales & Seaton, 1828.

20 p. 22.5 cm.

Creek Treaty—November 15, 1827. Message from the President of the United States transmitting the Information required by a Resolution of the House of Representatives of 22d ultimo, in relation to the Treaty with the Creek Nation of Indians, of the 15th of November last. Washington: Gales & Seaton, 1828.

26 p. 22 cm.

HILL, ISAAC

Brief Sketch of the Life, Character and Services of Major General Andrew Jackson. By a Citizen of New England. Concord, N.H.: Manahan, Hoag & Co., 1828.*

51 p. 14.5 cm. Printed wrappers. Frontisp. port.

With considerable attention to the Creek disturbances. A very fine copy.

MCKENNEY, THOMAS L.

To the Public. [Washington, 1828.]

16 p. 20.5 cm. Caption title.

A very scarce pamphlet, with details of Colonel McKenney's services at Green Bay and of his tour among the Creek and Chickasaw Indians.

Payments to Citizens of Georgia. Message from the President of the United States, transmitting Reports relating to Payments made to the Citizens of Georgia under the 4th Article of the Treaty with the Creek Nation, of 8th February, 1821, and the Disallowance of Certain Claims exhibited under that Treaty, &c. Washington: Gales & Seaton, 1828.

70 p. 22.5 cm.

Tennessee Militiamen. Report of the Committee on Military Affairs, to which were referred the Correspondence and Documents from the War Department, in relation to the Proceedings of a Court Martial ordered for the Trial of certain Tennessee Militiamen. Washington: Gales & Seaton, 1828.*

63 p. 25 cm. Uncut and unopened.

The investigation of the trial of the Tennessee soldiers for mutiny yielded considerable information on the Creek War.

1829

Treaty of San Lorenzo El Real. Letter from the Secretary of State, transmitting Copies of certain Letters of Andrew Ellicott, Commissioner, &c., relating to the Head or Source of St. Mary's River. [Washington, 1829.]*

18 p. 22.5 cm. Caption title.
Contains a highly important series of letters written in 1799 regarding the activities of William Augustus Bowles and Benjamin Hawkins, the English and French hostilities in Florida, and the course pursued by the Creeks and Seminoles.

1831

Claims. Citizens of Georgia vs. Creek Indians. [Washington, 1831.]
4 p. 22 cm. Caption title.
Creek depredations.

Creek Indians . . . A Memorial from several Head Men of the Creek Nation. [Washington, 1831.]
3 p. 23 cm. Caption title.
A claim by Creeks, forced to remove to Alabama, for losses suffered at the hands of whites in Georgia.

CROCKETT, DAVID

David Crockett's Circular. To the Citizens and Voters of the Ninth Congressional District in the State of Tennessee. [Nashville? 1831.]*
16 p. 22 cm. Caption title.
Contains Crockett's strictures on Jackson's Indian policy. Not in Sabin.

WILLETT, MARINUS

A Narrative of the Military Actions of Colonel Marinus Willett, taken chiefly from his own Manuscript. Prepared by his Son, William M. Willett. New York: G. & C. & H. Carvill, 1831.
[3], 162 p. 23.5 cm. Portrait, plan.
President Washington dispatched Colonel Willett in 1790 to negotiate a treaty with the Creeks. His narrative of this mission possesses the greatest importance. "Colonel Willett was an eminent partisan officer during the Revolution, serving principally on the frontiers of New York, in campaigns against the Six Nations. The narrative is therefore in great part composed of incidents connected with Indian warfare" (Field 1659). A fine copy.

1832

Clark—Adm'r of Seagrove et al. Indian Depredations. Memorial of Archibald Clark, Administrator of Robert Seagrove, deceased, for himself and other Citizens of Georgia. [Washington, 1832.]*
12 p. 24.5 cm. Caption title.
Creek Indian depredations about 1800.

Memorial of the Legislature of Alabama in behalf of Sundry Individuals belonging to the Creek Indians, praying for Assistance from the Government. [Washington, 1832.]
4 p. 22 cm. Caption title.

1833

BEAN, ELLIS

Columbus Enquirer. Extra. Letter from Ellis Bean, Colonel of Cavalry of the Mexican Republic. Nacogdoches, Texas, 24th Feb. 1833. [Columbus, Georgia, 1833.]*

Broadside. 26 cm.

The letter, with additional information from an unnamed source, possesses superlative interest and importance. It relates many otherwise unknown facts concerning Choctaw, Seminole, and Coushatte emigration and incursions into Texas and gives a lengthy account of a Creek Indian expedition into Texas led by Hopothleyohola and one Benjamin Hawkins with the object, evidently, of settling 28,000 Creek emigrants there. Unrecorded, and the only known copy.

ROBINSON, JOHN

The Savage. By Piomingo, a Headman and Warrior of the Muscogulgee Nation. Knoxville, Tenn. Republished at the "Scrap Book" Office. 1833.*

324 p. 17.5 cm.

Sabin does not list this edition. Excessively rare.

1834

Acts passed at the annual session of the General Assembly of the State of Alabama, begun and held in the town of Tuscaloosa, on the third Monday in November, one thousand eight hundred and thirty-three. Tuscaloosa: May & Ferguson, 1834.

205 p. 18.5 cm.

CROCKETT, DAVID

A narrative of the life of David Crockett, of the State of Tennessee. Written by himself. Philadelphia: E. L. Carey & A. Hart, 1834.

211 p. 19 cm.

Contains an account of Crockett's exploits in the Creek War.

FLEMING, JOHN

The Muskoko Imunaitsu. Muskokee (Creek) Assistant. Boston: Crocker & Brewster, 1834.

101 p. 14.5 cm.

The first book in the Creek language. It contains valuable linguistic material, including vocabulary and numerals. Excessively rare.

LEWIS, DIXON H., and SEABORN JONES

Remarks of the Hon. Dixon H. Lewis and Hon. Seaborn Jones on the Alabama Controversy, delivered in the House of Representatives, January 6, 1834. Washington, [1834].

16 p. 22.5 cm.

Controversy over the execution of the Creek treaty of 1832.

Memorandum respecting the Removal of Indians during the year 1834. [Washington, 1834.]

10 p. 20 cm. Caption title.

Specific instructions and regulations governing removal of Creeks, Cherokees and Quapaws.

1835

FLEMING, JOHN

A Short Sermon: also Hymns, in the Muskokee or Creek Language. By Rev. John

Fleming, Missionary of the American Board of Commissioners for Foreign Missions. Boston: Crocker & Brewster, 1835.

35 p. 14.5 cm.

Gen. Sanford, late Certifying Agent of the Chattahoochee District, Ala., will resume the Duties of his Former Station, so far as to Enquire into Certain Frauds, said to have been committed by False Representations of certain (Creek) Indians. [Tuskegee, Alabama? 1835.]*

Broadside. 15.5 cm. high × 23 cm. wide.

Unrecorded, and the only known copy.

1836

Chisolm, William, and Wm. S. Foster

Adjutant Pollard's Letter transmitting Col. Chisolm's Report to Col. Foster. [Mobile, Alabama, 1836.]

Broadside. 25.5 cm.

Highly important factual and detailed reports, nowhere else available, of engagements between the Alabama troops and the Creek Indians.

Lane, J. F.

Remarks upon an Editorial headed "The Army," published in the Courier & Enquirer of 26th July, 1836. [Columbus, Ga., 1836.]

[3] p. 25 cm. Caption title.

The author, a captain in the army, vigorously defends General Jesup's conduct of the Creek campaign. The letter, which is dated Creek Country, Aug. 8, 1836, contains highly important extracts from Jesup's own daily journal and offers valuable historical details, not elsewhere to be found, of military events of the Creek War immediately preceding Jesup's replacement by Winfield Scott. The importance of this document can scarcely be overestimated. No other copy can be traced.

Letter from the Secretary of War, transmitting Documents in relation to Hostilities of Creek Indians. [Washington, 1836.]

413 p. 22.5 cm. Caption title.

Letter from the Secretary of War, transmitting Documents in relation to Hostilities of Creek Indians. [Washington, 1836.]

13 p. 22.5 cm. Caption title.

Message from the President transmitting Documents relating to Frauds, &c., in the Sale of Indian Reservations of Land. [Washington, 1836.]*

388 p. 22.5 cm. Caption title.

A rich mine of information about the Creek land frauds.

Page, John

Order No. 47. Head Quarters, Army of the South, Tuskeegee, 21st July, 1836. [Tuskeegee, Alabama, 1836.]

Broadside. 25 cm.

Invitation for proposals from contractors for removing the Creek Indians. The requirements and plans are stated in considerable detail. John Page was superintendent of Creek Removal. Unrecorded, and the only known copy.

SCOTT, WINFIELD

Orders No. 29. Head Quarters, Army of the South, Columbus, Geo., July 7, 1836. [Columbus, Georgia, 1836.]*

Broadside. 25 cm.

General Scott turns over the command of his army to General Jesup and reviews the Creek campaign. Signed in autograph by General Scott. Unrecorded.

STANTON, HENRY

Head Quarters. Army of the South, Fort Mitchell, 25 July, 1836. Order No. 50. [Columbus, Georgia, 1836.]*

Broadside. 25.5 cm.

Provisions for the command of "a band of friendly Indian warriors" to be used against the hostile Creeks. Unrecorded, and the only known copy.

TRUMBULL, HENRY

History of the Discovery of America, of the Landing of our Forefathers at Plymouth, and of their Most Remarkable Engagements with the Indians in New England, from their First Landing in 1620, until the Final Subjugation of the Natives in 1679. To which is annexed the Particulars of almost every Engagement with the Savages at the Westward to the present day. Including the Defeat of Generals Braddock, Harmer and St. Clair, by the Indians at the Westward; the Creek and Seminole War, etc. Boston: George Clark, 1836.

256 p. 20.5 cm. Illustrated with woodcuts.

1837

Hostilities with Creek Indians. Message from the President of the United States, transmitting the Information required by a Resolution of the House of Representatives of the 1st of July last in relation to the Hostilities then Existing with the Creek Indians, &c. &c. [Washington:] Blair & Rives, [1837].

61 p. 22 cm. Caption title.

Proceedings of the Military Court of Inquiry, in the Case of Major General Scott and Major General Gaines. [Washington, 1837.]

734 p. 22.5 cm. 2 folded maps. 1 folded plan.

An encyclopedia of source material on the Creek and Seminole campaigns.

1838

Alleged Frauds on Creek Indians. Message from the President of the United States, transmitting Information in relation to Alleged Frauds on the Creek Indians in the Sale of their Reservations. [Washington:] Thomas Allen, printer, [1838].

102 p. 22.5 cm. Caption title.

Indian Depredations. [Washington:] Thomas Allen, print., [1838].

11 p. 25 cm. Caption title.

A review of Creek depredations in Georgia and Alabama.

Letter from the Secretary of War transmitting a Report from the Commissioner of Indian Affairs, accompanied by Copies of a Contract made between General Jesup, certain Creek Chiefs, and J. C. Watson & Co. [Washington, 1838.]
173 p. 22.5 cm. Caption title.

Report from the Secretary of War transmitting Copies of Correspondence with the Governor of Alabama, in reference to Hostilities with the Creek Indians. [Washington, 1838.]
7 p. 22.5 cm. Caption title.

ROBINSON, JOHN
The Savage, by Piomingo, a Headman and Warrior of the Muscogulgee Nation. Second edition. Philadelphia: John Ferral, 1838.
120 p. 22 cm.

1839

Sale of Indian Reservations, etc. Message from the President of the United States transmitting a Report on the Sales of Indian Reservations made under orders of the Courts of Alabama. [Washington, 1839.]
48 p. 22.5 cm. Caption title.

WYSE, JOHN M.
The Special Commissioner appointed to Investigate the Validity of the Assents of certain Creek Indians to the Contract made between Gen. Jesup, J. C. Watson and Co. and certain Chiefs of the Creek Nation . . . has adopted the following Regulations for the Government of the Proceedings before him. [Washington, 1839.]
Broadside. 24.5 cm.
No other copy can be traced.

1841

General Orders No. 80. War Department, Adjutant General's Office, Washington, Dec. 13th, 1841. [Washington, 1841.]
6 p. 19 cm. Caption title.
A review of the court martial acquittal of Captain John Page of charges of misusing funds due the Creek Indians. The document throws interesting light upon the relations between army officers and the Indians.

1843

BALDWIN, WILLIAM
Reliquiae Baldwinianae: Selections from the Correspondence of the late William Baldwin, M.D. Surgeon in the U.S. Navy. Compiled by William Darlington, M.D. Philadelphia: Kimber & Sharpless, 1843.
346, [1] p. 18.5 cm. Frontisp. portrait.
Baldwin made several botanical tours of Georgia and Florida between 1811 and 1817 and his letters describing the Creeks and Seminoles possess great interest and value. A scarce and little known book.

Claim of the Creek Indians. Letter from the Secretary of War, communicating a

Report of General Jesup, in relation to a Claim of the Creek Indians. [Washington, 1843.]

52 p. 25 cm. Caption title. Uncut and unopened.

1844

MALLARY, C. D.

Memoirs of Elder Jesse Mercer. New York: John Gray, 1844.

455, [1] p. Frontisp. port.

The volume contains interesting references to the Creeks and Cherokees. Mercer was a prominent Georgia preacher and politician.

Milly, an Indian Woman. Report of the Committee on Indian Affairs to whom was submitted a Communication from E. A. Hitchcock, and other Papers having reference to the Application on behalf of Milly, an Indian woman. [Washington, 1844.]

5 p. 22.5 cm. Caption title.

Milly, a daughter of the prophet Francis, a Creek chief executed by Jackson in 1818, in her girlhood saved the life of an American prisoner about to be burned by Creek warriors. Years later Colonel Hitchcock found her in Indian Territory living in want and interested himself in her behalf. Congress voted her a medal and a small pension, which were later presented to her heirs, Milly having died before the medal was struck.

1846

LOUGHRIDGE, R. M.

Mvskoko mopunvkv. Nakchokv setempohetv. Translation of the Introduction to the Shorter Catechism into the Creek Language. By R. M. Loughridge, Missionary to the Creek Indians. Park Hill: Mission Press: J. Candy & E. Archer, Printers. 1846.*

31 p. 13 cm.

Notice respecting the Re-opening, for Private Entry, of Lands in that portion of the Choctaw Cession of 1830, included in the Grenada District, in the State of Mississippi. [Washington, 1846.]*

Broadside. Folio.

Report of the Committee on Indian Affairs, to whom were referred the Public Documents and Testimony of James Erwin, of Arkansas, Soliciting Relief for himself, and for himself and the Heirs and Legal Representatives of his late Partner, Daniel Greathouse, now deceased. [Washington:] Ritchie & Heiss, [1846].

20 p. 22 cm. Caption title.

A claim for losses suffered under their contract for removal of Creek Indians. The document throws considerable light on the negotiation of such contracts.

1847

Circular to the United States' Registers and Receivers in Mississippi, Louisiana, Alabama, and Arkansas. [Washington, 1847.]

Broadside. 25.5 cm.

Relates to Choctaw land claims.

1848

HAWKINS, BENJAMIN

A Sketch of the Creek Country. Savannah, 1848.

88 p. 24 cm. Printed wrappers.

This most highly valued account forms Vol. 3, Pt. 1, of the Collections of the Georgia Historical Society. Rare in wrappers.

Report. The Committee on Indian Affairs, to whom was referred the Memorial of Benjamin Marshall, Tuckabatcha Micco, G. W. Stidham, and George Scott, Delegates of the Creek Nation of Indians, report, in part: . . . . [Washington, 1848.]

70 p. 22.5 cm. Caption title.

Report of the Secretary of War in answer to a resolution of the Senate calling for a List of the Creek Indian Warriors who were Killed, Wounded, or Died in the Service of the United States during the late War in Florida, with a Statement of the Arrears of Pay due them. [Washington, 1848.]

5 p. 22.5 cm. Caption title. Folded table.

1853

Muscogee or Creek Indians. Letter from the Commissioner of Indian Affairs: in reference to the Affairs of the Creek Indians. [Washington, 1854.]

[28] p. 21.5 cm. Caption title. Irregularly paged.

A rare volume, which contains a review of Creek relations with the United States.

1855

LOUGHRIDGE, R. M., tr.

Cesvs Klist, em-opunvkv-hera, Maro Coyvte. The Gospel according to Matthew. Translated into the Muskokee Language. Park Hill: Mission Press: Edwin Archer, Printer. 1855.

153, 7, [2] p. 12.5 cm.

MEEK, A. B.

The Red Eagle. A Poem of the South. New York: D. Appleton, 1855.

108 p. 19.5 cm.

The principal character in the poem is Weatherford, the Creek leader. P. P. Pitchlynn's copy, with his autograph.

1856

Creek and Seminole Treaty. Correspondence preliminary to the Treaty of August 7, 1856, between the United States and the Creek and Seminole Indians. Washington: Gideon, [1856].

117 p. 22.5 cm. Wrapper title.

A volume of the utmost importance for an understanding of Creek and Seminole relations and of the separation of the two tribes. No other copy can be traced.

1857

MILBURN, WILLIAM HENRY

The Rifle, Axe, and Saddle-bags, and other Lectures. New York: Derby & Jackson, 1857.

309 p. 19 cm. Frontisp. portrait.
Missionary experiences in the Middle West, with chapters on the history of the South and the Southwest. There are particularly interesting accounts of Alexander McGillivray and William Augustus Bowles.

1858

LOUGHRIDGE, R. M., and DAVID WINSLETT

Nakcokv setempohetv. Introduction to the Shorter Catechism. Translated into the Creek Language. By Rev. R. M. Loughridge, A.M. and Rev. David Winslett. Second edition. Philadelphia, 1858.

34 p. 15 cm.

Northern and Western Boundary Line of the Creek Country. Letter from the Secretary of War transmitting Reports of Captains Sitgreaves and Woodruff of the Survey of the Creek Indian Boundary Line. [Washington, 1858.]

32 p. 22.5 cm. Caption title. Large folded map.
With a most valuable account of the natural history of the country traversed.

ROBERTSON, W. S., and others

Come to Jesus. Cesvs a ok vtes. Erkenvkv hall coyvte, momen W. S. Robertson, John McKillop, Rev. David Winslett, esyomat Mvskoke empunvkv ohtvlecicet os. [New York, 1858?].

63 p. 15 cm.
Pilling, Muskhogean Bibliography, p. 79.

WIGHTMAN, WILLIAM M.

Life of William Capers, D.D., one of the Bishops of the Methodist Episcopal Church, South; including an Autobiography. By William M. Wightman, D.D., President of Wofford College. Nashville, Tenn., 1858.*

516 p. 18.5 cm. Frontisp. port.
The volume contains an account of the Capers mission to the Creeks of Georgia and Alabama and a sprightly description of a Creek ball play.

1859

WOODWARD, THOMAS SIMPSON

Woodward's Reminiscences of the Creek, or Muscogee Indians, contained in Letters to Friends in Georgia and Alabama. By Thomas S. Woodward, of Louisiana, (formerly of Alabama.) With an Appendix, containing Interesting Matter relating to the General Subject. Montgomery, Ala.: Barrett & Wimbish, 1859.

168 p. 21.5 cm. Printed wrappers.
A magnificent copy of a great rarity. Apparently unknown to Field. [See page 172.]

1860

BUCKNER, H. F.

A Collection of English Hymns for Creek Baptists: with a Few Original Pieces. New York, 1860.*

51, [1] p. 12 cm. Text in English.
Bound with the preceding volume. Excessively rare, and not noted by Pilling.

PRICE, 50 CENTS.

WOODWARD'S REMINISCENCES

OF THE

Creek, or Muscogee Indians,

Contained in Letters to Friends in

GEORGIA AND ALABAMA.

BY THOMAS S. WOODWARD, OF LOUISIANA,
(FORMERLY OF ALABAMA.)

WITH AN APPENDIX,
CONTAINING INTERESTING MATTER RELATING TO THE GENERAL SUBJECT.

MONTGOMERY, ALA.:
BARRETT & WIMBISH, BOOK AND GENERAL JOB PRINTERS.
1859.

BUCKNER, H. F., tr.

The Gospel according to John. Wpwnvkv hera Chanichwyvten, oksumkvlki irkinvkv, H. F. Buckner (ichwhwnvnwv), inyvtikv G. Herrod itipake Maskwke imwpwnvkv twhtvlhoechvtet wmis. Pwhesayechv Chesus hechkvte atekat whrwlwpe chwkpi rokkwhvmkin, chwkpi chinvpakin, pali-epakvtis. Marion, Ala.: Published by the Domestic and Indian Mission Board of the Southern Baptist Convention. 1860.

185, [5] p. 15 cm.

Excessively rare.

BUCKNER, H. F., and G. HERROD

A Grammar of the Maskoke, or Creek Language. To which are prefixed Lessons in Spelling, Reading, and Defining. By H. F. Buckner, a Missionary, under the patronage of the Domestic and Indian Mission Board of the Southern Baptist Convention; assisted by his Interpreter, G. Herrod, Superintendent of Public Instruction, etc., Micco Creek Nation. Marion, Ala.: Domestic and Indian Mission Board of the Southern Baptist Convention. 1860.*

138, [1] p.

Excessively rare.

BUCKNER, H. F., and G. HERROD

Maskoke Hymns. Original, collected, and revised. By H. F. Buckner, a Baptist Missionary, and G. Herrod, Interpreter. Marion, Ala.: Published by the Domestic and Indian Mission Board of the Southern Baptist Convention, 1860.

140 p. 12 cm. Text in Creek.

Pilling, Muskhogean Bib., p. 14.

Excessively rare.

1866

An Argument to the President of the United States on behalf of the 1st, 2d & 3d Indian Regiments, for Bounty, as provided for in the Act of July 22, A.D. 1861. Washington: Intelligencer Printing Establishment, 1866.*

12, [1] p. 22 cm. Printed wrappers.

Papers relating to the Negotiations between the United States and the Creek Indians, which resulted in the Treaty concluded at Washington, D.C., June 14th, 1866. Washington: Joseph L. Pearson, 1866.

54 p. 23 cm. Wrapper title.

A highly important volume. Unrecorded, and no other copy traced.

1868

STIDHAM, G. W., and S. W. PERRYMAN

Rooms of the Creek Delegation, Washington, August 15, 1868. To the Hon. N. G. Taylor, Commissioner of Indian Affairs. [Washington, 1868.]

8 p. 23 cm. Caption title. Plain wrappers.

A statement of Creek claims against the United States.

1869

BLUNT, JAMES G.

Report of James G. Blunt, Attorney for First Regiment (Creeks) Indian Brigade, relative to Alleged Frauds on Payments on Pensions, Bounties and Back Pay. Washington: Gibson Brothers, 1869.

70 p. 22 cm. Printed wrappers.

1871

ROBERTSON, W. S., and DAVID WINSLETT

Mvskoke nakcokv eskerretv esvhokkolat. Creek Second Reader. By Rev. W. S. Robertson and Rev. David Winslett. New York: American Tract Society, [1871].

90 p. 19 cm.

ROBERTSON, W. S., and DAVID WINSLETT

Nakcokv es kerretv enhvteceskv. Muskokee or Creek First Reader. By W. S. Robertson, A.M., and David Winslett. Fourth edition. New York, 1871.

48 p. 17.5 cm.

1872

Alleged Frauds against certain Indian Soldiers. [Washington, 1872.]*

590 p. 22.5 cm. Caption title.

A mine of detailed Civil War Service records of Creek and Cherokee members of the three regiments of Indian Home Guards.

Mvhayv. The Teacher. By the Tullahassee Boys and Girls. Creek Nation School Press, 1872.

[8] p. 15.5 cm.

One of only two known copies.

1874

CHAPPELL, ABSALOM H.

Miscellanies of Georgia, Historical, Biographical, Descriptive, &c. Columbus, Ga.: Thos. Gilbert, 1874.*

[4], 73, [2], 137, 24 p. 21.5 cm. In 3 parts, as issued. Printed wrappers.

An authoritative source of historical information on the Creek Indians. Very rare in wrappers.

CHAPPELL, ABSALOM H.

Miscellanies of Georgia, Historical, Biographical, Descriptive, etc. Atlanta: James F. Meegan, 1874.*

[4], 73, 137, 24 p. 21 cm.

[A Memorial, printed without title page or caption, of the Creek Delegation. N.p., 1874.]

12 p. 23 cm.

1875

General Funding Bond, Muscogee Nation, Indian Territory. $100. [1875].

Broadside, engraved. 34 cm.

ROBERTSON, ANN E. W.

[Three hymns in Creek. Tullahassee Mission Press, 1875?]*

Broadside. 15.5 cm. high × 23 cm. wide.

Signed: A. E. W. R. Tr.

The following manuscript note appears on the reverse: Printed for closing exercises of Tullahassee School. Unrecorded, and no other copy known.

Ross, William P.

Election Notice. Muskokee, C.N., Dec. 10, 1875. [Tullahassee Mission Press, 1875.]*

Broadside. 26.5 cm.

Imprint at end: Mission Press.

A call for a meeting of the stockholders of the Indian International Printing Company for the election of officers. Unrecorded, and the only known copy.

1876

Hodge, D. M.

Remarks of D. M. Hodge, Delegate of the Muscogee Nation of Indians, against the Establishment by Congress of a United States Government over the Indian Country without the Consent of the Indians. Washington: John L. Ginck, 1876.

23 p. 22.5 cm. Wrapper title.

Indian International Printing Company

"Notice." [Muskogee, 1876.]

Broadside. 12.5 cm.

A call for a meeting of the shareholders for the election of an editor of the Indian Herald, the first newspaper to be published in the Creek Nation. Accompanied by the stamped envelope in which it was originally addressed to P. P. Pitchlynn. Unrecorded, and the only known copy.

Memorial of the Creek Delegation in relation to Funds due the "Creek Orphans" under the Creek Treaty of 1832 and the Act of March 3, 1837. Washington: John L. Ginck, 1876.

14 p. 23 cm.

Maxwell, Thomas

Tuskaloosa, the Origin of its Name, its History, etc. Tuskaloosa, Alabama: Tuskaloosa Gazette, [1876].*

80 p. 22 cm. Printed wrappers. Map.

The volume is very scarce.

1877

Muskoke Baptist Association

Minutes. [N.p., 1877.]

12 p. 21 cm. Caption title.

Minutes of the fourth annual session, held at Big Arbor, Muskoke Nation, September 6, 1877.

1878

Freedmen's Baptist Association

Minutes of the Second Baptist Church of the Freedman Baptist Association held at Old Creek Agency, Muskoke Nation commencing November 22, 1877. Eufaula: Indian Journal Print, 1878.*

[2], 5, [2] p. 19 cm.

Not in Foreman, and no other copy known.

HODGE, DAVID M.

Argument of David Hodge before the Committee on Indian Affairs March 26th, 1878, in behalf of the Claims of the Loyal Creeks for Losses sustained during the late War, which have been examined, and awarded by a Commission composed of United States Officers. Washington: John L. Ginck, 1878.

10 p. 22.5 cm.

MUSKOKE BAPTIST ASSOCIATION

Minutes of the Fourth Annual Meeting (since the War) of the Muskoke (Creek Indian) Baptist Association held at Big Arbor North Fork Church, Muskoke (Creek) Nation, September 6, 7, 8, 9, 10 and 11, 1877. First Organized at Old North Fork Town, Creek Nation, Sept., 1851. Dallas, Texas: Texas Baptist Publishing House, 1878.

12 p. 22 cm. Caption title.

ROSS, WILLIAM P.

Early Creek History. Speech of Hon. William P. Ross at the Tullahassee Manual Labor Boarding School, July 18th, 1878. [Muskogee, 1878.]

4 p. 21 cm. Text in Creek.

Imprint at end: Printed at the Office of the Indian Journal.

A highly valued account of the tribe.

1879

FREEDMEN'S BAPTIST ASSOCIATION

Minutes of the Second Annual Session of the Freedmen's Baptist Association, of the Muskogee Nation, Indian Territory, held with the Blackjack Baptist Church, Thursday, August 1st, A.D., 1878. Muskogee: Indian Journal Print, 1879.

18 p. 21 cm.

Not in Foreman, and no other copy known.

WESTERN BAPTIST ASSOCIATION

Minutes of the Fifty-first Annual Session of the Western Baptist Association, held with the Church at Antioch, Meriwether Co., Ga., September 19th, 20th and 21st, 1879. West Point, Ga.: State Line Press Job Office, 1879.*

14, [2] p. 21.5 cm. Wrapper title.

Contains an account of the association's mission to the Creek Indians.

1880

Constitution and Laws of the Muskogee Nation. Published by Authority of the National Council. Saint Louis: Levison & Blythe Stationery Co., 1880.

142 p. 22 cm.

1881

Este-Maskoke em ahaka, momet ahaka-em-pataka. L. C. Perryman, etoh tal hoecate. Fotskat Talofan eshotop hoyatet os; ohrolop 1881 omof. [Fort Scott, Kansas, 1881.]

94 p. 22 cm. Title page in expert facsimile.
A translation into Creek of the preceding volume. One of only two known copies.

1882

Enactments of the National Council of the Muskogee Nation, during the Sessions of 1880 and 1881. St. Louis: Levison & Blythe Stationery Co., [1882].

20 p. 23 cm. Printed wrappers.
One of only four known copies, none of them in Oklahoma.

LATROBE, JOHN H. B.

Letters of Hon. John H. B. Latrobe to the Secretary of the Interior. October 28 and November 2, 1828. Washington: Thomas McGill & Co., [1882].

12 p. 22 cm. Wrapper title.
The letters relate to Creek orphan claims.

Message from the President of the United States, transmitting a Communication from the Secretary of the Interior, with Draft of a Bill and Accompanying Papers, in reference to the Proposition of the Creek Nation of Indians for the Cession of Certain of their Lands in the Indian Territory occupied by the Seminole Indians. [Washington, 1879.]

9 p. 23 cm. Caption title. Folded color map of Indian Territory.

1883

The Agreement and Recommendations between the Muskogee Gov't and Spiechee Party. [Muskogee, 1883.]*

Broadside. 26 cm.
The highly important agreement which ended the Spiechee Rebellion, or Green Peach War. One of only two known copies.

Enactments of the National Council of the Muskogee Nation, during the Sessions of 1880, 1881 and 1882. St. Louis: Levison & Blythe Stationery Co., [1883].

34 p. 23 cm. Printed wrappers.
One of only three known copies, the others being at the Chicago Law Institute and the Minnesota University Law School.

FISK, CLINTON B., and E. WHITTLESEY

Peace Ratified in the Creek Nation. Report of Commissioners Clinton B. Fisk and E. Whittlesey. Muscogee, I.T., August 11, 1883. Washington, 1883.

34 p. 22 cm.

1884

GATSCHET, ALBERT S.

A Migration Legend of the Creek Indians, with a Linguistic, Historic and Ethnographic Introduction. Vol. 1. Philadelphia: D. G. Brinton, 1884.*

251 p. 23 cm.
A work of the utmost importance.

GATSCHET, ALBERT S.

Tchikilli's Kasi'hta Legend in the Creek and Hitchiti Languages, with a Critical Commentary and Full Glossaries. [In Transactions of the Academy of Science of St. Louis. Vol. V, No. 1 & 2. St. Louis: R. P. Studley, 1888.]*

205 p. Original wrappers.

This volume forms the concluding portion of the preceding.

MUSKOKEE BAPTIST ASSOCIATION

Minutes of the Ninth Annual Meeting (since the War) of the Muskokee (Creek Indian) Baptist Association, held at Weokoofke Church, Muskokee Nation, August 15 and 16, 1884. First Organized at Old North Fork Town, Creek Nation, Sept. 1851. Dayton, Virginia: Ruebush, Kieffer & Co., 1884.

8 p. 22.5 cm. Printed wrappers.

ROBERTSON, A. E. W.

Mvskoke nettvcako cokv-heckv cokv esyvhiketv. Yvhiketv "punvkv-herv esyvhiketv" momet cokv eti aenkvpvket. The Muskokee S. S. Song-Book. From Gospel Songs and other Collections. By A. E. W. Robertson. New York, 1884.

96 p. 15 cm.

1885

Indian Journal Supplement. [Muskogee, 1885.]*

Broadsheet. 28 cm.

Devoted to news notes from Childers Station and to advertisements of Eufaula, Stringtown, and Muskogee merchants.

1886

MUSKOGEE, SEMINOLE, and WICHITA BAPTIST ASSOCIATION

Minutes of the First Annual Convention of the Muskogee, Seminole and Wichita Baptist Association, held with Greenleaf Church, Creek Nation, August 4, 5, 6 and 7, 1886. Muskogee: Indian Journal, 1886.

18 p. 22 cm. Printed wrappers.

1887

FREEDMEN'S BAPTIST ASSOCIATION

Minutes of the 9th Annual Session of the Freedmen's Baptist Association, held with the Second Baptist Church, Creek Nation. August 19, 20, 21 and 22, 1886. Muskogee, Indian Journal, 1887.*

14 p. 22 cm. Printed wrappers.

Not in Foreman, and no other copy located.

MUSKOGEE CITIZENS

Resolutions. [Muskogee, 1887.]

Broadside. 17 cm.

Resolutions of sorrow occasioned by the murder of Samuel Sixkiller, Captain of the U.S. Indian police. Unrecorded, and the only known copy.

OWEN, ROBERT L., and others

Muskogee, Ind. Ter., January 6th, 1887. Gentlemen: [Muskogee, 1887.]*

Broadside. 28 cm.
An appeal for contributions to a fund for the relief of the widow and children of Captain Samuel Sixkiller, the recently murdered Captain of U.S. Indian police. Unrecorded, and the only known copy.

1888

GRAYSON, G. W., and SPA HE CHA

Protest of Creek Delegation against the Passage of H.R. 1277. [Washington, 1888.]
5 p. 22.5 cm. Caption title.

POPE, JOHN

A Tour through the Southern and Western Territories of the United States of North America; the Spanish Dominions on the River Mississippi, and the Floridas; the Countries of the Creek nations; and many Uninhabited Parts. By John Pope. Richmond: Printed by John Dixon. For the Author and his Three Children, Alexander D. Pope, Lucinda C. Pope, and Anne Pope. M,DCC,XCII. [New York: Charles L. Woodward, 1888.]
104, iv p. 22 cm.
A type facsimile reprint, with an index.

1889

In the Matter of Attorney's Fees paid for Services in Establishing the Right of the Creek Nation to Certain Lands and Securing Pay for the same. 1889. Washington: Thomas McGill & Co.
35 p. 23 cm. Wrapper title.

TULLAHASSEE MANUAL LABOR SCHOOL

Catalogue Tullehassee Manual Labor School. 1888–'89. Muskogee, Creek Nation, Indian Territory. School will open Wednesday, Sept. 5, 1889. Muskogee: Phoenix Steam Print, June, 1889.
8 p. 21 cm. Printed wrappers.

1890

Constitution and Laws of the Muskogee Nation, as compiled by L. C. Perryman, March 1st, 1890. Muskogee, Indian Ter.: Phoenix Printing Co., 1890.
250 p. 21.5 cm.

HAMMERER, JOHN DANIEL

An Account of a Plan for Civilizing the North American Indians, proposed in the Eighteenth Century. By John Daniel Hammerer. Edited by Paul Leicester Ford. Brooklyn, N.Y.: Historical Printing Club, 1890.*
28 p. 17.5 cm. Printed wrappers.
Reprinted from a unique copy of the 1766 edition. Hammerer specifically proposed a mission to the Creeks in the colony of Georgia, and his references to the tribe are of great value.

HODGE, DAVID M.

To the Committee on Indian Affairs of the House of Representatives of the 51st

Congress. In the Matter of the Claims of the Loyal Creeks for Losses sustained by the Military Authorities of the United States during the late Rebellion. Washington: McGill & Wallace, [1890].

14 p. 23.5 cm. Wrapper title.

The document is signed by David M. Hodge, Is-ha-he-char (Isparhechar?), and Co-we Har-jo.

Loughridge, R. M., and David M. Hodge

English and Muskokee Dictionary. Collected from Various Sources and revised, by Rev. R. M. Loughridge, D.D., Missionary to the Creek Indians, and Elder David M. Hodge, Interpreter, Creek Mission, Indian Territory. St. Louis: J. T. Smith, 1890.*

[8], 236 p. 19.5 cm.

A fine copy.

Memorial to the United States Congress from the Creek Indian People of Eufaula, Indian Ter. Denison, Texas: Murray's Steam Printing House, 1890.

8 p. 22 cm. Printed wrappers.

The only known copy.

1891

Fulfilling Treaties with the Creeks. [Washington, 1891.]

4 p. 24 cm. Caption title.

Memorial of the Delegates of the Creek Nation of Indians praying for the Passage of the Bill providing for the Payment of Awards made to Creek Indians who Enlisted in the Federal Army, Loyal Refugees, and Freedmen. [Washington, 1891.]

6 p. 22.5 cm. Caption title.

Payment of Awards to Creek Indians who Enlisted in the Federal Army. [Washington, 1891.]

6 p. 23 cm. Caption title.

1892

Rules of the House of Warriors, compiled and translated by A. P. McKellop, Clerk of the House of Warriors. 1892. Muskogee: Phoenix Printing Co., [1892].

11 p. 14.5 cm. Printed wrappers. Text in English and in Cherokee. The only known copy.

1893

Constitution and Laws of the Creek Nation, as compiled and codified by A. P. McKellop, under Act of October 15, 1892. Muskogee, Indian Ter.: F. C. Hubbard, printer, 1893.

243 p. 22 cm.

1894

Acts and Resolutions of the Creek National Council of the Extra Session of April, 1894, and the Regular Session of October, 1894. Compiled and translated by D. C. Watson. Muskogee: E. H. Hubbard, 1894.*

19, 22, [1] p. 22 cm. Printed wrappers.

Acts and Resolutions of the National Council of the Muskogee Nation of 1893. Compiled by W. A. Rentie. Muskogee, Ind. Ter.: Phoenix Printing Co., 1894.
[2], ii, 21, [2], 28 p. 21.5 cm. Printed wrappers.

Este Maskoke etvlwv emvhakv empvtakv momet emvhakv. D. C. Watson, etohtvlhocvtet os ot'voskv rvkko ennetta 15, 1892, vjakv hakvte vcvkyen. Maskoke estecate etvlwv: E. H. Hubbard & Co., svnoricvlke, 1894. [Muskogee, 1894.]
[1], 192, xxvii, [1] p. 21.5 cm.
The 1893 compilation, translated into Creek. General Pleasant Porter's copy.

The New Constitution of the Muskogee Nation. Proposed under Act of the National Council, approved November 2, 1893. English and Indian. Eufaula, I.T.: Indian Journal Printing Co., 1894.*
25 p. 22 cm. Printed wrappers.
One of five known copies.

PERRYMAN, LEGUS CHOUTEAU

Este Maskoke, Tvlwv Vlke. Rasahee Rakko en Netta es 4n. 1894, Omof Omahv Nvkvfte Kake. Tvlwv Vlke Em Mekko, Opunvkv Cvpko Emwvkecvte Momen, Wvcenv en Kvmesvnvlke Tvlwv Vlke em Vyuposkvte. [Muskotee, 1894.]
12 p. 20 cm.
A translation into Creek of the preceding volume.

PERRYMAN, LEGUS CHOUTEAU

Message of the Chief of the Muskogees, and Reply to the National Council in Extraordinary Session April 4, 1894, to the Dawes Commission. Eufaula: Journal, [1894].
11 p. 21.5 cm. Wrapper title.
A document of high interest and rarity.

1895

Acts and Resolutions of the Creek National Council of the Extra Session of January, 1895. Compiled and translated by D. C. Watson. Muskogee, Ind. Ter.: E. H. Hubbard & Co., 1895.
12, 12 p. 22 cm. Printed wrappers. Text in English and Creek.

HALBERT, H. S., and TIMOTHY H. HALL

The Creek War of 1813 and 1814. By H. S. Halbert and T. H. Hall. Chicago: Donohue & Henneberry, 1895.
331, [3] p. Portraits and maps. 19 cm.
An authority on the subject. The large folded map, southwestern Alabama, past and present, T. H. Hall, usually lacking, is present in this copy.

PENDLETON, LOUIS

In the Okefenokee. A Story of War Time and the Great Georgia Swamp. Boston: Roberts Bros., 1895.*
182 p. 19 cm. Illus.
The Okefenokee Swamp was for many years a refuge of irreconcilable Creeks and

Seminoles. The volume is very scarce. The present copy formerly belonged to the Reverend J. S. Murrow, the Indian Territory Baptist missionary.

1896

Acts and Resolutions of the Creek National Council of the Called Session of August, and the Regular Session of October, 1896. With Creek Translation. Compiled and translated by D. C. Watson. Muskogee, Ind. Ter.: Phoenix Printing Co., 1896.*

23, 25 p. 21.5 cm.

One of only four known copies.

Acts and Resolutions of the Creek National Council of the Sessions of May, June, October, November and December, 1895. Compiled and translated by D. C. Watson. Muskogee: Phoenix Printing Co., 1896.

40 p. 21 cm.

One of four known copies.

WIGHTMAN, WILLIAM M.

Life of William Capers, D.D., one of the Bishops of the Methodist Episcopal Church, South; including an Autobiography. By William M. Wightman, D.D., President of Wofford College. Nashville, Tenn., 1896.*

516 p. 17.5 cm.

The volume contains valuable information on the first Methodist mission, established by Capers, to the Creeks of Georgia and Alabama, and a fine account of a Creek ball play.

1897

Agreement between the United States Commissioners to Negotiate with the Five Civilized Tribes and the Commissioners on the part of the Muscogee or Creek Nation. [Muskogee, 1897.]

[8] p. 23 cm. Caption title.

Agreement between the United States Commissioners to negotiate with the Five Civilized Tribes and the Commissioners on the part of the Muscogee or Creek Nation. [Washington, 1897.]

7 p. 22.5 cm. Wrapper title.

GRAYSON, G. W.

[A letter entirely in Creek, dated Tvlwv Hvtke, Ke-hvse 16, 1897, and signed Yvhv Tvstvnke.] [Muskogee? 1897.]

[2] p. 24 cm.

1899

Agreement between the United States Commissioners to negotiate with the Five Civilized Tribes and the Commissioners on the part of the Creek (or Muskogee) Nation. Concluded at Muskogee, Ind. Ter., February 1, 1899. [N.p., 1899.]

15 p. 22.5 cm.

ROBERTSON, A. E. W., tr.

Teleko-vhake opunvkv-svhopakv ofv pu hesayecvt opunvyecvte. Opunvkvherv maro coyvte 13:25-30. A. E. Robertson, tohtvlecicv, translator. Siloam Springs, Ark. Presbyterian Mission Press, Rev. F. L. Schaub, tvlemicv, 1899.

[4] p. 16.5 cm.

1900

Acts and Resolutions of the National Council of the Muskogee Nation of 1893 and 1899, inclusive. Muskogee, Ind. Ter.: Phoenix Printing Co., 1900.

94, iv p. 21 cm.

Permit Law of the Muskogee Nation, approved November 5, 1900. [Okmulgee, 1900.]

4 p. 21.5 cm.

One of only three known copies.

1901

An Act to Ratify and Confirm an Agreement with the Muscogee or Creek Tribe of Indians, and for other purposes. [Washington, 1901.]

13 p. 23 cm. Caption title.

1902

Creek Agreement. Proclamation. [Washington, 1902.]

Broadside. Folio.

A proclamation by President Theodore Roosevelt of the ratification of the Creek agreement of June 30, 1902.

The Creek Treaty. Passed by Congress, February, 1901. And Suplemental [sic] Creek Agreement ratified July 26, 1902, officially proclaimed, August 8, 1902. With Creek Translation. Muskogee: Phoenix Printing Co., [1902].

12, 18, 8, 9 p. 21.5 cm. Wrapper title.

Owen, Robert L.

Agricultural Contracts in the Creek Nation. Submitted by Robert L. Owen, etc. Washington: Judd & Detweiler, [1902].

12 p. 23.5 cm. Wrapper title.

1903

Rules of the House of Warriors. Adopted December 7, 1903. Okmulgee, Ind. Ter.: Chieftain Printing House, [1903].

15 p. 15 cm. Printed wrappers.

One of only four known copies.

1904

Cross, A. B., and others

A Souvenir of Muskogee, the Queen City of the Indian Territory. [Muskogee, 1904.]*

[36] p. 19.5 cm. Wrapper title.

Chiefly interesting for its thirty-four full pages of photographic views and scenes of Muskogee.

1907

SPECK, FRANK G.

The Creek Indians of Taskigi Town. Lancaster, Pa.: New Era Printing Co., 1907.*

[99]–164 p. 25 cm. Printed wrappers.

Memoirs of the American Anthropological Society, Vol. 2, part 2. An important paper.

1908

Equalization of Creek Allotments. Hearing before the Committee on Indian Affairs, House of Representatives. Washington, 1908.

52 p. 23 cm.

1914

A Memorial to Congress in the matter of the Preservation of the Creek Indian Council House at Okmulgee, Oklahoma. [Okmulgee, 1914.]

2 p. on 2 leaves broadside. 28.5 cm.

At the head of the first leaf is a photograph of the council house.

TIGER, MOTY

Message of Moty Tiger, Principal Chief of the Creek Nation, to the Extra Ordinary Session of the National Council of said Nation called by Authority of an Act of Congress, which convened at Okmulgee on September 1st, 1914. And the Actions and Proceedings thereof in the Creek and English Languages. Rendered into Creek by G. W. Grayson. Eufaula, Oklahoma: Indian Journal, printers, [1914].

64 p. 22.5 cm. Wrapper title.

The final official publication of the Creek government. The volume is very rare.

1916

HAWKINS, BENJAMIN

Letters of Benjamin Hawkins 1796–1806. Savannah, Ga., 1906.*

500 p. 24 cm. Folded map. Frontisp. port.

One of the most valuable source volumes on the Creek Indians.

Loyal Creek Claim. Hearings before a Subcommittee of the Committee on Indian Affairs of the House of Representatives. Washington, 1916.

37 p. 23 cm.

ROBERTSON, W. S., and DAVID WINSLETT

Nakcokv es kerretv enhvteceskv. Muskokee or Creek First Reader. Fifth edition. Philadelphia, 1916.

48 p. 17.5 cm.

1920

Handbook of the Alabama Anthropological Society. Compiled by the President. Montgomery, 1920.*

60 p. 22 cm. Printed wrappers.

Contains a valuable descriptive list of aboriginal towns in Alabama, with locations by county.

1922

PAINE, ROBERT

Life and Times of William McKendree, Bishop of the Methodist Episcopal Church. By Robert Paine, D.D., Bishop of the Methodist Episcopal Church, South. Nashville, Tenn., 1922.

549 p. 22 cm.

Contains an account of the establishment in 1821 by William Capers of the first Methodist mission to the Creeks, an important letter on the subject from Capers to McKendree, and narratives of visits by McKendree to the Wyandots and the Cherokees.

1926

MCQUEEN, A. S., and HAMP MIZELL

History of the Okefenokee Swamp. Clinton, S.C.: Jacobs and Company, [1926].

191 p. 19.5 cm. Map, plates.

The Okefenokee Swamp was long a refuge for irreconcilable Creeks and Seminoles. Printed in a small edition, the volume is very scarce.

Undated

ROBERTSON, ANN ELIZA WORCESTER

Fifty-third and Fifty-fifth Chapters of Isaiah. Cokv Owale Esivs Coyvte. [Muskogee? n.d.]*

[5] p. on one folded leaf. Caption title.

Translated into Creek.

ROBERTSON, ANN E. W., tr.

"Home Sweet Home." Hute Cvmpusat. [Muskogee? n.d.]*

Broadside. 11.5 cm.

Translated into Creek.

ROBERTSON, ANN E. W., tr.

"Kerkv here hvlvtaye tayat orusen hayvs." [New York, n.d.]*

12 p. 12 cm. Caption title.

A translation into Creek of a missionary tract entitled, "Make it so plain that I can get hold of it." Accompanied by a copy of the tract in English.

ROBERTSON, ANN E. W., tr.

Sele Estemerrat. A. E. W. R. tohtvlecicv. [New York, n.d.]*

12 p. 17.5 cm. Caption title.

"Poor Sarah," the long popular missionary tract, translated into Creek.

ROBERTSON, ANN E. W., tr.

Uewv Espaptisetv momet yafkehompetv. [Philadelphia, n.d.]*

8 p. 18 cm. Caption title.

At end: Presented to the Muskogee and Seminole people by Mrs. Thomas Stocks, Greensborough, Georgia, through J. S. Murrow, missionary.

DAKOTA INDIANS

1858

The Constitution of Minnesota in the Dakota Language, translated by Stephen R. Riggs, A.M. By Order of the Hazlewood Republic. Boston: T. R. Marvin & Son, 1858.

36 p. 19 cm.

The only instance known of the translation of a state constitution into an Indian language. Excessively rare. Pilling located only one copy.

1865

Hinman, Samuel Dutton

Ikce wocekiye wowapi. Oa isantanka makoce. Kin en token wohduze, qa okodakiciye wakan en tonakiya woecon kin, hena de he wowapi kin ee. Samuel Dutton Hinman, missionary to Dakotas. St. Paul: Pioneer Printing Company. 1865.

ix, 321 p. 21 cm.

Common prayer book, in the Santee language. Rare.

1869

Hinman, Samuel D.

Dakota Indians. To the Friends of the Santee Indian Mission. [Philadelphia, 1869.]

20 p. 22.5 cm. Caption title.

Pages 2–20 are devoted to a highly interesting journal kept by Hinman at Santee Mission.

1876

Sheridan, P. H.

[Reports on events in the Military Division of the Missouri. New Orleans, 1876.]*

7 p. on 7 leaves broadside. Folio.

A detailed and valuable report on the Indian troubles in Dakota, Montana, and Wyoming.

1879

Sheridan, P. H.

[Report of operations in the Military Division of the Missouri. Chicago, 1879.]*

4 p. Folio.

Detailed report on campaigns against hostile Indians in Dakota, New Mexico, Colorado, and Texas.

1885

Crow Creek Reservation, Dakota. Action of the Indian Rights Association, and Opinions of the Press, West and East, regarding its Recent Occupation by White Settlers, together with the Proclamation of the President commanding the Removal of the Settlers and restoring the Lands to the Indians. Philadelphia, 1885.*

45 p. 23.5 cm. Printed wrappers.

1888

Hare, William Hobart

Reminiscences. An Address delivered by William Hobart Hare, Missionary

Bishop of South Dakota, at a Service Commemorative of the Fiftieth Anniversary of his Consecration. Philadelphia: William F. Fell & Co., 1888.*

25 p. 23 cm. Printed wrappers.

1891

HARE, WILLIAM HOBART

South Dakota okna Niobrara Deanery omniciye kin 1891. [Sioux Falls, 1891.]*

[14] p. 22.5 cm. Wrapper title. Plates.

Rare.

1910

Papers relating to Talks and Councils held with the Indians in Dakota and Montana Territories in the years 1866–1869. Washington, 1910.

133 p. 23 cm. Printed wrappers.

A fine copy. Despite its fairly recent date, this valuable compilation is quite rare.

1934

Minutes of the Plains Congress. Rapid City Indian School, Rapid City, South Dakota, March 2–5, 1934. Lawrence, Kansas: Haskell Institute, 1934.*

[2], 149 p. 21.5 cm. Printed wrappers.

Very scarce.

DELAWARE INDIANS

1805

Message from the President of the United States transmitting Copies of Treaties, which have lately been entered into, and concluded, between the United States and the Delaware Tribe of Indians; the Piankeshaw Tribe of Indians; and the United Tribes of Sac and Fox Indians. Washington City: William Duane & Son, 1805.

22 p. 23 cm.

Very rare.

1834

Linapi'e lrkvekun, ave apwatuk. Wunhi nrtyrkvekrs, maneto. Jrpuna bni lipwrokun. Shawanoe Mission, J. Meeker, Printer, 1834.

48 p. 15 cm. Printed wrappers.

A primer in the Delaware language. Excessively rare and not recorded in the Union Catalog. Pilling located but one copy.

1837

ZEISBERGER, DAVID, and I. D. BLANCHARD

The History of Our Lord and Saviour Jesus Christ; comprehending all that the Four Evangelists have recorded concerning Him. Translated into the Delaware Language, in 1806, by Rev. David Zeisberger, Missionary of the United Bretheren. Retranslated, so as to conform to the Present Idiom of that Language, by I. D. Blanchard. J. Meeker, Printer, Shawanoe Baptist Mission. 1837.

221 p. 16 cm.

Pilling, Algonquian Bibliography, p. 547.

One of only three known copies.

1838

LUCKENBACH, A., tr.

Forty-six Select Scriptural Narratives from the Old Testament. Embellished with Engravings, for the Use of Indian Youth. Translated into Delaware Indian, by A. Luckenbach. New York: Daniel Fanshaw, 1838.

xiv, 304 p. 18 cm.

Pilling, Algonquian Bibliography, p. 318.

1846

PEERY, E. T.

Select Hymns with their Translations in the Delaware language on the Opposite Page. By Rev. E. T. Peery, with the Aid of Interpreters. Indian Manual Labor School, 1846.

84 p. 16.5 cm.

Not recorded by Pilling or by the Union Catalog, and probably the only known copy.

1867

BARTLING, H.

Timber Lands of Delaware Diminished Reserve! Public Notice. Tribune Print, Lawrence, [1867].

Broadside. Folio.

A warning against illegal cutting of timber on the reservation. Unrecorded, and the only known copy.

1890

Charles Journeycake, Principal Chief of the Delaware Indians, Plaintiff, v. The Cherokee Nation and the United States, Defendants. Suit under Provisions of Special Act of Congress. Washington: Gibson Bros., 1890.*

12 p. 23 cm. Wrapper title.

Tabulated Statement showing Financial Condition of Delaware Indians, in Indian Territory. April, 1890. [Muskogee, 1890.]

[8] p. 22.5 cm.

Not in Foreman, and no other copy traced.

1893

Protest against the Payment of Certain Moneys and the Interest thereon to either the Delaware or the United Tribe of Wea, &c., Indians. [Washington, 1893.]

3 p. 24.5 cm. Caption title.

1899

ADAMS, RICHARD C.

A Delaware Indian Legend and the Story of their Troubles. By Richard C. Adams, representing the Delaware Indians. Washington, 1899.

72, 3 p. 22 cm.

1903

Memorial of the Delaware Indians residing in the Cherokee Nation praying

Relief relative to the Rights in and Ownership of Certain Lands within the Boundaries of said Nation. [Washington, 1903.]

192 p. 23 cm. Caption title.

Contains Richard C. Adams' Brief History of the Delaware Indians.

1906

ADAMS, RICHARD C.

A Brief History of the Delaware Indians. [Washington, 1906.]

70 p. 23 cm. Caption title.

Besides the history of the tribe, the volume contains also the 1866 constitution of the Delaware Nation. Adams was himself a Delaware Indian and his account is reliable.

ADAMS, RICHARD C.

Memorial of the Delaware Indians to the Congress of the United States. [Washington, 1906.]

9 p. 21.5 cm. Wrapper title.

1910

Hearing held before the Committee on the Public Lands of the House of Representatives, December 19, 1910, on H.R. 22069 to compensate the Delaware Indians for Services rendered by them to the United States in Various Wars. Washington, 1910.

15 p. 23.5 cm.

FIVE CIVILIZED TRIBES

1894

Address of the United States Commission to the Five Tribes. [Muskogee, 1894.]

4 p. 22.5 cm. Caption title.

Very scarce.

Denial of Indians to Charges of Dawes Commission. Washington: Gibson Bros., 1894.

40 p. 23 cm. Printed wrappers.

A very scarce pamphlet.

Extra Census Bulletin. The Five Civilized Tribes in Indian Territory; the Cherokee, Chickasaw, Choctaw, Creek, and Seminole Nations. Washington: United States Census Printing Office, 1894.

70 p. 30 cm. Printed wrappers. Folded color map. Photographs.

A fine copy.

1895

An Appeal by the Delegates of the Five Civilized Nations of Indians to the Congress of the United States for Justice. [N.p., 1895.]

4 p. 22.5 cm. Wrapper title.

DUNCAN, W. A., and others

Remarks by Walter A. Duncan, Roach Young and Judge I. C. Parker before the House Judiciary Committee on change of Government for the Five Civilized Tribes

and Remonstrance of Indian Delegates. [N.p., 1895.]
38 p. 23 cm. Wrapper title.

TALIAFERRO, T. D.
Report of the Dawes Commission Analyzed and Statement Sharply Controverted. Washington: Gibson Bros., [1895].
19 p. 23.5 cm. Wrapper title.

1896

DAWES COMMISSION
Vinita, Indian Territory, July 8, 1896. To whom it may concern. [Vinita, 1896.]
3 p. 22 cm. Caption title.
Instructions to claimants to Indian citizenship. Unrecorded, and no other copy traced.

[Resolutions adopted at a meeting the delegates of the Five Civilized Tribes thanking the Legislature of Mississippi for its memorial to Congress in behalf of the Indians. N.p., 1896.]
Broadside. 25.5 cm.
No other copy traced.

1897

Commission to the Five Civilized Tribes. Annual Reports of 1894, 1895 and 1896. Also Correspondence with the Representatives of the Five Civilized Tribes from March 3, 1893, to January 1, 1897. [Washington, 1897.]
171 p. 22 cm. Printed wrappers.

1898

Annual Report of the Commission to the Five Civilized Tribes in the Indian Territory to the Secretary of the Interior. 1898. Washington, 1898.
42 p. 23 cm. Printed wrappers.

1899

JONES, W. A.
[Instructions to the Commission to the Five Civilized Tribes on the preparation of the final rolls of those tribes. Washington, 1899.]
Broadside. 26.5 cm.

1903

Chief Executives of Five Civilized Tribes adopt Plans for a Prohibition State. Protest against Territorial Form of Government or Annexation to Oklahoma. [Eufaula, 1903.]*
[6] p. 15.5 cm.
No other copy is known.

Chief Executives of Five Civilized Tribes adopt Plans for a Prohibition State. Protest against Territorial Form of Government or Annexation to Oklahoma. [N.p., 1903.]
[4] p. 16 cm. Printed wrappers.

Tenth Annual Report of the Commission to the Five Civilized Tribes to the

Secretary of the Interior for the Fiscal Year ended June 30, 1903. Washington, 1903.
192 p. 23 cm. Printed wrappers. Folded color maps.

1904

Eleventh Annual Report of the Commission to the Five Civilized Tribes to the Secretary of the Interior, for the year ended June 30, 1904. Washington, 1904.*
202 p. 23 cm. Printed wrappers. 7 large folded color maps.

1906

Index to the Annual Reports of the Commission to the Five Civilized Tribes for the years 1894 to 1905, inclusive. Washington, 1906.
136 p. 23 cm. Printed wrappers.
An indispensable tool.

Legislation relating to Five Civilized Tribes. Fifty-ninth Congress, First Session. [Carlisle, Pa.: Carlisle Indian School, 1906.]
17 p. 23 cm. Caption title.

Report of the Commissioner to the Five Civilized Tribes for the year ended June 30, 1906. Washington, 1906.
71 p. 23 cm. Printed wrappers.

1907

Amendments to Existing Regulations for Leasing Allotted Land in the Five Civilized Tribes. [N.p., 1907.]
[4] p. 20.5 cm. Caption title.

The Final Rolls of Citizens and Freedmen of the Five Civilized Tribes in Indian Territory. [Muskogee, 1907.]
[2], 634 p. 23 cm.

Index to the Final Rolls of Citizens and Freedmen of the Five Civilized Tribes in Indian Territory. Muskogee, [1907].
[2], 634, [2] p. 23 cm. 3 p. of errata inserted at front.

Report of the Commissioner to the Five Civilized Tribes to the Secretary of the Interior for the Fiscal Year ended June 30, 1907. Washington, 1907.
48 p. 23 cm. Printed wrappers.

1908

An Act for the Removal of Restrictions from part of the Lands of Allottees of the Five Civilized Tribes, and for other purposes. [Washington, 1908.]
6 p. 22.5 cm. Caption title.

Report of the Commissioner to the Five Civilized Tribes to the Secretary of the Interior, for the Fiscal Year ended June 30, 1908. Washington, 1908.
74 p. 23 cm. Printed wrappers.

1913

Five Civilized Tribes in Oklahoma. Reports of the Department of Interior and

Evidentiary Papers in support of S. 7625, a Bill for the Relief of Certain Members of the Five Civilized Tribes in Oklahoma. Washington, 1913.

666 p. 23.5 cm. Printed wrappers.

1914

Report of the Commissioner to the Five Civilized Tribes, accompanied by the Reports of the Superintendent of the Union Agency and the Supervisor of Schools, for the Fiscal Year ended June 30, 1914. Washington, 1914.

112 p. 23 cm. Printed wrappers.

Rules of Procedure, Five Civilized Tribes. Rules of Procedure in Probate Matters adopted by the County Judges of the Five Civilized Tribes portion of Oklahoma, together with the Resolutions and Statements of approval thereto attached. [Washington, 1914.]

8 p. 24.5 cm. Caption title.

FUR TRADE

1824

Mr. Benton, from the Committee on Indian Affairs, communicated the Following Documents. [Washington, 1824.]*

20 p. 22.5 cm. Caption title.

A report of the highest importance, with valuable information on the fur trade with the western Indians. Half the document is devoted to a statement by Joshua Pilcher.

Mr. Benton, from the Committee on Indian Affairs, laid on the table the Following Documents. [Washington, 1824.]*

6 p. 22 cm. Caption title.

Letters on Arikara and Mandan attacks upon traders and agents of the Missouri Fur Company and the Columbia Fur Company.

1826

Mr. Benton, from the Committee on Indian Affairs, reported a bill "For the Better Regulation of the Fur Trade," and laid on the table the Following Documents in relation thereto. [Washington, 1826.]

12 p. 21.5 cm. Caption title.

The documents include letters from Bernard Pratte, Robert Stuart, Lewis Cass, and Thomas L. McKenney.

1828

Mr. Benton made the Following Report: The Committee on Indian Affairs, to whom was referred the Resolution instructing them to inquire into the Present Condition of the Fur Trade, and to report what Measures, if any, are necessary to be adopted for the Safe and Successful Prosecution of that Trade by American Citizens, report.... [Washington, 1828.]

19 p. 20.5 cm. Caption title.

The document contains communications, whose importance can scarcely be exaggerated, from William Clark, Lewis Cass, W. H. Ashley, C. C. Cambreleng, and John Jacob Astor.

1832

Message from the President of the United States, in compliance with a Resolution of the Senate, concerning the Fur Trade and Inland Trade to Mexico. [Washington, 1832.]*

86 p. 22.5 cm. Caption title.

Wagner-Camp 46.

An invaluable document. Letters and reports by Joshua Pilcher, John Jacob Astor, A. P. Chouteau, Henry R. Schoolcraft, and Alphonso Wetmore. Among the most interesting is Wetmore's diary of a journey made in 1828 from Missouri to New Mexico.

1937

Kurz, Rudolph Friederich

Journal of Rudolph Friederich Kurz. An Account of His Experiences among Fur Traders and American Indians on the Mississippi and the Upper Missouri Rivers during the years 1846 to 1852. Translated by Myrtis Jarrell. Edited by J. N. B. Hewitt. Washington, 1937.*

ix, 382 p. 23.5 cm. Printed wrappers.

GEORGIA INDIANS

1739

Whitfield, George

A Continuation of the Reverend Mr. Whitfield's Journal from his Arrival at Savannah to his Return to London. The Second Edition. London: W. Strahan, 1739.

[4], 38 p. 21 cm.

Contains an account of a visit by Whitfield to the dying Tomochichi.

1741

Martyn, Benjamin

An Impartial Enquiry into the State and Utility of the Province of Georgia. London: W. Meadows, 1741.

[4], 104 p. 22 cm.

A fine, uncut copy of the rare first edition, complete with half title. Contains a valuable account of the Indians. George Grenville's copy, with his book plate. Grenville was the author of the Stamp Act.

1742

Stephens, William

A State of the Province of Georgia, attested upon Oath in the Court of Savannah, November 10, 1740. London: W. Meadows, 1742.

[4], 32 p. 22 cm.

A fine, uncut copy of the rare first edition, complete with half title. An important account of the Indians living on the frontiers of the colony. George Grenville's copy. [See page 194.]

1743

Stephens, Thomas

A Brief Account of the Causes that have Retarded the Progress of the Colony of

A STATE OF THE Province of *Georgia*,

Atteſted upon OATH

IN THE

COURT of SAVANNAH,

November 10, 1740.

LONDON:
Printed for W. MEADOWS, at the *Angel* in *Cornhill.*
MDCCXLII.

Georgia, in America; attested upon Oath. Being a Proper Contrast to a State of the Province of Georgia, attested upon Oath; and some other Misrepresentations on the same Subject. London, 1743.*

[4], 24, 101 p. 20 cm.

The rare first edition, complete with half title. Contains valuable notices of trade with the Creek and Chickasaw Indians. George Grenville's copy.

1748

THORESBY, RALPH

The Excellency and Advantage of Doing Good; represented in a Sermon preached before the Honourable Trustees for Establishing the Colony of Georgia in America. To which is annex'd a Letter of Samuel Loyd, Esq. concerning the Nature and Goodness of the Georgia Silk. London: W. Meadows, 1748.

[2], [5]–21, [1] p. 21.5 cm.

Collates perfect, in agreement with the De Renne copy. Contains highly interesting references to the inroads of the Spanish Indians to the South.

1800

An Address and Remonstrance of the Legislature of the State of Georgia. [Louisville, Georgia? 1800.]

18 p. 22.5 cm.

A presentation of Georgia's claim to the Western Territory then occupied by the Indians.

1811

MCCALL, HUGH

The History of Georgia. Savannah: Seymour & Williams, 1811–1816.

2 vols. Original boards.

Rare in any condition and excessively rare in the original printed boards. Written by a contemporary, it is the foundation of much of our present day knowledge of the history of Georgia and its Indians.

1816

Acts of the General Assembly of the State of Georgia, passed at Milledgeville at an Annual Session in November and December, 1816. Published by Authority. Milledgeville: S. & F. Grantland, 1816.*

122, viii p. 20 cm.

Important resolutions and memorials on Indian affairs and Indian lands.

Journal of the Senate of the State of Georgia at an Annual Session of the General Assembly, begun and held at Milledgeville, the Seat of Government, in November and December, 1816. Milledgeville: S. & F. Grantland, State Printers, [1816].

71 p. 26.5 cm. Folded table.

Important reports on extinguishment of Indian land titles in Georgia.

1817

Acts of the General Assembly of the State of Georgia, passed at Milledgeville, at an Annual Session in November and December, 1817. Published by Authority. Milledgeville: S. & F. Grantland, 1817.*

164, v p. 20 cm.

Provisions for the disposition of lands lately acquired or about to be acquired from the Creeks and Cherokees.

1818

Acts of the General Assembly of the State of Georgia, passed at Milledgeville, at an Annual Session, in November & December, 1818. Published by Authority. Milledgeville: S. & F. Grantland, 1818.

235, v p. 20 cm.

Important acts relating to Indians and Indian lands. This is one of the rarest of all Georgia laws, the great collector, W. J. DeRenne, having never succeeded in obtaining a copy.

1821

Acts of the General Assembly of the State of Georgia, passed at Milledgeville, at an Annual Session, in November and December, 1821. Published by authority. Milledgeville: Camak & Hines, 1821.*

163 p. 20 cm.

1822

Message from the President of the United States upon the Subject of the Extinguishment of the Indian Title to Land within the State of Georgia. Washington: Gales & Seaton, 1822.

3 p. 22.5 cm.

1824

Acts of the General Assembly of the State of Georgia, passed at Milledgeville, at an Annual Session in November and December, 1823. Published by Authority. Milledgeville: Camak & Ragland, 1824.

270 p. 23.5 cm. Plain wrappers.

Legislation and reports on Indian matters.

Message of the President of the United States transmitting certain papers relating to the Compact between the U. States & the State of Georgia of 1802, &c. Washington: Gales & Seaton, 1824.

82 p. 22.5 cm.

By the Compact of 1802, Georgia ceded her western lands, then occupied by Cherokee, Creek, Choctaw, and Chickasaw Indians, to the United States. The volume contains many pertinent documents bearing upon the negotiations of the Georgia commissioners with the Indians.

Report of the Select Committee to which was referred the President's Message, of the 30th of March, 1826, relating to the Compact of 1802 between the United States and the State of Georgia; also, a Memorial of the Legislature of the said State upon the same subject. [Washington, 1824.]

18 p. 22.5 cm. Caption title.

1826

Acts of the General Assembly of the State of Georgia, passed in Milledgeville, at an Annual Session in Nov. and Dec. 1826. Milledgeville: Camak & Ragland, 1826.

248 p. 23 cm. Plain wrappers. Uncut and unopened.

Contains important laws and reports relating to the Indians. [See page 197.]

ACTS

OF THE

General Assembly,

OF

THE STATE OF GEORGIA,

PASSED IN MILLEDGEVILLE,

AT AN ANNUAL SESSION

IN NOV. AND DEC.

1826.

MILLEDGEVILLE:
PRINTED BY CAMAK & RAGLAND

1826.

1830

Acts of the General Assembly of the State of Georgia, passed in Milledgeville at an Annual Session in November and December, 1829. Published by Authority. Milledgeville: Camak & Ragland, 1830.

299 p. 23.5 cm. Plain wrappers.

Important acts relating to the Indians.

1831

Acts of the General Assembly of the State of Georgia, passed at Milledgeville at an Annual Session in October, November and December, 1830. Published by Authority. Milledgeville: Camak & Ragland, 1831.

312, 16 p. 24 cm. Uncut and unopened. Plain wrappers.

Important acts relating to the Indians.

1844

Elliott, Stephen

A High Civilization the Moral Duty of Georgians. A Discourse delivered before the Georgia Historical Society on the Occasion of its Fifth Anniversary. Savannah, 1844.

21 p. 24.5 cm.

Contains important observations on Georgia's Indian policy.

1877

Smith, George G., Jr.

The History of Methodism in Georgia and Florida, from 1785 to 1865. By Geo. G. Smith, Jr., of North Georgia Conference. Macon, Ga.: Jno. W. Burke & Co. 1877.

530 p. 18.5 cm. Portraits.

Important for its background of frontier and Indians. Ex-library copy.

1878

Jones, Charles Colcock, Jr.

The Dead Towns of Georgia. Savannah: Morning News, 1878.

263 p. 23.5 cm.

Information on Indian forays and depredations in the eighteenth century.

1883

Jones, Charles Colcock, Jr.

The History of Georgia. Boston: Houghton Mifflin & Co., 1883.

2 vols. Maps and plates.

A prime source of information about Georgia Indians in the Colonial and Revolutionary periods. This is one of the very best American colonial histories. A fine copy.

1887

Report of the Committee appointed by the General Assembly of South Carolina in 1740, on the St. Augustine Expedition under General Ogelthorpe. Charleston: Walker, Evans & Cogswell, 1887.*

178 p. 23.5 cm.

Considerable information on General Ogelthorpe's employment of Indians in the war against the Spaniards.

1932

Georgia Colonial Laws, 17th February 1755–10th May 1770. Savannah: James Johnston, 1763–1770. Washington: Reprinted by the Statute Law Book Co., 1932.

[564] p. 28 cm.

Highly important laws, whose text is nowhere else available, relating to trade and intercourse with the Indians. A facsimile reprint, on all rag paper, of the unprocurable original sessional issues. One of only thirty copies issued.

1942

BARTRAM, JOHN

Diary of a Journey through the Carolinas, Georgia, and Florida, from July 1, 1765, to April 10, 1766. Annotated by Francis Harper. Philadelphia: American Philosophical Society, 1942.

[4], 120 p. 30 cm. Printed wrappers. Plates.

This and the companion volume, which follows, contain highly important observations on the Georgia and Florida Indians. The annotations are a model of their kind.

1943

BARTRAM, WILLIAM

Travels in Georgia and Florida, 1773–74. A Report to Dr. John Fothergill. Annotated by Francis Harper. Philadelphia: American Philosophical Society, 1943.

[2], 121–242 p. 30 cm. Printed wrappers. Plates.

Undated

PATTERSON, ISABEL GARRARD

Archaeology of Georgia. Athens, Ga. [N.d.]*

16 p. Mimeographed. Wrapper title.

GREER COUNTY

1883

ROBERTS, O. M.

Message of the Governor. Greer County. [Austin, Texas, 1883.]

8 p. 23.5 cm. Wrapper title. 4 maps.

An able presentation of the State of Texas' title to the disputed Greer County. Rare.

Title of Greer County Investigated by John M. Swisher, with Opinions of Ex-Gov. E. M. Pease and Major Wm. M. Walton. Austin, Texas: American Sketch Book Publishing House, 1883.

16 p. 22 cm. Wrapper title.

Very scarce.

1884

Letter from the Secretary of the Interior transmitting Information concerning the Status of Certain Lands in the Indian Territory. [Washington, 1884.]*

18 p. 23 cm. Caption title.

SWISHER, JOHN M.

Greer County. [Austin, Texas, 1884.]

17 p. 21.5 cm. Wrapper title.

A review by the Governor of Texas of his state's claim to Greer County. Autographed by the author. Rare.

1887

WORKS, J. S. (BUCKSKIN JOE)

February Report of the Texas Oklahoma Homestead Colony. Organized December, 1885. Office at Queen City, Texas. [Queen City, 1887.]*

Broadsheet. 27 cm.

The colony was organized with the object of making a settlement in Greer County. The only known copy.

1888

Free Home Excursion to Greer County in the New Oklahoma leaves Kansas City April 4th, May 9th, June 6th, 1888. Kansas City: Kimberly & Hudson, [1888].

Broadsheet. 23 cm.

The beauties, advantages, and virtues of the country are set forth. The only known copy.

1894

[Record in the Greer County Case. i.e., the suit brought by the United States against the State of Texas to determine the status of Greer County. Washington: Judd & Detweiler, 1894.]

2 vols. Scores of maps.

Foreman: "The trial of this law suit developed more of historical interest touching the State of Oklahoma than any other law suit ever tried. Within the printed record of fourteen hundred pages is compressed more historical material concerning Oklahoma otherwise unpublished and unknown than is to be found in any other printed document." Perhaps the most valuable single publication on the early history of Oklahoma and its Indians.

HAIDA INDIANS

1889

[The Lord's Prayer, translated into Haida by Charles Harrison. Masset, 1889?].*

Card. 10.7 × 8 cm.

One of only two known copies. See Butler, Checklist (1941), Haida 9.

SAM HOUSTON

1855

HOUSTON, SAM

Speeches of Sam Houston, of Texas, on the subject of an Increase of the Army, and the Indian Policy of the Government, delivered in the Senate of the United States, January 29 and 31, 1855. Washington: Printed at the Office of the Congressional Globe, 1855.

20 p. 24 cm.

A fine, uncut copy.

1859

Life of General Sam Houston. [Washington: J. T. Towers, 1859.]

15 p. 24 cm. Caption title.
A fine copy, uncut and unopened. Very scarce.

IDAHO

1864

Laws of the Territory of Idaho, First Session; convened the 7th day of December, 1863, and adjourned on the 4th day of February, 1864, at Lewiston. Also, containing the Territorial Organic Act, Declaration of Independence, the Federal Constitution, the Pre-emption, and Naturalization Laws, etc., etc. Lewiston: James A. Glascock, 1864.

686, xxxvi p. 20.5 cm.
Contains highly important acts, resolutions, and memorials on Indian affairs. The first Idaho laws.

1874

Proposed Indian Reservations in Idaho and Washington Territories. [Washington, 1874.]*

11 p. 22 cm. Caption title.

INDIAN HOSTILITIES

1838

GRAHAM, JAMES

Speech of Mr. James Graham, of North Carolina, on the Bill making an Appropriation to Prevent and Suppress Indian Hostilities. Delivered in the House of Representatives, May 24, 1838. Washington: Gales & Seaton, 1838.

14 p. 22.5 cm.

Indians Hostile on Western Frontier. Letter from the Secretary of War upon the subject of a Hostile Disposition upon the part of the Indians on the Western Frontier. [Washington, 1838.]

10 p. 24.5 cm. Caption title.

TOWNS, GEORGE WASHINGTON BONAPARTE

Speech of Mr. Towns, of Georgia, on the bill making Appropriations for Suppressing Indian Hostilities. Delivered in the House of Representatives of the United States, May 23, 1838. Washington: Printed at the Globe Office. 1838.

14 p. 22.5 cm.

TURNEY, HOPKINS LACY

Speech of Mr. Turney, of Tennessee, on the Bill to Suppress Indian Hostilities. [Washington, 1838.]

7 p. 25 cm. Caption title.

1858

Head Quarters of the Army, June 29, 1858. General Orders, No. 17. [New York, 1858.]*

4 p. 19 cm.

Re-assignment of troops, freed by the collapse of Mormon resistance in Utah, to theatres of Indian hostilities.

Head-quarters of the Army, New York, November 10, 1858. General Orders, No. 22. [New York, 1858.]*

11 p. 20 cm. Caption title.

A summary of combats with hostile Indians in 1857 and 1858.

1859

Head-quarters of the Army, New York, November 10th, 1859. General Orders, No. 5. [New York, 1859.]

8 p. 20 cm. Caption title.

Summary of combats with hostile Indians in 1858 and 1859.

1860

Head-quarters of the Army, New York, November 23, 1860. General Orders, No. 11. [New York, 1860.]

19 p. 20 cm. Caption title.

Summary of combats with hostile Indians in 1859 and 1860.

1865

Head-Qrs. Dist. of the Upper Arkansas, Fort Riley, Kansas, June 29th, 1865. General Orders No. 22. [Fort Riley, 1865.]

Broadside. 20 cm.

Official notice of an attack by a large body of Indians upon a mail coach a few miles from Cow Creek Station and of the pursuit and defeat of the marauders by Lieutenant Richard W. Jenkins and seven of his men.

Head-Qrs. Dist. of the Upper Arkansas, Fort Riley, Kansas, July 20th, 1865. General Orders No. 30. [Fort Riley, 1865.]

[3] p. 20 cm. Caption title.

Rules to be observed in fighting the Indians.

1888

Annual Report of Brigadier General W. Merritt, U.S. Army, commanding Department of the Missouri. [Fort Leavenworth, 1888.]

13 p. 19.5 cm. Wrapper title.

Notices of Indian disturbances and of the busy cattle traffic. A very rare volume.

1891

Chronological List of Actions, &c., with Indians. January 1, 1866, to January, 1891. Office Memoranda. Adjutant General's Office. [Washington, 1891.]*

65 p. 23.5 cm. Printed wrappers.

1892

Record of Engagements with Hostile Indians within the Military Division of the Missouri, from 1868 to 1882, Lieutenant General P. H. Sheridan, commanding. Compiled at Headquarters Military Division of the Missouri from official records. Washington, 1882.*

112 p. 24.5 cm.

Valuable official summary of all engagements between Indians and regular troops for the period named.

1906

McReynolds, Robert

Thirty Years on the Frontier. Colorado Springs: El Paso Publishing Co., 1906.
256 p. 18.5 cm. Illustrations.

1908

Godfrey, Edward S.

General George A. Custer and the Battle of the Little Big Horn. New York: The Century Co., [1908].

38 p. 25 cm. Printed wrappers. Illustrations and photographs.
With a preface by General Custer's widow.

1909

Military Record of Colonel Hugh L. Scott, U.S. Army, Superintendent U.S. Military Academy, West Point, New York. [N.p., 1909.]*

39 p. 23 cm. Printed wrappers.
Half the volume is devoted to a recital of Scott's experiences with the Indians of the West.

1910

Hardin, C. B.

The Sheepeater Campaign. By Major C. B. Hardin, U.S.A., retired. Governor's Island, N.Y.H., 1910.*

Pp. 26–40. Printed wrappers. Maps.

INDIAN SIGN LANGUAGE

1890

Hadley, Lewis F.

A Lesson in Sign Talk. Designed to Show the Use of the Line Showing the Movement of the Hands in the Indian Gesture Language. By In-go-nom-pa-shi. Fort Smith, Ark., 1890.

10, [2] p. 17.5 cm. Portrait.
One of only two known copies, the other being at the Library of Congress.

Hadley, Lewis F.

Wolf Lame and the White Man. By In-go-nom-pa-shi. Fort Smith, Ark., 1890.
8 p. 17.5 cm.
Text in sign language, with interlinear English. One of only two known copies, the other being at the New York Public Library.

1926

Tomkins, William

Universal Indian Sign Language of the Plains Indians of North America, together with a Dictionary of Synonyms covering the Basic Words represented, also a Codification of Pictographic Word Symbols of the Ojibway and Sioux Nations. San Diego: William Tomkins, [1926].

77 p. 25 cm. Printed wrappers.

INDIAN TERRITORY

1827

McCoy, Isaac

Remarks on the Practicability of Indian Reform, embracing their Colonization. By Isaac M'Coy. Boston: Lincoln & Edmands, December, 1827.

47 p. 21 cm.

Scarce.

McCoy, Isaac

Remarks on the Practicability of Indian Reform, embracing their Colonization. By Isaac M'Coy. Boston: Lincoln & Edmands, 1827.

47 p. 23 cm. Plain wrappers.

A slightly different issue from the preceding. Scarce.

1829

McCoy, Isaac

Remarks on the Practicability of Indian Reform, embracing their colonization; with an appendix. By Isaac M'Coy. Second edition. New York: Gray & Bunce, 1829.*

72 p. 21.5 cm.

McCoy, Isaac

Remove Indians Westward. [Washington, 1829.]*

48 p. 24 cm. Caption title.

A very fine copy, entirely uncut and unopened, of this foundation document. Wagner-Camp notes only an edition of twenty-three pages.

Order No. 68. Adjutant General's Office, Washington, Oct. 20, 1829. [Washington, 1829.]

10 p. 19.5 cm. Caption title.

A review of the court martial conviction of Major R. B. Hyde for various offenses committed at Fort Towson and Fort Arbuckle.

1830

Report of the Committee on Indian Affairs to whom was referred that part of the President's Message, dated the eighth day of December last, which relates to Indian Affairs . . . . [Washington, 1830.]*

9 p. 22 cm. Caption title.

This important report, one of the fundamental documents on Indian Territory, recommends removal of the great southern tribes to some area in the West to be chosen for the purpose.

1831

McCoy, Isaac

Address to Philanthropists in the United States, generally, and to Christians in particular, on the Condition and Prospects of the American Indian. [N.p., 1831.]

8 p. 20 cm. Caption title.

Dated: Surveyor's Camp, Neosho River, Indian Territory, Dec. 1, 1831. Excessively rare.

Philip Everhard; or, A History of the Baptist Indian Missions in North America. Boston: T. R. Marvin, 1831.

108 p. 14 cm.

Interesting and valuable accounts of the activities among the western and southern Indians of Isaac McCoy and other early Baptist missionaries. Two copies, in different original bindings. The volume is very scarce.

1832

McCoy, Isaac

Country for Indians West of the Mississippi. Letter from the Secretary of War, transmitting a Copy of a Report made by Isaac McCoy, upon the subject of the Country reserved for the Indians West of the Mississippi. [Washington, 1832.]

15 p. 25 cm. Caption title.

A valuable description of Indian Territory.

1834

Gaines, Edmund Pendleton

Order No. 11. Head-quarters Western Department. Memphis, Tenn. Feb. 28, 1836.]

Broadsheet. 20 cm.

Indian Territory and other frontier defenses. The leaf is the earliest known example of printing in Memphis. Unrecorded, and the only known copy.

1835

McCoy, Isaac

The Annual Register of Indian Affairs within the Indian (or Western) Territory. Published by Isaac M'Coy. Shawanoe Baptist Mission House, Ind. Ter. January 1, 1835. Shawanoe Mission, J. Meeker, Printer, 1835.

48 p. 20.5 cm. Printed wrappers.

Peter P. Pitchlynn's copy. Pp. 5–8 are lacking.

Issues of this periodical are very rare. It contains highly important particulars regarding the Indian emigrant's advent into the new country, his adaption to his surroundings, and his prospects.

1836

Cass, Lewis, and Andrew Jackson

Important Document. Discharge of the Volunteers. [Nashville, Tennessee, 1836.]

Broadside. Folio.

Headed: Banner-Extra. Nashville, Saturday Morning, August 6th, 1836.

Official communications by Lewis Cass, Andrew Jackson, and C. A. Harris on General Gaines' call for state troops to combat Indian hostilities on the western frontier. Unrecorded, and the only known copy.

CASS, LEWIS, and ANDREW JACKSON

Military. [Louisville, Kentucky, 1836.]

Broadside. Folio.

Correspondence between Lewis Cass, Andrew Jackson, and C. A. Harris regarding General Gaines' call for volunteers to resist the nonexistent Indian uprising in Indian Territory. Unrecorded, and the only known copy.

HARDEMAN, THOMAS

Executive Order. [Nashville, Tennessee, 1836.]

Broadside. 28 cm.

Executive order by the governor of Tennessee and General Order by the adjutant general of the state calling into service the troops required by General Gaines for the suppression of threatened hostilities in Indian Territory. Unrecorded, and no other copy known.

McCOY, ISAAC

The Annual Register of Indian affairs within the Indian (or Western) territory. No. 2. Published by Isaac McCoy. Shawanoe Baptist Mission House, Indian Territory, January 1, 1836. Shawanoe Baptist Mission, Ind. Ter. J. Meeker, printer. 1836.

88 p. 21 cm.

Field 983.

Very rare.

1837

GAINES, EDMUND PENDLETON

Hd. Qrs. Western Division, As't. Adjutant General's Office, St. Louis Arsenal, Dec. 6, 1837. Special Orders No. 23. [St. Louis, 1837.]

6 p. 20.5 cm.

A highly important letter, in which General Gaines expresses his views on the establishment of a new military post on Red River "considerably in advance of Fort Towson, for the purpose of affording more complete protection to the emigrating and other Indians." Unrecorded, and the only known copy.

McCOY, ISAAC

The annual register No. 3 of Indian Affairs within the Indian (or Western) Territory. Published by Isaac McCoy. Shawanoe Baptist Mission House, Indian Territory, May, 1837. Shawanoe Baptist Mission, Ind. Ter. J. G. Pratt, printer. 1837.

81 p. 21 cm.

Field 983.

Very rare.

1838

GAINES, EDMUND PENDLETON

Defence of the Western Frontier. A Plan for the Defence of the Western Frontier, furnished by Major General Gaines. [Washington:] Thomas Allen, printer, [1838].*

58 p. 22.5 cm. Caption title. Folded map.

Scarce.

GAINES, EDMUND P.

To the Young Men of the States of the American Union, Civil and Military. [New Orleans? 1838.]*

88 p. 22.5 cm. Caption title.

Contains a presentation of his plan for Indian Territory and other frontier defenses. Very rare.

LUMPKIN, JOSEPH HENRY

Speech of Mr. Lumpkin, of Georgia, on the Indian Territory Bill. Delivered in the Senate of the United States, April 30, 1838. Washington: Printed at the Globe Office. 1838.

7 p. 22 cm.

Field 960.

1840

Biography of Edmund Pendleton Gaines, Major General, U.S. Army, condensed from the Best Authorities, by a Friend. [N.p., 1840.]

10 p. 23 cm. Caption title. Plain wrappers.

Contains a notice of his plan for Indian Territory and frontier defenses. Rare.

GAINES, EDMUND PENDLETON

Memorial of Edmund Pendleton Gaines, to the Senate and House of Representatives of the United States in Congress assembled. Memphis, Tenn.: Enquirer Office, 1840.*

30 p. 21 cm.

General Gaines' defense plan included the construction of a railroad to Fort Gibson. Unrecorded, and the only known copy.

MCCOY, ISAAC

History of Baptist Indian Missions: embracing Remarks on the Former and Present Condition of the Aboriginal Tribes; their Settlement within the Indian Territory, and their Future Prospects. Washington: William M. Morrison, 1840.

611 p. 22 cm.

Wagner-Camp 81.

A valuable record of the personal experiences of the missionary, his family, and his friends from 1818 on. While McCoy touches upon practically all the tribes of the Middle West and of Indian Territory, his book is particularly instructive in regard to the Ottawas and the Pottawatomies.

1842

GAINES, EDMUND P.

[A Plan for National Defence. Washington, 1842.]*

18 p. 22.5 cm. Printed without title page or caption.

Proceedings of the Western Baptist Convention, held in Cincinnati, Ohio, October 27th, 28th, and 29th, 1842. Louisville, Ky.: J. Eliot & Co.'s Power Press, 1842.

32 p. 23 cm. Printed wrappers.

Contains valuable notices of Indian Territory missions. Very rare.

57 House and Senate Bills and Joint Resolutions. [Washington, 1842–1888.]*
Variously paged. Folio.
Bills and resolutions relating to affairs of the Cherokee, Creek, Choctaw, and Chickasaw tribes; to Indian Territory boundary and railroad matters; to the extension of United States jurisdiction over certain offenses in Indian Territory; to the proposed establishment of a territorial government over the Indian tribes; and to erection of the Territory of Oklahoma. Many of the pieces were the property of former Choctaw Principal Chief Peter P. Pitchlynn and several of them bear his autograph. One of them, relating to a boundary dispute between Arkansas and the Choctaw Nation, bears a long manuscript addition in the hand of Albert Pike.

1843

Proceedings of the First Annual Meeting of the American Indian Mission Association, held at Louisville, Ky., Oct. 26, 27, 28, 1843. Louisville, 1843.
59 p. 21 cm.
This and the subsequent proceedings listed here (see 1844, 1845, 1846, 1847, and 1848) comprise a valuable and strangely neglected source of information on Indian Territory of the period. Isaac McCoy was the leading spirit in the Association. Very rare.

1844

Proceedings of the Second Annual Meeting of the American Indian Mission Association; held at Louisville, Ky. October 31, November 1, 2, 1844. Louisville: Buck's Steam Power Press, 1844.
60 p. 22.5 cm.
Very rare.

1845

Journal of the Proceedings of the Southwestern Convention, begun and held at the City of Memphis, on the 12th November, 1845. Memphis, Ten., 1845.
127 p. 22 cm. Printed wrappers.
A volume of the highest importance and rarity. Among many documents on the economic resources and prospects of the Southwest are reports on railroad and river transportation, military roads to the Indian country, and forts and defenses of the Western Indian frontier.

Proceedings of the Semi-annual meeting of the American Indian Mission Association, held at Forsyth, Georgia, May 17, 18, and 19, 1845. Louisville, Ky.: Monsarrat's Steam Power Press, 1845.
24 p. 21 cm. Printed wrappers.
Excessively rare.

Proceedings of the Third Annual meeting of the American Indian Mission Association. Held at Louisville, Ky., Oct. 30, 31, and Nov. 1, 2, 1845. Louisville: Geo. H. Monsarrat's Power Press, 1845.
52 p. 22 cm.
Very rare.

1846

Proceedings of the Fourth Annual Meeting of the American Indian Mission

Association, held in Louisville, Kentucky, October 29th, 30th, 31st. Louisville: G. H. Monsarrat & Co., 1846.

35 p. 22 cm.
Very rare.

1847

Proceedings of the Fifth Annual Meeting of the American Indian Mission Association. Held at Nashville, Tenn. October, the 28th, 29th, 30th. Louisville, Ky.: Monsarrat & Co.'s Steam Press, 1847.

32 p. 20 cm. Printed wrappers.
Very rare.

1848

Proceedings of the Sixth Annual Meeting of the American Indian Mission Association, held at Augusta, Georgia, October 26, 27th and 29th, 1848. Louisville: The Baptist Banner Office, 1848.

27 p. 20.5 cm.
Very rare.

Indian Territory, West of the Mississippi. [Washington, 1848.]

14 p. 22 cm. Caption title.

1850

Copway, George

Organization of a New Indian Territory East of the Missouri River. Arguments and Reasons submitted to the Honorable the Members of the Senate and House of Representatives of the 31st Congress of the United States, by the Indian Chief Kah-ge-ga-gah-bouh, or Geo. Copway. New York: S. W. Benedict, 1850.

32 p. 22 cm. Printed wrappers.
Copway, a Chippewa chief, advocated the erection of a new Indian Territory which should be an improvement upon the old, by offering an asylum to Northern bands only, and by providing at the outset for Indian self-government.

Resolutions and Address adopted by the Southern Convention, held at Nashville, Tennessee, June 3d to 12th, inclusive, in the year 1850. Published by order of the Convention. Nashville, Tenn.: Harvey M. Watterson, 1850.*

21 p. 23 cm.
Some of the documents have an important bearing upon Indian Territory.

1851

Sixth Annual Report of the Missionary Society of the Methodist Episcopal Church, South. Louisville, Kentucky.: Morton & Griswold, 1851.

131 p. 20.5 cm.
This and the subsequent reports of the Society listed here (8th, 1853, and 9th, 1854), contain interesting and valuable reports on Indian Territory missions.

1853

Eighth Annual Report of the Missionary Society of the Methodist Episcopal Church, South. Louisville, Ky.: Morton & Griswold, 1853.*

172 p. 20.5 cm.

1854

Ninth Annual Report of the Missionary Society of the Methodist Episcopal Church, South. Louisville, Ky.: Morton & Griswold, 1854.*

202 p. 20.5 cm.

Report of the Committee on Territories to whom was referred the Bill to Establish and Organize the Territories of Cha-la-kee, Muscogee and Cha-ta. [Washington, 1854.]*

31 p. 23 cm. Caption title.

1856

ECHOTA

The Proposed Territory of Neosho. [New York, 1856.]

Broadside. Folio.

Headed: The Aboriginal. New York, July, 1856. Justice, Civilization, Liberty. A proposal to grant territorial status to the larger Indian Territory and to organize an aboriginal department of the government. Excessively rare.

Proceedings of the M. W. Grand Lodge of the Most Ancient and Honorable Fraternity of Free and Accepted Masons of the State of Arkansas, held at Little Rock, Nov. 6, 1855. Little Rock: William Woolford, 1856.

75 p. 22 cm. Printed wrappers.

Contains directories of early Indian Territory lodges, then under Arkansas jurisdiction.

1858

JOHNSTON, JOSEPH E.

Southern Boundary Line of Kansas. Letter from the Secretary of War transmitting the Report of Colonel Johnston's Survey of the Southern Boundary Line of Kansas. [Washington, 1858.]*

3 p. 24 cm. Caption title. Large and valuable folded map.

1861

WHIPPLE, CHARLES K.

Relation of the American Board of Commissioners for Foreign Missions to slavery. By Charles K. Whipple. Boston: R. R. Wallcut, 1861.

247 p. 19 cm.

Valuable for its authoritative reports on slavery among the Indian Territory tribes.

1863

PHILLIPS, WILLIAM A.

Head Quarters, Districts of Western Arkansas and Indian Ter're, Fort Gibson, May 16, 1863. General Orders No. 17. [Fort Gibson, 1863.]

Broadside. 19.5 cm.

"The Post formerly known, and abandoned as Fort Gibson, and now known formally by the Cherokee name of Ke-to-wa . . . shall hereafter be known as Fort Blunt, Cherokee Nation," etc. Unrecorded, and the only known copy.

1865

BLUNT, JAMES G.

Fort Gibson, C.N. May 11, 1865. General Orders No. 6. [Fort Gibson, 1865.]
Broadside. 20.5 cm.

Assumption of command of the military district including Indian Territory and establishment of headquarters at Fort Gibson. Unrecorded, and the only known copy.

[Instructions to the Fort Smith Commissioners. Washington, 1865.]
4 p. 32.5 cm.

The highly important instructions to the commissioners sent to Fort Smith in the summer of 1865 to negotiate treaties with the Indian Territory tribes who had allied themselves with the Confederate states.

Report of the Proceedings of the Council with the Indians of the West and Southwest, held at Fort Smith, Ark., in September, 1865. [Fort Smith, 1865.]*
37 p. 23 cm. Caption title.

Easily one of the rarest and most important volumes in this entire collection. The proceedings of this momentous treaty council contain speeches, statement, and pleas by the principal men of Indian Territory and of the wild tribes, which are nowhere else available. Unrecorded, and one of only two known copies.

1866

INDIAN TERRITORY FREEDMEN COMMISSION

Circular No. 1. [Fort Smith, 1866.]
4 p. 20.5 cm. Caption title.
Dated: Head Quarters, Commission for regulating Relations between Freedmen of Indian Territory and their former Masters. Fort Gibson, January 1st, 1866.

This and the three following circulars are unrecorded, and no other copies are known.

INDIAN TERRITORY FREEDMEN COMMISSION

Circular No. 2. [Fort Smith, 1866.]
Broadside. 21 cm.
Imprint at end: New Era, Print.
Dated: Head Quarters, Commission to regulate Relations between Freedmen of Indian Territory, and their former Masters. Fort Gibson, January 2d, 1866.

INDIAN TERRITORY FREEDMEN COMMISSION

Circular No. 3. [Fort Smith, 1866.]
Broadside. 20.5 cm.
Imprint at end: Fort Smith New Era, Print.
Dated: Head Quarters, Commission for regulating Relations between Freedmen of the Indian Territory and their former Masters. Boggy Depot, Choctaw Nation, Jan. 17, 1866.

INDIAN TERRITORY FREEDMEN COMMISSION

Circular No. 4. [Fort Smith, 1866.]
Broadsheet. 20.5 cm.
Imprint at end: Fort Smith New Era, Print.

Dated: Head Quarters, Commission for regulating Relations between Freedmen of the Indian Territory and their former Masters. Fort Smith, Ark., January 27th, 1866.

1867

Circular. Union. Liberty, Equality, Fraternity. No Expatriation. Citizen's Rights for the Red Men. [Chicago, 1867.]

Broadside. 19 cm.

Proposal of a new and large Indian Territory in the West designed to put an end to Indian troubles, "notwithstanding the Union Pacific Railroad and Smoky Hill Route."

Floyd-Jones, De Lancey

Headquarters, District of the Indian Territory, Fort Gibson, C.N., November 17, 1867. General Orders No. 9. [Fort Gibson, 1867.]

Broadside. 20.5 cm.

Indian Territory was left in such disorganized condition at the close of the Civil War that practically all normal activities, including printing, were suspended for four or five years afterward. This leaf is the only known example of printing there in the year 1867. Unrecorded, and the only known copy.

1868

Bryant, Montgomery

Headquarters, District of the Indian Territory, Fort Gibson, C.N., January 20th, 1868. General Orders No. 1. [Fort Gibson, 1868.]

Broadside. 16 cm.

Assumption of command of the district. The only known example of printing in Indian Territory in the year 1868. Unrecorded, and the only known copy.

1870

Contract for Wagon Transportation in Indian Territory for 1870–71. [Fort Leavenworth, 1870.]

3 p. Folio. Caption title.

Contract between the chief quartermaster of the Department of the Missouri and Percival G. Lowe, of Leavenworth. Unrecorded, and the only known copy.

1871

Journal of the General Council of the Indian Territory, composed of Delegates duly elected from the Indian Tribes legally resident thereof, assembled in Council at Okmulgee, in the Indian Territory. Lawrence, Kansas: Excelsior Book and Job Printing Office, 1871.

64 p. 20.5 cm. Printed wrappers.

This and the subsequent journals of the so-called Okmulgee Council possess the highest degree of historical importance. One of but five known copies.

Message of the President of the United States communicating a Copy of the Proceedings of the Council of Indian Tribes held at Okmulgee, in December, 1870. [Washington, 1871.]

23 p. 23 cm. Caption title.

Second Annual Report of the Associated Executive Committee of Friends on Indian Affairs. Eighth Month 26th, 1871. Philadelphia: Sherman & Co., 1871.*

23, [1] p. 20 cm. Wrapper title.

Valuable information about the Wild Tribes.

1872

BOUDINOT, ELIAS CORNELIUS

The Manners, Customs, Traditions, and Present Condition of the Civilized Indians of the Indian Territory. [Tahlequah? 1872?].

43 numbered leaves, broadside. 23.5 cm. Caption title.

Ms. note on first page: This lecture was written in 1872 by E. C. Boudinot.

A highly important discussion by one of Indian Territory's leading men. Unrecorded, and the only known copy.

Journal of the Third Annual Session of the General Council of the Indian Territory, composed of Delegates duly elected from the Indian Tribes legally resident therein, assembled in Council at Okmulgee, Indian Territory, from the 3d to the 18th (inclusive) of June, 1872. Lawrence, Kansas: Journal Book and Job Printing House, 1872.

34 p. 21 cm. Printed wrappers.

One of only five known copies.

SHANKS, JOHN P. C.

Indian Affairs. Speech of Gen. John P. C. Shanks, of Indiana, in the House of Representatives, on April 13, 1872. Washington City: Judd & Detweiler, 1872.

30 p. 22 cm.

An important speech, almost wholly devoted to the condition and affairs of the principal tribes in Indian Territory.

Survey of Lands in the Indian Territory. Protest of the Indian Delegates to the Survey of their Lands in the Indian Territory, as proposed in the Indian Appropriation Bill. [Washington, 1872.]

4 p. 24 cm. Caption title.

3 Special Field Orders, dated Field Headquarters Department of Texas. [Fort Sill and Fort Gibson, 1872.]

Broadsides. 20 cm.

The first two orders were issued at Fort Sill, the third at Fort Gibson. Unrecorded, and the only known copies.

To the Congress of the United States. [Washington, 1872.]

4 p. 23 cm. Caption title.

A protest by Cherokee, Choctaw, and Creek delegates against consolidation of the Indian tribes and the establishment of a territorial government over them.

1873

General Orders 98. War Department, Adjutant General's Office, Washington, October 3, 1873. The following Opinion of the Attorney General of the United States is published for the Information of all concerned: Opinion. [Washington, 1873.]

4 p. 19.5 cm. Caption title.

An official answer to the question, What is the Indian Country? The document possesses great importance.

Journal of the Fourth Annual Session of the General Council of the Indian Territory, composed of Delegates duly elected from the Indian Tribes legally resident therein, assembled in Council at Okmulgee, Indian Territory, from the 5th to the 15th (inclusive) of May, 1873. Lawrence, Kansas: Journal Steam Book and Job Printing House, 1873.

38 p. 20 cm. Printed wrappers.
One of only four known copies.

Peace Policy among the Indians. Third Annual Report of the Associated Executive Committee of Friends on Indian Affairs, Eighth Month 26th, 1872. New Vienna, O.: A. H. Hussey, 1873.*

[2], 26 p. 18 cm. Printed wrappers.
Quaker educational activities in Indian Territory and Kansas among the Kickapoos, Shawnees, Pottawatomies, Kaws, Great and Little Osages, Quapaws, Sacs and Foxes, Cheyennes and Arapahoes, Wichitas, Kiowas, Comanches, and Apaches.

Peace Policy among the Indians. Fourth Annual Report of the Associated Executive Committee of Friends on Indian Affairs. Eighth Month 1st, 1873. Richmond, Ind. Telegram Steam Printing Co., 1873.

16, [1] p. 18.5 cm. Wrapper title.

1874

Boudinot, Elias Cornelius

Division of Lands, United States Courts, a Delegate in Congress for the Civilized Indians of the Indian Territory. Speech of Elias C. Boudinot, of the Cherokee Nation, delivered at Vinita, Indian Territory, August 29th, 1874. St. Louis: Barns & Beynon, 1874.*

40 p. 21.5 cm.
Rare.

Boudinot, Elias Cornelius

A Territorial Government for the Civilized Indians of the Indian Territory. If They Must be Subjected to the Responsibilities of Citizens of the United States, They should have their Privileges also. [N.p., 1874?]*

26 p. on 26 leaves, broadside. 21.5 cm.
Rare.

Fifth Annual Report of the Associated Executive Committee of Friends on Indian Affairs. Eighth Month 7th, 1874. Richmond, Indiana: The Telegram, 1874.

12, [1] p. 18.5 cm. Wrapper title. Folded map.
Report on missions in Indian Territory and Kansas. The map, an excellent one, shows distribution of tribes, agency locations, and railroad and stage routes. Rare.

Headquarters Mil. Div. of the Missouri, Cheyenne Agency, I.T., October 27, 1874. Special Field Orders No. 1. [Cheyenne and Arapahoe Agency, 1874.]

Broadside. 22.5 cm.
Unrecorded, and the only known copy.

Journal of the Fifth Annual Session of the General Council of the Indian Territory, composed of Delegates duly elected from the Indian Tribes legally resident therein, assembled in Council at Okmulgee, Indian Territory, from the 4th to the 14th (inclusive) of May, 1874. Lawrence, Kansas: Journal Steam Book and Job Printing House, 1874.*

58 p. 21 cm. Printed wrappers.
One of but six known copies.

Journal of the Fourth Annual Session of the General Council of the Indian Territory, composed of Delegates duly elected from the Indian Tribes legally resident therein, assembled in Council at Okmulgee, Indian Territory, Dec. 1st, 1873. [Boggy Depot, 1874.]

34 p. 22.5 cm. Printed wrappers.
One of only two known copies.

Moore, J. H.

The Political Condition of the Indians and the Resources of the Indian Territory. St. Louis: Southwestern Book and Publishing Co., 1874.

62 p. 23 cm. Printed wrappers.
In a protective case. An important conspectus.

23 Special Field Orders, dated Field Headquarters Department of Texas. [Fort Sill and Caddo, 1874.]

Broadsides. 20 cm.
One of the orders was issued at Caddo; the others at Fort Sill. They relate to troop movements in the Indian country, military messenger, and telegraph lines, the employment of Indian scouts, etc. Unrecorded, and the only known copies.

1875

Journal of the Adjourned Session of the Sixth Annual General Council of the Indian Territory, composed of Delegates duly elected from the Indian Tribes legally resident therein, assembled in Council at Okmulgee, Indian Territory, from the 1st to the 9th (inclusive) of Sept., 1875. Lawrence, Kansas: Journal Steam Book and Job Printing House, 1875.

35 p. 21 cm. Printed wrappers.
One of but five known copies.

Journal of the Sixth Annual Session of the General Council of the Indian Territory, composed of Delegates duly elected from the Indian Tribes legally resident therein, assembled in Council at Okmulgee, Indian Territory, from the 3d to the 15th (inclusive) of May, 1875. Lawrence, Kansas: Republican Journal Steam Printing Establishment, 1875.

114 p. 21 cm. Printed wrappers.
A fine copy.

Objections of the Indian Delegations to Bill H. R. 2687 and Kindred Measures in the Congress of the United States, providing for a Delegate in Congress from the Indian Territory. [N.p., 1875?].

7 p. 23 cm. Caption title.
Signed by representatives of the five principal tribes.

Proceedings of the Most Worshipful Grand Lodge, A. F. & A. M. of the Indian Territory. Held September 7th and 8th, 1875. Printed at the Office of the "Oklahoma Star," Caddo, I.T., [1875].

26 p. 20 cm. Printed wrappers.

The earliest Masonic publication in Indian Territory and Oklahoma. Rare.

Protest of the Indian Delegation against the Establishment by Congress of a Territorial Government of the United States over the Indian Territory. [Washington, 1875.]

5 p. 22 cm. Caption title.

Signed by delegates of the Cherokee, Choctaw, Chickasaw, Muscokee, and Seminole nations.

[Resolutions of citizens of Chetopa, Kansas. Chetopa, 1875.]

Broadside. Folio.

The resolutions deplore the growing lawlessness in Indian Territory and urge the establishment of a federal court with jurisdiction over Indian Territory crimes, the survey and division in severalty of Indian Territory lands, the granting of legislative powers to the Okmulgee Council, and the election of an Indian Territory delegate to Congress. The only known copy.

Statement of Facts relating to the Indian Territory. [N.p., 1875.]

19 p. 22 cm. Caption title.

No other copy can be traced.

1876

Bryan, Joel M.

Argument of Colonel Joel M. Bryan, of the Cherokee Nation, before the Committee on Indian Affairs of the House of Representatives of the United States, March 8, 1876, in Opposition to the Territorial Bill, H. R. No. 1923, entitled "A Bill to provide a Government for the Indian Territory." [N.p., 1876.]

8 p. 22.5 cm. Caption title.

De Semalle, Rene

Considerations on the Establishment in the Indian Territory of a New State of the American Union. By R. De S. Versailles: E. Aubert, 1876.

8 p. 21 cm. Printed wrappers.

The original edition.

Proceedings of the Second Annual Communication of the M. W. Grand Lodge of the Indian Territory, held in the Town of Caddo, commencing first Tuesday in September, A.D. 1876, A. L. 5876. Memphis, Tenn.: Southern Baptist Publication Society Print, 1876.

45, [1] p. 21.5 cm. Printed wrappers.

Protest of the Lawful Delegates of the Civilized Nations of Indians of the Indian Territory (herein named) on their behalf and on behalf of the Indian Race against the Passage of a Law by Congress Transferring them and their Property to Military Control. Washington: Gibson Bros., 1876.

12 p. 23 cm. Wrapper title.

Remonstrance of the Cherokee, Creek, Choctaw and Seminole Delegations against the Organization of the Indian Territory into a Territory of the United States. It is Unlawful, and Destructive to the Rights of the Citizen Population of said Territory. Washington: John L. Ginck, 1876.

24 p. 22.5 cm.

1877

GALPIN, S. A.

Report upon the Condition and Management of certain Indian Agencies in the Indian Territory, now under the Supervision of the Orthodox Friends. Washington, 1877.

41 p. 23 cm.
Autograph inscription by the author.

Proceedings of the M. W. Grand Lodge of Ancient, Free and Accepted Masons, of the Indian Territory. Third Annual Communication held at Vinita Sept. 4, 5, A. L. 5877. Memphis: Southern Baptist Publication Society, 1877.

52 p. 22 cm. Printed wrappers.

1878

The Indians Opposed to the Transfer Bill. United Action of the Delegations of the Cherokee, Creek, Seminole, Chickasaw, and Choctaw Nations in Opposition to the Measure. They Protest against it, and Give their Reasons for so doing. Washington: Gibson Bros., 1878.

21 p. 22.5 cm. Printed wrappers.
Very scarce.

Letter from the Secretary of the Interior communicating Information in relation to the Decisions of that Department upon the Rights of Indians to Impose Taxes in the Indian Territory. [Washington, 1878.]

55 p. 23 cm. Caption title.

Memorial of the Delegates from the Indian Territory, presented by Hon. H. L. Muldrow, in the House of Representatives, April 22, 1878. [Washington, 1878.]

4 p. 23 cm. Caption title.
Signed by delegates of the Choctaw, Cherokee, Creek, and Seminole nations.

Supplementary Objections of the Indian Delegates of the Indian Territory to Bill S. No. 107, 45th Congress. [N.p., 1878.]

5 p. 23.5 cm. Caption title.
A protest signed by the delegates of the five principal tribes against the provisions of a bill looking to Indian citizenship in the United States.

1879

BOUDINOT, ELIAS CORNELIUS

Indian Territory. Argument of Elias C. Boudinot, submitted to the Senate Committee on Territories, January 17, 1879. Washington: Thomas McGill & Co., 1879.

73 p. 23.5 cm. Wrapper title.
Very scarce.

GARVIN, I. L.

Memorial of I. L. Garvin, Principal Chief of the Choctaw Nation, Remonstrating against the Establishment of Territorial Governments in the Indian Nations, Indian Territory. [Washington, 1879.]

3 p. 24 cm. Caption title.

PARKER, ISAAC C.

Timber in the Nations. Decision of Judge Parker. United States vs. Ben Reese. [Fort Smith? 1879.]*

11 p. 22 cm. Caption title.

Protest of Indian Delegates against Organization of Territorial Government over the Indian Country. Protest of the Delegates from the Cherokee, Creek, and Choctaw Nations, against the Organization of a United States Territorial Government over the Indian Territory. [Washington, 1879.]

7 p. 23 cm. Caption title.

[Report on Indian Territory, with particular reference to railroads and civil government. Washington, 1879.]*

813, 325, [1] p. 23 cm.

A document of the highest importance and one indispensable to a knowledge of conditions among the tribes of Indian Territory at the time. Copies are seldom encountered.

ROSS, WILLIAM P.

Indian Territory. Remarks of William P. Ross, of the Cherokee Delegation, before the Committee on Territories of the United States Senate, on the Subjects referred to in the Resolutions of Mr. Voorhees, as delivered in part January 17, 1879, and submitted in full January 23, 1879. Washington: Gibson Bros., 1879.

42 p. 23 cm. Wrapper title.

1880

Memorial of the Indian Delegates against the Passage by Congress of any Act providing for the Organization of a United States Territorial Government over the Indian Country. No Territorial Government of the United States can be Organized over the Indian country without the Express Consent of the Indian Nations to be affected; nor can their Lands be Allotted except by their Consent as provided by Treaty Stipulation. Washington: John L. Ginck, [1880].

16 p. 22 cm. Wrapper title.

The protest is signed by delegates of the Cherokee, Creek, and Choctaw nations.

Memorial of Indian Delegates, remonstrating against the Passage of an Act providing for the Organization of a United States Territorial Government over the Indian Country. [Washington, 1880.]

9 p. 23 cm. Caption title.

1881

GANNETT, HENRY

Indian Territory. By Henry Gannett. New York: Charles Scribner's Sons, 1881.

11 p. 16.5 cm. Printed wrappers. Map.
An excellent description of the country and its inhabitants.

Proceedings of the Grand Lodge of the Indian Territory for 1881. Including Reprints of Proceedings for the years 1874, 1875 & 1877. [Sedalia, Mo.: Democrat Steam Book and Job Printing House, 1881.]
25, 30, 65, 52 p. 23 cm. Printed wrappers.

1882

Fort Supply, Indian Territory, February 21st, 1882. Orders No. 29. [Fort Supply, 1882.]
Broadside. 19.5 cm.
The order relates to the military telegraph line from Red River via Fort Supply to Fort Elliott, Texas. Unrecorded, and the only known copy.

Letter and Accompanying Documents transmitted by the Secretary of Interior as to Existence of Lands in the Indian Territory Available for Settlement by the Colored Population. [Washington, 1882.]
5 p. 23 cm. Caption title.

Letter from the Secretary of the Interior transmitting Copy of Report in reference to the Right of Occupation by Settlers on any Portion of the Indian Territory. [Washington, 1882.]
4 p. 24.5 cm. Caption title.

1883

Fort Supply, Indian Territory, Sept. 10, 1883. Orders No. 151. [Fort Supply, 1883.]
Broadside. 18 cm.
Special assignments. Unrecorded, and the only known copy.

Proceedings of the M. W. Grand Lodge of the Indian Territory. Ninth Annual Communication held at Fort Gibson, November 6th and 7th, 1883. Sedalia, Mo.: Democrat Steam Printing House, 1883.
151, [1] p. 23 cm. Printed wrappers.

Third Annual Catalogue of the Officers and Students of the Indian University, Tahlequah, Ind. Ter., 1882–83. New Bedford, Mass.: Knight & Howland, 1883.
23 p. 20.5 cm.
Rare.

Third Annual Commencement of the Indian University, June 1st, 1883. [Muskogee, 1883.]*
Broadside. 31.5 cm.
Program of exercises. The only known copy.

1884

Fourth Annual Catalogue. Indian University. Tahlequah, Indian Territory. 1883–84. New Bedford, Mass.: Paul Howland, Jr., 1884.
24 p. 20 cm. Wrapper title.
Rare.

Letter from the Secretary of the Interior, transmitting Copies of Documents and Correspondence relating to Leases of Lands in the Indian Territory to Citizens of the United States for Cattle-grazing and other purposes. [Washington, 1884.]
160 p. 23 cm. Caption title. Maps.

Proceedings of the M. W. Grand Lodge A. F. & A. M. of the Indian Territory. Tenth Annual Communication, held at A-to-ka, Choctaw Nation, November 4th, 5th, and 6th, 1884. Sedalia, Mo.: Democrat Steam Printing House and Book Bindery, 1884.
70, 91, [1] p. 23 cm. Printed wrappers.

1885

By-Laws of O-ho-yo-homa Chapter No. 1, O. E. S. Located at A-to-ka, Choctaw Nation, Ind. Ter., chartered by the General Grand Chapter, O. E. S. of the United States. [Atoka, 1885.]*
8 p. 13.5 cm. Printed wrappers.
Very scarce.

By-Laws of the Oklahoma Council, R. & S. M. No. 1, located at Atoka, Choctaw Nation, Indian Territory, chartered by the General Grand Council Royal and Select Masters of the United States. Muskogee, I.T.: Indian Journal Steam Print, 1885.*
12 p. 13.5 cm. Printed wrappers.

Letter of the Secretary of the Interior transmitting Report relative to the Leasing of Indian Lands in the Indian Territory. [Washington, 1885.]
220 p. 23 cm. Caption title. Folded color map.

[An Opinion, addressed by the Attorney General to the Secretary of the Interior, on the validity of Indian grazing leases. Washington, 1885.]*
3 p. 24 cm.

Proceedings of the Baptist Territorial Convention, of the Indian Territory, held with the church at Tahlequah, Cherokee Nation, June 1 & 2, 1883, and with the Church at High Hill, Choctaw Nation, July 12, 13 & 14, 1884. Muskogee, I.T.: Indian Journal Steam Printing House, 1885.*
8 p. 19.5 cm. Printed wrappers.
Not in Foreman.

Proceedings of the International Territorial Convention. [Eufaula, 1885.]*
4 p. 22 cm. Caption title.
Excessively rare.

Proceedings of the M. W. Grand Lodge A. F. & A. M. of the Indian Territory. Eleventh Annual Communication. Held at McAlester, Choctaw Nation, November 3d, 4th and 5th, A.D. 1885. [Muskogee? 1885.]
74, [1], 135 p. 22.5 cm. Wrapper title.

1886

Fort Supply, Indian Territory, March 2, 1886. Circular. [Fort Supply, 1886.]
Broadside. 19 cm.
Unrecorded, and the only known copy.

Proceedings of the Baptist Missionary and Educational Convention of the Indian Territory. Held with the Hillibee Baptist Church, Creek Nation, June 5th and 6th, 1885, and with the Spring Baptist Church, Seminole Nation, July 15th, 16th and 17th, 1886. 1886. Kessler & Sumner, printers. Ottawa, Kansas.*

15 p. 19.5 cm. Printed wrappers.

Proceedings of the M. W. Grand Lodge A. F. & A. M. of the Indian Territory. Twelfth Annual Communication held at A-to-ka, Choctaw Nation, November 2nd, 3d and 4th, 1886. Denison, Texas: Murray's Steam Printing House, 1886.

68, 50, [1] p. 23 cm. Printed wrappers.

Report of the Committee on Indian Affairs, United States Senate, on the Condition of the Indians in the Indian Territory, and other Reservations. Washington, 1886.*

3 vols. 22.5 cm.

Testimony taken by the Committee on Indian Affairs of the United States Senate in relation to the Condition of the Indian Tribes in the Indian Territory, and upon other Reservations, under Resolutions of the Senate of June 11 and December 3, 1884, and February 23, 1885. Washington, 1886.*

467, 597 p. 23 cm.

A mine of information on social and economic conditions in Indian Territory.

1887

Allotment of Lands. Defense of the Dawes Indian Severalty Bill. [Philadelphia, 1887.]*

7 p. 23 cm. Caption title.

The Dawes Land in Severalty Bill and Indian Emancipation. [Philadelphia, 1887.]*

7 p. 21 cm. Caption title.

Headquarters Department of the Missouri, Fort Leavenworth, Kansas, March 26, 1887. Circular No. 4. [Fort Leavenworth, 1887.]

4 p. 20.5 cm.

A list of crimes for which Indian Territory intruders may be arrested and expelled, and instructions detailing procedure against them. Unrecorded, and the only known copy.

Proceedings of the International Council of Indians of the Indian Territory held at Eufaula, Indian Territory, June 6, 7, 8 and 9, 1887. The Next Session will be held at Fort Gibson, Cherokee Nation, Ind. Ter. commencing first Tuesday in May, 1888. Eufaula: Indian Journal Steam Print, 1887.*

7 p. 22 cm. Wrapper title.

One of but two known copies.

Seventh Annual Catalogue of the Officers and Students of Indian University, Muskogee, Indian Territory, 1886–7. Ottawa, Kansas: J. B. Kessler, 1887.

26 p. 21 cm.

1888

Eighth Annual Catalogue of the Officers and Students of Indian University.

Bacone, Indian Territory. 1887–1888. Muskogee, I.T.: Phoenix Steam Book and Job Print, 1888.

34 p. 20 cm.

Eighth Annual Commencement of Indian University, June 21, 1888. Exercises begin at 9:30 a. m. [Muskogee, 1888.]*

[3] p. 16 cm.

Program of exercises. The only known copy.

Indian University. Exhibition of the Academic Department, June 20, 1888. Exercises begin at 7:30 p. m. [Muskogee, 1888.]

[3] p. 16 cm.

Recital program. The only known copy.

Memorial and Resolutions adopted by the Convention for the Opening of the Indian Territory, held at Kansas City, Mo. February 8, 1888. [Kansas City, 1888.]

16 p. 23 cm. Wrapper title.

Of the highest importance, and of very great rarity.

Painter, C. C.

The Condition of Affairs in Indian Territory and California. A Report by Prof. C. C. Painter. Philadelphia, 1888.

114, [2] p. 22 cm. Printed wrappers.

Proceedings of the Convention to Consider the Opening of the Indian Territory, held at Kansas City, Mo. February 8, 1888. With an Appendix. Kansas City, Mo.: Ramsey, Millett & Hudson, 1888.*

80 p. 22 cm. Printed wrappers.

Of great importance and of excessive rarity.

Thayer, James B.

The Dawes Bill and the Indians. [Boston, 1888.]*

Pp. [315]–322. 24 cm. Caption title.

A reprint from the *Atlantic Monthly*.

Vinita, Cherokee Nation. Citizens.

Memorial of the Citizens of Vinita, Ind. Ter., to the Hon. Senate aud [sic] House of Representatives of the United States of America in Congress assembled: In the matter of the Establishment of a Federal court in the Indian Territory. [Vinita, 1888.]

[4] p. 19.5 cm. Caption title.

Unrecorded, and the only known copy.

1889

Minutes of the Indian Mission Conference of the Methodist Episcopal Church, South. Forty-fourth session held in Atoka, Ind. Ter., October 2–7, 1889. Muskogee: Our Brother in Red Pub. Co., [1889].

26 p. 23.5 cm. Printed wrappers. Folded table.

Not in Foreman.

Ninth Annual Catalogue of the Officers and Students of Indian University. Bacone, Indian Territory, and other Baptist Indian Schools. 1888–1889. Muskogee: Phoenix Steam Book and Job Print, 1889.

36 p. 21 cm. Printed wrappers.

Post of Fort Reno, I.T., July 29, 1889. Orders No. 122. [Fort Reno, 1889.]

Broadside. 21 cm.

Unrecorded, and the only known copy.

Post of Fort Reno, I.T., August 13, 1889. Orders No. 127. [Fort Reno, 1889.]

Broadside. 21 cm.

Unrecorded, and the only known copy.

Post of Fort Reno, I.T., August 16, 1889. Orders No. 130. [Fort Reno, 1889.]

Broadside. 21 cm.

Unrecorded, and the only known copy.

Proceedings of the Baptist Missionary and Educational Convention of the Indian Territory. Held with the South Canadian Baptist Church, Choctaw Nation, September 9th and 10th, 1887. With the Big Arbor Baptist Church, Choctaw Nation, Septemtember 11th, 1888. With the Atoka Baptist Church, Choctaw Nation, September 13th and 14th, 1889. Ottawa, Kansas: J. B. Kessler, Proprietor Herald and Book and Job Printer. 1889.

20 p. 19.5 cm. Printed wrappers.

Proceedings of the M. W. Grand Lodge of the Indian Territory, at its Sixth Annual Communication, held at Atoka, Nov. 2nd and 3d, 1880. Sedalia, Mo.: Democrat Steam Book and Job Printing House, 1889.*

53 p. 22.5 cm. Printed wrappers.

1890

Constitution of the Industrial Union of the Indian Territory. 1890. "Territorial Topic" Job Print, Purcell, Ind. Ter.

24 p. 13.5 cm.

The only known copy, and the earliest known Purcell imprint.

De Semalle, Rene

Considerations on the Establishment in the Indian Territory of a New State of the American Union. Versailles: E. Aubert, 1890.*

8 p. 22 cm. Printed wrappers.

The 1890 reprint is rarer than the original edition of 1876.

Letter from the Secretary of the Interior addressed to the Chairman of the Committee on Indian Affairs, transmitting Copy of a Communication from the Commissioner of Indian Affairs and accompanying Papers relative to Coal Leases in the Indian Territory. [Washington, 1890.]*

36 p. Caption title.

Letter from the Secretary of the Interior transmitting the Compilation concerning the Legal Status of the Indians in Indian Territory. [Washington, 1890.]

31 p. 23 cm. Caption title. Large folded color map.

An important discussion.

Minutes of the Eighth Annual Meeting of the Baptist Missionary and Educational Convention of Indian Territory. Held with the Atoka Baptist Church, October 23, 24, 25 and 26, 1890. 1890. Indian Citizen Print, Atoka, Ind. Ter.*

22 p. 19.5 cm. Printed wrappers.
Not in Foreman.

Minutes of the Second Session of the Indian Mission Conference of the Methodist Episcopal Church, held at Oklahoma City, I.T., February 6–10th, 1890. Oklahoma City: Times Book and Job Print, 1890.*

25, [23] p. 18.5 cm. Printed wrappers.
Not in Foreman.

Proceedings of the First Annual Meeting of the Grand Chapter of the Order Eastern Star of the Indian Territory. Muskogee: Phoenix Printing Co., 1890.

32 p. 21 cm. Printed wrappers.
Unrecorded.

Tenth Annual Catalogue of the Officers and Students of Indian University, Bacone, Indian Territory, and other Baptist Indian Schools. 1889–90. Muskogee: Phoenix Printing Co., [1890].

38 p. 20.5 cm.

1891

Blackall, Mrs. C. R.

Two Weeks among Indians and Glimpses of Work in their Behalf. Chicago, 1891.

15, [1] p. 13 cm. Printed wrappers.
A missionary tour of Indian Territory.

Eleventh Annual Catalogue of the Officers and Students of Indian University, Bacone, Indian Territory, and other Baptist Indian Schools. 1890–91. Muskogee: Phoenix Printing Co., [1891].

38 p. 20.5 cm. Printed wrappers.

Minutes of the ninth annual meeting of the Baptist Missionary and Educational Convention of Oklahoma and Indian territories. Held with the First Baptist Church of Muskogee, October 22–25, 1891. 1891. Baptist Publishing Company Print, Oklahoma City, O.T.*

26 p. 19.5 cm. Printed wrappers.
Not in Foreman.

Minutes of the Third Session of the Indian Mission Conference of the Methodist Episcopal Church, held at Guthrie, Oklahoma Ty., January 15th to 19th, 1891. Arkansas City, Kansas: Traveler, [1891].

50 p. 22 cm. Printed wrappers.
The imprint is on the front wrapper.

Proceedings of the M. W. Grand Lodge of Indian Territory, at an Emergent Communication held at Eufaula, March 22, 1891, and of the Seventeenth Annual Communication held at Oklahoma City, Oklahoma Dist., August 18–19, 1891. Muskogee: Phoenix Steam Printing Co., 1891.

121, 117, [9], iii p. 21 cm. Printed wrappers.

1892

Certain Indian Lands in Indian Territory and Oklahoma. Letter from the Secretary of the Interior with Information as to what Indian Lands in Indian Territory and Oklahoma are now Occupied for Grazing Purposes. [Washington, 1892.]

17 p. 22.5 cm. Caption title.

McCormick, Calvin

The Memoir of Miss Eliza McCoy. By Calvin McCormick, A.M. Dallas, Texas: Published by the author. 1892.*

162 p. 19.5 cm. Frontisp. port.

Eliza McCoy was a niece of Isaac McCoy, and was herself a missionary to the Pottawatomies and Weas. Scarce.

Minutes of the Fourth Session of the Indian Mission Conference of the Methodist Episcopal Church, held at Norman, Ok., Jan. 7–11, 1892. Guthrie: State Capital Printing Co., 1892.

34 p. 22 cm. Printed wrappers. 3 folded tables.

Not in Foreman.

Minutes of the Tenth Annual Meeting of the Baptist Missionary and Educational Convention of Oklahoma and Indian territories, held with First Baptist Church, Oklahoma City, O.T. October 20–23, 1892. 1892. Baptist Publishing Company Print, Oklahoma City, O.T.*

34 p. 19.5 cm. Printed wrappers.

Not in Foreman.

Proceedings of the Third Annual Convocation of the Grand Royal Arch Chapter of Indian Territory, held at Tahlequah, Cherokee Nation, August 18th, A.D. 1892. Muskogee: Phoenix Printing Co., 1892.

38, ii p. 21.5 cm. Printed wrappers.

Report from the Committee on Indian Affairs. [Washington, 1892.]*

35 p. 22.5 cm. Caption title. 18 maps.

A report on the Choctaw and Chickasaw Leased District.

Twelfth Annual Catalogue of the Officers and Students of Indian University, Bacone, Indian Territory, and Preparatory Schools, 1891–1892. Muskogee: Phoenix Printing Co., 1892.

33, [1] p. 21 cm.

1893

Constitution and By-Laws of the M. E. Grand Royal Arch Chapter of Indian Territory, also the By-Laws, for the Government of Subordinate Chapters, in Indian Territory. Atoka: Indian Citizen Pub. Co., [1893].

25, [2] p. 15.5 cm. Wrapper title.

Indian University, Bacone, Indian Territory. [Muskogee, 1893.]*

16 p. 13 cm.

A description of the school and letters from successful graduates. Unrecorded, and no other copy known.

Minutes of the Eleventh Annual Meeting of the Baptist Missionary and Educational Convention of Oklahoma and Indian Territories held with First Baptist Church, So. McAlester, I.T. June 22–24, 1893. Baptist Publishing Company Print, Oklahoma City, O.T. 1893.*

36 p. 19.5 cm. Printed wrappers.
Not in Foreman.

Thirteenth Annual Catalogue of the Officers and Students of Indian University, Bacone, Indian Territory, and its Preparatory Schools, 1892–1893. Muskogee: Phoenix Printing Co., [1893].

50 p. 21 cm.

1894

Annual Report of the Mine Inspector for Indian Territory for the Fiscal Year ending June 30, 1894. Washington, 1894.

20 p. 23 cm. Printed wrappers.

Duncan, Walter A.

Letter to the President, touching Statehood for Indian Territory. By Walter A. Duncan, Delegate of Cherokee Nation. Second edition. Washington: Gibson Bros., 1894.*

34 p. 23 cm. Printed wrappers.
Rare and important.

Fourteenth Annual Catalogue of the Officers and Students of Indian University, and its Preparatory Schools, 1893–1894. Muskogee: Phoenix Printing Co., 1894.

63 p. 21.5 cm.

Holmes, William Henry

An Ancient Quarry in Indian Territory. Washington, 1894.*

19 p. 24.5 cm. Printed wrappers. Plates.

Minutes of the Twelfth Annual Meeting of the Baptist Missionary and Educational Convention of Oklahoma and Indian Territories, held with First Baptist Church, Ardmore, Indian Territory, June 1–3, 1894. Muskogee, Ind. Ter.: The Phoenix Printing Company, 1894.*

46 p. 19.5 cm. Printed wrappers.
Not in Foreman.

1895

Annual Report of the Mine Inspector for Indian Territory to the Secretary of the Interior for the year ending June 30, 1895. Washington, 1895.

24 p. 23 cm. Printed wrappers.

Fifteenth Annual Catalogue of the Officers and Students of Indian University, Bacone, Indian Territory, and its Preparatory Schools. 1894–1895. Muskokee: E. H. Hubbard & Co., 1895.

53 p. 21 cm.

Minutes of the Thirteenth Annual Meeting of the Baptist Missionary and Educational Convention of Oklahoma and Indian Territories, held with First Baptist Church, Vinita, Indian Territory, June 20–22, 1895. Baptist Standard Print, Waco. [1895].*

32 p. 19.5 cm. Printed wrappers.

WYETH, WALTER N.

Isaac McCoy. Early Indian Missions. Isaac McCoy—Christiana McCoy. A Memorial. By Walter N. Wyeth, D.D., Philadelphia, Pa. Philadelphia: W. N. Wyeth, [1895].*

236 p. 19.5 cm. Portraits.

1896

MILLER, BENJAMIN S.

Ranch Life in Southern Kansas and Indian Territory as told by a Novice. How a Fortune was made in Cattle. New York: Fless & Ridge Printing Co., 1896.*

163, [1] p. 20.5 cm. Printed wrappers.
An interesting and valuable account.

Minutes of the Fourteenth Annual Meeting of the Baptist Missionary and Educational Convention of Oklahoma and Indian Territories. Held with First Baptist Church, Oklahoma City, O.T. June 25–27th, 1896. Hicks Print, Oklahoma City. [1896].*

70 p. 19.5 cm. Printed wrappers.
Not in Foreman.

WEED, JOHN J.

Ex-parte in the Matter of Charles Johnson. Brief and Argument for Petitioner. [N.p., 1896.]*

23 p. 23 cm. Wrapper title.
An important argument on the jurisdiction of the United States courts over capital offenses in Indian Territory.

1897

Minutes of the Fifteenth Annual Meeting of the Baptist Missionary and Educational Convention of Indian and Oklahoma Territories, held with 1st Baptist Church, South McAlester, I.T., June 23–27, 1897. [1897.]*

52 p. 19.5 cm. Printed wrappers.

1898

Graduating Exercises Willie Halsell College. Wednesday, June 1st, 10 a.m. College Chapel. 1898.*

[4] p. 15 cm.
Unrecorded.

RICHARDS, W. L.

Digest of Decisions of the United States Supreme Court, United States Circuit Court of Appeals, Indian Territory Court of Appeals. On Appeals from the United

States Courts in the Indian Territory. Edited by W. L. Richards, of the Indian Territory Bar. Atoka: Choctaw Champion Print, 1898.

[2], 155 p. 23 cm. Printed wrappers.

A fine copy of a very scarce volume.

1900

Journal of the Indian Mission Conference, Methodist Episcopal Church, South. Fifty-fifth Session held at Vinita, Indian Territory, October 25 to 29, 1900. J. M. Porter, editor. Vinita: Leader Printing Co., 1900.*

[4], 25, [28] p. 23 cm. Printed wrappers.

Not in Foreman.

The Petition of a People for Relief. The Convention of the People of the Indian Territory, held at South M'Alester, Feb. 22 and 23, 1900. Its Proceedings, Resolutions and Memorial. [South McAlester, 1900.]

18, 21 p. 25 cm. Wrapper title.

Rare.

Proceedings of the Grand Commandery of Knights Templar of Indian Territory. Held at Ardmore, Indian Territory, April 18th, 1900. Muskogee: Evening Times Print, 1900.

32 p. 23 cm. Printed wrappers.

1901

Memorial Reciting Condition of the Four Hundred Thousand People in the Indian Territory and Respectfully Appealing to Congress for Immediate Relief. The Wrongs of Four Hundred Thousand Free Born American Citizens Graphically Depicted and Redress of same Demanded with Justified Earnestness. Purcell, I.T.: The Register Power Printing House, 1901.

12 p. 21 cm. Printed wrappers.

Rare.

Murrow, J. S.

Some Plain Facts about our Indian Mission Work. [Muskogee, 1901.]

12 p. 16 cm.

Status of Southern Baptist missionary work in Indian Territory. Unrecorded.

Proceedings of the Grand Commandery of Knights Templar of Indian Territory, Muskogee, April 25th, 1901. Muskogee: Evening Times Print, 1901.

52, [1] p. 23 cm. Printed wrappers. Frontisp. port.

1902

Annual Report of the United States Indian Inspector for the Indian Territory. Washington, 1902.

229 p. 23 cm. Printed wrappers. Maps. Photographs.

Proceedings of the Grand Commandery of Knights Templar of Indian Territory, South McAlester, April 10th, 1902. Muskogee: Evening Times Print, 1902.

[2], 43, [1] p. 23 cm. Printed wrappers. Frontisp. portrait.

Proceedings of the M. Ill. Grand Council of Royal and Select Masters of Indian Territory. Eighth Annual Assembly held at Oklahoma City, Okla. Ter. April 9th, 1902. Muskogee: Evening Times, 1902.

16, [1] p. 23 cm. Printed wrappers.

Proceedings of the Thirteenth Annual Convocation of the M. E. Grand Royal Arch Chapter of Indian Territory, held at Oklahoma City, Oklahoma Territory, April 8, 1902. Muskogee: Evening Times, 1902.

54 p. 22.5 cm. Printed wrappers. Frontisp. portrait.

1903

Annual Report of the Mine Inspector for Indian Territory to the Secretary of the Interior for the year ended June 30, 1903. Washington, 1903.

171 p. 23 cm. Printed wrappers. Folded maps.

Proceedings of the Fourteenth Annual Convocation of the M. E. Grand Royal Arch Chapter of Indian Territory, held at Guthrie, Oklahoma Territory, April 14, 1903. Atoka: Indian Citizen, 1903.*

88 p. 23 cm. Printed wrappers. Frontisp. portrait.

Proceedings of the Grand Commandery of Indian Territory, Ardmore, April 16, 1903. Atoka: Indian Citizen, 1903.

37, [1] p. 23 cm. Printed wrappers. Frontisp. portrait.

Proceedings of the M. Ill. Grand Council of Royal and Select Masters of Indian Territory. Ninth Annual Assembly held at Guthrie, Oklahoma, April 15th, 1903. Atoka: Indian Citizen, 1903.

21, [1] p. 23 cm. Printed wrappers. Photographs.

1904

Alleged Abuses and Irregularities in the Public Service of the Indian Territory. Message from the President of the United States, transmitting a Letter from the Secretary of the Interior, with accompanying Report of Charles J. Bonaparte and Clinton Rogers Woodruff, Special Inspectors, in the matter of Alleged Abuses and Irregularities in the Public Service of the Indian Territory, and inclosing a Memorandum of the work of the Commission to the Five Civilized Tribes. [Washington, 1904.]

48 p. 23 cm. Caption title.

Annual Report of the United States Indian Inspector for the Indian Territory, together with the Reports of the Indian Agent in charge of the Union Agency, the Superintendent and Supervisors of Schools in that Territory, the Mining Trustees for Choctaw and Chickasaw Nations, and the Supervising Engineer, Indian Territory Town Sites, to the Secretary of the Interior for the Fiscal Year ended June 30, 1904. Washington, 1904.

290 p. 23 cm. Printed wrappers.

Baker, H. G.

Did the Government of the United States ever Pledge itself to give Separate Statehood to Indian Territory? [Muskogee, 1904.]

Broadside. Folio.

A strong argument for separate statehood for Indian Territory. Unrecorded, and the only known copy.

Indian Territory, dealing particularly with those Portions of it along the Lines of the Rock Island System. Chicago, 1904.
31, [1] p. 23 cm. Printed wrappers. Photographs. Map.

Letter to the President from the Secretary of the Interior transmitting the Report of Col. Charles J. Bonaparte and Clinton R. Woodruff regarding the Public Service in Indian Territory. Washington, 1904.
48 p. 23 cm. Printed wrappers.

OWEN, ROBERT L.
Statehood for Indian Territory and Oklahoma. Remarks of Robert L. Owen, of Muscogee, Ind. T., before the Committee on the Territories of the House of Representatives. Washington, 1904.*
160 p. 23 cm.
Important and very scarce.

Proceedings of the Fifteenth Annual Convocation of the Grand Royal Arch Chapter of Indian Territory. Held at Muskogee, Indian Territory, April 12, 1904. Denison, Texas: Herald Press, 1904.
159 p. 22.5 cm. Printed wrappers. Frontisp. photograph.

1905

DEWITZ, PAUL W. H.
Notable Men of Indian Territory at the Beginning of the Twentieth Century, 1904–1905. Edited by Paul W. H. Dewitz. Muskogee, [1905].
186 p. 24 cm. Portraits.
Of considerable reference value.

GANNETT, HENRY
A Gazetteer of Indian Territory. Washington, 1905.
70, ii p. 23 cm.

HUNT, M. P.
Mission Work among the Indians. [Atlanta, 1905.]*
11, [1] p. 13.5 cm.
An exposition of Southern Baptist missionary work in Indian Territory. Unrecorded.

Official Proceedings of the Thirty-second Annual Communication of the M. W. Grand Lodge, Ancient, Free and Accepted Masons of Indian Territory, held at Tulsa, Creek Nation, Aug. 8 and 9, 1905. Atoka: Indian Citizen Pub. Co., 1905.
97, 30, 29, 149, [2], errata slip. 23 cm. Printed wrappers. Frontisp. port.

Report of the Mine Inspector for Indian Territory to the Secretary of the Interior for the year ended June 30, 1905. Washington, 1905.
68 p. 23 cm. Printed wrappers.

1906

BACHE, FRANKLIN

Suggestions for Disposition of the Segregated Coal Lands in the Indian Territory made to the Special U.S. Senate Committee by Franklin Bache, President of the Bache-Denman Company. Fort Smith: Weldon, Williams & Lick, [1906].*

4 p. 24 cm. Wrapper title.

Indian Territory. Regulations for Tribal Indian Schools among the Five Civilized Tribes. Washington, 1906.

9 p. 23 cm. Printed wrappers.

Oil Lands in Indian Territory and Territory of Oklahoma. Hearings before the Secretary of the Interior on Leasing of Oil Lands and Natural Gas Wells in Indian Territory and Territory of Oklahoma. Washington, 1906.

84 p. 23 cm. Printed wrappers.

Prominent Indians' Views of the Political Parties of the Day. Showing the Abuses the Indian has received at the Hands of the Republican Party. Setting forth Cogent Reasons why the Indian will Cast his Vote with the Democratic Party. Some History not Generally known, which has Sufficient Weight to cause the Indian to Vote the Democratic Ticket. [N.p., 1906?].*

64 p. 23 cm. Printed wrappers.

Statements by prominent members of the Five Tribes urging their fellow citizens to align themselves with the Democratic Party in the imminent State of Oklahoma. The statements by the Choctaw leaders appear in both English and Choctaw. No other copy has been traced.

Report of the United States Indian Inspector for the Indian Territory for the year ended June 30, 1906. Washington, 1906.

102 p. 23 cm. Printed wrappers. Folded map.

1907

HITCHCOCK, ETHAN ALLEN

Statement of Hon. Ethan Allen Hitchcock, Secretary of the Interior. Washington, 1907.

77 p. 23 cm. Printed wrappers.

Affairs in Indian Territory.

Official Proceedings of the Thirty-fourth Annual Communication of the M. W. Grand Lodge of Indian Territory, held at South McAlester, Choctaw Nation, August 13 and 14, 1907. Address of the Grand Secretary, J. S. Murrow, Atoka, Indian Territory. Atoka, I.T.: Indian Citizen Publishing Co., 1907.

108, [2], 34, [4] p. 23 cm. Printed wrappers. Photographs.

Report of the Select Committee to Investigate Matters connected with Affairs in the Indian Territory, with Hearings November 11, 1906–January 9, 1907. Washington, 1907.*

2 vols. continuously paged. 2165 p. 22 cm.

Of great value for its picture of the economic and social condition of the Indian tribes just before statehood.

Report of the United States Indian Inspector for the Indian Territory to the Secretary of the Interior. 1907. Washington, 1907.

58 p. 23 cm. Printed wrappers.

1908

Official Proceedings of the Thirty-fifth Annual Communication of the M. W. Grand Lodge of Indian Territory. Address of the Grand Secretary, J. S. Murrow. Atoka: Indian Citizen, 1908.

292, [2] p. 23 cm. Printed wrappers.

Proceedings of the Grand Commandery of Knights Templar of Indian Territory. McAlester, April 23, 1908. Atoka: Indian Citizen Pub. Co., 1908.

49, 83, [1], ii p. 23 cm. Printed wrappers. Frontisp. portrait.

1909

Littleheart, Oleta

The Lure of the Indian Country and a Romance of its Great Resort. By Oleta Littleheart, Sulphur, Okla. Sulphur: A. Abbott, [1909].*

153, [1] p. 17.5 cm. Printed wrappers.

1910

Murrow, J. S.

A Savings Bank. [Atoka, 1910?].*

[4] p. 13 cm.

An appeal for funds for the Indian orphans' home.

1912

Murrow, J. S.

The Indian's Side. [Atoka: Atoka Press, 1912.]

39 p. 23 cm. Wrapper title.

Murrow, J. S.

Why the Indian is Poor and Lazy. [Ardmore:] Indian Territory Baptist Print, [1912].

[2], 11 p. 13 cm.

1916

Anti-Horse Thief Association

Proceedings of the 14th Annual Session of the Anti-Horse Thief Association, I.T. Division, held at Miami. St. Paul, Kansas: News, [1916].

18, [8] p. 19.5 cm. Printed wrappers. Portraits.

1918

Anti-Horse Thief Association

Proceedings of the 16th Annual Session of the Anti-Horse Thief Association, I.T. Division, Oklahoma, held at Ada. St. Paul, Kansas: Weekly News, [1918].

16, [4] p. 20 cm. Printed wrappers. Portraits.

1919

Anti-Horse Thief Association

Proceedings of the 17th Annual Session of the Anti-Horse Thief Association, I.T. Division, Oklahoma, held at Hugo. St. Paul, Kansas: The News, [1919].

21, [6] p. 20 cm. Printed wrappers. Portraits.

1920

Anti-Horse Thief Association

Proceedings of the 18th Annual Session of the Anti-Horse Thief Association, I.T. Division, Oklahoma, held at McAlester. St. Paul, Kansas: The News, [1920].

18, [4] p. 20 cm. Printed wrappers.

1922

Anti-Horse Thief Association

Proceedings of the 20th Annual Session of the Anti-Horse Thief Association, I.T. Division, held at Dewey. St. Paul, Kansas: The News, [1922].

19, [3] p. 20 cm. Printed wrappers.

1923

Anti-Horse Thief Association

Proceedings of the 21st Annual Session of the Anti-Horse Thief Association, I.T. Division, held at Checotah. St. Paul, Kansas: The Rural Digest, [1923].

14, [4] p. 19 cm. Portraits.

1924

Anti-Horse Thief Association

Proceedings of the 22nd Annual Session of the Anti-Horse Thief Association, East Oklahoma Division, held at Stilwell. St. Paul, Kansas: The Rural Digest, [1924].

12, [2] p. 19 cm. Printed wrappers.

1925

Anti-Horse Thief Association

Proceedings of the 23d Annual Session of the Anti-Horse Thief Association, East Oklahoma Division, held at Wagoner. St. Paul, Kansas, [1925].

15 p. 20 cm. Printed wrappers.

1926

Anti-Horse Thief Association

Proceedings of the 24th Annual Session of the Anti-Horse Thief Association, East Oklahoma Division, held at Bartlesville. St. Paul, Kansas: The News, [1926].

19 p. 20 cm.

1927

Anti-Horse Thief Association

Proceedings of the 25th Annual Session of the Anti-Horse Thief Association of the East Oklahoma Division, held at Coweta. St. Paul, Kansas: The News, [1927].*

16 p. 19.5 cm. Printed wrappers.

1928

ANTI-HORSE THIEF ASSOCIATION

Proceedings of the 26th Annual Session of the Anti-Horse Thief Association of the East Oklahoma Division, held at Tahlequah. St. Paul, Kansas: The News, [1928].*

15 p. 19.5 cm. Printed wrappers.

1929

ANTI-HORSE THIEF ASSOCIATION

Proceedings of the 27th Annual Session of the Anti-Horse Thief Association of the East Oklahoma Division, held at Dewey. St. Paul, Kansas: News, [1929].*

17 p. 19.5 cm. Printed wrappers.

1930

ANTI-HORSE THIEF ASSOCIATION

Proceedings of the 28th Annual Session of the Anti-Horse Thief Association of the East Oklahoma Division, held at Stilwell. St. Paul, Kansas: The News, [1930].*

14 p. 19.5 cm. Printed wrappers.

ROFF, JOE T.

A Brief History of Early Days in North Texas and the Indian Territory. By Joe T. Roff, Roff, Oklahoma. [N.p.], 1930.

40 p. 17.5 cm. Printed wrappers.

INDIAN TRADE

1800

Report of the Committee appointed to Enquire into the Operation of the Acts making Provision for the Establishment of Trading Houses with the Indian Tribes, and into the Expediency of Reviving and Continuing the said Acts in force. [Washington, 1800.]

18 p. 22.5 cm. Folded tables.

1818

Message from the President of the United States transmitting a Report from the Secretary of War containing a List of the Names of the Several Agents of Indian Affairs and of the Agents of Indian Trading Houses, with the Pay and Emoluments of the Agents respectively. Washington: E. De Krafft, 1818.

8 p. 21.5 cm.

Report of the Secretary of War of a System, providing for the Abolition of the Existing Indian Trade Establishments of the United States, and providing for the Opening of the Trade with the Indians to Individuals, under Suitable Regulations. Washington: E. De Krafft, 1818.

14 p. 24 cm.

1820

Letter from the Secretary of War, transmitting Statements of the Amounts and Costs of Goods furnished annually to Indian Trading Houses since the year 1815.

Specifying, also, the Kinds and Quantity of Furs, &c., annually received since that period, of said Factories. Washington: Gales & Seaton, 1820.

4 p. 24 cm. Folded table.

Letter from the Superintendent of Indian Trade to the Chairman of the Committee on Indian Affairs, communicating a Report in relation to Indian Trade. Washington: Gales & Seaton, 1820.

8 p. 24 cm.

[Report of the Committee on Indian Affairs on Trade and Intercourse with the Indian Tribes. Washington, 1820].

9 p. 24 cm.

Important letters from Thomas Biddle and Henry Atkinson on trade with the Indians on the Missouri River.

1821

Letter from the Secretary of War transmitting a Statement of the Amount of Merchandise on hand at the Different Indian Trading Houses and in the hands of the Superintendent of Indian Trade in Georgetown. Washington: Gales & Seaton, 1821.

8 p. 23.5 cm.

Message from the President of the United States transmitting a Statement of Expenditures and Receipts in the Indian Department; also, the Nature and Extent of Contracts entered into from March 2, 1811, to the present period. Washington: Gales & Seaton, 1821.

10 p. 23.5 cm. Folded table.

1822

Documents relative to Indian trade. Submitted to the Senate by the Committee on Indian Affairs. Washington: Gales & Seaton, 1822.

62 p. 22.5 cm. Folded tables.

An important document.

Letter from the Secretary of War transmitting Sundry Statements in relation to the Indian Department. Washington: Gales & Seaton, 1822.

20 p. 22.5 cm. 2 folded tables.

1824

Report of the Committee on Indian Affairs, upon the subject of the Execution of the Act to Abolish the Indian Trading Establishments, &c. &c. [Washington, 1824.]

32 p. 22.5 cm. Caption title.

1825

Letter from the Secretary of War, transmitting a Report of the Second Auditor in relation to the Disbursements of Indian Agents from 1st September, 1823, to the 1st September, 1824. Washington: Gales & Seaton, 1825.*

94 p. 22 cm. Many folded tables.

An extremely valuable source of information on the Indian trade.

Message from the President of the United States, transmitting an Abstract of

Licenses granted to Persons to Trade in the Indian Country, during the year ending January 17, 1825. Washington: Gales & Seaton, 1825.

[4] p. 22 cm. 3 folded tables.

Message from the President of the United States transmitting a Report of the Progress made in the Execution of the Act to Abolish the Indian Trading Establishments, &c. Washington: Gales & Seaton, 1825.

36 p. 22 cm.

1834

An Act to Regulate Trade and Intercourse with Indian Tribes, and to Preserve Peace on the Frontiers. Approved June 30, 1834. [Washington, 1834.]

8 p. 24.5 cm. Caption title.

An important and far-reaching act.

1853

Ewing, W. G., and G. W. Ewing

For Sale. W. G. & G. W. Ewing will sell a large and commodious Brick Store, situated in Westport, Jackson County, Mo. . . . Also, a Large Stock of Indian and Citizens' Goods, etc. [Westport, Mo., 1853.]

Broadside. Folio.

The Ewings conducted a large Indian trade. The only known copy.

1889

[Report of Senate Committee on Indian Traderships. Washington, 1889.]*

601 p. 23 cm.

An important document.

1935

The Southern Indian Trade. Being particularly a Study of Material from the Tallapoosa River Valley of Alabama by Peter A. Brannon. Montgomery: The Paragon Press, 1935.

87 p. 23 cm. Printed wrappers.

A valuable and well illustrated monograph.

IOWA INDIANS

1843

Hamilton, William, and S. M. Irvin

An Elementary Book of the Ioway Language, with an English Translation. By Wm. Hamilton and S. M. Irvin, under the Direction of the B. F. Miss. of the Presbyterian Church. J. B. Roy, Interpreter. Ioway and Sac Mission Press. Indian Territory. 1843.

101 p. 15 cm. The English title is preceded by one in the Iowa language.

Pilling, Siouan Bibliography, p. 32.

The first book in the Iowa language. One of only two copies located, the other being at the New York Public Library. [See page 237.]

AN

ELEMENTARY BOOK

OF THE

IOWAY LANGUAGE,

WITH AN

ENGLISH TRANSLATION.

BY

WM. HAMILTON,

AND

S. M. IRVIN.

Under the direction of the B. F. Miss. of the

PRESBYTERIAN CHURCH.

J. B. ROY, INTERPRETER.

IOWAY, AND SAC MISSION PRESS.

INDIAN TERRITORY.

1843.

1848

HAMILTON, WILLIAM, and S. M. IRVIN

An Ioway Grammar, illustrating the Principles of the Language used by the Ioway, Otoe and Missouri Indians. Prepared and printed by Rev. Wm. Hamilton and Rev. S. M. Irvin. Under the Direction of the Presbyterian B. F. M. Ioway and Sac Mission Press. 1848.

152 p. 15 cm.

Pilling, Siouan Bibliography, p. 33.

The Union Catalog locates only three copies.

1850

HAMILTON, WILLIAM, and S. M. IRVIN

We-wv-hae-kju. [Ioway and Sac Mission Press, 1850.]*

29 p. 14.5 cm. Caption title.

Pilling, Siouan Bibliography, p. 33.

Catechism in the Iowa language. One of only three known copies, the others being at the Library of Congress and the Newberry Library.

HAMILTON, WILLIAM, and S. M. IRVIN

Wv-ro-haw. [Ioway and Sac Mission Press, 1850.]*

24 p. 14.5 cm. Caption title.

Pilling, Siouan Bibliography, p. 33.

Prayers in the Iowa language. One of only three known copies, the others being at the Library of Congress and the Newberry Library.

1890

Message from the President of the United States transmitting an Agreement between the Cherokee Commission and the Iowa Indians in the Indian Territory. [Washington, 1890.]

23 p. 23 cm. Caption title.

1895

Petition of the Iowa Indians to the Senate and House of Representatives, with a Letter to the Honorable Commissioner of Indian Affairs. 1895. [Guthrie: Daily Leader Press, 1895.]

6 p. 22 cm. Printed wrappers.

Unrecorded, and no other copy traced.

KANSAS INDIANS

1834

Proceedings of the General Meeting of Western Baptists at Cincinnati, commencing on the sixth of November, 1833. Cincinnati: N. S. Johnson, 1834.*

80 p. 21 cm.

Contains an account of Indian missions supported by the Baptist board, with particular notice of the appointment of Jotham Meeker as missionary to Indians in the present Kansas and the purchase of a printing press and types for his use. Very rare.

1846

Articles of a Treaty made and concluded at the Methodist Mission, in the Kanzas Country, between Thomas H. Harvey and Richard W. Cummins, Commissioners of the United States, and the Kanzas Tribe of Indians, on the 14th of January, 1846. [Washington, 1846.]

19 p. 25 cm. Caption title.

The rare preliminary confidential printing, which contains the important journal of the treaty council.

1847

A Memorial to Congress on the subject of Organizing a Territory West of the State of Missouri. [Jefferson City? 1847.]*

Broadsheet. 25.5 cm.

An important memorial of the Missouri legislature asking the expulsion of all Indians from the present Kansas, the opening of that country to white settlement, and the formation of a territorial government there. The only known copy.

1855

Montgomery, John

Notice to Intruders on the Kansas Indian Reservation. [Leavenworth, 1855.]

Broadside. 25 cm.

An unrecorded and extremely early Kansas imprint, and the only known copy.

1856

Greene, Max

The Kanzas Region: Forest, Prairie, Desert, Mountain, Vale, and River. Descriptions of Scenery, Climate, Wild Productions, Capabilities of Soil, and Commercial Resources; Interspersed with Incidents of Travel and Anecdotes Illustrative of the Character of the Traders and Red Men; to which are added Directions as to Routes, Outfit for the Pioneer, and Sketches of Desirable Locations for Present Settlement. New York; Fowler & Wells, 1856.

192, 4, 4, 4 p. 19 cm. 2 maps.

Wagner-Camp 276. Field 628.

1857

Vanderslice, D.

Iowa Trust Lands. Great Nemaha Agency, Kansas Territory, 1857.

Broadside. 15 cm.

A warning against intrusion upon Indian lands. Unrecorded, and the only known copy. No other Great Nemaha Agency imprint is known.

Walker, R. J.

Inaugural Address of R. J. Walker, Governor of Kansas Territory. Delivered in Lecompton, K.T., May 27, 1857. "Union" Office, Lecompton, May, 1857.

24 p. 21 cm.

Proposes immediate seizure and occupation of Indian Territory. A rare and early Kansas Territory imprint.

1861

Rules and Regulations to be observed in the Execution of Conveyances of Lands which have been or shall be assigned in severalty to Indians within the Territory of Kansas, and for which Patents shall be issued. [Washington, 1861.]

2 p. 34 cm. Caption title.

1865

Head-Qrs. Dist. of the Upper Arkansas, Fort Riley, Kansas, July 20th, 1865. General Orders No. 29. [Fort Riley, 1865.]

2 p. 20 cm. Caption title.

Instructions regarding operations against the Indians.

1874

Copy of the Original Papers recommending an Appropriation for Mrs. O. F. Short, whose Husband and Son were Killed by Indians during the summer of 1874. Lawrence, Kansas: Republican Journal Steam Printing Establishment, 1874.

8 p. 22 cm. Printed wrappers.

Extremely rare.

1900

GOODLANDER, C. W.

Memoirs and Recollections of C. W. Goodlander of the Early Days of Fort Scott from April 29, 1858, to January 1, 1870, covering the time prior to the Advent of the Railroad and during the days of the Ox-team and Stage Transportation. And Biographies of Col. H. T. Wilson and Geo. A. Crawford, the Fathers of Fort Scott. Fort Scott, Kansas: Monitor Printing Co. 1900.

145, [4] p. 16 cm. Frontisp. port. Plates.

A very scarce volume.

1908

DUNBAR, JOHN B.

The White Man's Foot in Kansas. An Address at the Pawnee Village, Republic County, Kansas. Topeka, 1908.

62 p. 23 cm. Printed wrappers. Folded map.

KENTUCKY INDIANS

1802

TOULMIN, HARRY

A Collection of all the Public and Permanent Acts of the General Assembly of Kentucky which are now in force. By Harry Toulmin, Secretary to the Commonwealth of Kentucky. Frankfort: William Hunter, 1802.

lxiv, 507, [2] p. 16 cm.

Contains the highly repressive laws governing "Slaves, Free Negroes, Mulattoes, and Indians."

1818

KENTUCKY GENERAL ASSEMBLY

[Resolution asking extinguishment of Indian title to lands in Kentucky. Frankfort, 1818.]*

Broadside. 25 cm.
Unrecorded, and the only known copy.

KIOWA INDIANS

1864

CARLETON, JAMES H.

Head-Quarters, Department of New Mexico, Santa Fe, N.M., October 22, 1864. General Orders No. 32. [Santa Fe, 1864.]

Broadsheet. 19 cm.
Organization of an expedition, under the command of Colonel Kit Carson, "to move against the Kioway and Comanche Indians, who, during last summer, attacked trains on the roads leading from New Mexico to the States." Unrecorded, and the only known copy.

1865

CARLETON, JAMES H.

Cuarteles Generales, Dep'to de Nuevo Mejico, Santa Fe, Enero 31 de 1865. Ordenes Generales No. 2. [Santa Fe, 1865.]

Broadside. 20 cm.
A translation into Spanish of the following order. Unrecorded, and the only known copy.

CARLETON, JAMES H.

Head-Quarters, Department of New Mexico, Santa Fe, N.M., January 31, 1865. General Orders No. 2. [Santa Fe, 1865.]

Broadside. 20 cm.
An order forbidding traders to go among the hostile Kiowas and Comanches. Unrecorded, and the only known copy.

1867

Headquarters Military Division of the Missouri. St. Louis, Mo., Nov. 2, 1867. General Orders No. 10. [St. Louis, 1867.]

Broadside. 20.5 cm.
Announcement of terms of treaties with the Kiowa, Comanche, and Apache tribes, and with the Cheyennes and Arapahoes.

1872

Statement of Henry Warren. Claims for Indian Depredations. Kiowa and Cheyenne Tribes. Weatherford, Texas. 1872.*

8 p. 22 cm.
An extremely rare and valuable and wholly unrecorded account of the famous Warren wagon-train massacre perpetrated May 18, 1871, by the Kiowas under the leadership of Satanta and that of August, 1871, perpetrated by the Cheyennes.

1878

HAWORTH, J. M.

Proposals for Breaking Prairie. Sealed Proposals will be received at the Office of the Kiowa and Comanche Agency, Indian Territory for breaking two hundred and fifty acres of Prairie Land for Indian Farms, etc. [Fort Sill, 1878.]

Broadside. 15.5 cm. high × 28 cm. wide.

Unrecorded, and the only known copy.

Hunt, P. B.

Proposals for School and Commissary Buildings. Office Kiowa, Comanche and Wichita Agency, Anadarko P. O., Ind. Ter., Sept. 16, 1878. [Anadarko? 1878.]

Broadside. 10 cm.

Unrecorded, and the only known copy.

1879

Hunt, P. B.

Sealed Proposals. Office of Indian Agent, Kiowa, Comanche and Wichita Agency, Anadarko, Indian Territory, March 25, 1879. Sealed Proposals will be received at this Office until 12 M. Thursday, May 1st, 1879, for the Delivery at the Agency on or before July 1st, 1879, of 500 Native or Northern Texas Yearling Heifers, 10 Short-Horn Bulls, 5 Short-Horn Heifers, etc. Wichita: Eagle Steam Print, [1879].

Broadside. Folio.

The only known copy.

1891

Howry, Charles B.

George H. Giddings vs. The United States and the Kiowa, Comanche, and Apache Tribes of Indians. Supplemental Brief and Argument. [Washington? 1891.]

123 p. 23 cm. Caption title.

A suit to recover damages suffered in the 1860's from repeated depredations by the Kiowas, Comanches, and Apaches upon Giddings' mail and stage coaches running between San Antonio, El Paso, and Yuma. The volume contains letters, documents, and depositions offering valuable detail. No other copy can be traced.

1895

Howry, Charles B.

Don A. Sanford vs. The United States and the Kiowa and Comanche Indians. Brief for Defendants. [Washington, 1895.]*

33 p. 23.5 cm. Wrapper title.

A claim for the value of a large herd of cattle stolen from Sanford in 1872 while he was driving it from San Saba, Texas, to California, by a party of Kiowa and Comanche Indians. The evidence is set forth in valuable detail.

1897

Clouse, H. H., and M. J. Reeside

The First Kiowa Hymn-Book. Translated by Miss M. J. Reeside. Compiled by Rev. H. H. Clouse, 1897. Shell Rock, Iowa: D. L. Clouse, [1897].

[8] p. 18.5 cm. Wrapper title.

The first book in the Kiowa language. Unrecorded, and the only known copy. [See page 243.]

THE FIRST

KIOWA HYMN-BOOK.

Translated by Miss. M. J. Reeside.
Compiled by Rev. H. H. Clouse.

1897.

D. L. Clouse, Print. Shell Rock, Iowa.

1899

METHVIN, J. J.

Andele, or the Mexican-Kiowa Captive. A Story of Real Life among the Indians. By J. J. Methvin, Superintendent of Methvin Institute, Anadarko, O.T. 1899: Pentecostal Herald Press, Louisville, Ky.

185 p. 18 cm.

1900

John S. Hagler, Administrator of Tip Mooney, vs. The United States and the Kiowa and Comanche Indians. Evidence for Defendants. [Washington, 1901.]*

Pp. 33–70. 23 cm. Caption title.

The estate of Mooney, a cattle raiser in Texas, claimed that a herd of two thousand head of cattle was stolen by the Kiowa and Comanche Indians in 1866. The many depositions here printed offer interesting and valuable detail.

WEED, JOHN J.

John S. Hagler, Administrator of the Estate of Tip Mooney, vs. The United States and the Kiowa and Comanche Indians. Brief for Claimant. [N.p., 1900.]*

45 p. 21 cm. Wrapper title.

Claim for a large herd of cattle stolen from Mooney in 1866 by the Kiowas and Comanches. The evidence is set forth in valuable detail.

1901

Lone Wolf, Chief of Kiowas, Eshitie, Principal Chief of Comanches, et al., Appellants, vs. Ethan A. Hitchcock, Secretary of the Interior, et al. Appeal from the Supreme Court of the District of Columbia. Reply Brief of Appellants. Washington: Gibson Bros., 1901.*

17 p. 23 cm. Wrapper title.

The litigation arose from provisions of the treaty concluded at Medicine Lodge Creek in 1867. James Mooney's copy, with his signature on the title page.

Lone Wolf, Principal Chief of Kiowas; Eshitie, Principal Chief of Comanches; White Buffalo, Ko-Koy-Taudle, Mar-Mo-Sook-Car-Wer, Nar-Wats, Too-Wi-Car-Ne, William Tivis, Delos K. Lonewolf, Appellants, vs. Ethan A. Hitchcock, Secretary of the Interior, William A. Jones, Commissioner of Indian Affairs, and Binger Hermann, Commissioner of the General Land Office. Appeal from the Supreme Court of the District of Columbia. Brief and Argument of Appellants. Washington: Gibson Bros., 1901.

33 p. 23 cm. Wrapper title.

James Mooney's copy, with his signature.

1902

Proposals for Leasing the Surplus Grazing Lands of the Kiowa, Comanche, and Apache Indians, in Oklahoma. [Washington, 1902.]

Broadside. Folio.

1903

Kiowa Indian Agency. Letter from the Secretary of the Interior, transmitting the

Results of an Investigation into the Affairs of the Kiowa Indian Agency. Washington, 1903.

49 p. 22.5 cm. Printed wrappers.

1905

Proposals for Leasing the Surplus Grazing Lands of the Kiowa, Comanche, and Apache Indians in Oklahoma. [Washington, 1905.]

Broadside. Folio.

1910

BARDE, F. A.

In Camp. A Description of an Indian Camp Meeting in Oklahoma. [New York, 1910.]*

[24] p. 16 cm. Photographs.

A Baptist camp meeting held at Short Teeth's allotment on Kingfisher Creek and attended by people of the Kiowa, Comanche, Cheyenne, Arapahoe, Apache, Wichita, Caddo, Delaware, Pawnee, and Osage tribes.

LOUISIANA TERRITORY

1803

An Account of Louisiana, being an Abstract of Documents in the offices of the Departments of State and of the Treasury. Philadelphia: William Duane, 1803.

30 p. 21 cm. Folded table.

A valuable account of the newly acquired empire.

1804

Account of Louisiana, laid before Congress by direction of the President of the United States, November 14, 1803: comprising an Account of its Boundaries, History, Cities, Towns, and Settlements; of the Origin, Number and Strength of its Inhabitants; of its Rivers, Canals, Mountains, Minerals, and Productions of Soil; of the Different Tribes of Indians, and the Number of their Warriors; and of its Navigation and Laws under the Spanish Government, &c. &c. Providence: Printed by Heaton & Williams. [1804].

72 p. 16.5 cm.

A rare and important volume.

RAMSAY, DAVID

An Oration on the Cession of Louisiana to the United States, delivered on the 12th May, 1804, in St. Michael's Church, Charleston, South-Carolina, at the Request of a Number of the Inhabitants, and Published at their Desire. By David Ramsay, M.D. Charleston: W. P. Young, M.DCCCIV.

27 p. 20 cm.

1808

The Laws of the Territory of Louisiana. Comprising all those which are now actually in force within the same. Published by Authority. St. Louis (L.): Printed by Joseph Charless, Printer to the Territory, 1808.*

376, [58] p. 21.5 cm. Title page in expert facsimile.

The first laws for the government of the vast area comprising the Louisiana Purchase, and the first printing in the United States west of the Mississippi River. The volume contains laws regulating trade with the Indians. Of superlative rarity.

1812

STODDARD, AMOS

Sketches, Historical and Descriptive, of Louisiana. By Major Amos Stoddard. Philadelphia: Matthew Carey, 1812.

488 p. 21 cm.

Field 1505.

An important and detailed account, with extended notices of the Indian tribes.

1922

SIBLEY, JOHN

A Report from Natchitoches in 1807, by Dr. John Sibley. Edited, with an Introduction, by Annie Heloise Abel. New York: Heye Foundation, 1922.

102 p. 17 cm. Printed wrappers. Plates.

With highly useful annotations.

Undated

Observations on the Nature of French, British, and Spanish Grants of Land in Louisiana, for the Better Understanding the Report, made by the Land Commissioners, under authority of the Act of 25th April, 1812. [N.p., n.d.]

Broadside. Folio.

No other copy can be traced.

MAPS

1591

Floridiae Americae Provinciae Recens & Exactissima Descriptio Auctore Iacobo le Moyne. [1591].

14 in. × 18.

Generally acknowledged as the most important map of the sixteenth century showing the region between Cape Hatteras and the Florida keys.

1653

America Septentrionalis. Amstelodami: Excudit Ioannes Iansonius. [1653].

20 in. × 24.

1657

Americque Septentrionale. Par N. Sanson. [Paris, 1657.]

8½ in. × 13. Colored.

Audience de Guadalajara, Nouveau Mexique, Californie, &c. Par N. Sanson. [Paris, 1657.]

8½ in. × 11. Colored.

Audience de Mexico. Par N. Sanson. [Paris, 1657.]

8½ in. × 12½. Colored.

Le Canada, ou Nouvelle France, &c. Par N. Sanson. [Paris, 1657.]

8½ in. × 13½. Colored.

1667

Nova Virginiae Tabula. Ex Officina Guiljelmi Blaeuw. [Amsterdam, 1667.]
18 in. × 23.
Inset: Status Regis Powhatan quando Prefectus Smith Captivus illi daretur. The Amsterdam reproduction of the famous John Smith map.

Virginiae Partis Australis, et Floridae Partis Orientalis, Interjacentiumque Regionum Nova Descriptio. [Amsterdam: J. Blaeu, 1667.]
19 in. × 22. Colored.

1671

Nova Virginiae Tabula. [London, 1671.]
13½ in. × 17.
A reproduction of the Smith map.

1690

[A detailed map of Tidewater Virginia and Carolina. London: I. Thornton? 1690?].
26 in. × 20½.
Locates Indian settlements. Not in Phillips.

1717

A Map of Mexico or New Spain, Florida now called Louisiana &c. and Part of California &c. By H. Moll, Geographer. [London, 1717.]
8½ in. × 12.

A Map of New France, containing Canada, Louisiana &c. in North America. By H. Moll, Geographer. [London, 1717.]
8½ in. × 12.
Valuable for its notations of Indian settlements.

1752

A New & Accurate Map of the Provinces of North & South Carolina, Georgia, &c. Drawn from Late Surveys and Regulated by Astronl. Observations. By Eman. Bowen. [London, 1752.]
16 in. × 19.
Of great value for its location of Indian tribes, settlements, and trails.

1763

A New Map of North & South Carolina, & Georgia. By T. Kitchin, Geogr. [London, 1763.]
9 in. × 11.
Georgia and the Carolinas extended at the time to the Mississippi River. Notations of Indian tribes and settlements.

1764

A New Map of Georgia, with Part of Carolina, Florida and Louisiana. Collected by Eman. Bowen, Geographer to His Majesty. [London, 1764.]
16½ in. × 19.
Valuable for its notations of Indian tribes, settlements, and trails in Georgia, Florida, Alabama, Mississippi, Tennessee, and Louisiana.

1765

A Draught of the Cherokee Country, on the West Side of the Twenty Four Mountains, commonly called Over the Hills; taken by Henry Timberlake, when he was in that Country, in March 1762. Likewise the Names of the Principal or Headmen of Each Town, and what Number of Fighting Men they Send to War. [London, 1765.]

19 in. × 11½.

The large paper issue of the important map which appeared, trimmed to fit the volume, in Timberlake's Memoirs [London, 1765].

1768

North America, from the French of Mr. d'Anville. Improved with the Back Settlements of Virginia and Course of Ohio. Illustrated with Geographical and Historical Remarks. [London, 1768.]

19 in. × 20½. Colored.

A map of very great value.

1777

Carte detaillee des Possessions Angloises dans l'Amerique Septentrionale. Construite d'apres les dernieres relations et les Cartes particulieres de ces Provinces pour l'intelligence de la Guerre actualle entre les Anglois et leurs Colonies. A Paris ches Esnauts et Rapilly, 1777.

21 in. × 30½. Colored. Backed with muslin.

Inset: Florida and the West Indies.

1795

Georgia, from the Latest Authorities. W. Barker, sculp. [Philadelphia, 1795.]

15 in. × 18.

Georgia at this time embraced Alabama and Mississippi, and the map notes Indian tribes, settlements, and trails in this vast area.

1805

Map of the Southern, Western & Middle Provinces of the United States. London: J. Mawman, 1805.

16 in. × 21.

Notations of Indian tribes and settlements. Not in Phillips.

1812

Carte des Etats-Unis de Amerique Septentrionale. Copiee et Cravee sur celle d'Arrowsmith. Paris: P. F. Tardieu, 1812.

50 in. × 29½. Colored. Backed with muslin.

An inset Plan of the City of Washington, and an inset view of Niagara Falls, with two Indians on the river bank.

A map of the highest value.

1813

Map of the Seat of War in North America. Second Edition, with Additions and Improvements. John Melish, del. [Philadelphia, 1813.]

17 in. × 22½. Colored.

Shows location of Indian tribes in the Great Lakes region.

A Map of the Southern Section of the United States, including the Floridas & Bahama Islands. Showing the Seat of War in that Department. Drawn by John Melish. Engraved by H. S. Tanner. Philadelphia: John Melish, March, 1813.

17 in. × 12. Colored.

Information of great value on Indian tribes and settlements of the South and Southwest.

1814

Mississippi Territory. [1814?].*

17 in. × 22. Colored.

Mississippi Territory at the time included Alabama. The map shows Indian tribes, settlements, and trails.

The State of Georgia. [1814].*

21 in. × 17. Colored. 2 different issues.

Particularly valuable for showing settlements and trails in the Creek country. Not in Phillips.

The State of Tennessee. [1814?].

17 in. × 22. Colored.

1818

Map of the State of Georgia. Prepared from Actual Surveys and other Documents for Eleazer Early, by Daniel Sturges. Savannah: E. Early, 1818.

44 in. × 56. Colored. In four sections; backed with muslin.

With its wealth of authoritative detail, this map is easily one of the most important ever made showing the Indian country of Georgia, eastern Alabama, and northern Florida.

1826

Map of the United States, drawn from the most approved Surveys. New York: Solomon Schoyer, 1826.

17 in. × 21½. Colored. Folded into a leather case.

Arkansas Territory includes present Oklahoma. Missouri Territory includes the vast Northwest. Indian tribes and settlements are indicated. Not in Phillips.

1830

Map of the State of Georgia, drawn from Actual Surveys and the most Authentic Information. By Carleton Wellborn (Late Surveyor General) and Orange Green, 1830. Engraved by W. Hoogland. New York, [1830].

31½ in. × 27. Colored. Backed with muslin.

Shows the northern portion of the state still occupied by the Cherokee Indians. Not in Phillips.

1831

A Map of the Route pursued by an Exploring Party from Cantonment Gibson under the Direction of Mr. McCoy.

16 in. × 17.

Negative photostat of the original manuscript map in the National Archives.

1832

Map of North and South Carolina and Georgia. Compiled from the Latest Authorities. Published by S. Augustus Mitchell. Philadelphia, [1832].

17 in. × 21. Colored. Folded into a leather case.

Shows the country of the Cherokee Indians in northwestern Georgia.

1835

Mitchell's Map of the United States, showing the Principal Travelling, Turnpike and Common Roads; on which are given the Distances in Miles from one Place to another; also the Courses of the Canals & Railroads throughout the Country, carefully compiled from the Best Authorities. Philadelphia: S. A. Mitchell, 1835.

19 in. × 23.

In Mitchell, Compendium [Philadelphia, 1835].

General Ethan A. Hitchcock's copy.

1836

Map showing the Lands Assigned to Emigrant Indians West of Arkansas and Missouri. [Washington? 1836.]

20 in. × 15. Colored.

With a statement of the area of land assigned, the numbers of emigrants by tribes, the numbers by tribes of Indians already living in the West, etc. The map shows portions of the Santa Fe and Osage Trails and the Texas Road, and the old western boundary of Arkansas. The only known copy of the first map of Indian Territory.

1837

Map of Florida by J. Lee Williams, 1837. Lithographed by Greene & McGowran, New York. [1837].

35½ in. × 30½. Backed with muslin.

Of great value for its notation of Indian tribes and settlements.

1838

Georgia. Engraved by G. W. Boynton. [Boston, 1838].

19.5 in. × 15.5. Colored.

Probably the earliest map to show Georgia entirely devoid of Indians. Not in Phillips.

Map of the Indian Territory, corrected according to the Latest Surveys. By Isaac McCoy, 1838.*

A positive photostat, in 4 sections, each 25 in. × 18, of the manuscript original in the National Archives.

I do not think that this map has ever been reproduced. The Indian Territory depicted is the larger Indian Territory.

Mitchell's Traveller's Guide through the United States. A Map of the Roads, Distances, Steam Boat and Canal Routes, &c. Philadelphia: Published by A. Augustus Mitchell, 1838.

17½ in. × 22. Colored.

In Mitchell's Traveller's Guide. [Philadelphia, 1838].

Shows location of Indian tribes on the western borders.

1842

Traveller's Guide. A Map of the Ohio and Mississippi Rivers. Extending from Pittsburgh to the Gulf of Mexico. By J. Duff. Cincinnati: George Conclin, 1842.

24 in. × 9½. Folded into a stiff paper cover.

With a table of distances.

General E. A. Hitchcock's copy, with his bookplate. Not in Phillips.

1847

Mapa de los Estados Unidos de Mejico. Revised Edition. Nueva York: J. Disturnell, 1847.

30½ in. × 41. Colored. Folded into a cloth cover.

A fine copy, bright and fresh, of this important and magnificent map. Mexico at the time included a large part of the present far western United States. Together with a facsimile (marked: "The Earliest of Five or More 1847 Editions") issued by the U.S. State Department about 1935.

1851

Map of the Territory of New Mexico, compiled by Bvt. 2nd. Lt. Jno. G. Parke, U.S.T.E., assisted by Mr. Richard H. Kern, by Order of Bvt. Col. Jno. Munroe, U.S.A., Comdg. 9th Mil. Dept. Drawn by R. H. Kern. Santa Fe, N.M., 1851. New York: J. & D. Major, [1851].

27 in. × 38.

1855

Map of the Survey of a Route for the Pacific Railroad near the 32nd Parallel between the Rio Grande and Red River. By Bvt. Capt. Jno. Pope, Topgl. Engrs., assisted by Lieut. K. Garrard, 1st Dragoons. Philadelphia: D. Chillas, [1855].

34 in. × 88.

A large and detailed map of the country between Fulton, Arkansas, and the Rio Grande, with locations of Indian tribes and trails, emigrant roads, and mail routes. In a protective case. Not in Phillips.

1859

Stevenson & Morris, New Sectional Map of Kansas. Stevenson & Morris, St. Louis, 1859.

29½ in. × 21½. Colored. Folded into a cloth case.

Shows the Osage and Cherokee lands, and the Otoe, Iowa, Kickapoo, Delaware, Wyandot, Sac and Fox, Ottawa, Peoria, Kaskaskia, Piankeshaw, and Wea reservations. Not in Phillips.

1863

Map of Mexico & California. Compiled from the Latest Authorities by Jules Hutawa. 2nd Edition. St. Louis, 1863.

24½ × 20 in. Colored.

1864

Hartley's Map of Arizona. New York, [1864].

31 in. × 36. Colored. Folded into a cloth case.

An exceptionally fine map, showing in valuable detail all the settlements, rivers, mountains, mines, wagon roads, and Indian tribes. General E. A. Hitchcock's copy, with his bookplate. Not in Phillips.

1866

Indian Territory, with part of the Adjoining State of Kansas. Prepared from the Map of Dan'l. C. Major, U.S. Astr., showing the Boundaries of the Choctaw and Chickasaw Nations, the Creek, Seminole, and Leased Indian Country established by Authority of the Commrs. of Indian Affairs in 1858–'59; and from Lieut. Col. J. E. Johnston's Map of the Southern Boundary of Kansas in 1857; the Map of the Creek Country by Lieut. I. C. Woodruff, Topl. Engrs., in 1850–51. [Washington,] October, 1866.

21 in. × 27.

Manuscript and water color additions show proposed reservations for the Cheyennes and Arapahoes and for the Kiowas, Comanches, and Apaches. A second copy, backed with muslin. With interesting manuscript and water color additions.

1867

Map of the Routes of the Union Pacific Railroads with their Eastern Connections. Compiled from Authorized Explorations, Public Surveys, and other Reliable Data. November, 1867. Washington: J. F. Gedney, [1867].

16 in. × 40½. Colored.

1869

Watson's New Map of the Western States, Territories, Mexico, and Central America. New York: Gaylord Watson, [1869].

38 in. × 29. Colored. Folded into a cloth case.

Not in Phillips.

1873

Colton's New Map of the State of Texas, the Indian Territory, and Adjoining Portions of New Mexico, Louisiana and Arkansas. Compiled by Prof. A. R. Roessler. New York: G. W. & C. B. Colton, 1873.*

33½ in. × 37. Colored. Backed with muslin.

Western Territories. Sheet No. 1. Prepared by Major J. W. Barlow, Corps of Engineers, U.S.A. [Washington, 1873.]

30 in. × 22.

With additional notations in manuscript. Nebraska, Iowa, Dakota, and Minnesota in valuable detail.

1875

New Map of the State of Texas, prepared and published for the Bureau of Immigration of the State of Texas, by A. R. Roessler, Civil and Mining Engineer. New York, 1875.

16½ in. × 19. Colored.

Shows practically all of Indian Territory on the North. Greer County is shown as a part of Texas. The Texas Panhandle is divided between Bexar Territory and Young Territory. Not in Phillips.

1876

Map of the States of Kansas and Texas, and Indian Territory, with Parts of the

Territories of Colorado and New Mexico. From the Most Recent Official Surveys and Explorations and other Authentic Information. Third Edition, with Corrections. Prepared in the Office of the Chief of Engineers, U.S. Army. [Washington,] 1876.*

2 sections, each 26 in. × 38. Colored.

With many additional notations in manuscript.

A large and detailed map, of the highest importance, showing Indian tribes, trails, and settlements, army posts, railroads, stage routes, military telegraph lines, and routes of all military tours of exploration from that of S. H. Long in 1819.

Western Territories. Sheet No. 2. Prepared by Major G. L. Gillespie, Corps of Engr's. [Washington,] 1876.

28 in. × 21½. Colored.

With additional notations in manuscript.

Indian Territory, Texas, Kansas, in authoritative detail.

Western Territories. Sheet No. 3. Prepared by Major G. L. Gillespie, Corps of Engineers. January, 1876. [Washington, 1876].

30½ in. × 22.

With additional notations in manuscript.

Wyoming and Nebraska in valuable detail.

1879

Boudinot, E. C.

Map of Indian Territory. [By E. C. Boudinot. N.p., 1879].

19 in. × 24. Colored.

With Boudinot's famous letter describing the fourteen million acres of land in Indian Territory purchased by the government from the Indian tribes to become a part of the public lands of the United States. The letter and map, widely distributed, were among the chief instruments which started the ultimately roaring rush of settlers to Oklahoma. Not in Phillips, and excessively rare.

Indian Territory. New York: Julius Bean, 1879.

27 in. × 34. Colored.

Not in Phillips.

1880

Thayer's Map of New Mexico. Published by H. L. Thayer, Denver, Col. 1880.

31 in. × 27. Colored. Folded into a cloth case.

Indian reservations and land grants.

1881

Military Map of the Indian Territory. Compiled under the direction of Capt. E. H. Ruffner, Engineers, Chief Engineer, Department of the Missouri. [Fort Leavenworth,] 1881.

47½ in. × 58.

The northwest, northeast, and southeast sections of this rare and important map, which was issued in four sections. The southwest section is not present.

1882

Cherokee Indian Reservation, Indian Territory. [Washington?] 1882.
19½ in. × 15½.
Shows towns, rivers, roads, mountains, etc.

1883

Indian Territory, 1883. [Washington, 1883.]
27 in. × 34. Colored. Backed with muslin.
Roads, railroads, cattle trails, military posts, towns, etc., of Indian Territory and Oklahoma. Not in Phillips.

1885

The Kansas State Journal Map of Oklahoma, compiled by S. N. Wood, Editor Kansas State Journal. Topeka Litho. Co., Topeka, Kans., [1885].
24 in. × 36. Colored. Backed with muslin.
Phillips 637.
One of the most interesting features of the map is the clear marking of cattle trails. The first map of Oklahoma, and a prime rarity.

Military Map of Oklahoma. Prepared under the direction of 1st Lieut. H. L. Ripley, 24th Infantry, Acting Chief Engineer Dep. Mo., by W. H. Stair. November, 1885.*
18 in. × 15½.
Positive photostat of the original manuscript in the National Archives.

1887

Indian Territory, 1887. [Washington, 1887.]
27 in. × 34½. Colored.
Roads, railroads, cattle trails, towns, etc., of Indian Territory and Oklahoma.

Map of the Atchison, Topeka, and Santa Fe Railroad Company and its Leased Lines and Connections. Chicago: Rand, McNally & Co., [1887].
14 in. × 22. Colored.
The whole of present Oklahoma, with the exception of the Panhandle, is marked Indian Territory.

Map of the Indian Territory, showing the Railways Built and Projected within its Boundaries. [Washington, 1887.]
21 in. × 28½.
Not in Phillips.

Map of Part of Indian Territory. [El Reno, 1887.]
Blueprint. 39½ in. × 22. Backed with muslin.
Cheyenne, Arapahoe, Pottawatomie, Wichita, Kiowa, Comanche, and Apache lands and settlements, and the western portion of the Chickasaw Nation. Military posts, Indian agencies, towns, railroads, and cattle trails are marked. Unrecorded, and the only known copy.

1889

Harrison, Oklahoma. [Wichita, Kansas, 1889.]
18 in. × 12.

The first map of Guthrie, issued just before the opening of April, 1889, by the Harrison Town Company, which ambitiously planned to occupy the site which later became Guthrie and to lay out streets and dispose of lots according to the survey and plan here set forth. Unrecorded, and the only known copy.

Map of the Indian Territory, showing the Railways Built and Projected within its Boundaries. [Washington, 1889.]
24½ in. × 28.
Not in Phillips.

Map of Oklahoma City, Indian Ter. Made from the Official Map drafted by Chas. Chamberlain, City Engineer, and approved by the City Council. [Oklahoma City, 1889.]
17½ in. × 12.
The first map of Oklahoma City. The map was issued within a month of the settlement of the town and shows the conflicting surveys north and south of Grand Avenue. Unrecorded, and the only known copy.

1891

Indian Territory. New York: Julius Bien & Co., 1891.
32 in. × 29. Colored.
2 copies.
Not in Phillips.

1892

Map of the Cheyenne, Arapahoe, and Wichita Reservations, I.T. Published by the Southwestern Map Publishing Company, Wichita, Kansas. March, 1892.
24 in. × 32. Colored. Backed with muslin.
Insets: Distances, population by tribes, and abstract of land laws, and directions for finding locations.
Excessively rare.

1894

Map of Oklahoma Territory. Boston and New York: Forbes Co., [1894].
29 in. × 41. Colored.

Oklahoma County, O.T. Compiled from Public Records and Published by D. C. Emley, OK City, O.T. Jan. '94.
Blueprint. 40 in. × 49.
A large and detailed map showing the name of the owner of every quarter section. No other copy can be traced.

1897

Fort Sill and Vicinity, Oklahoma. [Fort Sill, 1897.]
32½ in. × 32.
A valuable and detailed map, apparently produced by some photographic process. Unrecorded, and no other copy traced.

Map showing the Location of the Houses and Farms of the Apache Prisoners of

War, Military Reservation at Fort Sill, Oklahoma. Drawn under direction of Captain H. L. Scott, 7th Cavalry. Jan. & Feb., 1897. [Fort Sill, 1897.]

38 in. × 70. Backed with muslin.

Blueprint, irregularly shaped. Scale: 4 in., 1 mile.

Unrecorded, and no other copy known.

Sectional Map of the Kiowa, Comanche and Apache Reservation, Oklahoma, U.S.A. Kansas City: Hudson-Kimberly Publishing Co., [1897].

22 in. × 16. Colored. Folded into a stiff paper cover.

Another copy, headed: B. V. Cummins, Kingfisher, Okla. Ter., etc.

1898

Indian Territory. Compiled under the direction of Charles H. Fitch, Topographer in charge of the Indian Territory Surveys. [Washington,] 1898.

35½ in. × 33.

Not in Phillips.

1899

Map of the Indian Territory. Washington: A. B. Graham, 1899.

24 in. × 23. Colored.

2 copies.

Not in Phillips.

1901

Map of the Wichita Indian Reservation, Oklahoma Territory, showing Lands to be Opened for Entry on August 6, 1901. [Washington,] Norris Peters Co., [1901].

28 in. × 24. Colored.

Headed: Preliminary Edition.

Wichita Mountains. Johnson's New Map showing the Mineral Belt of the Great Wichita Mountains. The Most Valuable Undeveloped Mineral Region in the World. [Chickasha, 1901.]*

Blueprint. 33½ in. × 29. Backed with muslin.

Unrecorded, and the only known copy.

1905

Rand McNally & Co.'s Oklahoma and Indian Territory. [Chicago, 1905.]

21½ in. × 28. Colored. Folded into a cloth case.

With 38 pages of text.

1906

Proposed State of Oklahoma. Washington: Andrew B. Graham Co., 1906.

24 in. × 44½. Colored.

1907

Map of Oklahoma. Compliments of First National Bank, Muskogee, Oklahoma. [Chicago, 1907.]

20½ in. × 27. Colored. Folded into a stiff paper cover.

United States, showing Routes of Principal Explorers and Early Roads and Highways. Washington: Andrew & Graham, 1907.*

25 in. × 34. Colored.
A very useful map.

MINNESOTA INDIANS

1850

Acts, Joint Resolutions and Memorials passed by the First Legislative Assembly of the Territory of Minnesota, at its First Session, begun and held at St. Paul on the third day of September, 1849. Published by Authority of the Legislative Assembly. Saint Paul: James M. Goodhue, 1850.

213 p. 25 cm.
Contains important acts relating to the Indians. This is the first publication of Minnesota laws, an early example of printing in that territory, and a very rare volume.

Pembina Settlement. Letter from the Secretary of War, transmitting Report of Major Wood, relative to his Expedition to Pembina Settlement, and the Condition of Affairs on the North-Western Frontier of the Territory of Minnesota. [Washington, 1850.]

55 p. 25 cm. Caption title.
A fine copy, uncut and unopened.

1863

Missionary Paper by the Bishop Seabury Mission. Number Twenty-Eight. Christmas 1863. The Indian System. Faribault, Minn.: Central Republican Book and Job Office, 1863.

10 p. 20 cm.
Devoted to An Appeal to Reform the Present Indian System, by H. B. Whipple, Bishop of Minnesota.

MISCELLANEOUS

1684

Esquemeling, John

Bucaniers of America: of, a True Account of the Most Remarkable Assaults Committed of Late Years upon the Coasts of the West Indies, by the Bucaniers of Jamaica and Tortuga, both English and French. Now faithfully rendered into English. London: William Crooke, 1684.

[12], 115, 151, [1], 124, [11] p. 24 cm. Two of the nine engraved plates are lacking, a defect to which copies of this volume seem to be especially susceptible.
The rare first English edition.

1704

Engraved bookplate, dated 1704, for marking volumes sent to Indian mission libraries in America by the Society for the Propagation of the Gospel in Foreign Parts. The plate depicts a sailing vessel, on whose bow stands a robed clergyman holding up a Bible, approaching a hilly shore on which stands a group of gesticulating Indians.* Excessively rare.

1794

Loskiel, George Henry

History of the Mission of the United Bretheren among the Indians of North America. By George Henry Loskiel. Translated from the German by Christian Ignatius La Trobe. London, 1794.

xii, 159, 234, 233, 22 p. 20 cm. Folded map.

An important account based upon narratives of the Moravian missionaries.

1804

Gallatin, Albert

Letter from the Secretary of the Treasury, addressed to William Lattimore, on the subject of Lands South of the State of Tennessee. Washington: William Duane and Son, 1804.

8 p. 21 cm.

1816

Latour, A. LaCarriere

Historical Memoir of the War in West Florida and Louisiana in 1814–15. With an Atlas. By Major A. LaCarriere Latour, Principal Engineer in the late Seventh Military District United States' Army. Written originally in French, and translated for the Author by H. P. Nugent, Esq. Philadelphia, 1816.

xx, 264, cxc p. 21 cm. Frontisp. port.

The atlas, consisting of a title page and nine maps and plans, is bound in at the end.

A Narrative of Five Youth from the Sandwich Islands, now Receiving an Education in this Country. New York: J. Seymour, 1816.*

44 p. 21.5 cm.

The youths attended the famous mission school at Cornwall, Connecticut, where Elias Boudinot and John Ridge, among other Southern Indians, were educated.

1819

Report of the Committee to whom was referred so much of the President's Message as relates to the Civilization of the Indian Tribes. [Washington, 1819.]

3 p. 22 cm. Caption title.

1820

Letter from the Secretary of the Treasury transmitting a Statement of Money annually appropriated and paid since the Declaration of Independence for Purchasing from the Indians, Surveying, and Selling the Public Lands; showing the Quantities of Land which have been purchased, etc. Washington: Gales & Seaton, 1820.

27 p. 23.5 cm.

Letter from the Secretary of the Treasury transmitting a Statement of the Money expended in each year, since the Declaration of Independence in holding Conferences, and making Treaties with the Indian Tribes. Washington: Gales & Seaton, 1820.

14 p. 23.5 cm. 3 folded tables.

1822

LEWIS, Z.

Letter to a Member of Congress in relation to Indian Civilization. New York: Daniel Fanshaw, 1822.

15 p. 22 cm.

McKENNEY, THOMAS L.

[Communication on Indian Affairs. Washington, 1822.]

12 p. 22.5 cm. Folded table.

Message from the President of the United States, transmitting a Report of the Secretary of War of the Expenditures made under the Act to Provide for the Civilization of the Indian Tribes. Washington: Gales & Seaton, 1822.

9 p. 22 cm. Folded table.

A New Society for the Benefit of Indians, Organized at the City of Washington, February, 1822. [Washington: Davis & Force, 1822.]*

12 p. 20 cm.

1823

Letter from the Secretary of War transmitting Copies of the Accounts of Superintendents and Agents for Indian Affairs. Washington: Gales & Seaton, 1823.

4 p. 22.5 cm. 15 folded tables.

1824

The First Annual Report of the American Society for Promoting the Civilization and General Improvement of the Indian Tribes in the United States. New Haven: S. Converse, 1824.

74 p. 24 cm. Printed wrappers.

Contains valuable vocabularies.

Letter from the Secretary of War transmitting Information in relation to the Surveying of the Public Lands, North and South of Red River. Washington: Gales & Seaton, 1824.

20 p. 22.5 cm.

Report of the Committee on Indian Affairs, who were instructed, by a Resolution of the House of Representatives, to Inquire into the Expediency of repealing the Act making Provision for the Civilization of the Indian Tribes, adjoining the Frontier Settlements of the United States. [Washington, 1824.]

5 p. 22.5 cm. Caption title. Folded table.

Strictures addressed to James Madison on the Celebrated Report of William H. Crawford, recommending the Intermarriage of Americans with the Indian Tribes. Ascribed to Judge Cooper, and originally published by John Binns, in the Democratic Press. Philadelphia: Jesper Harding, 1824.

22 p. 21 cm.

Rare.

1826

Civilization of the Indians. Letter from the Secretary of War, to the Chairman of the Committee on Indian Affairs, transmitting a Report of General Clark, Superintendent of Indian Affairs, in relation to the Preservation and Civilization of the Indians. Washington: Gales & Seaton, 1826.

7 p. 25 cm. Uncut and unopened.
Remarkably humane views.

Donations by Indians to Government Agents. Message from the President of the United States respecting Proposed Donations of Land by Indian Tribes to any Agent or Commissioner of the United States. Washington, 1826.

14 p. 24.5 cm.

Intercourse with the Indians. [Washington, 1826.]

10 p. 22 cm. Caption title. 2 folded tables.

Preservation and Civilization of the Indians. Letter from the Secretary of War to the Chairman of the Committee on Indian Affairs, accompanied by a Bill for the Preservation and Civilization of the Indian Tribes within the United States. Washington: Gales & Seaton, 1826.

12 p. 22 cm.

Report of the Register and Receiver of the Land District South of Red River, in Louisiana, upon the Land Claims situated between the Rio Hondo and the Sabine. Washington: Gales & Seaton, 1826.

139 p. 22.5 cm. Folded table.

1829

Documents and Proceedings relating to the Formation and Progress of a Board in the City of New York, for the Emigration, Preservation, and Improvement of the Aborigines of America, July 22, 1829. New York: Vanderpool & Cole, 1829.

48 p. 22.5 cm. Printed wrappers.
The contents include the constitution of the board, correspondence with Thomas L. McKenney about its organization, Jackson's talk to the Creeks, and his talk to the Cherokee delegation, etc.

Letter from the Secretary of War transmitting Information in relation to our Indian Affairs generally. [Washington, 1829.]*

120 p. 22.5 cm. Caption title.

1831

HERRING, ELBERT

Report from the Superintendent of Indian Affairs. November, 1831. [Washington, 1831.]

7 p. 21 cm.
The separate issue is very rare.

1832

Board of Commissioners—Foreign Missions. Memorial of the Prudential Committee of the American Board of Commissioners for Foreign Missions, respecting the Property of the Board in the Choctaw Nation. [Washington, 1832.]

17 p. 22 cm. Caption title.

Interesting letters, reports, and statistics.

Indian Annuities. Letter from the Secretary of War transmitting Information in relation to the Payment of Indian Annuities during the years 1830 and 1831. [Washington, 1832.]

19 p. 22.5 cm. Caption title.

Message from the President of the United States, in compliance with a Resolution of the Senate concerning the Public Lands, etc. [Washington, 1832.]

6 p. 22.5 cm. Caption title.

Report from the Superintendent of Indian Affairs. December, 1832. [Washington, 1832.]

8 p. 21 cm.

The rare separate printing.

Rules and Regulations for the Government of the Mounted Rangers. Washington: Francis J. Blair, [1832].

23 p. 19 cm. Printed wrappers.

Small Pox among the Indians. Letter from the Secretary of War upon the subject of the Small Pox among the Indian Tribes. [Washington, 1832.]

9 p. 22 cm. Caption title.

1833

HERRING, ELBERT

Report of the Commissioner of Indian Affairs. [Washington, 1833.]

24 p. 22.5 cm.

The rare separate printing.

1834

DRAKE, SAMUEL G.

Biography and History of the Indians of North America. Third Edition. Boston: O. L. Perkins, 1834.

[2], vi, [1], 28, 120, 132, 72, 158, [1], 18, 12 p. 22.5 cm.

Report from the Commissioner of Indian Affairs. [Washington, 1834.]

30 p. 22.5 cm. Caption title.

The rare separate issue.

1836

EVERETT, HORACE

Speech of Horace Everett, of Vermont: delivered in the House of Representatives, in Committee of the Whole, on the Indian Annuity Bill, Friday, June 3, 1836. Washington: National Intelligencer Office. 1836.

23 p. 23 cm.

GILLETT, RANSOM H.

Speech of Mr. Gillett, of New York, on the Bill to Authorize the President to Accept the Service of Volunteers. Washington: Blair & Rives, 1836.

7 p. 24 cm. Uncut and unopened.

The bill under discussion proposed the raising and organizing of an additional regiment of dragoons or mounted riflemen for the purpose of subduing the Indians.

A Sketch of the Life and Public Services of William Henry Harrison, Commander in Chief of the North Western Army during the War of 1812, &c. New York: Harper & Bros., 1836.

32 p. 21.5 cm. Printed wrappers.

Considerable attention is devoted to Harrison's Indian campaigns.

WHITE, JOSEPH M.

Speech of Mr. White, of Florida, upon the Indian Appropriation Bill. Washington: Gales & Seaton, 1836.

15 p. 22.5 cm.

1837

Indians in Military Service. Letter from the Secretary of War in relation to Indians Employed in the Military Service. [Washington, 1837.]

13 p. 22 cm. Caption title.

1838

Report from the Secretary of the Treasury transmitting a Report from the Register and Receiver of the Land Office at Ouachita, with a Statement of the Claims presented to them, together with the Opinion of the Commissioner of the General Land Office on the Validity of the said Claims. [Washington, 1838.]

290 p. 24.5 cm. Caption title. Maps. Uncut and unopened.

1842

On Repealing the Act of 1819 for the Civilization of the Indians, &c. [Washington, 1842.]

19 p. 24.5 cm. Caption title. Uncut and unopened.

1846

Report of the Committee on the Judiciary, who were instructed by a resolution of the Senate to Inquire into the Expediency of Extending the Criminal Laws of the United States over the Indian Territories. [Washington:] Ritchie & Heiss, [1846].

11 p. 23 cm. Caption title.

1847

Regulations (governing the introduction of intoxicating liquors into the Indian country). [Washington, 1847.]

2 p. 22.5 cm. Caption title.

1849

GAMMELL, WILLIAM H.

History of American Baptist Missions. Boston: Gould, Kendall & Lincoln, 1849.

359 p. 19 cm. Maps.

SCHOOLCRAFT, H. R.

A Bibliographical Catalogue of Books, Translations of the Scriptures, and Other Publications in the Indian Tongues of the United States, with Brief Critical Notices. Washington: C. Alexander, 1849.*

27 p. 22.5 cm.

Field 1376.

An early attempt at a bibliography of American Indian linguistics. The pamphlet is rare.

1855

Les Hommes Rouges de l'Amerique du Nord. Rapport a M. le Ministre de l'Interieur des Etats Unis, M. le Chef du Bureau des Affaires Indiennes. Paris: Imprimerie Administrative de Paul Dupont, 1855.

27 p. 22 cm. Printed wrappers.

A fine copy.

MANYPENNY, GEORGE W.

Letter from the Commissioner of Indian Affairs to Colonel Benton. Washington: Union Office, 1855.

15 p. 22 cm.

1856

COLES, EDWARD

History of the Ordinance of 1787. Philadelphia, 1856.

33 p. 22.5 cm. Printed wrappers.

1857

Office Copy of the Laws, Regulations, etc., of the Indian Bureau. 1850. Washington: A. O. P. Nicholson, 1857.*

96 p. 23 cm.

1860

FOSTER, THOMAS

Letter of Dr. Thomas Foster, of Minnesota, to the Committees of Indian Affairs and of Appropriations, relative to the Appointment of a Historiographer of the Indian Department, to prepare an Encyclopedia of Indian Affairs and to Organize an Indian Archaeological Museum. [N.p., 1860.]*

Broadside. Folio.

Memorandum of Stocks held in Trust for Indian Tribes by the Secretary of the Interior; showing the Proportion in which the Stocks of the several States are distributed among the various Tribes, the Time and Place of payment of Interest thereon, etc. [Washington, 1860.]

3 p. 25 cm. Caption title.

Statistics which take on an added importance in view of the imminence of the Civil War and the United States policy toward the southern tribes.

1861

Memorial Volume of the First Fifty Years of the American Board of Commissioners for Foreign Missions. Fourth Edition. Boston, 1861.

xiv, 462 p. 22.5 cm.

Valuable information about Indian missions.

1865

DONNELLY, IGNATIUS

Reform of the Indian System. Speech of Hon. Ignatius Donnelly, of Minnesota. [Washington, 1865.]

8 p. 24.5 cm. Caption title.

1867

HANCOCK, W. S.

Headquarters Department of the Missouri. Fort Leavenworth, Kansas, January 26th, 1867. General Orders No. 16. [Fort Leavenworth, 1867.]

3 p. 20 cm.

An order prohibiting the sale by traders of arms and ammunition to hostile Indians in the West. Unrecorded.

Indian Affairs. Letter from the Secretary of War, addressed to Mr. Schenck, chairman of the Committee on Military Affairs, transmitting a Report by Colonel (Eli) Parker on Indian Affairs. [Washington, 1867.]

11 p. 22 cm. Caption title.

Indian Atrocities. Narratives of the Perils and Sufferings of Dr. Knight and John Slover, among the Indians, during the Revolutionary War, with Short Memoirs of Col. Crawford & John Slover. And a Letter from H. Brackinridge, on the Rights of the Indians, etc. Cincinnati: U. P. James, Publisher. (Reprint from the Nashville edition of 1843.) 1867.

72 p. 20 cm. Printed wrappers.

A fine copy.

MANYPENNY, GEORGE W.

Letter of Hon. Geo. W. Manypenny in regard to Treatment of the Indians, January 31, 1867. [Columbus, Ohio? 1867.]

7 p. 23 cm. Wrapper title.

Report of the Secretary of the Interior communicating Information in relation to the Indian Tribes of the United States. [Washington, 1867.]

50 p. 22.5 cm. Caption title.

A valuable census and description of the Indian tribes of the United States.

SUMNER, CHARLES

Speech of Hon. Charles Sumner, of Massachusetts, on the Cession of Russian America to the United States. Washington, 1867.

48 p. 23 cm. Printed wrappers. Large folded map.

The map is valuable.

1868

DODDRIDGE, JOSEPH

Logan, the Last of the Race of Shikellemus, Chief of the Cayuga Nation. A Dramatic Piece. To which is added The Dialogue of the Backwoodsman and the Dandy, first recited at the Buffaloe Seminary, July the 1st, 1821. By Dr. Joseph Doddridge. Reprinted from the Virginia edition of 1823, with an appendix relating to the Murder of Logan's Family, for William Dodge, by Robert Clarke & Co. Cincinnati, 1868.

76 p. 22 cm.

Very scarce.

[Memorial to Congress by the General Committee of the United States Indian Commission. New York, 1868.]*

2 leaves broadside. 40 cm.

A protest against mistreatment of the Indians and a discussion of the causes of Indian wars.

TAYLOR, N. G.

Effort and Failure to civilize the Aborigines. Letter to N. G. Taylor, Commissioner of Indian Affairs, from Edward D. Neill. Washington, 1868.

15 p. 23 cm. Printed wrappers.

Presentation copy from the author, with an inscription.

1870

Rules and Regulations of the Humanitarian Pioneers' Association. New York: Journeymen Printers' Co-operative Association, 1870.

14 p. 14.5 cm.

The communistic Utopia was to be established in the southwest. The only known copy.

WEEKS, GRENVILLE M.

Introductory Summary of Facts Forming the Basis of Accompanying Specific Plan for the Treatment of the Indians. [New York, 1870.]

15 p. 21.5 cm. Caption title.

A plan proposed at a convention at Cooper Institute, New York City.

1871

BLUNT, JAMES G.

Statements of James G. Blunt, in Reply to the Allegations of Members of "The Peace Commission." Washington: Powell & Ginck, [1871].

22 p. 21.5 cm. Wrapper title.

Quapaw frauds.

CHIPMAN, N. P.

Investigation into Indian Affairs, before the Committee on Appropriations of the House of Representatives. Argument of N. P. Chipman, on behalf of Hon. E. S. Parker, Commissioner of Indian Affairs. Washington: Powell, Ginck & Co., 1871.

121 p. 22 cm. Wrapper title.

Report of the Delegates representing the Yearly Meetings of Philadelphia, New

York, Baltimore, Indiana, Ohio, and Genesee, on the Indian Concern, at Baltimore, Tenth Month, 1871. New York, 1871.
18 p. 18 cm. Printed wrappers.

WELSH, WILLIAM

Summing Up of Evidence before a Committee of the House of Representatives, charged with the Investigation of Misconduct in the Indian Office. Washington: H. Polkinhorn & Co., 1871.
67 p. 21.5 cm. Printed wrappers.

1872

BARTLETT, S. C.

Sketches of the Missions of the American Board. By S. C. Bartlett, D.C., Professor in Chicago Theological Seminary. Boston: Published by the Board, 1872.
v, [1], 233 p. 18.5 cm.
Pages 175–216 present an excellent historical sketch of the missions to the American Indians.

Copy of Law regulating Trade and Intercourse with the Indian Tribes, approved June 30, 1834; of Several Acts of Congress relative to Claims for Depredations by Indians; of Decision of Supreme Court of the United States, December Term, 1865, in the matter of Indictments; of Opinion of United States Attorney General, December 21, 1830, relative to Citizens who become Members of an Indian Tribe by Adoption, not being Exempt from the Laws of the United States. [Washington, 1872.]*
14 p. 30 cm. Wrapper title.

Indians, Soldiers and Civilization. New York, 1872.
11 p. 22 cm.

The Thirty-fifth Annual Report of the Board of Foreign Missions of the Presbyterian Church of the United States of America. New York: Mission House, 1872.
24, [4] p. 21.5 cm.
Informative reports on missions to the American Indians.

Twenty-seventh Annual Report of the Domestic and Indian Mission Board to the Southern Baptist Convention, in session, Raleigh, N.C., May 9th, 1872. Atlanta, Georgia: Franklin Steam Printing House, 1872.
20 p. 22.5 cm.
Contains a report on Indian missions.

1873

CONDICT, J. ELLIOT

Is there any Justice for Indians. [New York? 1873.]
7 p. 22.5 cm. Wrapper title.

Journal of the Second Annual Conference of the Board of Indian Commissioners with Representatives of the Religious Societies cooperating with the Government, and Reports of their Work among the Indians. Washington, 1873.*
64 p. 23 cm. Printed wrappers.

1874

Investigation on the Conduct of Indian Affairs. [Washington, 1874.]
283 p. 23 cm. Caption title.
A report on a House Committee investigation of fraud in connection with contracts for supplies for Western Indians.

List of Indian Agencies assigned to the Several Religious Bodies. [N.p., 1874?].*
Broadside. Folio.

What the Government and the Churches are doing for the Indians. Washington, 1874.*
24 p. 23.5 cm. Printed wrappers.

1875

Alphabet for use in Recording Indian Languages. [Washington, 1875?].
[3] p. 16 cm.

Alphabet to accompany Second Edition of "Introduction to the Study of Indian Languages." [N.p., 1875?].
[3] p. 15.5 cm.

Sixth Annual Report of the Board of Indian Commissioners for the year 1874. Washington, 1875.*
14 p. 23 cm. Printed wrappers.

1876

CONDICT, J. ELLIOT
The Indian Question. [Princeton? 1876.]
16 p. 22 cm. Wrapper title.

MACMAHON, RICHARD RANDOLPH
The Anglo-Saxon and the North American Indian. By Richard Randolph MacMahon, of Alexandria, Virginia. Baltimore: Kelly, Piet & Co., 1876.
50 p. 23 cm. Printed wrappers.

Seventh Annual Report of the Board of Indian Commissioners for the year 1875. Washington, 1876.*
164 p. 23.5 cm.

The Seventh Annual Report of the Superintendent and Agents of the Central Indian Superintendency, with a carefully revised Statistical Table indicating the Advancement of the Indians in their Industrial Pursuits, Education and Wealth, compared with that of 1868. Lawrence, Kansas: Journal Steam Book and Job Printing House. 1876.*
79, [1] p. 21.5 cm.
Very rare.

TAYLOR, N. G.
Remarks of Hon. N. G. Taylor, President Indian Peace Commission, and Com-

missioner of Indian Affairs, on the question of the Transfer of the Indian Bureau from the Interior to the War Department. [Washington,] J. L. Pearson, [1876].*
6 p. 23 cm. Wrapper title.

WILSHIRE, WILLIAM W.

Transfer of the Indian Bureau. Speech of Hon. William W. Wilshire, of Arkansas, in the House of Representatives, April 19, 1876. Washington, 1876.
20 p. 21 cm.

1877

WHITE, BARCLAY

Report of Barclay White, Special Agent of the Society of Friends, on the Condition of the Indians in the Northern Superintendency. Philadelphia, 1877.
16 p. 23 cm. Folded table. Printed wrappers.

1878

Les Annales de la Propagation de la Foi chez les Sauvages des Etats-Unis publiees par le Bureau des Missions Indiennes Catholiques Washington, D.C. 1er Octobre 1878. Montreal: Plinguet & Fils, 1878.
64 p. 21 cm.
Important reports from missions to the western and far western tribes. Very scarce.

A Bill providing for the Extension of Civil and Criminal Law over the Indian Reservations. [N.p., 1878.]
4 p. 25 cm. Caption title.

Need of Law on the Indian Reservations. Issued by the Associated Executive Committee of Friends on Indian Affairs. Philadelphia: Sherman & Co., 1878.
52 p. 23.5 cm. Wrapper title.

Ninth Annual Report of the Board of Indian Commissioners, for the year 1877. Washington, 1878.*
101 p. 23.5 cm. Printed wrappers. Folded color map.

Report of Board of Inquiry convened by Authority of Letter of the Secretary of the Interior of June 7, 1877, to Investigate Certain Charges against S. A. Galpin, Chief Clerk of the Indian Bureau, and concerning Irregularities in said Bureau. Washington, 1878.*
65 p. 23 cm.

1879

Report of the Joint Committee appointed to Consider the Expediency of Transferring the Indian Bureau to the War Department. Washington, 1879.
20 p. 23 cm.

Testimony taken by the Joint Committee appointed to take into consideration the Expediency of Transferring the Indian Bureau to the War Department. Washington, 1879.*
406 p. 22.5 cm.
This little known document contains a wealth of detailed information about troubles with the uncivilized tribes.

Transfer of the Indian Bureau to the War Department. Report of Four Members of the Joint Committee appointed by the Two Houses of Congress, at its last Session, to take into consideration the Expediency of Transferring the Management of Indian Affairs from the Interior to the War Department. [Washington, 1879.]
20 p. 23 cm. Caption title.

1880

Eleventh Annual Report of the Board of Indian Commissioners for the year 1879. Washington, 1880.*
129 p. 23 cm. Printed wrappers.

MANYPENNY, GEORGE W.

Our Indian Wards. By George W. Manypenny, Commissioner of Indian Affairs from March, 1853, until March, 1857; and Chairman of the Sioux Commission of 1876. Cincinnati: Robert Clarke & Co., 1880.
23 cm. xxvi, 436 p.
An authoritative volume.

1881

NEWLIN, JAMES W. M.
Proposed Indian Policy. [Philadelphia, 1881.]
113 p. 23 cm. Wrapper title.

1882

An Act to Provide for the Allotment of Lands in Severalty to Indians on the Various Reservations, and to Extend the Protection of the Laws of the States and Territories over the Indians, and for other Purposes. [Philadelphia, 1882.]
5 p. 24 cm. Caption title.

DODGE, RICHARD I.

A Living Issue. By the Author of "Our Wild Indians." Washington: Francis B. Mohun, 1882.
37 p. 23 cm. Printed wrappers.
Inscribed by the author. Rare.

Prevention of Trespass on Indian Lands. Message from the President of the United States, transmitting a Communication from the Secretary of the Interior relative to the more Adequate Prevention of Trespass upon Indian Lands. [Washington, 1882.]
3 p. 24 cm. Caption title.

1883

DE SEMALLE, RENE

Mouvement de la Population chez les Indiens des Etats-Unis par Rene de Semalle. Paris: Societe de Geographie, 1883.
11 p. 22 cm. Wrapper title.

Rules governing the Court of Indian Offenses. [Washington, 1883.]
8 p. 22 cm. Caption title.

1884

An Act to Provide for the Establishment of Courts of Criminal Jurisdiction upon Indian Reservations, to Define their Powers and the Offenses of which they may take cognizance, to Affix Penalties to the Commission of such Offenses, and for other purposes. Prepared by the Committee on Legislation and Legal Matters of the Indian Rights Association. Philadelphia, 1884.

4 p. 22.5 cm. Wrapper title.
A proposed act.

PANCOAST, HENRY S.

Indian Land in Severalty, as provided by the Coke Bill. Philadelphia, 1884.*

7 p. 22 cm.

1885

COOK, JOSEPH

The Prelude to the One Hundred and Seventy-fifth Lecture of Joseph Cook. Frontier Savages, White and Red. Delivered in the Tremont Temple. Philadelphia, [1885].

14 p. 22.5 cm.

The Opinions of the Press on the Need for Legislation for Indians by the present Congress. [Philadelphia, 1885.]

8 p. 19 cm. Caption title.

1886

DUNN, J. P.

Massacres of the Mountains. A History of the Indian Wars of the Far West. New York: Harper & Bros., 1886.*

784 p. 21.5 cm. Illustrated.

1887

HARRISON, J. B.

The Latest Studies on Indian Reservations. Philadelphia: Indian Rights Association, 1887.*

233 p. 18 cm.

RHOADS, JAMES E.

Our Next Duty to the Indians. Philadelphia, 1887.

5 p. 21 cm. Wrapper title.

1889

VINCENT, H.

The Plot Unfolded! A History of the Famous Coffeyville Dynamite Outrage, October 18, 1888. Winfield, Kansas: American Nonconformist, 1889.

xvi, 101, [3] p. 21 cm. Printed wrappers.
Rare.

1890

Employment of Indian Scouts. Message from the President of the United States

transmitting a Communication from the Secretary of State, with accompanying papers, relative to the Employment of Indian Scouts. [Washington, 1890.]
9 p. 23 cm. Caption title.

PILLING, JAMES CONSTANTINE

Bibliographic Notes on Eliot's Indian Bible and on his other Translations and Works in the Indian Language of Massachusetts. Washington, 1890.
58 p. 31.5 cm. Printed wrappers. Photographs of title pages.
The large paper edition.

1891

An Address of the Representatives of the Religious Society of Friends, for Pennsylvania, New Jersey and Delaware, to their Fellow Citizens, on behalf of the Indians. Philadelphia, 1891.
55 p. 18.5 cm. Wrapper title.

MORGAN, THOMAS J.

The Present Phase of the Indian Question. Boston: Frank Wood, 1891.
23 p. 23.5 cm. Printed wrappers.

1892

Regulations concerning Cattle Transportation. [Washington, 1892.]
4 p. 22.5 cm. Caption title.

1894

Annual Report of the Assistant Attorney-General of the United States in charge of Indian Depredation Claims. Washington, 1894.
17 p. 23 cm. Printed wrappers.

MOONEY, JAMES

The Siouan Tribes of the East. Washington, 1894.
101 p. 25 cm. Printed wrappers.
A standard authority.

Report on Indians Taxed and Indians Not Taxed in the United States (except Alaska) at the Eleventh Census: 1890. Washington, 1894.*
683 p. 29 cm. Many portraits in color, plates, and folded maps.
An extremely valuable publication.

TURNER, FREDERICK J.

The Significance of the Frontier in American History. By Prof. Frederick J. Turner, of the University of Wisconsin. Washington, 1894.*
[31] p. 24.5 cm. Printed wrappers.
Inscribed copy of the first separate appearance of this important essay.

1895

PILLING, JAMES C.

The Writings of Padre Andres de Olmos in the Languages of Mexico. Washington: Judd & Detweiler, 1895.*
18 p. 24 cm. Wrapper title.

1897

Coues, Elliott

In Memoriam Sergeant Charles Floyd. Sioux City: Perkins Bros., 1897.*

58 p. 22 cm. Printed wrappers.

Floyd was a sergeant on the Lewis and Clark Expedition. This memorial volume yields many particulars of the journey of exploration and of his life.

1898

Dorsey, George A.

A Bibliography of the Anthropology of Peru. Chicago, 1898.*

206 p. 25 cm. Printed wrappers.

1899

Statistics of Indian Tribes, Indian Agencies, and Indian Schools of Every Character. Corrected to January 1, 1899. Washington, 1899.

172 p. 18 cm. Printed wrappers.

An important compilation.

1901

Digest of Decisions relating to Indian Affairs. Compiled by Kenneth S. Murchison. Vol. 1. Washington, 1901.*

667 p. 22.5 cm.

Vol. 2 was never published.

A valuable compilation.

Eighth Annual Report of the Commission to the Five Civilized Tribes to the Secretary of the Interior for the Fiscal Year ended June 30, 1901. Washington, 1901.*

219 p. 23 cm. Printed wrappers. Folded color maps. Photographs.

1906

Densmore, Frances

The Plea of our Brown Brother, and Ke-wa-kun-ah, the Homeward Way. Two Indian Sketches. Chilocco, Oklahoma: Indian Print Shop Press, 1906.*

[15] p. 25 cm. Printed wrappers. Photographs.

With presentation inscription by the author.

Leupp, Francis E.

Segregation of Indian Tribal Funds. Washington, 1906.

12 p. 23 cm.

Wegelin, Oscar

A List of the Separate Writings of William Gilmore Simms of South Carolina, 1806–1870. New York, 1906.

31 p. 12.5 cm.

Simms's interest in the Southern Indians is strongly reflected in this useful guide.

1908

Boggess, Arthur Clinton

The Settlement of Illinois 1778–1830. Chicago, 1908.

267 p. 23.5 cm. Folded map.
An authoritative volume, with considerable attention to the Indian tribes.

HOLMES, W. H.

Biographical Memoir of Lewis Henry Morgan, 1818–1881. Washington: Judd & Detweiler, 1908.*

[2], 221–39 p. Printed wrappers. Portrait.
Contains a bibliography of Morgan's contributions to American Indian ethnology.

1909

Regulations for Applications for Tribal Funds under Act of March 2, 1907. [Washington, 1909.]*

4 p. 23 cm. Caption title.

1910

COX, ISAAC JOSLIN

The Indian as a Diplomatic Factor in the History of the Old Northwest. Cincinnati, 1910.*

[2], 209–35 p. 21 cm. Printed wrappers.

1911

FITZPATRICK, T. J.

Rafinesque. A Sketch of his Life with Bibliography. Des Moines, 1911.

241 p. 24 cm. Plates.
An important bibliography.

1916

KETCHAM, WILLIAM H.

The Indians and Catholic Indian Missions of the United States. [N.p., 1916.]

16 p. 15.5 cm.

1917

DE PUY, HENRY F.

A Bibliography of the English Colonial Treaties with the American Indians, including a Synopsis of Each Treaty. New York: Lenox Club, 1917.

50 p. 25 cm.
A scarce and indispensable bibliography. The title of each item described is reproduced.

1919

Bibliotheca Americana. Catalogue of the John Carter Brown Library in Brown University, Providence, Rhode Island. Providence, 1919–1931.

5 vols. Ex-library copy.

All published; the catalogue will not be continued.
Scholarly bibliographical descriptions of this library's highly important holdings, up through 1674, of books relating to America. The volumes are now out of print and difficult to come by.

1926

GATES, WILLIAM

A Gage of Honor. The Development and Disruption of the Department of Middle American Research of Tulane University at New Orleans. March, 1926. [N.p.]*

70 p. 24.5 cm. Printed wrappers.

A highly scurrilous pamphlet which was rigidly suppressed at the time of its publication.

1930

WAR BOW

[4 poems. Geary, 1930.]*

Broadsheet. 22.5 cm.

War Bow is here described as a blanket Indian.

1931

KARPINSKI, LOUIS C.

Bibliography of the Printed Maps of Michigan, 1804–1880. With a Series of over One Hundred Reproductions of Maps, constituting an Historical Atlas of the Great Lakes and Michigan. Lansing, 1931.

539 p. 23 cm.

Of great value for the location of Indian tribes.

1932

BUSHNELL, DAVID I., JR.

Seth Eastman: The Master Painter of the North American Indian. Washington, 1932.*

18 p. 24.5 cm. Printed wrappers. 15 plates.

1933

LANGFELD, WILLIAM R.

Washington Irving. A Bibliography. New York, 1933.

ix, 90, [1] p. 26 cm. Portrait and plates.

The definitive bibliography, rich in minute detail.

1935

DUNCAN, WINTHROP HILLYER

Josiah Priest, Historian of the American Frontier. A Study and Bibliography. Worcester, Mass.: 1935.

60 p. 25 cm. Printed wrappers.

An important study. Priest wrote voluminously on the Indians.

1937

MARTIN, LAWRENCE

Disturnell's Map. Washington, 1937.*

Pp. [337]–70. 25 cm.

A valuable monograph, describing in minute detail the twenty-four editions of this famous map. Only a few copies were issued in this separate form (with a special title page) and the volume is now unobtainable.

Undated

Indian Titles. [N.p., n.d.]*
26 p. 22.5 cm. Printed wrappers.
A valuable historical and legal examination of Indian land titles.

Warning! This is Indian Land. [Washington, n.d.]*
Broadside, on white cloth. Folio.

MISSISSIPPI INDIANS

1801

Papers in relation to the Official Conduct of Governour Sargent. Published by particular desire of his friends. Boston: Thomas & Andrews, 1801.
64 p. 22 cm.
Affairs in Mississippi Territory with important references to the Indians within its borders.

1803

DUANE, WILLIAM

Mississippi Question. Report of a Debate in the Senate of the United States on Certain Resolutions concerning the Violation of the Right of Deposit in the Island of New Orleans. Philadelphia: W. Duane, 1803.
[2], 198 p. 23 cm.
The discussion touched upon the important role played by the Southern Indians in the intrigues and collisions between the great powers.

1814

Report of the Committee to whom was referred the Bill from the Senate entitled "An Act providing for the Indemnification of Certain Claimants of Public Lands in the Mississippi Territory." Washington: A. & G. Way, 1814.
29 p. 21 cm.

1815

At the Annual Meeting of the Foreign Mission Society for the County of Litchfield, on the 15th day of February, 1815. [Litchfield, Connecticut, 1815.]
[3] p. 34.5 cm. Caption title.
The society commissioned Daniel Smith "to go and preach the gospel to the people of Natchez" and to the neighboring Indians.

MISSOURI INDIANS

1817

EASTON, RUFUS

To the People of the Territory of Missouri. [St. Louis, 1817.]
3, [2] p. Folio. Caption title.
A lengthy and important review of frontier affairs and problems, including that of Indian depredations. Unrecorded, and the only known copy.

1818

GEYER, HENRY S.

A Digest of the Laws of Missouri Territory. An Elucidation of the Title of the United States to Louisiana; Constitution of the United States; Treaty of Cession; Organic Laws; Laws of Missouri Territory (alphabetically arranged); Spanish Regulations for the Allotment of Lands; Laws of the United States for adjusting Titles to Lands, &c. To which are added a Variety of Forms, useful to Magistrates. St. Louis: Joseph Charless, 1818.

xii, 486, xxvi, 30 p. 20 cm.

Contains important laws relating to Indians and Indian traders.

Memorial of the Legislature of Missouri for a Division of the Territory, &c. Washington: E. De Krafft, 1818.

7 p. 22 cm.

1826

Memorial of the State of Missouri, and Documents in relation to Indian Depredations upon Citizens of that State. Washington: Gales & Seaton, 1826.

90 p. 22.5 cm. Folded tables.

MOHAWK INDIANS

1839

Ne kaghyadonghsera ne royadadokenghdy ne Isiah. New York: Printed for the American Bible Society. D. Fanshaw, printer. 1839.

243 p. 15 cm.

Pilling, Iroquoian Bibliography, p. 128.

1856

JOGUES, ISAAC

Narrative of a Captivity among the Mohawk Indians, a Description of New Netherlands in 1642–3, and Other Papers, by Father Isaac Jogues, of the Society of Jesus. With a Memoir of the Author, by John Gilmary Shea. New York: Richard Dunigan & Bro., 1856.

69 p. 23.5 cm. Printed wrappers.

Field 781. Newberry-Ayer 161.

MONTAGNAIS INDIANS

1852

DUROCHER, FLAVIEN

Ir mishiniigin. Eku omeru tshe apatstats ishkuamishkornuts, uiapokornuts, uashaornuts, ekuandjornuts, mashkuarornuts, shikotimiornuts kie piokuamiornuts. Moniants (Montreal): Akonikano nte etat Louis Perrault, 1852.*

168 p. 16.5 cm.

Prayers, songs, and hymns, in Montagnais. Printed for the use of the Indians at the trading posts of the Hudson Bay Company along the northern shore of the St. Lawrence, and on the Saguenay River, Eskoumoun River, Mashkuaro, Chicoutimi,

Lake St. John, etc. With the four-page table at the end which was apparently lacking from the two copies which Pilling saw in Canada.

Tshipiatoko-meshkanakanots. [Montreal? 1852?].*
18 p. 16.5 cm. Caption title.
Religious songs in the Montagnais language, with headings in French. Pilling located but one copy, and that in Canada.

1856

DUROCHER, FLAVIEN

L. J. C. et M. I. Aiamieu kukuetshimitun misinaigan. Kaiakonigants nte opistikoiats. Nte etat Aug. Cote et Cie. 1856. [Quebec.]*
72 p. 16.5 cm.
Catechism, credo, commandments, etc., in Montagnais. Pilling located but two copies, both in Canada.

DUROCHER, FLAVIEN

L. J. C. et M. I. Aiamieu kushkushkutu mishinaigan. Kaiakonigants nte opistikoiats. Nte etat Aug. Cote et Cie. 1856. [Quebec.]*
104 p. 16.5 cm.
Chants for mass with words in the Montagnais language and headings in French. With music. Pilling located but two copies, both in Canada.

MONTANA INDIANS

1866

Acts, Resolutions and Memorials of the Territory of Montana passed by the First Legislative Assembly. Convened at Bannack, December 12, 1864. Virginia City, Montana: D. W. Tilton, 1866.
viii, 721, xli p. 22.5 cm.
The rare first laws of Montana, which include important acts and resolutions on Indian affairs.

NEBRASKA INDIANS

1855

Territory of Nebraska. Laws, Resolutions and Memorials, passed at the Regular Session of the First General Assembly of the Territory of Nebraska, convened at Omaha City, on the 16th day of January, Anno Domini, 1855. Together with the Constitution of the United States, the Organic Law, and the Proclamations issued in the Organization of the Territorial Government. Published by Authority. Omaha City, N.T.: Sherman & Strickland, 1855.
517 p. 21 cm. Errata slip.
Contains important acts, resolutions, and memorials on Indian affairs. The earliest Nebraska laws and perhaps the first book printed in that territory.

1891

COLBY, L. W.

Report of Brig. Gen'l. L. W. Colby, Commanding the Nebraska National Guard in the Indian Campaign of 1890–91, to the Adjutant General, N.N.G. Lincoln, Neb.: Calhoun & Woodruff, 1891.

23 p. 22.5 cm. Printed wrappers.

NEW MEXICO INDIANS

1848

New Mexico and California. Message from the President of the United States, transmitting Reports from the Secretaries of State, Treasury, War, and Navy. [Washington, 1848.]

49 p. 22.5 cm. Caption title.

Largely reports from New Mexico and California territorial officers. Considerable attention is paid to Indian affairs.

1850

Munroe, John

Proclamation. [Santa Fe, 1850.]

Broadside. 22.5 cm.

Call for a territorial election for voting on the proposed constitution. Excessively rare.

Munroe, John, and James S. Calhoun

A los caciques Gobernadorcillos y otras autoridades de los Pueblos de Indios del Territorio de N. Mejico. [Santa Fe, 1850.]

Broadside. 25.5 cm.

Excessively rare.

1852

Laws of the Territory of New Mexico, passed by the First Legislative Assembly in the City of Santa Fe at a Session begun and held on the second day of June, 1851; and at a Session begun and held on the first day of December, 1851; to which are prefixed the Constitution of the United States, and the Act of Congress Organizing New Mexico as a Territory. City of Santa Fe: James L. Collins, 1852.

442, [1] p. 21.5 cm. Text in English and Spanish.

This and the subsequent New Mexico laws and journals in the collection are of incalculable value for a study of the Indians of the Southwest.

1853

Las actas de la camera de representantes del Territorio de N. Mejico; siendo la segunda de la primera asamblea legislativa comenzada y tenida en la ciudad de Santa Fe, Diciembre 1º de 1851. Santa Fe: Collins, Kephart & Ca., 1853.*

265 p. 22 cm. Text in Spanish.

Contains resolutions regarding Indian hostilities.

Laws of the Territory of New Mexico, passed by the Second Legislative Assembly in the City of Santa Fe, at a Session begun on the Sixth Day of December, 1852. Santa Fe: James L. Collins & Co., 1853.

160 p. 23 cm. Text in English and Spanish.

Important acts and resolutions affecting the Indians.

1854

Laws of the Territory of New Mexico, passed by the Third Legislative Assembly in the City of Santa Fe, at a Session begun on the Fifth Day of December, 1853. Santa Fe: J. L. Collins, 1854.*

219 p. 23 cm. Text in English and Spanish.
Acts and resolutions touching upon Indian affairs.

1855

Laws of the Territory of New Mexico, passed by the Fifth Legislative Assembly, in the City of Santa Fe, at a Session begun on the Fourth Day of December, 1854. Printed in the Santa Fe Gazette Office, 1855.

147 p. 24 cm.
Important acts, resolutions, and memorials relating to Indian hostilities.

1856

Laws of the Territory of New Mexico. Passed by the Legislative Assembly, 1855–56. Santa Fe: Santa Fe Weekly Gazette Office, 1856.*

176 p. 23 cm. Text in English and Spanish.
Contains important resolutions and memorials on Indian hostilities.

1857

Laws of the Territory of New Mexico. Passed by the Legislative Assembly 1856–57. Santa Fe: Office of the Democrat, 1857.

112 p. 23.5 cm. Text in English and Spanish.
Important acts and resolutions regarding hostile Indians.

1860

Laws of the Territory of New Mexico. Passed by the Legislative Assembly, Session of 1859–60. Santa Fe: O. P. Hovey, 1860.

141 p. 22.5 cm. Text in English and Spanish.
Important resolutions on Indian affairs.

1861

Connelly, Henry

The First Annual Message of Governor Connelly, delivered before the Legislative Assembly of the Territory of New Mexico, December 4th, 1861. Santa Fe: Printed in the Gazette Office, 1861.

13 p. 21 cm.
Contains an important discussion of the necessity of regulating the Indian tribes in the territory. Excessively rare.

1866

Headquarters District of New Mexico. General Orders, No. 21. 1866. Organizing Battalion of New Mexican Volunteers. [Fort Union, 1866.]

10 p. 19 cm.
Kit Carson was selected to command the battalion.

1868

HAZEN, WILLIAM B.

Headquarters District of New Mexico, Santa Fe, New Mexico, August 1, 1868. Circular No. 10. [Santa Fe, 1868.]

Broadsheet. 18.5 cm.

Detailed instructions to scouts on how to pursue and kill or capture hostile Indians. Unrecorded.

1869

ARNY, W. F. M.

Abiquiu Indian Agency, Rio Arriba County, New Mexico. September 23rd, 1869. His Excellency U. S. Grant, President of the United States. Sir. [Abiquiu Indian Agency, 1869.]

7 p. 20 cm. Caption title.

Recommendations for the welfare of the Indians of the United States in general and the New Mexico Navajoes, Utahs, and Jicarilla Apaches in particular. Excessively rare.

1880

Petition to Congress made by the Heirs of Dr. John Charles Beales and the Howard University of Washington for the Confirmation of the Title to a Certain Grant of Land in New Mexico known as the Arkansas Grant. New York: S. C. Law, 1880.*

107 p. 23 cm. Printed wrappers. Maps.

Of superlative interest and value for its authoritative documents, nowhere else available, on the history of the important land grant by the States of Coahuila and Texas to Beales and Royuela. Included are Alexander Le Grand's "Field Notes and Journal of Survey," which are extraordinarily valuable for their notices of Indians, wild game, terrain, etc., of western Texas and New Mexico. Unrecorded, and no other copy traced.

1890

Message from the President of the United States transmitting a Report relative to the Proposed Removal of Certain Indians in New Mexico. [Washington, 1890.]

8 p. 23 cm. Caption title.

1914

FEWKES, J. WALTER

Archaeology of the Lower Mimbres Valley, New Mexico. Washington, 1914.*

53 p. 24.5 cm. Printed wrappers. Plates.

1917

FEWKES, J. WALTER

Archaeological Investigations in New Mexico, Colorado, and Utah. Washington, 1917.*

38 p. 24.5 cm. Printed wrappers. Plates.

NEWSPAPERS, INDIAN TERRITORY AND OKLAHOMA

THE ATOKA INDEPENDENT [Atoka, Choctaw Nation]

1877: Oct. 5.
1878: Aug. 16.

THE CADDO FREE PRESS [Caddo, Choctaw Nation]

1878: Aug. 8; Oct. 4, 11, 18, 25.
1879: March 21; April 11, 18, 25; May 16, 30; July 4, 18, 25; Aug. 1.

THE CHEROKEE ADVOCATE [Tahlequah, Cherokee Nation]

1845: March 20, 27.
1872: Sept. 21.
1873: June 7.
1878: Jan. 12; Oct. 26.
1879: Dec. 17.

THE CHEROKEE ADVOCATE. COUNCIL EDITION. TRI-WEEKLY. [Tahlequah, Cherokee Nation]

1877: Nov. 13.

The only known copy of the only known issue. Not recorded by Foreman, Gregory, or Ray.

THE CHOCTAW NEWS [Chahta-Tamaha, Choctaw Nation]

1878: Oct. 10, 11, 12, 15, 17, 18, 19, 20, 30; Nov. 7, 8.

The only known copies of the only known issues. The paper, which is not recorded by Foreman, Gregory, or Ray, was published at the Choctaw capital during a session of the Choctaw council, and its columns are occupied almost exclusively by official reports of council proceedings.

THE DAILY INDIAN JOURNAL [Muskogee, Creek Nation]

1876: Oct. 18, 19.

Each issue is marked Extra Edition. The second and third numbers of the first daily newspaper published in Oklahoma. Not recorded by Gregory or Ray. Foreman saw one privately owned copy of each of the two issues above. No copy of the first issue is known to exist.

THE DAILY OKLAHOMAN [Oklahoma City]

1895: Jan. 30.

THE EVENING GAZETTE [Oklahoma City]

1889: Nov. 23; Dec. 23.

THE GUTHRIE TIMES [Guthrie]

1889: June 4.

THE INDIAN CHAMPION [Atoka, Choctaw Nation]

1885: May 2.

THE INDIAN JOURNAL [Muskogee, Creek Nation]

1876: June 1, 8, 15, 22, 29; July 6, 13; Aug. 3, 10, 24, 31; Sept. 7, 14; Oct. 26; Dec. 7, 14, 21.

THE INDIAN JOURNAL [Eufaula, Creek Nation]

1877: April 5; June 28; July 5, 26; Aug. 2, 11, 18; Sept. 8, 15; Dec. 8.
1878: Feb. 13; June 19; Oct. 16; Dec. 15.
1879: April 17.

THE INDIAN PROGRESS [Muskogee, Creek Nation]

1875: Oct. 22.

One of only two known copies, the other being at the Oklahoma Historical Society. Not in Gregory.

THE NATIONAL REGISTER [Boggy Depot, Choctaw Nation]

1861: June 1.

The only known copy of the only known issue, and the sole known example of a newspaper printed in Confederate Indian Territory. The paper is not recorded by Foreman, Gregory, or Ray.

THE OKLAHOMA DAILY CAPITAL [Guthrie]

1889: June 2.

THE OKLAHOMA DAILY STAR [Oklahoma City]

1895: Jan. 27.

THE OKLAHOMA GAZETTE [Oklahoma City]

1889: May 23.

THE OKLAHOMA STAR [Caddo, Choctaw Nation]

1874: Feb. 20, 27; March 6; May 1; June 5; July 24.
1875: Jan. 29; Feb. 12; Sept. 3.
1876: Nov. 2.

THE STAR-VINDICATOR [McAlester, Choctaw Nation]

1877: Feb. 24; March 3, 17, 24; Aug. 18, 25; Sept. 1, 8, 29; Oct. 6, 13, 20; Nov. 6, 10, 24; Dec. 1, 8, 15, 22, 29.
1878: Jan. 5, 12; Feb. 16, 23; March 9, 23, 30; April 6, 13, 20, 27; May 4, 11, 18, 25; June 1, 8, 15, 22, 29; July 6, 13, 27; Aug. 3, 17, 24, 31; Sept. 7, 14, 21; Oct. 12, 19; Nov. 2; Dec. 7.

THE STAR-VINDICATOR [Blanco City, Texas]

1879: March 1, 15, 22; April 5; May 3; June 7; July 19.

Moved from McAlester to Blanco City, the newspaper soon perished. Blanco City issues are excessively rare.

THE TERRITORIAL ADVOCATE [Beaver City, Neutral Strip, or No Man's Land]

1887: Dec. 14.

The only known copy of the only known issue in the period in which No Man's Land was completely without organization or law. This is said to have been the only newspaper ever published wholly beyond the legal jurisdiction of any government. Ray (p. 112) saw only a copy, whose location is not stated, of the issue of Jan. 12, 1891. Foreman (p. 272–3) saw no copy. Gregory (p. 558) locates no copy of any issue.

The Vindicator [Atoka, Choctaw Nation]

1872: Sept. 14, 28; Oct. 5, 12, 19, 26; Nov. 2, 23.
1875: Sept. 25; Dec. 22, 29.
1876: Jan. 5; Feb. 16; April 19; June 7, 14; July 12; Aug. 30; Sept. 13; Nov. 15, 22; Dec. 20.

The Vindicator [New Boggy, Choctaw Nation]

1872: March 28.
1873: Aug. 27; Oct. 18.

NEZ PERCÉ INDIANS

1876

Monteith, John B.

The Status of Young Joseph and his Band of Nez-Perce Indians under the Treaties between the United States and the Nez-Perce Tribe of Indians, and the Indian Title to Land. Portland, Oregon: Assistant Adjutant General's Office. Department of the Columbia, 1876.

49 p. 18.5 cm.

1877

Howard, O. O.

Annual Report. Headquarters Department of the Columbia, in the Field, Camp Ebstein, Henry Lake, Idaho Territory, August 27, 1877. [N.p., 1877.]*

25 p. 20.5 cm. Caption title.

A detailed report on Nez Percé hostilities. The volume is rare.

An Impudent Indian. [New York, 1877.]*

3 p. 20.5 cm. Caption title.

A defense of Chief Joseph.

The Indian War. [New York? 1877.]*

4 p. 20 cm. Caption title.

An explanation of the origins of the Nez Percé uprising.

A Lesson from the Nez Perces. [New York, 1877.]*

3 p. 20.5 cm. Caption title.

Reflections on the Nez Percé War.

The Nez Perces. [New York? 1877.]*

3 p. 20.5 cm. Caption title.

Remarks, signed by H. C. W., on the Nez Percé uprising.

26 Field Circulars issued by General O. O. Howard, commanding the Department of the Columbia, during the pursuit of the Nez Perce Indians under Chief Joseph, from July 3 to September 17, 1877.*

The earliest circular was issued at Mountain Camp, Canoe Landing Trail, Idaho Territory, and the latest at Camp Leary, on Yellowstone River, Montana Territory. The rapidity of the chase may be judged from the fact that of the twenty-six circulars, twenty-three were issued at different camps. A valuable record, not only for the history of the campaign, but for the history of printing in Idaho and Montana.

1878

Supplementary Report (Non-Treaty Nez-Perce Campaign) of Brigadier-General O. O. Howard, Brevet Major-General U.S. Army, commanding Department of the Columbia. January 26, 1878. Portland, Oregon: 1878.

68 p. 19.5 cm.

Narratives and reports of the greatest importance. The volume is very rare.

OKLAHOMA

1866

Interesting Incident. [Washington, 1866.]

Broadside. 25.5 cm.

The account of a visit at Washington in 1866 of the Choctaw delegation to the home of Commissioner of Indian Affairs Cooley for the purpose of presenting a gold-headed cane to the commissioner. Former Principal Chief Peter P. Pitchlynn made the speech of presentation, which is quoted, and Cooley responded with a speech in the course of which he spoke of the recent treaty "which is to make you the nucleus of an Indian State—Oklahoma, 'the home of the red people'—and thus bring you into more intimate relationship with the United States." This is the earliest known printed application of the name Oklahoma to the future state. The only known copy.

1870

Memorial of the Delegates of the Cherokee, Creek, and Choctaw Nations of Indians, remonstrating against the Passage of the Bill to Organize the Territory of Oklahoma, Consolidate the Indian Tribes under a Territorial Government, and Carry Out Provisions of the Treaties of 1866 with certain Indian Tribes. [Washington, 1870.]

12 p. 22.5 cm. Caption title.

With an autograph inscription by P. P. Pitchlynn.

1871

Dr. F. P. Cleary. [Darlington? 1871.]*

Broadsheet. 20.5 cm.

Testimonials by Indian Territory army officers and Indian agents to the professional and social accomplishments of Dr. Cleary.

1872

Ross, William P.

The Indian Territory. Arguments of William P. Ross, of the Cherokee Delegation, delivered before the Committee on Territories of the House of Representatives, in Opposition to Bills before the Committee to Establish the Territory of Oklahoma, on the 1st day of February and the 5th day of March, 1872. Washington: Chronicle Publishing Co., 1872.

32 p. 22 cm.

1873

McKee, George C.

Territory of Oklahoma. Speech of Hon. George C. McKee, of Mississippi, in the House of Representatives, January 16, 1873. [Washington:] Congressional Globe Office, [1873].

8 p. 24 cm. Caption title.

1874

Boudinot, Elias Cornelius

Remarks of Elias C. Boudinot, of the Cherokee Nation, in behalf of the Bill to Organize the Territory of Oklahoma, before the House Committee on Territories, May 13, 1874. McGill & Witherow, Washington, [1874].*

18 p. 21.5 cm. Wrapper title.
Bound with others.

Ross, William P.

Indian Territory. Remarks in Opposition to the Bill to Organize the Territory of Oklahoma, by Wm. P. Ross, Principal Chief of the Cherokee Nation, before the Committee on Territories of the House of Representatives, Monday, February 9th, 1874. Washington: Gibson Bros., 1874.

30 p. 23 cm. Printed wrappers.

1875

Oklahoma. Report of the Committee on Indian Affairs to whom was referred the Bill which looked to Providing for the Organization of a Territorial Form of Government over the Country usually known as the Indian Territory. [Washington, 1875.]

8 p. 22.5 cm. Caption title.

1876

Adair, William P.

Remarks of W. P. Adair, Cherokee Delegate, in relation to the Expediency and Legality of Organizing the Indian Country into a Territory of the United States, to be called the Territory of "Ok-la-ho-ma," made before the Committee on Territories of the House of Representatives of the United States, January 31, 1876. [N.p., 1876.]

37 p. 23 cm. Caption title.

Boudinot, Elias C.

Oklahoma. An Argument by E. C. Boudinot, of the Cherokee Nation, delivered before the House Committee on Territories, February 3, 1876. Washington City: M'Gill & Witherow, 1876.

20 p. 23 cm. Wrapper title.

Hubbard, Gardiner G.

Argument of Hon. Gardiner G. Hubbard before the Committee on Territories on a Territorial Government for Oklahoma. Washington City: Beardsley & Snodgrass, 1876.

20 p. 20.5 cm.

Ross, William P.

Indian Territory. Remarks in Opposition to Bills to Organize the Territory of Oklahoma, by Wm. P. Ross, of the Cherokee Nation, before the Committee on Indian Affairs of the House of Representatives, Wednesday, March 8th, 1876. Washington: Gibson Bros., 1876.

23 p. 23 cm. Printed wrappers.

1877

The Territory of Oklahoma. Report of the Committee on Territories. [Washington, 1877.]

13 p. 23 cm. Caption title.

1878

Boudinot, E. C.

Oklahoma. Argument of Col. E. C. Boudinot before the Committee on Territories, January 29, 1878. Alexandria, Va.: G. H. Ramey & Son, 1878.

69 p. 22.5 cm. Wrapper title.

Grafton, B. F.

Argument before the Committee on the Territories, House of Representatives, January 26, 1878, on the Bill (H.R. No. 1596) to Provide for the Organization of the Territory of Oklahoma. B. F. Crafton, Counsel. Washington City: Thomas McGill & Co., 1878.

36 p. 22.5 cm. Wrapper title.

1879

Boudinot, E. C.

Col. Boudinot's Letter, showing the Status of the United States Lands in the Indian Territory. [Baltimore, 1879.]

Broadside. Folio.

It was this momentous letter, originally published in a Chicago newspaper, which first focused the attention of the country upon Oklahoma. Excessively rare, and a fine copy.

Hayes, Rutherford B.

Message from the President of the United States communicating Information in relation to an Alleged Occupation of a Portion of the Indian Territory by White Settlers. [Washington, 1879.]

34 p. 23 cm. Caption title. Folded color map.

The beginning of troubles with the Kansas intruders. The map of Indian Territory is a highly important one and shows the Unassigned Lands, about this time becoming an object of loud clamor on the part of land seekers.

Hayes, Rutherford B.

Message from the President of the United States communicating Information in relation to Lands in the Indian Territory acquired by the Treaties of 1866. [Washington, 1879.]*

6 p. 23 cm. Caption title.

HAYES, RUTHERFORD B.

[Proclamation by President R. B. Hayes forbidding intrusion upon Indian lands in Indian Territory. Washington, 1879.]*

[4] p. 34 cm. Printed in script.

HAYES, RUTHERFORD B.

Unauthorized Settlement in the Indian Territory. [Washington, 1879.]*

Broadside. 28 cm.

A proclamation, brought forth by the threat of a Payne boomer invasion, forbidding intrusion upon the Indian lands, together with a letter of Carl Schurz on the subject.

The Organization of the Territory of Oklahoma. [Washington, 1879.]

38 p. 23 cm. Caption title.

1880

HAYES, RUTHERFORD B.

By the President of the United States of America. A Proclamation. [Washington, 1880.]*

3 p. Folio. Printed in script.

A proclamation, aimed at D. L. Payne and his followers, prohibiting settlement in the Unassigned Lands. Excessively rare.

The Oklahoma Town Company, Wichita, Kansas. Certificate of Capital Stock. St. Louis: C. Hamilton & Co., [1880?].

Broadsheet, engraved. 18 cm. high × 26.5 cm.

Signed, in autograph, by D. L. Payne.

2 copies.

PAYNE, DAVID L.

Last Chance for Cheap Homes. Headq'rs of the Southwest Colonization Association, Wichita Kansas, January 1, 1880.

Broadside. Folio.

A glowing description of the territory to be colonized and an invitation to membership in the colony. A highly important document. Excessively rare, and a fine copy.

PAYNE, D. L.

Payne's Oklahoma Colony Pledge. [Wichita? 1880?].

Broadside. Folio.

The heading above is printed over the cancelled original heading: Southwest Colony Pledge.

PAYNE, DAVID L.

[A ticket of admission to Payne's lecture on Oklahoma, and Payne's business card, which described him as "President Payne Oklahoma Colony" and gives his address as "Oklahoma, Indian Territory."]

2 pieces.

Southwest Colony Town and Mining Company. Incorporated under the Laws of Kansas. Certificate for Capital Stock. $100. Wichita, Kansas, February 28, 1880.

Broadside. 17 cm. high × 21.5 cm. wide.

The certificate entitled the holder to "protection in securing 160 Acres of land in Indian Territory."

1881

PRICE, T. D.

[A circular promoting Payne's Oklahoma Colony. Spencer, Indiana, 1881.]

Broadside. 19 cm.

The only known copy.

1882

Certificate of Membership. Payne's Oklahoma Colony. Wichita, Kansas. Caldwell, Kansas: Caldwell Commercial and Job Printing Office, [1882].*

Broadside. 10.5 cm.

Dated July 10th, 1882.

Signed, in autograph, by D. L. Payne.

Certificate of Membership. Payne's Oklahoma Colony. [Wichita, Kansas, 1882?].

Broadside. 9 cm. high × 21.5 cm. wide.

Signed, in autograph, by D. L. Payne.

PARKER, I. C.

Decision of District Judge I. C. Parker on the Status of Lands in the Indian Territory. United States vs. D. L. Payne. In the District Court of the United States for the Western District of Arkansas, at the May term thereof, A.D. 1881. [Fort Leavenworth, 1882.]*

12 p. 21.5 cm. Wrapper title.

A highly important document of which no other copy can be traced.

PARKER, ISAAC C.

Decision of Judge I. C. Parker on the Status of Lands in the Indian Territory. Interior Department: Branch Printing Office. 1882.*

12 p. 23.5 cm.

Rare.

PAYNE, DAVID L.

To Our Oklahoma Colonists. Those who wish a Home in that Beautiful Country. [Wichita, Kansas, 1882.]*

[4] p. 22 cm. Caption title.

A highly important document in the history of the boomer movement, and a glowing picture of the wonders and delights awaiting those who would join Payne's colony. Excessively rare.

1883

PAYNE, DAVID L.

Oklahoma Colony. [Wichita, Kansas? 1883.]

Broadside. 10 cm. high × 14 cm. wide.

Announcement of an expedition into Oklahoma set for June 25, 1883. Excessively rare.

PAYNE, DAVID L.

On to Oklahoma! [Wichita, Kansas? 1883.]

Broadside. 10 cm. high × 14.5 cm. wide.

Invitation for members to join an expedition into Oklahoma on June 25, 1883. Excessively rare.

1884

ARTHUR, CHESTER A.

By the President of the United States of America. A Proclamation. [Washington, 1884.]*

Broadsheet. Folio. Printed in script.

A proclamation, aimed at the persistent D. L. Payne and his followers, forbidding unauthorized settlement upon Oklahoma lands.

ARTHUR, CHESTER A.

Headquarters of the Army, Adjutant General's Office, Washington, July 31, 1884. General Orders. No. 83. By the President of the United States of America. A Proclamation. [Washington, 1884.]

Broadside. 20.5 cm.

Another issue of the preceding proclamation.

Headquarters Department of the Missouri, Fort Leavenworth, Kansas, June 10, 1884. General Orders No. 8. [Fort Leavenworth, 1884.]

Broadside. 19 cm.

An order constituting the Military District of Oklahoma and providing for the expulsion of intruders. Unrecorded.

Lithograph portrait of David L. Payne, with an inset view titled "Captain Payne's Home in Oklahoma." Kansas City: Ramsey, Millett & Hudson, Lithographers. [1884?].*

63.5 cm.

Oklahoma War-Chief. The Oklahoma War-Chief will resume publication as a breeze newspaper, Saturday, April 26, 1884. [Arkansas City, Kansas, 1884.]

Broadside. 8 cm. high × 21 cm.

Excessively rare.

Payne's Oklahoma Colony. Certificate of Location. Wichita, Kansas, June 7, 1884. Topeka: Geo. W. Crane & Co., [1884?].

Broadsheet. 19.5 cm. high × 25.5 cm. wide.

Signed, in autograph, by D. L. Payne.

1885

Cleveland, Grover

By the President of the United States of America. A Proclamation. [Washington, 1885.]*

Broadsheet. Folio. Printed in script.

Another proclamation aimed at D. L. Payne and his colonists.

Jackson, A. P., and E. C. Cole

Oklahoma! Politically and Topographically described. History and Guide to the Indian Territory. Biographical Sketches of Capt. David L. Payne, W. L. Couch, Wm. H. Osborn, and others. A Complete Guide to the Indian Territory, illustrated with a Map, Hunting and Fishing Grounds. Kansas City: Ramsay, Millett & Hudson, [1885].

150, [2] p. 19 cm. Portraits, plates. The map is missing.

Excessively rare.

Message from the President of the United States, transmitting Communications from the Secretary of War and the Secretary of the Interior, relative to Certain Lands in the Indian Territory acquired by Treaty from the Creek and Seminole Indians. [Washington, 1885.]*

71 p. 23 cm. Caption title. 2 folded color maps.

Important information on the Payne invasion and other intrusions.

Osburn, W. H.

To Our Oklahoma Colonists: Those who wish a Home in that Beautiful Country. [Burrton, Kansas, 1885.]

Broadsheet. 28 cm.

Encouraging words to the boomers, and a glowing promotional description of Oklahoma calculated to attract new members to the colony. No other copy can be traced.

Potter, Joseph H.

Fort Supply, Indian Territory. October 14, 1885. Orders No. 211. [Fort Supply, 1885.]

Broadside. 15.5 cm.

Post firefighting regulations. Unrecorded, and the only known copy.

1886

Reply of the Chickasaw, Choctaw, Seminole, Creek, and Cherokee Indians, to Arguments submitted by Hon. J. B. Weaver and Hon. Sidney Clarke, in favor of the Bill to Organize the Territory of Oklahoma. [N.p., 1886.]

29 p. 23 cm. Wrapper title.

1887

Objections of the Delegates of the Chickasaw, Cherokee and Creek Nations to the Bill (S. 54) entitled "An Act for the Allotment of Lands in Severalty to Indians on the various Reservations, and to Extend the Protection of the Laws of the United States and of the Territories over the Indians, and for other purposes," now pending in the Senate of the United States. Washington: Gibson Bros., 1887.*

5 p. 23 cm. Wrapper title.

1888

From the Topeka Daily Capital. August 23, 1888. [Topeka, 1888.]*
Broadside. 31 cm.
An account of the murder in No Man's Land of Sheriff Cross, of Stevens County, Kansas, and the historical background explaining the complete absence of legal jurisdiction over crimes committed in that territory. Unrecorded, and the only known copy.

HARKINS, GEORGE W.

Argument of George W. Harkins, Delegate of the Chickasaw Nation, in Opposition to the Bill introduced by Mr. Springer to provide for the Organization of the Territory of Oklahoma, and for other purposes. Washington: Gibson Bros., 1888.
16 p. 23.5 cm. Wrapper title.

"Oklahoma," and the Rights of the Five Tribes of the Indian Territory. Submitted to Congress by the Cherokee Delegation. Washington, D.C.: Gray & Clarkson, 1888.
13 p. 23 cm. Printed wrappers.

PAINE, VEEDER B.

Oklahoma, its Climate, Acreage, Soil, and Title. Veeder B. Paine, Saginaw, Mich. East Saginaw, Mich.: Evening News, 1888.*
21 p. 19 cm.
A racy and witty account. Unrecorded, and the only known copy.

SIMS, LIEUT. A. K.

Saffron Sol, the Man with a Shadow. Or, The Tigers of No Man's Land. New York: Beadle's Half Dime Library, 1888.
14, [2] p. 17 cm.
The scene is laid in No Man's Land, or the Neutral Strip.

Was it Murder? Was John M. Cross, Sheriff of Stevenson County and the Men with him Murdered? If so, who were responsible? [Topeka, 1888.]
Broadsheet. Folio.
A highly interesting case. Sheriff Cross and his deputies were enticed across the Kansas line into No Man's Land, where they were murdered. No Man's Land, or the Unorganized Territory, was completely detached and without law, and not a single territorial, state, or Federal court in the United States could assert jurisdiction in the case. Unrecorded, and the only known copy.

1889

HARRISON, BENJAMIN

A Proclamation (opening the Unassigned Lands to settlement). [Washington, 1889.]*
3 p. 24 cm. Caption title.
It was this momentous proclamation that authorized the celebrated Oklahoma run of April 22, 1889.

JEFFERSON, H. E.

Oklahoma, the Beautiful Land. An Exciting Narrative of the Scenes Incident to the Occupation of Oklahoma. A Complete History of the Country and its Wondrous Development. By H. E. Jefferson of the Chicago Press. Chicago, 1889.

202 p. 18.5 cm. Printed wrappers.

A valuable account. Very rare.

Library of Tribune Extras. War Ships Sunk in Samoa. With the Settlement of Oklahoma. An Account of the Johnstown Disaster, and other Articles from the New-York Daily Tribune. New York: Tribune Association, 1889.

104 p. 26 cm. Wrapper title.

Pages 21–51 contain sprightly and entertaining accounts by eyewitnesses of the opening of Oklahoma.

MATTHEWS, W. B.

The Settler's Map and Guide Book. Oklahoma. A Brief Review of the History, Government, Soil, and Resources of the Indian Territory, Oklahoma proper, the Public Land Strip, and Cherokee Outlet. Washington: Wm. H. Lepley, 1889.

66 p. 23.5 cm. Printed wrappers. Folded map.

A very scarce volume.

MERRITT, WESLEY

Annual Report of Brigadier General W. Merritt, U.S. Army, commanding Department of the Missouri, 1889. [Fort Leavenworth, Kansas, 1889.]*

6 p. 20 cm. Wrapper title.

General Merritt established field headquarters at Oklahoma City in April, 1889, and was in command of the troops there during the opening and settlement. His official report of the event possesses therefore the greatest authority and importance. Unrecorded, and no other copy traced.

MERRITT, WESLEY

Circular. To the Settlers in Oklahoma. [Oklahoma City, 1889.]

Broadside. 20 cm.

An announcement, printed the day before the celebrated run and hence the day before the settlement of Oklahoma City, of the arrival of United States troops and of their determination to maintain law and order during the opening. This and the following Field Order No. 1 share the honor of being the first printing executed in Oklahoma City. Unrecorded, and the only known copy.

MERRITT, WESLEY

Headquarters Department of the Missouri (In the Field). Oklahoma, I.T., April 21, 1889. Field General Orders No. 1. [Oklahoma City, 1889.]

Broadside. 19.5 cm.

An order requiring troops to cooperate with United States marshals in keeping order and preventing traffic in liquor during the opening and settlement. Unrecorded, and the only known copy.

Oklahoma. Information for Congress. Townsite Frauds. Don't Legalize Town

Acts, nor give them any force: Copies of Ordinances, Judgements and Records. Oklahoma City: Daily Times print, 1889.*

19 p. 20.5 cm.

The first book printed in Oklahoma City. It contains the earliest Oklahoma City ordinances. Of the utmost rarity.

PAINTER, C. C.

The Oklahoma Bill, and Oklahoma. [Philadelphia, 1889.]

6 p. 23 cm. Caption title.

WARNE, PHILIP S.

Oklahoma Hi, the Blue Coat Scout; or, The Boomer's Last Battle. A Tale of the Beautiful Land. New York: Beadle's Half Dime Library, 1889.

16 p. 29 cm.

The scene is laid in Oklahoma.

WHEELER, E. L.

Deadwood Dick Jr. in No-Man's Land, or, Golconda, the Gladiator. New York: Beadle's Half Dime Library, 1889.

14, [2] p. 30 cm.

The scene is laid in No Man's Land, or the Neutral Strip.

1890

An act to Provide a Temporary Government for the Territory of Oklahoma, to Enlarge the Jurisdiction of the United States Court in the Indian Territory, and for other purposes. [Washington, 1890.]

21 p. 22.5 cm. Caption title.

One of the fundamental documents on Oklahoma.

BADGER, JOS. E., JR.

Dandy Darling, Detective; or, The Boomers of Big Buffalo. New York: Beadle's New York Dime Library, 1890.

30 p. 31 cm.

The action takes place during the opening of Oklahoma in 1889.

First Annual Session. Minutes of the Central Baptist Association, held with the Oklahoma City Baptist Church on Monday, December 22, 1890. Guthrie: L. F. Leach & Son. 1890.

9, [1] p. 21.5 cm. Printed wrappers.

Not in Foreman.

GEFFS, IRVING

The First Eight Months of Oklahoma City. By Bunky. Oklahoma City: McMaster Printing Co., 1890.

110 p. 21.5 cm.

The original edition. This classic is excessively rare.

Land Office at Guthrie, Oklahoma. Letter from the Secretary of the Interior,

transmitting Correspondence relating to Methods of Locating Homesteads and Town Sites at the Land Office at Guthrie, Oklahoma. [Washington, 1890.]
11 p. 22.5 cm. Caption title.

Letter from the Secretary of the Interior transmitting, in response to the Resolution of the Senate of December 17, 1889, Copies of Certain Reports on the Settlement of Oklahoma, etc. [Washington, 1890.]
30 p. 23 cm. Caption title.
The wild scramble for lots in Oklahoma City and Guthrie.

Letter from the Secretary of War, transmitting, in response to a Resolution of the 4th instant, a Letter from the Adjutant-General, with Copies of Correspondence on file in his office, relating to Affairs at Guthrie and Oklahoma City, Ind. Ter. [Washington, 1890.]
61 p. 22.5 cm. Caption title.
Important for its authoritative picture of early conditions.

Oklahoma Territorial Bill approved May 2, 1890. Oklahoma Townsite Bill, approved May 15, 1890. [Oklahoma City, 1890.]
14, [9] p. 21 cm. Wrapper title.
A highly important volume. Not in Foreman, and no other copy known.

Proceedings of the First Annual Session of the General Association of Oklahoma Territory, held at the Second Baptist Church, Guthrie, Ok. November 6, 7 & 8, 1890. Guthrie: State Capital print, [1890].
18 p. 19.5 cm. Printed wrappers.
Not in Foreman, and no other copy located.

ROCK, MARION TUTTLE

Illustrated History of Oklahoma, its Occupation by Spain and France, its Sale to the United States, its Opening to Settlement in 1889, and the Meeting of the First Territorial Legislature. Topeka: C. B. Hamilton & Son, 1890.
xii, 277, [1] p. Many portraits and views.
A very fine copy. Most of the edition is said to have been destroyed in a fire at Topeka.

WORKS, J. S. (BUCKSKIN JOE)

To Renters. [Mangum? 1890?].*
Broadside. 22 cm.
A warning to those renting lands from Indians of unproved citizenship. Unrecorded, and the only known copy.

1891

BRYANT, MONTGOMERY

Fort Supply, I.T. August 17, 1891. Orders No. 108. Extract. [Fort Supply, 1891.]
Broadside. 20 cm.
Regulations governing the hunting of deer, grouse, and wild turkeys in the vicinity of the post. Unrecorded, and the only known copy.

HARRISON, BENJAMIN

[Proclamation throwing open to settlement the reservations just acquired from the Sac and Fox, Iowa, Pottawatomie, and Shawnee Indians. Washington, 1891.]*

[4] p. 34 cm. Caption title.

MEEK, ANDREW H.

The Belief and Requirements of the True Church. Kingfisher, 1891.

20 p. 17 cm. Wrapper title.

One of the earliest Kingfisher imprints. Not in Foreman.

STEELE, GEORGE W.

Report of the Governor of Oklahoma to the Secretary of the Interior. 1891. Washington, 1891.

15 p. 23 cm. Printed wrappers.

STEVENS, D. W.

The James Boys in No Man's Land: or, The Bandit King's Last Ride. New York: The New York Detective Library, 1891.

30, [2] p. 32.5 cm.

1892

BUCKSKIN JOE

Mass Meeting! How many willing Workers have we in Comanche? How many Men are there here who want to see a City built here? [Comanche? 1892?].

Broadside. 21.5 cm.

Unrecorded, and the only known copy.

Business and Resident Directory of Guthrie and Logan County, Ok. For the year commencing Sept. 1st, 1892. Embracing an Index of Residents in Guthrie, together with the names of all Homesteaders in Logan County, giving quarter section, township and range. Frank G. Prouty, Publisher, Guthrie, Oklahoma. [1892].*

152 p. 24.5 cm.

Rare.

CLARKE, SIDNEY

Speech of Hon. Sidney Clarke at Oklahoma City, October 6, 1892, upon the Vital Local Questions of the Territory. [Oklahoma City, 1892.]

16 p. 22 cm. Caption title.

Not in Foreman.

Hennessey Clipper—Supplement. Hennessey, Kingfisher County, Oklahoma, April 22, 1892.

Broadsheet. 30 cm. Printed on red paper.

Contains an account of the land opening and rush at Kingfisher. No other copy is known.

Oklahoma and Indian Territory Baptist Year Book, 1892. Oklahoma City: Baptist Publishing Co., 1892.

21 p. 22 cm. Wrapper title.

Not in Foreman, and no other copy located.

Proceedings of the Oklahoma Convention held at Iowa Park, Texas, Jan. 1, 1892. [Iowa Park, 1892.]

Broadside. 22.5 cm.

Resolutions proposed by Captain J. S. Works (Buckskin Joe), demanding the immediate opening to Texas cattlemen of the Kiowa and Comanche reservations. Unrecorded, and the only known copy.

Seay, Abram J.

Report of the Governor of Oklahoma to the Secretary of the Interior. 1892. Washington, 1892.

15 p. 23 cm. Printed wrappers.

1893

First Biennial Report of the Territorial Board of Health of the Territory of Oklahoma, from April 16th, 1891, to December 1st, '92. Kingfisher: Kingfisher Free Press, 1893.

36 p. 21.5 cm.

Not in Foreman.

The James Boys among the Boomers; or, Old King Brady and Carl Greene Fighting the Outlaws in Oklahoma. By a N.Y. Detective. New York: Detective Library, 1893.*

30, [2] p. 32 cm.

Lyman, L. B.

Free Common Sense Ideas. For All People. Guthrie, O.T.: State Capital Printing Co., 1893.

37 p. 21.5 cm.

Not in Foreman.

Renfrow, William C.

Report of the Governor of Oklahoma Territory for the fiscal year ending June 30, 1893. Washington, 1893.

11 p. 23 cm. Printed wrappers.

Seay, Abram J.

Governor's Message to the Second Legislative Assembly of the Territory of Oklahoma. Delivered January 19, 1893. Guthrie: State Capital Printing Co., [1893].

11 p. 22 cm. Wrapper title.

1894

In the Supreme Court of the Territory of Oklahoma. J. J. Burke and E. E. Brown vs. the Territory of Oklahoma. Brief of Defendant in Error. Oklahoma City: Press-Gazette Print, 1894.

7 p. 20.5 cm. Wrapper title.

Not in Foreman.

Oklahoma Town Sites. Regulations provided by the Secretary of the Interior for the Guidance of Trustees in the Execution of their Trust. [Washington, 1894.]

14 p. 22.5 cm. Wrapper title.

Opinions of the Oklahoma Press and People of Oklahoma regarding the Cockrell-Flynn "Sooner Bill" (S. Bill No. 2038, and H. Bill No. 7943). As Published in Recent Issues. El Reno, Oklahoma Territory: Globe Print, [1894].

26 p. 20.5 cm. Wrapper title.
Not in Foreman, and no other copy known.

RENFROW, WILLIAM C.

Report of the Governor of Oklahoma to the Secretary of the Interior. 1894. Washington, 1894.

18 p. 23 cm. Printed wrappers.

Report of the President of the Oklahoma Agricultural and Mechanical College . . . and the Biennial Report to the Governor of Oklahoma, December 31, 1894. Guthrie: Representative Print, 1895.

24, [1] p. 23.5 cm. Printed wrappers.
Not in Foreman.

1895

Free Home League. Constitution for Local Leagues, Issued by Order F.H.L. Convention, held Feb. 12, 1895. Guthrie: State Capital Printing Co., [1895].

8 p. 19.5 cm. Printed wrappers.
Not in Foreman.

Ordinances of the City of Norman, Cleveland County, Oklahoma Territory. 1895. Norman, O.T.: Press of the People's Voice, [1895].

64 p. 14.5 cm. Printed wrappers.
Not in Foreman, and no other copy known. [See page 298.]

Report of Territorial University. Exhibit "C" of Governor's Message to the Third Legislative Assembly of the Territory of Oklahoma. January 8, 1895. [Guthrie, 1895.]

6 p. 22 cm. Printed wrappers.

1896

HOUSTON, J. J.

Free Home Convention. [Perry, Oklahoma Territory, 1896.]

Broadside. 22 cm.
Call for a convention of the Free Home League to meet at Guthrie January 12, 1897.
Not in Foreman, and no other copy located.

RENFROW, WILLIAM C.

Report of the Governor of Oklahoma to the Secretary of the Interior. 1896. Washington, 1896.

23 p. 23 cm. Printed wrappers.

1897

BARNES, CASSIUS M.

Report of the Governor of Oklahoma to the Secretary of the Interior. 1897. Washington, 1897.

41 p. 23 cm. Printed wrappers.

ORDINANCES

OF THE

CITY OF NORMAN

Cleveland County,

OKLAHOMA TERRITORY.

1895.

COOK, T. R.

The Ft. Sill, Kansas City & St. Louis Land, Townsite and Mining Association. By Capt. T. R. Cook. Full Description of the Wichita, Comanche and Kiowa Reservations. How to Acquire Land and Enter Townsites. "All is not gold that glitters," but Gold and Silver do Exist in the Wichita Mountains. 1897. Noble County Sentinel Print. Perry, Oklahoma.*

67 p. 22 cm. Frontisp. port. Plates. Printed wrappers.
Unrecorded, and apparently the only known copy.

COOK, T. R.

Read the Record. The Fort Sill, Kansas City and St. Louis Land, Townsite and Mining Association, organized by and for the Common People to secure for themselves the Best Results possible in the Opening of the Indian Lands to Settlement, etc. [Perry, 1897.]*

Broadside. Folio.
Unrecorded, and no other copy located.

Government Lands. The Comanche, Kiowa and Apache Lands soon to be Opened for Settlement. A Tract of Land rich in Mineral, with fine Timber and good Water; a Tract of Land beautiful in Scenery and rich for Agricultural Purposes. [Perry, Oklahoma, 1897.]*

4 p. 15 cm. Caption title.
A glowing description. The only known copy.

Office of the Ft. Sill, Kansas City & St. Louis Land, Townsite and Mining Association. Perry, O.T. [Perry, 1897.]

Broadside. 14.5 cm.
A blank membership certificate.

Reports in Governor's Message to the Fourth Legislative Assembly of Oklahoma Territory. Guthrie: Daily Leader, 1897.

161 p. 23.5 cm. Printed wrappers.

True Facts regarding Oklahoma. [N.p., 1897.]

Broadsheet. Folio.
Promotional literature of the Free Home League.

1898

BARNES, CASSIUS M.

Report of the Governor of Oklahoma to the Secretary of the Interior for the Fiscal Year ended June 30, 1898. Washington, 1898.

76 p. 23 cm. Printed wrappers. Folded color map. Plates.

1899

BARNES, CASSIUS M.

Message of the Governor of Oklahoma to the Fifth Legislative Assembly. January 11, 1899. [Guthrie: State Capital Printing Company, 1899.]

32, [3] p. 23 cm. Printed wrappers.

1900

CUMMINS, B. V.

A Description of the Kiowa, Comanche and Apache Indian Reservation, Oklahoma Territory. "Soon to be Opened for Settlement." [Kingfisher, 1900.]*

7 p. on 7 leaves broadside. Folio. In script, and apparently the product of a letter duplicator.

A glowing description by a vigorous promoter. Not in Foreman, and no other copy known.

CUMMINS, B. V.

A Free Home awaits the Old Soldier in the Rich and Fertile Country of the Kiowa, Comanche and Apache Reservations, which will be thrown open for settlement by the United States not later than June 6th, 1901, and possibly not later than December of this year. [Kingfisher, 1900.]*

Broadside. Folio.

Not in Foreman, and no other copy traced.

CUMMINS, B. V.

Free Homes! Free Homes! For "Old Soldiers" and their Widows. Accept your Last Chance, or Forever Hold Your Peace. [Kingfisher, 1900.]

Broadsheet. 30 cm.

Not in Foreman, and no other copy traced.

CUMMINS, B. V.

General Provisions of the Homestead Laws. [Kingfisher, 1900.]

Broadside. Folio.

An offer to file claims in the Kiowa, Comanche, Apache, and Wichita Reservation. Not in Foreman, and no other copy traced.

CUMMINS, B. V.

Oklahoma. Free Homes for Old Soldiers and their Widows. Accept your Last Chance or forever Hold your Peace. The Kiowa, Comanche, Apache and Wichita Reservations are soon to be Opened for Settlement. [Kingfisher, 1900.]

Broadside. Folio.

Unrecorded, and the only known copy.

DUNCAN, M. M.

The Time is Short! Oklahoma. The Last Chance! The Kiowa, Comanche, Apache, and Wichita Reservation will soon be Opened to Settlement. [Kingfisher, 1900.]

Broadside. 27 cm.

A glowing promotional circular. Unrecorded, and the only known copy.

HALE, JAMES H.

Pawnee, County and Town. Its Location, Wealth and Advantages. Pawnee, Oklahoma Territory, August 15, 1900. Pawnee: Times-Democrat, [1900].*

8 p. on a folded leaf. 14 cm.

Not in Foreman, and no other copy located.

Jay M. Jackson & Co.

Free Lands for Soldiers in Oklahoma. [Oklahoma City, 1900.]*
Broadside. 27.5 cm.
A promotional circular directed to prospective settlers on the Kiowa, Comanche, and Apache Reservation. Not in Foreman, and no other copy traced.

The Minstrel. Minco, I.T., December 21, 1900. Volume 1, Number 8.
[16] p. 23 cm. Wrapper title.
The leading article is one entitled "Anadarko in 1885." Copies of this obscure publication are very seldom found.

Morgan, Dick T.

Free Home Address of Hon. Dick T. Morgan, of Perry, O.T., President of the Free Home League of Oklahoma, before its Annual Convention held at El Reno, Oklahoma, February 16, 1900. Resolutions and Proceedings of Convention. [Perry, 1900.]
11 p. 22 cm. Printed wrappers.
Not in Foreman.

1901

Barnes, Cassius M.

Message of the Governor of Oklahoma to the Sixth Legislative Assembly. January 9, 1901. Guthrie: State Capital Printing Co., [1901].
28, [5] p. 22.5 cm. Printed wrappers.

Dickerson, Philip J.

History of Anadarko, O.T. Its Past and Present and Bright Future. [Anadarko, 1901.]
60 p. 19 cm. Wrapper title.
Not in Foreman.

Dickerson, Philip J.

History of Lawton, O.T. What it is, and what it may be. Guthrie: State Capital Printing Co., [1901].
[56] p. 19.5 cm. Wrapper title.

Memorial to Congress and proceedings of the Statehood Convention of Oklahoma and Indian territories held at South McAlester, I.T., December 10, 1900. Guthrie: State Capital Printing Co., 1901.
10 p. 21.5 cm. Printed wrappers.
Rare.

Pawnee County Business Directory. Brief History of Pawnee County and her Business Men. [Pawnee:] Davis & Gould, [1901].
32 p. 22 cm. Wrapper title.
Not in Foreman.

Proceedings of the Grand Commandery, 1901. Knights Templar of the Territory of Oklahoma. Perry, Oklahoma. June 10, 1901. [Perry? 1901.]*
32 p. 23.5 cm. Printed wrappers. Frontisp. portrait.

Report of the Assistant Commissioner of the General Land Office to the Secretary of the Interior respecting the Opening to Settlement and Entry of the Kiowa, Comanche and Apache, and Wichita Lands in Oklahoma Territory. Washington, 1901.
16 p. 23 cm. Printed wrappers. Folded color map. 20 full page photographs.
A scarce and valuable document.

1902

DICKERSON, PHILIP J.
History of Mountain View, O.T. Washita County. [N.p., 1902.]
28 p. 19 cm. Wrapper title.

The Negro Problem. Notice! We, the citizens of Guthrie and Surrounding Country have determined to Boycot All Business Men and Employers who hereafter Employ or in any way Patronize the Negro, etc. [Guthrie, 1902?].
Broadside, on orange paper. Folio.
Unrecorded, and the only known copy.

New Statehood Bill. Hearings before the Subcommittee of the Committee on Territories on House Bill 12543, to Enable the People of Oklahoma, Arizona, and New Mexico to Form Constitutions and State Governments and be Admitted into the Union on an Equal Footing with the Original States. Washington, 1902.
394 p. 23 cm.
A valuable picture of conditions in Oklahoma Territory.

1903

BLACKBURN-HASKETT, ANNETTE
A Souvenir of Hennessey, Oklahoma, by Mrs. Annette Blackburn-Haskett. Hennessey, Oklahoma: Clipper Office, 1903.
29 p. 19.5 cm. Wrapper title.
Almost wholly devoted to the life and death of Pat Hennessey. Rare.

Constitution and By-Laws of the Guthrie Building and Loan Association, of Guthrie, Oklahoma. Chartered June 26, 1890. Guthrie: Daily Leader Printing Co., 1903.
22 p. 16.5 cm. Printed wrappers.
Not in Foreman.

Proceedings of the Grand Commandery 1903. Knights Templars of the Territory of Oklahoma. Guthrie, Oklahoma, February 12, 1903. [Guthrie? 1903.]
43 p. 21 cm. Wrapper title.

1905

CURTIS, WILLIAM E.
Oklahoma, Indian Territory, Texas. A Series of Articles by William E. Curtis, published in the Record-Herald of Chicago, Ill. [St. Louis, 1905.]
31, [1] p. 22.5 cm. Printed wrappers.

FERGUSON, THOMPSON B.
Governor's Message to the Eighth Legislative Assembly of the Territory of Oklahoma convening January 10, 1905. Guthrie: State Capital Co., 1905.
30 p. 22 cm. Printed wrappers.

Hearing on Prohibition in the Proposed State of Oklahoma, before the Committee on the Territories, House of Representatives. Washington, 1905.

87 p. 23 cm.

Testimony by General Pleasant Porter, Paschal Ridge, and other prominent Indians.

ROGERS, W. C., and others

Statehood Constitutional Call. [Muskogee, 1905.]

Broadside. Folio.

An important document, issued by the chiefs of the Cherokee, Choctaw, Creek, and Seminole nations. Unrecorded, and no other copy located.

1906

Proceedings of the second annual meeting of the Oklahoma and Indian Territory Bar Association. Guthrie: State Capital Co., 1906.*

248 p. 22 cm.

Proclamation and Regulations Opening and Prescribing the Method of the Sale of the Pasture and Wood Reserve Lands in the Kiowa, Comanche, and Apache Indian Reservations in Oklahoma. [Washington, 1906.]*

32 p. 23 cm. Caption title.

PUCKETT, J. L., and ELLEN PUCKETT

History of Oklahoma and Indian Territory and Homeseekekers' (sic) Guide, by J. L. and Ellen Puckett. Vinita: Chieftain Publishing Co., 1906.

149, [2] p. 22 cm. Printed wrappers.

A fine copy. Very scarce.

1907

CAMPBELL, W. P.

Neenie, the Coffeyman's Daughter. Storyette in Two Parts. By W. P. Campbell, Oklahoma City, Okla. Waukomis, Okla.: The Hornet, [1907].

57 p. 18 cm. Printed wrappers.

Early Oklahoma fiction.

The Constitution (of the State of Oklahoma). Guthrie: Leader Printing Co., [1907].

64 p. 22 cm. Wrapper title.

The first printing.

EGAN, CHARLES H.

In the Supreme Court of Oklahoma Territory. Board of County Commissioners of the County of Greer vs. Constitutional Delegate Convention et al. Brief of Plaintiff. Mangum: Mangum Job Print, 1907.

10 p. 22 cm. Printed wrapper.

Not in Foreman.

Opera House To-Night. [Waukomis, 1907.]*

Broadside, on green paper. 27.5 cm.

A play-bill. Not in Foreman, and no other copy traced.

Proceedings of the Third Annual Meeting of the Oklahoma and Indian Territory Bar Association. Oklahoma City, December 1906. McAlester: Capital Ptg. Co., [1907].*

[2], 176, [1] p. 22.5 cm.

Report concerning Indians in Oklahoma, Oregon and Pennsylvania. [N.p., 1907.]

[58] p. 24.5 cm. Wrapper title.

The volume is a rather crude job of printing and is probably the product of one of the Indian school presses.

1908

Constitution of the State of Oklahoma. Washington, 1908.

80 p. 23 cm.

Emergency Laws passed by the First Legislature, State of Oklahoma, 1907–1908. Ardmore: Ardmoreite Press, [1908].*

75 p. 22 cm. Printed wrappers.

1910

HUGHES, MARION

Oklahoma Charley. Arkansaw Corndoctor, Cowboy, Knightherder, Missourian, Miner, Indian Scout, Invalid, Prospector, Polygamist, Soldier, Saloonkeeper, Snake-charmer, Horsetrader, Hillbillie, Hayseed, Haweater, Hobo, Bookagent, Bullwhacker, Bearhunter, Bartender, Bootlegger and Boozefighter. St. Louis: John P. Wagner & Co., [1910].

159 p. 18.5 cm. Printed wrappers.

The second edition of this classic of low humor.

1911

HAMRICK, GEMES L'MON

Terressa. A Thrilling Western Romance. By Gemes L'Mon Hamrick, Author and Publisher. Tuttle, Oklahoma, 1911.

280 p. 15.5 cm. Printed wrappers. Illustrations.

Very scarce example of native Oklahoma fiction.

1912

STARR, EMMET

Encyclopedia of Oklahoma. Based on the 1910 Census. Issued at least annually. Volume 1. Oklahoma City, 1912.

148 p. 21.5 cm. Printed wrappers.

Almost the entire edition was destroyed by the printer. The volume was printed on cheap paper which has now turned quite brittle, and most of the very few copies which survived are in bad condition. This is a fine copy, perhaps the very finest in existence. Very rare.

1914

MOTT, M. L.

The Act of May 27, 1908, placing in the Probate Courts of Oklahoma Indian Jurisdiction a National Blunder. This Jurisdiction was conferred by Congress; there and there alone lies the Power to withdraw it. In the light of the Incontrovertible Record herein, can Congress fail to do it. Compiled and Presented by M. L. Mott, National Attorney for the Creek Tribe of Indians in Oklahoma for the period of ten years beginning in 1904 and ending in 1914. [N.p., 1914.]

77 p. 23 cm. Printed wrappers.

1927

Horton, Roderic

The Sooners. A romance of early Oklahoma. Los Angeles, [1927].*

280 p. 20 cm. Illustrated.

1937

Botkin, B. A.

The American Play-party Song. With a Collection of Oklahoma Texts and Tunes. Lincoln, Nebraska: The University, 1937.*

400 p. 23 cm. Printed wrappers.

An excellent study.

OMAHA INDIANS

1860

Code of Laws, as adopted by the Chiefs and Members of the Omaha Tribe of Indians, in Council assembled, the 11th day of May A.D. 1860. [Omaha, Nebraska, 1860.]

4 p. 13 cm. Caption title.

The only known copy.

1881

John Elk, Plaintiff in Error, vs. Charles Wilkins, Defendant in Error. Brief and Argument of Defendant in Error. [Omaha, 1881.]*

18 p. 21 cm.

The case arose from the refusal of Omaha, Nebraska, authorities to allow John Elk, who had surrendered his Indian citizenship, to vote in a municipal election.

1885

Fletcher, Alice C.

Historical Sketch of the Omaha Tribe of Indians of Nebraska. Washington: Judd & Detweiler, 1885.*

12 p. 23.5 cm. Illustrations. Map.

OREGON INDIANS

1846

New Indian Territory in Oregon, &c., &c. Memorial of the Board of Managers of the American Indian Mission Association. [Washington, 1846.]

6 p. 24.5 cm. Caption title.

1851

Message of the President of the United States, communicating the Correspondence in relation to the Possessory Rights of the British Hudson's Bay Company in Oregon. [Washington, 1851.]

18 p. 25 cm. Caption title.

1855

Articles of Agreement and Convention made and concluded at Dayton, Oregon Territory, by Joel Palmer, Superintendent of Indian Affairs, on the part of the United States, and the following named Chiefs of the Confederated Bands of Indians residing in the Willamette Valley . . . . [Washington, 1855.]

6 p. 22.5 cm. Caption title.

Headed: Confidential.

The rare confidential printing which preceded the official folio printing of the ratified treaty.

By the Governor of the Territory of Oregon. A Proclamation. Whereas certain Indians have been guilty of the commission of Criminal Offences, and have combined and are now engaged in Hostilities that Threaten the Peace and Security of the Frontier, etc. [Portland, Oregon, 1855.]

Broadside. Folio.

The proclamation calls for eight companies of mounted volunteers to suppress Indian hostilities. Unrecorded, and the only known copy.

Special Laws passed by the Legislative Assembly of the Territory of Oregon, at the Sixth Regular Session thereof, begun and held at Salem, December 4, 1854. Corvallis, Oregon: Asahel Bush, 1855.

65, [2] p. 22 cm.

Memorials relating to the Snake Indian massacre.

1858

Laws of the Territory of Oregon: enacted during the Ninth Regular Session of the Legislative Assembly begun December 7, 1857; concluded February 5, 1858. Salem, Oregon: Asahel Bush, 1858.

64, 112, 23, 8 p. 23 cm.

Interesting and important memorials on Indian affairs.

1860

The Constitution; together with the Session Laws of Oregon, enacted during the First Regular Session of the Legislative Assembly of Oregon, begun Sept. 10, 1860. Salem, Oregon: Asahel Bush, 1860.

111, 9, 5, 6, [1] p. 21.5 cm.

Important memorials on military roads through the Indian country and protection of immigrants from Indian depredations.

1874

Report of Governor Grover to General Schofield on the Modoc Work, and Reports of Maj. Gen. John F. Miller and General John E. Ross, to the Governor. Also a Letter of the Governor to the Secretary of the Interior on the Wallowa Valley Indian Question. Salem, Oregon: Mart. V. Brown, 1874.

68 p. 21.5 cm. Printed wrappers.

SIX INDIENS
rouges
DE LA TRIBU
DES GRANDS OSAGES,

ARRIVÉS DU MISSOURI

Au Havre, le 27 Juillet 1827,

SUR LE NAVIRE AMÉRICAIN

NEW-ENGLAND, CAP. HUNT.

Seconde Édition, revue, corrigée et augmentée.

AU HAVRE,
CHEZ S. FAURE, IMPRIMEUR.

1892

Brown, J. Henry

Brown's Political History of Oregon. Provisional Government. Treaties, Conventions, and Diplomatic Correspondence on the Boundary Question; Historical Introduction of the Explorations on the Pacific Coast; History of the Provisional Government from Year to Year, with Election Returns and Official Reports; History of the Cayuse War, with Original Documents. Volume 1. Portland, Oregon: Lewis & Dryden Printing Co., 1892.

viii, 462 p. 21.5 cm. Map. Portrait. Facsimile.

Valuable for its treatment of the Cayuse War. Volume 2 was never published. Rare.

1904

Dodge, Orvil

The Heroes of Battle Rock, or the Miners' Reward. A Short Story of Thrilling Interest. How a Small Canon Done its Work. Port Orford, Oregon, the Scene of the Great Tragedy. A Desperate Encounter of Nine White Men with Three Hundred Indians. Miraculous Escape after Untold Hardships. Historically True. Savages Subdued and Rich Gold Mines Discovered. January 1904. [N.p.]

21 p. 23.5 cm. Wrapper title.

Undated

Lockley, Fred

To Oregon by Ox-Team in '47. The Story of the Coming of the Hunt Family to the Oregon Country and the Experiences of G. W. Hunt in the Gold Diggings of California in 1849. Portland, [N.d.].

16 p. 23 cm. Printed wrappers.

Inscribed by the author.

OSAGE INDIANS

1827

Six Indiens rouges de la Tribu des Grand Osages, arrivés du Missouri au Havre, le 27 Juillet 1827, sur le Navire Américain New-England, Cap. Hunt. Seconde Edition. Havre: S. Faure, [1827].

28 p. 21 cm. Plain wrappers. Folded color plate.

[See page 307.]

Six Indiens Rouges de la Tribu des Grands Osages, arrivés du Missouri au Havre, le 27 Juillet 1827, sur le Navire Américain New-England, Cap. Hunt. Troisieme Edition. Paris: Delaunay, 1827.*

36 p. 21 cm. Color plate.

Vissier, Paul

Histoire de la tribu des Osages. Paris, 1827.

92 p. 22 cm. Printed wrappers.

Rare. [See page 309.]

HISTOIRE

DE LA TRIBU

DES OSAGES,

PEUPLADE SAUVAGE DE L'AMÉRIQUE SEPTENTRIONALE,
DANS L'ÉTAT DE MISSOURI,
L'UN DES ÉTATS-UNIS D'AMÉRIQUE;

ÉCRITE D'APRÈS LES SIX OSAGES ACTUELLEMENT A PARIS;

PAR M. P. V.

Suivie de la Relation du Voyage de ces Sauvages, et d'une Notice historique sur chacun de ces Indiens célèbres dans leur tribu par leurs exploits guerriers.

PARIS,
CHEZ CHARLES BÉCHET, LIBRAIRE,
QUAI DES AUGUSTINS, Nº 57,
ET CHEZ LES MARCHANDS DE NOUVEAUTÉS.
A RENNES, CHEZ DUCHESNE, LIBRAIRE, RUE ROYALE.

1827.

Imprimerie de C. J. TROUVÉ, rue Notre-Dame-des-Victoires, nº 16.

1834

Washashe wageressa pahugreh tse. The Osage First Book. Boston: Crocker & Brewster, 1834.

126 p. 15 cm.

The first book in the Osage language, and a rare volume.

1835

WÜRTTEMBERG, PAUL WILHELM, PRINCE OF

Erste Reise nach dem nördlichen Amerika in den Jahren 1822 bis 1824, von Paul Wilhem, Herzog von Württemberg. Stuttgart und Tübingen, J. G. Cotta, 1835.

vi, 394, [2] p. 22.5 cm.

Of great rarity. Wagner-Camp 58 locates but three copies. Prince Paul visited the Osages and made a trip up the Missouri to Council Bluffs, afterward visiting the Pawnees and Otoes.

1837

Letter from the Secretary of War to the Chairman of the Committee on Indian Affairs recommending Measures for the Relief of the Osage Indians. [Washington, 1837.]

10 p. 22.5 cm. Caption title.

1868

CLARKE, SIDNEY

Remonstrance against the Treaty with the Great and Little Osage Indians. Gross Injustice done the Settler. The School Fund Despoiled, and Land Monopoly Created. Washington: Gibson Bros., 1868.

11 p. 22 cm.

1871

Agreement between the United States and the Great and Little Osage Indians for the Sale of their Lands in Kansas, and for the Purchase of a New Reserve in the Indian Territory. 1870. Lawrence, Kansas: Journal Book and Job Printing Office, 1870.

8 p. 22 cm. Printed wrappers.

CURTIS, B. R.

In the Matter of the Osage Ceded Lands in Kansas. Argument of Mr. B. R. Curtis before the Secretary of the Interior. December 18, 1871. Washington: Judd & Detweiler, [1871].

28 p. 22 cm. Wrapper title.

LAWRENCE, WILLIAM

The Osage Ceded Lands. Who Owns Them? The Settler vs. the Railroads. Views of Judge Lawrence, of Ohio. [Parsons, Kansas: Reynolds & Perry, 1871.]

8 p. 24.5 cm. Caption title.

1872

Decision of the Secretary of the Interior and Opinion of the Assistant Attorney General in the Matter of the Osage Ceded Lands in Kansas. Washington, 1872.

16 p. 23 cm. Wrapper title.

Erste Reise

nach dem

nördlichen Amerika

in den Jahren 1822 bis 1824

von

Paul Wilhelm, Herzog von Württemberg.

Stuttgart und Tübingen,
Verlag der J. G. Cotta'schen Buchhandlung.
1835.

1874

History of the Land Grants of the Leavenworth, Lawrence and Galveston Railroad, with the Laws and Documents pertaining thereto. Prepared by John W. Scott, Land Commissioner. Lawrence, Kansas: Journal Steam Printing Establishment, 1874.*

40 p. 21 cm. Printed wrappers.

The title to the railroad's lands rested upon a disputed clause in the 1867 treaty with the Osages.

Protest of the Osage Nation of Indians, against the Establishment by Congress of a Territorial Government of the United States, over the Indian Nations. [N.p., 1874.]*

7 p. 22 cm. Caption title.

Two issues, one with a very crude woodcut at the end.

1875

Adair, W. P.

Hon. Clinton B. Fisk, Chairman; and Members of the Honorable Board of Indian Commissioners. [Washington, 1875.]*

4 leaves, broadside. The galley proofs.

A statement of the Adair claim against the Osage Indians.

Evidence in the Matter of a Requisition of the Osage National Council on their Funds in the Keeping of the United States. Washington: R. O. Polkinhorn, [1875].

28 p. 23 cm. Wrapper title.

The Osage Troubles in Barbour County, Kansas, in the Summer of 1874. Correspondence between the State Government and the Interior Department—Testimony relative to the Killing of Four Osage Indians. Topeka, Kansas: Geo. W. Martin, 1875.

68 p. 22 cm.

A scarce volume.

1879

Indian raids of 1878. The Report of the Commission appointed in pursuance of the provisions of Senate Joint Resolution No. 1, relating to Losses sustained by Citizens of Kansas, by the Invasion of Indians during the year 1878. Topeka, Kansas: Geo. W. Martin, Kansas Publishing House, 1879.*

58 p. 22 cm.

A scarce volume.

1880

To the Congress of the United States. Statement of the Account of Adair and Vann with the Osage Nation of Indians. [N.p., 1880.]

24 p. 20.5 cm. Caption title.

1883

The Constitution and Laws of the Osage Nation, passed at Pawhuska, Osage Nation, in the years 1881 and 1882. Washington: R. O. Polkinhorn, 1883.

29 p. 23.5 cm. Wrapper title.

The finest of the four known copies.

1885

Laws of the Osage Nation, passed at Pawhuska, Osage Nation, in the years 1883, 1884, and 1885. Muskogee, I.T.: By the Indian Journal Steam Job Office, 1885.
12 p. 22 cm. Printed wrapper.
The only known copy.

Vann & Adair vs. The United States and the Osage Nation of Indians. Petition. Washington: W. H. Moore, [1885].
4 p. 23 cm. Wrapper title.

1895

Treaties and Laws of the Osage Nation, as passed to November 26, 1890. Compiled by W. S. Fitzpatrick. Cedar Vale, Kansas: Cedar Vale Commercial, 1895.
[15], 103 p. 23 cm.
Two copies, one in the usual sheep and the other in the rare wrappers, the back wrapper, however, having been lost.

1897

George M. Adams and Alvin C. Cadwell, Partners Doing Business under the Firm Name and Style of Adams & Cadwell, Plaintiffs in error, vs. H. B. Freeman, Agent of the Osage Indian Reservation, and Morris Robacker, Chief of Police of said Osage Indian Reservation. Brief of Defendants in error. Guthrie: Daily Leader, [1897].*
41 p. 22 cm. Wrapper title.
Unrecorded, and no other copy located.

1898

Osage Annuity Roll Contested Cases. Washington, 1898.
74, 6 p. 23 cm.

1903

Bailey, Lorenzo A.

Watson Stuart vs. The United States and the Osage Nation of Indians. Plea and Brief of Osage Nation with Statement as to Findings requested by Claimant and Request for Additional Findings of Fact. Washington, D.C.: Beresford, 1903.
Pp. 115–41. 24 cm. Printed wrappers.
Answer of the Osage Nation to a suit brought in the Court of Claims for services rendered the tribe in selling their lands.

1905

Petition to the President and Congress of the United States relative to a Fraudulent Claim of $180,000 against the Osage Nation. Washington: Gibson Bros., 1905.
7 p. 23.5 cm.

1906

Dickerson, P. J.

History of the Osage Nation, its People, Resources and Prospects. The Last Reservation to Open in the New State. [Pawhuska, 1906.]
141, [1] p. 23.5 cm. Wrapper title.

Osage Townsite Bill. Passed, as an Amendment to Indian Appropriation Bill, March 3, 1906. [Pawhuska, 1906.]

[4] p. 14 cm. Caption title.

Headed: W. M. Dial, E. W. King. The Pioneers in the Capital of the Osage Nation, the Metropolis of Northeastern Oklahoma.

The only known copy.

1907

The Osage Nation, Contestant, vs. John D. Atkin, et al., (composing the "Omaha Family"), Contestees. In re Fraudulent Enrollment of Contestees. Statement, Brief and Argument, on Behalf of Contestees, also their Reply Brief and Argument, by H. C. McDougal, their Attorney. [Kansas City, 1907.]

49, [1], 32 p. 25 cm. Wrapper title.

1924

The Osage Nation of Indians vs. The United States. Evidence for the Defendant. [Washington, 1924.]

Pp. 119–24. 23 cm. Caption title.

The government's reply to the suit brought by the Osage Nation in the Court of Claims for monies arising from the sale of lands under the treaty of 1865.

The Presentation of the President's Certificate honoring the Osages. [Pawhuska, 1924.]

22 p. 22 cm. Printed cloth wrapper. Photographs.

Undated

Sue M. Rogers, as Executrix of the Estate of William P. Adair, and Cullus Mayes, as Administrator of the Estate of Clement N. Vann, Petitioners, vs. The Osage Nation of Indians, Defendant. Brief for Defendant. Washington: J. D. Milans & Son. [N.d.]

Pp. 844–997. 23 cm. Wrapper title.

OTTAWA INDIANS

1829

Report of the Judiciary Committee on the Missionary Institution at Mackinac. Detroit: Gazette Office, 1829.

26 p. 23.5 cm.

An investigation into the mercantile activities of the missionaries to the Ottawas. A fine, untrimmed copy, and the only one known.

1832

Treaties with Indian Tribes. Message from the President of the United States, transmitting Copies of Treaties with several Indian Tribes. [Washington, 1832.]

25 p. 22.5 cm. Caption title.

Treaties with the Ottawa, Wyandot, Creek, Shawnee, and mixed Seneca and Shawnee Indians.

1841

Meeker, Jotham, tr.

The New Testament of Our Lord and Saviour Jesus Christ; translated into the

Ottawa Language by Jotham Meeker, Missionary of the Amer. Bap. Board of For. Missions. Carefully revised, and compared with the Greek, by Rev. Francis Barker, A.M., Baptist Missionary to the Shawanoes. Shawanoe Baptist Mission Press, J. G. Pratt, Printer, 1841.*

125 p. 16.5 cm.

Pilling, Algonquian Bibliography, p. 351.

McMurtrie-Allen locates only the Huntington Library and Boston Athenaeum copies.

1844

MEEKER, JOTHAM, tr.

The Gospel according to John, translated into the Ottawa Language by Jotham Meeker, Missionary of the Amer. Bap. Board of For. Missions. Revised, and compared with the Greek, by Rev. Francis Barker, A.M., Baptist Missionary to the Shawanoes. Press of the Amer. Baptist Board of For. Missions. Shawanoe. 1844.*

98 p. 16.5 cm.

Pilling, Algonquian Bibliography, p. 351.

McMurtrie-Allen locates but three copies.

1864

WILSON, JOHN

Notice to the People! The Town Site of Ottawa, Franklin Co., Kansas, as now located, is on my Land, owned by me, and fully recognized by my Tribe many years since, etc. [Ottawa, 1864.]*

Broadside. Folio.

The only known copy.

1887

History of the Ottawa and Chippewa Indians of Michigan; a Grammar of their Language, and Personal and Family History of the Author. By Andrew J. Blackbird, Late U.S. Interpreter, Harbor Springs, Emmet Co., Mich. Ypsilanti, Mich.: Ypsilantian Job Printing House, 1887.*

128 p. 17 cm. Printed wrappers.

A very scarce volume.

PACIFIC NORTHWEST INDIANS

1921

SMITH, CHARLES W.

Pacific Northwest Americana. A Checklist of Books and Pamphlets relating to the History of the Pacific Northwest. Compiled by Charles W. Smith. Second edition, revised and enlarged. New York: H. W. Wilson, 1921.

xi, 329 p. 26 cm.

An indispensable bibliography.

1938

BUSHNELL, DAVID I., JR.

Drawings by George Gibbs in the Far Northwest, 1849–1851. Washington, 1938.*

28 p. 24.5 cm. Printed wrappers. 18 plates.

PAH-UTE [PAIUTE] INDIANS

1872

Bateman, C. A.

[Second annual Report as U.S. Indian Agent of Nevada. Wadsworth, Navada, 1872.]

10 p. on 10 leaves broadside. 26 cm.

An important report on the Pah-Utes of Pyramid Lake and Walker River. No other copy can be traced.

PAPAGO INDIANS

1914

Eliot, Samuel A., and William H. Ketcham

Report on Conditions among the Papago Indians. [Washington, 1914.]

4 p. 23 cm.

PAWNEE INDIANS

1875

Correspondence of the Hon. Secretary of the Interior and the Commissioner of Indian Affairs relative to the Removal and Necessities of the Pawnee Indians. Washington, 1875.*

16 p. 23 cm. Printed wrappers.

PENNSYLVANIA INDIANS

1764

A Dialogue between Andrew Trueman and Thomas Zealot; about the Killing the Indians at Canestoge and Lancaster. Printed at Ephesus. [Philadelphia: Anthony Armbruster, 1764.]

7 p.

Evans 9634; Hildeburn 1972.

Excessively rare.

1938

Van Doren, Carl, and Julian P. Boyd, editors

Indian Treaties printed by Benjamin Franklin 1736–1762. With an Introduction by Carl Van Doren and Historical & Bibliographical Notes by Julian P. Boyd. Philadelphia: The Historical Society of Pennsylvania, 1938.

lxxxviii, [2], 340 p. 39.5 cm. Facsimiles.

A handsome and valuable publication. This copy bears the autographs of the editors.

ALBERT PIKE

1834

Pike, Albert

Prose Sketches and Poems, Written in the Western Country, by Albert Pike. Boston: Light & Horton, 1834.

200 p. Height of title page: 18.8 cm. Height of binding: 19.7 cm.

In original cloth, with red label. One of the finest copies in existence. [See page 317.]

PROSE SKETCHES

AND

POEMS,

Written in the Western Country,

BY ALBERT PIKE.

BOSTON:
LIGHT & HORTON.
1834.

1852

PIKE, ALBERT

The Muscogee or Creek Nation of Indians versus the United States. Petition. Philadelphia: King & Baird, [1852].

16 p. 23 cm. Wrapper title.

Not recorded in the Union Catalog, and no other copy traced.

1854

PIKE, ALBERT

To the Honorable (————), a Principal Chief of the (Choctaw) Nation. [Little Rock, 1854.]*

[6] p. 25 cm. The salutation above, which forms the only title, is printed with space left blank for filling in the name of the chief addressed and that of his tribe.

An address to the Indians by a committee, of which Albert Pike was the chairman, of the Southern and Western Commercial Convention, which met at Charleston in April, 1854, urging them to grant a right of way through Indian Territory to the proposed Southern Pacific Railroad. Dated, addressed, and corrected in Albert Pike's hand. This copy was sent to Peter P. Pitchlynn, the prominent Choctaw. Of the greatest importance and rarity. No other copy is known.

1857

PIKE, ALBERT

Overland Route to the Pacific. [N.p., 1857.]

[2], 66 p. Caption title.

The preliminary leaf is devoted to a letter to Honorable Gwin, signed "A Citizen of Arkansas." Not recorded in the Union Catalog, not mentioned by Wagner-Camp, and no other copy traced.

1861

PIKE, ALBERT

State or Province? Bond or Free? Addressed Particularly to the People of Arkansas. [Little Rock:] 1861.

40 p. 23 cm. Printed wrappers.

Rare.

1862

PIKE, ALBERT

Albert Pike's Letter addressed to Major General Holmes. [Little Rock, 1863.]

7 p. 19.5 cm. Caption title.

Pike's eloquent defense of his operations in Indian Territory, and a stern indictment of Holmes's neglect of the Indian troops in Confederate service. Not recorded in the Union Catalog, and no other copy traced.

PIKE, ALBERT

Headquarters Dep't. Ind. Ter. Fort McCulloch, June 27th, 1862. Sir: You are aware that I have been for two months endeavoring to erect field-works here, to make a fortress that will enable me, with a small force, to hold this place against a large one. [Fort McCulloch: Confederate Military Press, 1862.]*

Broadside. 21.5 cm.
Signed, in autograph, by Albert Pike, and addressed in his hand to Col. P. P. Pitchlynn, Eagletown.

An appeal to the Indians to lend him their Negro slaves for work on the fortification. Colonel Pitchlynn, to whom the copy was addressed, was one of the largest slave-holders in Indian Territory. Unrecorded, and the only known copy.

PIKE, ALBERT

Regulations for the Government of the Forces of the Confederate States in Department of Indian Territory. Part II. Respecting the Rights, Duties, and Business of the Officer and Soldier. Promulgated at Fort McCulloch, 1st July, 1862. [Fort McCulloch, 1862.]*

36 p. 21 cm. Marbled paper wrappers.

No copy of Part I is known. Unrecorded, and the only known copy.

PIKE, ALBERT

To the Chiefs and People of the Cherokees, Creeks, Seminoles, Chickasaws, and Choctaws. [Fort McCulloch, 1862.]

Broadside. Folio.

A paper of superlative interest and importance. Pike undertook here to explain to the Indians his inability, which he imputed to the meddling of his superior officers, to carry out the terms of the treaties of alliance which he negotiated in 1861 on behalf of the Confederate States. Had the South won the war, the publication of this address would most certainly have resulted in the trial of Pike on charges of insubordination if not of treason. Unrecorded, and the only known copy.

1863

PIKE, ALBERT

Address. To the Senators and Representatives of the State of Arkansas in the Congress of the Confederate States. [Shreveport, Louisiana, 1863.]

20 p. 21.5 cm. Caption title.

A renewal of charges against General Hindman. Not recorded in the Union Catalog, and apparently the only known copy.

PIKE, ALBERT

Charges and Specifications preferred August 23, 1862, by Brigadier General Albert Pike, against Major Gen. Thos. C. Hindman. Richmond, Va.: Smith, Bailey & Co., printers, 1863.

13 p. 22 cm.

Pike charged Hindman with betraying the Confederate Indian allies. Excessively rare, only two other copies being known.

PIKE, ALBERT

Second Letter to Lieut.-General Theophilus H. Holmes. [Richmond, 1863.]

20 p. 22 cm. Caption title.

An extension by Pike of his charges against Holmes of interfering with the defense of Indian Territory and of criminally neglecting the Confederate Indian troops. Not recorded in the Union Catalog, and no other copy traced.

1870

PIKE, ALBERT

Elias C. Boudinot and Stand Watie, Citizens of the Cherokee Nation, vs. the United States. Error to the District Court of the United States for the Western District of Arkansas. Argument for Plaintiffs in Error. Albert Pike, Robert W. Johnson, of Counsel. [Washington, 1870.]

A valuable analysis of Cherokee treaty rights and obligations.

1871

PIKE, ALBERT

Vindication of the Ancient and Accepted Scottish Rite against Certain Libels. (From the Memphis Appeal, as published in 1867.) Washington: Cunningham & McIntosh, 1871.

93 p. 22 cm. Printed wrappers.

1872

PIKE, ALBERT

The Choctaw Nation vs. The United States. Is an Award against the United States, made under a Treaty that Declares it shall be Final, Binding upon the Conscience of the Nation? Washington: David McIntosh, 1872.

205 p. 22 cm. Printed wrappers.

Largely written by Albert Pike.

PIKE, ALBERT

Letter of Albert Pike to the Choctaw People. Washington: Cunningham & McIntosh, 1872.

25, 14 p. 22 cm. Printed wrappers.

Rare.

1873

PIKE, ALBERT

A Letter from Tvshka-Homma to the Choctaw People. August, 1873. [N.p., 1873.]*

17 p. 22.5 cm.

Rare.

1878

PIKE, ALBERT, and JAMES W. DENVER

Before the Congress of the United States, 45th Congress, 2d Session. The Choctaw Nation of Indians vs. The United States of America. For Payment of Judgment in the Last Resort. Plaintiff's Brief. Washington: Judd & Detweiler, [1878].*

9 p. 26 cm. Wrapper title.

No other copy can be traced.

1917

PIKE, ALBERT

Narrative of a Journey in the Prairie. [In Publications of the Arkansas Historical Association, Vol. 4. Conway, Arkansas, 1917.]*

Pp. 66–129.

"In 1835 General Pike published the 'Narrative of a Journey in the Prairie' as a serial in the columns of his paper, 'The Arkansas Advocate,' whence it is resurrected and reproduced here." The newspaper appearance was a serial reprint of the narrative portion of the Boston 1834 edition of Pike's Prose Sketches and Poems. This 1917 reprint is quite rare, but few copies, apparently, have been issued.

PONCA INDIANS

1880

SCHURZ, CARL

Removal of the Ponca Indians. Open Letter to Hon. John D. Long, Governor of Massachusetts, by Hon. Carl Schurz, Secretary of the Interior. Washington, 1880.

17 p. 22.5 cm.

1881

SCHURZ, CARL

An Open Letter in Answer to a Speech of Hon. H. L. Dawes, United States Senate, on the Case of Big Snake, by Hon. Carl Schurz, Secretary of the Interior. Washington, 1881.

14 p. 22.5 cm.

1887

The Ponca Chiefs. An Indian's Attempt to Appeal from the Tomahawk to the Courts. A Full History of the Robbery of the Ponca Tribe of Indians, with all the Papers Filed and Evidence Taken in the Standing Bear Habeas Corpus Case, and Full Text of Judge Dundy's Celebrated Decision, with some Suggestions towards a Solution of the Indian Question. By Zylyff. With an Introduction by Inshtatheamba (Bright Eyes), and Dedication by Wendell Phillips. Second Edition. Boston: Lockwood, Brooks, and Company, 1880. [1887].*

[8], 146 p. 17 cm. Printed wrappers.

POTTAWATOMIE INDIANS

1830

Anthony Rollo, the Converted Indian. Philadelphia, [1830?].

[12] p. 17.5 cm. Wrapper title.

Anthony Rollo was a young Pottawatomie Indian who died at the Carey Missionary Station in Michigan Territory in 1828.

1837

EDMONDS, J. W.

Report of J. W. Edmonds, United States' Commissioner, upon the Disturbance at the Potawatamie Payment, September, 1836. New York, 1837.

47 p. 23 cm.

Excessively rare.

1844

LYKINS, JOHNSTON, tr.

The Gospel according to Matthew, and the Acts of the Apostles; translated into the Putawatomie language. By Johnston Lykins. Carefully compared with the Greek text. Published under the patronage of the American and Foreign Bible Society, by the Board of Managers of the American Indian Mission Association. Louisville, Ky. William C. Buck, printer. 1844.

240 p. 16.5 cm.

Sabin 42770.

Excessively rare.

1846

A. M. D. G. Pewani ipi Potewatemi missinoikan, eyowat nemadjik, Catholiques endjik. Baltimoinak: John Murphy, okimissinakisan ote missinoikan, 1846.

31 p. 13.5 cm. Printed wrappers.

Very rare.

1851

Opinion of the Second Comptroller of the Treasury on a Claim of Alexis Coquillard, Assignee of Joseph Bertrand, for a Debt against the Potawattomie Indians. Washington: Gideon & Co., 1851.

24 p. 22.5 cm. Printed wrappers.

1866

GAILLAND, MAURICE

Potewatemi nemewinin ipi nemenigamowinin. Rev'd. Maurice Gailland, S.J. Wespanionag. St. Louis, Mo.: Francis Saler, okimisinakisan. 1866.

119 p. 10 cm. Eng. frontisp.

Pilling, Algonquian Bibliography, p. 198.

Very rare.

1870

CATON, JOHN DEAN

The Last of the Illinois, and a Sketch of the Pottawatomies. Chicago, 1870.

36 p. 22.5 cm.

Authoritative. Caton wrote, as a contemporary, living in the neighborhood, of the removal of the Pottawatomies.

1887

ELLIS, E. JOHN

Argument before the Department of the Interior and Committees of Congress in the Matter of the Claims of the Pottawatomie Indians against the United States. By E. John Ellis, of Counsel for the Citizens Band of Pottawatomies. Washington: Rufus H. Darby, 1887.

15 p. 22.5 cm. Wrapper title.

1888

In the Matter of the Removal of the Cattle of Catherine Greiffenstein from the Pottawatomie Lands in the Indian Territory. Appeal from the Decision of the Honorable Secretary of the Interior, dated July 7, 1888. Washington: Gibson Bros., 1888.

31 p. 22.5 cm. Wrapper title.

QUAPAW INDIANS

1825

Message from the President of the United States, transmitting Copies of Treaties between the United States and the Quapaw and Choctaw Nations of Indians. Washington: Gales & Seaton, 1825.

11 p. 22 cm.

Submitted in this form to the Senate for ratification or rejection, this printing preceded the official folio printing of the ratified treaties.

1827

Quapaw Indians. Letter from the Secretary of War transmitting Information in relation to the Present Condition of the Quapaw Nation of Indians. Washington: Gales & Seaton, 1827.

15 p. 25 cm.

1855

Message from the President of the United States communicating a Treaty with the Quapaw Tribe of Indians. [Washington, 1855.]

2, 4 p. 24.5 cm. Caption title.

The first printing of the treaty. In this preliminary and confidential form it was submitted to the Senate for ratification or rejection and it of course preceded the official folio printing of the ratified treaty. Public documents marked "confidential" are rare.

1864

Quapaw Indians. Letter from the Secretary of the Interior, recommending an Appropriation for the Quapaw Indians, now in Kansas. [Washington, 1864.]

13 p. 22.5 cm. Caption title.

1896

In the Matter of the Allotment and Leasing of Lands in the Quapaw Agency. Brief and Argument by A. W. Abrams and Samuel J. Crawford. 1896. [N.p., 1896.]

8 p. 23 cm. Wrapper title.

Headed: Before the Honorable the Secretary of the Interior.

RAILROADS

1854

Report of the Chief Engineer of the Little Rock and Fort Smith Branch of the Cairo and Fulton Railroad, made to the Company, August 22d, 1854. Little Rock: True Democrat Office, 1854.

29 p. 20.5 cm.

The growth and development of Arkansas railroads exercised a profound influence upon the Indians on the western border of that state. Rare.

Report of the Chief Engineer on the Experimental Surveys of the Arkansas Midland Railroad. Little Rock: True Democrat Office, 1854.

12 p. 20.5 cm.

Rare.

Reports of the President and Chief Engineer of the Arkansas Pacific Railroad Co. Little Rock: True Democrat Office, 1854.

15 p. 20.5 cm.
Excessively rare.

1855

Proceedings of the Second Annual Meeting of the Stockholders of the Cairo and Fulton Railroad Company, held in Little Rock, Arkansas, May 7th, 1855. With an Appendix. Little Rock: True Democrat Office, 1855.

32 p. 22 cm. Printed wrappers. Maps.
Rare.

1858

Letter from Albert H. Campbell to Hon. Guy M. Bryan, of Texas, in relation to the Pacific Railroad. Washington, 1858.

18 p. 24 cm.

1863

Exhibit of the Union Pacific Railway (Eastern Division), Kansas, U.S.A., containing Charters of the Leavenworth, Pawnee & West. R.R. Co., Indian Treaties for Lands, Act of Congress Granting Aid, Statistics, Reports, &C. New York: Hosford & Ketcham, 1863.

65 p. 23 cm. Printed wrappers.

1868

Explanatory Notes and Map showing the Route of the International Pacific Rail-Road, from Cairo, Illinois, to San Blas, on the Pacific Coast. New York: Wm. L. Stone & J. T. Barron, 1868.

6 p. 24.5 cm. Folded map.
A very rare pamphlet.

Memorial of the Memphis, El Paso and Pacific Railroad Company, of Texas, praying for a Grant of Public Lands, and a Loan of United States Bonds, to Aid in Constructing a Continuous Line of Railroad and Telegraph from Jefferson, in Texas, to San Diego, in California, by the way of El Paso, with Authority to make such Railroad Connections as to Reach San Francisco, Guaymas, Memphis, and Virginia City, on the Harbor of Norfolk, in Virginia, or any other Point on the Atlantic Coast, and Washington City, under the Title of the Southern Trans-Continental Railroad. Philadelphia: King & Baird, 1868.

29, 72 p. 23.5 cm. Printed wrappers. Folded map.
Contains an important description of the country to be traversed. The volume is very rare.

1870

Executive Document. Railroads through the Indian Territory. [Washington, 1870.]

11 p. 23 cm.

Executive Documents in relation to the Missouri, Kansas and Texas Railway Company, running through the Indian Territory. New York: Evening Post Steam Presses, 1870.

32 p. 23 cm. Wrapper title.

The Great Railroad Route to the Pacific and its Connections, showing the Relation of the Alabama and Chattanooga Railroad to the Proposed Southern Route to the Pacific. Boston: Alfred Mudge & Son, 1870.

10 p. 23 cm. Printed wrappers. Large folded map.
Rare.

PHILLIPS, WILLIAM A.

In the Matter of the Claim of the Missouri, Kansas & Texas Railway Company to Build Another Railroad in the Indian Territory. [N.p., 1870?].

10 p. 23 cm. Caption title.

1872

FINN, DANIEL C.

Argument of Daniel C. Finn. [N.p., 1872.]

24 p. 22 cm. Caption title.
An argument against a grant of Indian Territory lands to railroad companies.

FINN, DANIEL C.

Argument of Daniel C. Finn, of Arkansas, on House Resolution 1132. A Bill repealing Acts and parts of Acts granting Lands and certain Privileges to Railroad Companies. Washington City: Powell, Ginck & Co., 1872.

24 p. 22 cm. Wrapper title.

LAUGHLIN, W. R.

Argument of W. R. Laughlin, of Kansas, on House Resolution 1132. A Bill repealing Acts and parts of Acts granting Lands and certain Privileges to Railroad Companies. Washington City: Powell, Ginck & Co., 1872.

19 p. 22 cm. Wrapper title.

1874

Memorial of the Indian Delegates to Congress, asking the Repeal of so much of Certain Railroad Charters as grand Conditional Grants of Indian Lands to Railroads. [N.p., 1874.]

6 p. 22.5 cm. Caption title.

1877

THROCKMORTON, JAMES W.

Texas and Pacific Railway. Speech of Hon. James W. Throckmorton, of Texas, in the House of Representatives, March 1, 1877, together with the Report of the Hon. L. Q. C. Lamar. Washington, 1877.

29 p. 21.5 cm.

1878

REAVIS, L. U.

The Texas and Pacific Railway or a National Highway along the Path of Empire. By L. U. Reavis. New York: Baker & Godwin, 1878.

32 p. 23 cm. Printed wrappers.

Peter P. Pitchlynn's copy.

1881

Message from the President of the United States, transmitting a Communication from the Secretary of the Interior, in reference to the Application of the Chicago, Texas and Mexican Central, and the St. Louis and San Francisco Railway Companies, for a Right of Way across the Lands of the Choctaw Nation, in the Indian Territory. [Washington, 1881.]

22 p. 23 cm. Caption title.

1882

Executive Correspondence and Decisions in reference to Rights of Atlantic & Pacific R. R. Co. in Indian Territory, and elsewhere. [N.p., 1882.]

Hon. Hiram Price, Commissioner of Indian Affairs. [Washington, 1882.]*

20 p. 23 cm. Caption title.

Communications from the Cherokee Delegation, and other documents, relating to the plans and proposals of the Atlantic and Pacific Railroad Company.

In Re. Bills to Forfeit the Grant of Lands to the Atlantic & Pacific R. R. Co. [N.p., 1882.]

18 p. 23 cm. Caption title.

Right of Way to Saint Louis and San Francisco Railroad through the Indian Territory. [Washington, 1882.]

5 p. 25 cm. Caption title.

1883

A Bill to Grant a Right-of-way through the Choctaw Nation to the Saint Louis and San Francisco Railway. [Atoka? 1883.]

[2] p. 33.5 cm. Caption title.

Unrecorded, and the only known copy.

1888

An Act to authorize the Choctaw Coal and Railway Company to construct and operate a Railway through the Indian Territory, and for other purposes. [Washington, 1888.]

4 p. 22.5 cm. Caption title.

1890

Brief of the Choctaw Coal and Railway Company, Lessee, in the matter of Senate Joint Resolution 119, H.R. Joint Resolution 206, relating to Coal Leases in the Indian Territory. Washington: Beresford, [1890].*

CHOCTAW COAL AND RAILWAY COMPANY

Choctaw Coal and Railway Co. First mortgage coal lease bond. Total issue, $1,000,000. Allen, Lane & Scott, Philadelphia, [1890].

26 leaves, printed broadside. 29.5 cm.

1895

To the Honorable the Secretary of the Interior, Washington, D.C. [N.p., 1895.]

13 p. 21.5 cm. Caption title.

A letter on company matters from the president of the Choctaw, Oklahoma, and Gulf Railroad.

1901

Brief of the Western Oklahoma Railroad Company in re Protest of the Denison and Northern Railway Company. Philadelphia: Allen, Lane & Scott, [1901].

26 p. 23.5 cm. Wrapper title.

REMOVAL OF THE INDIANS

1825

Message from the President of the United States, transmitting Sundry Documents in relation to the Various Tribes of Indians within the United States, and recommending a Plan for their Future Location and Settlement. Washington: Gales & Seaton, 1825.

13 p. 22 cm. 4 folded tables.

Calhoun's momentous proposals. Two issues.

1827

Removal of the Indians Westward. Letter from the Secretary of War, transmitting Information in relation to the Disposition of the several Tribes of Indians to Emigrate West of the Mississippi. Washington: Gales & Seaton, 1827.

13 p. 22 cm.

Devoted to a long and informative letter on the subject by Thomas L. McKenney.

1828

Message from the President of the United States transmitting a Report from the Secretary of War in relation to the Removal of the Indian Agency, from Fort Wayne, in Indiana. Washington: Duff Green, 1828.*

27 p. 22.5 cm.

VINTON, SAMUEL F.

Speech of Mr. Vinton on the Emigration of Indians. Washington: Gales & Seaton, 1828.

28 p. 18 cm.

WOODS, JOHN

Speech of Mr. Woods, of Ohio, on the Emigration of Indians. Washington: Gales & Seaton, 1828.

20 p. 19.5 cm.

1829

EVARTS, JEREMIAH

Essays on the Present Crisis in the Condition of the American Indians; First Published in the National Intelligencer, under the Signature of William Penn. Boston: Perkins & Marvin, 1829.

112 p. 21 cm.

Field notes only the Philadelphia edition the next year.

1830

ADAMS, ROBERT H.

Speech of Mr. Adams, of Mississippi, on the Bill to Remove the Indians West of the Mississippi. Delivered in the Senate of the United States, April, 1830. Washington: Duff Green, 1830.

31 p. 25 cm.

BATES, ISAAC CHAPMAN

Speech of Mr. Bates, of Massachusetts, on the Indian Bill. [N.p., 1830.]

24 p. 22.5 cm. Caption title.

EVARTS, JEREMIAH, ed.

Speeches on the Passage of the Bill for the Removal of the Indians, delivered in the Congress of the United States, April and May, 1830. Boston: Perkins & Marvin, 1830.

viii, 304 p. 19.5 cm.
Field 1468.

A valuable compilation.

EVERETT, EDWARD

Speech of Mr. Everett, of Massachusetts, on the Bill for Removing the Indians from the East to the West Side of the Mississippi. Delivered in the House of Representatives on the 19th of May, 1830. Boston: Office of the Daily Advertiser, 1830.

46 p. 24.5 cm.

A presentation copy, signed by the author.

EVERETT, EDWARD

Speech of Mr. Everett, of Massachusetts, on the Bill for Removing the Indians from the East to the West side of the Mississippi. Delivered in the House of Representatives on the 19th May, 1830. Washington: Gales & Seaton, 1830.

32 p. 22.5 cm.
Field 513.

FRELINGHUYSEN, THEODORE

Speech of Mr. Frelinghuysen, of New Jersey, delivered in the Senate of the United States, April 6, 1830, on the Bill for an Exchange of Lands with the Indians residing in any of the States or Territories, and for their Removal West of the Mississippi. Washington: National Journal, 1830.

44 p. 22 cm.
Field 564.

Chancellor Kent's copy.

LAMAR, H. G.

Speech of Mr. H. G. Lamar, of Georgia, on the Bill to Remove the Indians West of the Mississippi. Delivered in the House of Representatives of the United States, May, 1830. Washington: Duff Green, 1830.

20 p. 25 cm.

LUMPKIN, WILSON

Speech of Mr. Wilson Lumpkin, of Georgia, on the Bill providing for the Removal of the Indians. Washington: Duff Green, 1830.

19 p. 25 cm.

Important because of former Governor Lumpkin's active participation in the removal of the Georgia Indians.

Removal of Indians. [Washington, 1830.]
32 p. 22.5 cm. Caption title.

Rights of the Indians. [Boston, 1830.]*
16 p. 23 cm. Caption title.

SPRAGUE, PELEG

Speech of Mr. Sprague, of Maine: delivered in the Senate of the United States, 16th April, 1830, in reply to Messrs. White, McKinley, and Forsyth, upon the Subject of the Removal of the Indians. Washington: Published at the Office of the National Journal. Peter Force, print., 1830.

36 p. 22 cm.
Field 1474.

A Statement of the Indian Relations; with a Reply to the Article in the sixty-sixth number of the North American Review, on the Removal of the Indians. New York: Clayton & Van Norden, 1830.

21 p. 21 cm.

STORRS, HENRY

Speech of Mr. Storrs, of New York, on the Bill for the Removal of the Indians West of the Mississippi. Utica: Northway & Porter, 1830.

53 p. 22 cm.

Very rare.

WILDE, RICHARD HENRY

Speech of Mr. Wilde, of Georgia, on the Bill for Removing the Indians from the East to the West Side of the Mississippi. Delivered in the House of Representatives on the 20th May, 1830. Washington: Gales & Seaton, 1830.

66 p. 24 cm.
Field 1658.

Wilde enjoyed a considerable literary reputation in Georgia and the South, a fact which makes this one of the most sought after speeches on Indian removal.

1832

An Examination of the Indian Question. [Washington, 1832.]

16 p. 26 cm. Caption title.

A discussion of Indian removal.

Message from the President of the United States with a Report from the Secretary of War in relation to the Employment of Agents among the Indians for their Removal, &c. &c. [Washington, 1832.]

20 p. 22.5 cm. Caption title.

Regulations concerning the Removal of the Indians. [Washington, 1832.]

15, [16] p. 19.5 cm. Wrapper title.

Important, and very rare.

1834–35

Correspondence on the subject of the Emigration of Indians. Washington: Duff Green, 1834–1835.

5 vols., aggregating over 4200 pages.

The rare and famous "Document 512," the very cornerstone of the literature of the subject. Its thousands of documents, affidavits, depositions, and letters by army officers, Indian agents, state officials, and the Indians themselves comprise a source that must forever remain the ultimate authority. Even Field (see his Nos. 369 and 370) managed to obtain only three odd volumes of the set.

1837

Revised Regulations. No. 5. Concerning the Emigration of Indians. Adopted May 13, 1837. [Washington, 1837.]*

32 p. 25 cm. Caption title.

Very rare.

SAC AND FOX INDIANS

1833

Kirby, E.

Iowa Volunteers. Galena, 1833.

Broadside. 24.5 cm.

Provision for "payment to the Nineteen Companies of Iowa County, Michigan Volunteers, commanded by Col. Henry Dodge," who took part in the Black Hawk War. Unrecorded, and the only known copy.

1838

Wisconsin Territorial Council

An Act for the Partition of the Half-Breed Lands, & for other purposes. [Madison? 1838.]

4 p. 26.5 cm.

Partition of lands reserved for the half bloods of the Sac and Fox tribe. Unrecorded, and the only known copy.

1848

Indian Trade. The Late Sac and Fox Payment. [Washington:] Congressional Globe Office, [1848].

16 p. 22.5 cm. Caption title.

No other copy can be traced.

Report of the Secretary of War transmitting Documents in relation to the Difficulties which took place at the payment of the Sac and Fox Annuities, last fall. [Washington, 1848.]

128 p. 22.5 cm. Caption title.

1863

Treaty concluded at the Sac and Fox Agency, in Kansas, on the 2d day of September, 1863, between William P. Dole, Commissioner of Indian Affairs, Commissioner on the part of the United States, and the New York Indians, represented by duly authorized Members of the Bands of said Tribe. [Washington, 1863.]

[4] p. 23.5 cm. Caption title.

Headed: Confidential.

The rare preliminary confidential printing.

1887

Constitution and Laws of the Sac and Fox Nation, Indian Territory. The Constitution of the Sac and Fox Nation prepared by the Authorized Committee and adopted by the National Council. Washington: National Free Press, 1887.

30 p. 23 cm. Wrapper title.

One of only two known copies.

1890

Letter from the Secretary of the Interior transmitting, in further response to Senate Resolution of March 3, 1890, Certain Reports and Papers relative to the Membership of the Sac and Fox Indians. [Washington, 1890.]

80 p. 22.5 cm. Caption title.

Message from the President of the United States, transmitting an Agreement between the Cherokee Commission and the Sac and Fox Indians in the Indian Territory. [Washington, 1890.]

21 p. 23 cm. Caption title.

1906

The Sac and Fox Indians of the Mississippi, in Iowa, Claimants, vs. the Sac and Fox Indians of the Mississippi, in Oklahoma, and the United States, Defendants. For the Adjustment of Claims arising from Unequal Apportionment of the Annuities of the Confederated Tribes of Sac and Fox Indians of the Mississippi, between the Two Branches of the Tribes. Brief on behalf of the Claimant Indians and Answer to Defendants' Brief, by R. V. Belt, Attorney for Sac and Fox Indians in Iowa. Washington, [1906].

61 p. 23.5 cm. Wrapper title.

A valuable review of the relations between the two branches of the tribe.

1907

Belt, R. V.

The Sac and Fox Indians of the Mississippi in Iowa, Claimants, vs. The Sac and Fox Indians of the Mississippi in Oklahoma and the United States, Defendants. Amended Petition. Washington: Judd & Detweiler, [1907].*

28 p. 23.5 cm. Wrapper title.

1913

Green, C. R.

Early days in Kansas. In Keokuk's time on the Kansas reservation. Being various incidents pertaining to Keokuk, the Sac & Fox Indians (Mississippi band), and tales of the early settlers, life on the Kansas reservation, located on the head waters of the Osage River, 1846–1870. Charles R. Green. Olathe, Kansas. January, 1913.

[4] p, 68, [3] p. 21 cm. Diagram and 19 plates.
Very scarce.

1914

Green, C. R.

Sac and Fox Indians in Kansas. Mokohoko's Stubbornness. Some History of the Band of Indians who staid behind their Tribe for 16 yrs. as given by Pioneers. By C. R. Green, Olathe, Kan. Nov. 1914. [Olathe, 1914.]

[22] p. 21 cm. Printed wrapper title. Plates.
The wrappers are pink, the title page is on green paper, and the text on white paper. Very scarce.

SEMINOLE INDIANS

1811

Dickenson, Jonathan

Narrative of a Shipwreck in the Gulph of Florida: showing God's Protecting Providence, Man's Surest Help and Defence in Times of Greatest Difficulty, and Most Imminent Danger. Faithfully related by One of the Persons concerned therein, Jonathan Dickenson. Burlington, N.J. Printed at the Lexicon Press of D. Allinson & Co., 1811.

107 p. 16 cm.
Very rare.

1818

Message from the President of the United States, transmitting a Report from the Secretary of War respecting the Requisitions that were made on the Contractors for Deposites of Provisions, in advance, at the Several Posts on the Frontiers of Georgia, and the adjoining Territory. Washington: E. De Krafft, 1818.

26 p. 21 cm. Folded table.

Message from the President of the United States transmitting a Report from the Secretary of War in relation to the Manner the Troops in the Service of the United States, now operating against the Seminole Tribe of Indians, have been subsisted,

whether by Contract or otherwise, and whether they have been regularly furnished with Rations. Washington: E. De Krafft, 1818.
8 p. 21.5 cm.

Message from the President of the United States transmitting Copies of Documents referred to in his Communication of the seventeenth ultimo, in relation to the Seminole War, &c. Washington: E. De Krafft, 1818.
165 p. 22 cm.
One of the foundation documents on the Seminole War.

1819

CLAY, HENRY

Speech of Hon. Henry Clay in the House of Representatives of U.S. on the Seminole War. [Washington, 1819.]
30 p. 18 cm. Caption title.

Message from the President of the United States transmitting a Letter from Gov. Bibb to Gen. Jackson, connected with the late Military Operations in Florida. Washington: E. De Krafft, 1819.
6 p. 23 cm.

Message from the President of the United States transmitting Information of Certain Correspondence between the Department of War, and the Governor of Georgia, and of the said Department, with General Andrew Jackson. Washington City: E. De Krafft, 1819.*
7 p. 21.5 cm.

Message from the President of the United States, transmitting such further Information in relation to our Affairs with Spain as, in his opinion, is not Inconsistent with the Public Interest to Divulge. Washington: E. De Krafft, 1819.
215 p. 22 cm.

Report of the Committee on Military Affairs to whom was referred so much of the President's Message of 17th November last as relates to the Proceeding of the Court Martial in the trial of Arbuthnott and Armbrister and the Conduct of the Seminole War. [Washington, 1819.]
4 p. 21.5 cm. Caption title.

TALLMADGE, JAMES, JR.

Speech of the Honorable James Tallmadge, Jr. of Duchess County, N. York, in the House of Representatives of the United States on the Seminole War. New York: E. Conrad, 1819.
31 p. 21 cm.
Field 1529.

Views of the Minority of the Committee on Military Affairs, on the subject of the Seminole War, and the Trial and Execution of Arbuthnott and Armbrister. [Washington, 1819.]
12 p. 22 cm. Caption title.

1821

[Official folio printing of the Treaty of February 22, 1819, between the United States and Spain, by which Spain ceded Florida to the United States. Washington, 1821.]

9 p. 34.5 cm. Text in English and Spanish.
A treaty of momentous import to the southern tribes.

TURNBULL, NICOL, and others

[Memorial asking examination and confirmation of their title to lands in East Florida. Charleston, S.C., 1821.]

Broadside. Folio.
No other copy is recorded.

1823

Letter from the Secretary of War to the Chairman of the Committee on Indian Affairs transmitting Sundry Documents and Correspondence in relation to the Indians of Florida. Washington: Gales & Seaton, 1823.

19 p. 22.5 cm.

1826

BURCH, DANIEL E.

Sealed Proposals. Will be received by me at Jacksonville in Florida on the first day of July next, for opening by contract a Public Road in Florida, leading from the Ferry at Camp Pinckney on the St. Mary's River (where it is crossed by the "Kings Road,") to the Ferry on Black Creek. [Tallahassee, 1826.]*

Broadside. 25 cm.
Unrecorded.

DICKENSON, JONATHAN

The Shipwreck and Dreadful Sufferings of Robert Barrow, with Divers Other Persons, amongst the Inhuman Cannibals of Florida; faithfully related to Jonathan Dickenson, who was concerned therein. To which are added Some Remarks & Observations, made by a Person who Renounced Deism: also the Dying Expressions of Some Persons of Eminence & Learning, who had Embraced the Same Principles. Salem (C.) Republished by Joshua Shinn, Robert Fee, Printer. 1826.

120 p. 16 cm.

Florida Indians. Letter from the Secretary of War in relation to the Florida Indians. Washington: Gales & Seaton, 1826.

39 p. 22 cm.
A fine copy, uncut and unopened.

Treaty with the Florida Indians. Letter from the Secretary of War in relation to the instructions given to the commissioners for negotiating with the Florida Indians, &c. &c. Washington: Gales & Seaton, 1826.

109 p. 22.5 cm.

1828

Exposition of the Titles to the Lands in Florida, commonly known by the name of Forbes' Purchase. Washington: Printed at the Office of J. Elliot, Pennsylvania Avenue, 1828.

28 p. 23.5 cm.

Rare and important. The title rested upon Indian deeds, which are quoted in full.

PERKINS, SAMUEL

General Jackson's Conduct in the Seminole War, delineated in a History of that Period, affording Conclusive Reasons why he should not be the next President. Brooklyn, Con.: Advertiser Press, John Gray, Jr., 1828.

39 p.

1831

Acts of the Legislative Council of the Territory of Florida, passed at the Ninth Session commencing January third, and ending February thirteenth, 1831. With also, the Resolutions of a Public or General Character, adopted by the Legislative Council at said Session. Published by Authority. Tallahassee: Gibson & Smith, 1831.*

123 p. 22.5 cm.

Contains highly important acts regulating trade with and extending territorial laws over the Indians.

Correspondence between Gen. Andrew Jackson and John C. Calhoun, President and Vice-President of the U. States, on the subject of the Course of the Latter, in the Deliberations of the Cabinet of Mr. Monroe, on the Occurrences in the Seminole War. Washington: Duff Green, 1831.

52 p. 24.5 cm.

The letters and documents comprise an important review of Jackson's Seminole campaign and of the whole Seminole question.

1832

Acts of the Legislative Council of the Territory of Florida, passed at the 16th Session, commencing January 2d, and ending February 12th, 1832. Published by Authority. Tallahassee: William Wilson, 1832.

[5], 162 p. 20 cm.

Contains important acts relating to trade with and employment of Indians.

1836

Acts of the Governor and Legislative Council of the Territory of Florida: passed at the Fourteenth Session, begun and held at the City of Tallahassee, on Monday January 4th, and ended Sunday February 14th, 1836. Published by Authority. Tallahassee: William Wilson, 1836.

iv, 71 p. 20.5 cm.

Important acts and resolutions regarding Seminole hostilities.

BARR, JAMES

A Correct and Authentic Narrative of the Indian War in Florida, with a Description of Maj. Dade's Massacre, and an Account of the Extreme Suffering, for want of provisions, of the Army—having been obliged to eat horses' and dogs' flesh, &c &c. By Capt. James Barr. New York: J. Narine, 1836.

32 p. 15 cm.

The rarest and most desirable of all the Seminole War narratives. Only two other copies appear to be known. [See page 337.]

Foster, Wm. S.

Camp Georgia, Territory of Florida, 9th April 1836. To General D. L. Clinch, Com'g. Right Wing, Army of Florida. Sir: [Tallahassee? 1836.]

Broadside. 25.5 cm.

Sprightly account of an engagement with the Seminole Indians on March 31, 1836. "This force met the Indians posted in a 'Hammock', and drove them through it for a mile and a half without giving them a moments respite, the troops constantly firing and pushing forward, and cheering so loudly as completely to overpower and silence the Indian Yell, etc." Unrecorded, and the only known copy.

General Orders No. 61. Headquarters of the Army, Adjutant General's Office, Washington, Sept. 16, 1836.

Broadside. 20 cm.

Official announcement of the attack by Major Pierce upon a large body of Seminole Indians collected at the site of old Fort Drane, Florida.

Resolution authorizing the President to Furnish Rations to certain Inhabitants of Florida. [Washington, 1836.]

3 p. 33.5 cm. Caption title.

The rations were to be given to citizens who had been driven from their homes by Seminole depredations. Appended are the regulations governing the distribution of rations.

Seminole Hostilities. Message from the President of the United States, transmitting a Supplemental Report respecting the Causes of the Seminole Hostilities and the Measures taken to suppress them. [Washington, 1836.]

272 p. 24.5 cm. Caption title.

Sketch of the Seminole War, and Sketches during a Campaign. By a Lieutenant of the Left Wing. Charleston: Dan. J. Dowling, 1836.

iv, [2], 311, [1] p. 20 cm.

In a protective case. The volume is excessively rare.

1837

General Order No. 13. Head Quarters of the Army, Adjutant General's Office, Washington, March 21, 1837.

14 p. 20 cm. Caption title.

Opinions of the Court of Inquiry convened at Frederick, Maryland, to examine the causes and failure of the Seminole campaigns in Florida.

General Orders No. 24. Head Quarters of the Army, Adjutant General's Office, Washington, April 25, 1837.

2 p. 20 cm. Caption title.

Review of a general court-martial acquittal at Savannah, Georgia, of Major William Gates, who had been charged with disgraceful conduct when attacked by a body of Seminole Indians at Fort Barnwell, Volusia, on the St. John's River, Florida, on April 14, 1836.

A

CORRECT AND AUTHENTIC

NARRATIVE

OF THE

INDIAN WAR IN FLORIDA,

WITH A

DESCRIPTION

OF

MAJ. DADE'S MASSACRE,

AND AN

ACCOUNT OF THE EXTREME SUFFERING,
FOR WANT OF PROVISIONS, OF THE ARMY—HAVING BEEN
OBLIGED TO EAT HORSES' AND DOGS' FLESH, &c. &c.

BY CAPT. JAMES BARR.

NEW YORK:
J. NARINE, PRINTER, 11 WALL ST.

1836.

A Narrative of the Life and Sufferings of Mrs. Jane Johns, who was Barbarously Wounded and Scalped by Seminole Indians, in East Florida. Published exclusively for her Benefit. Baltimore: Jas. Lucas & E. K. Deaver, 1837.

24 p. 22.5 cm. Printed wrappers.
No other copy seems to be recorded.

St. Augustine: Saturday, Dec. 30, 1837. [St. Augustine, 1837.]

Broadside. 25 cm.
Reports of engagements with the Seminoles, together with a list of Seminole prisoners, among them Osceola, to be taken on the morrow from Fort Marion to Sullivan's Island. "They go with great reluctance." Unrecorded, and the only known copy.

1838

Acts of the Legislative Council of the Territory of Florida, passed at its Sixteenth Session, commencing Monday January 1st, and ending Sunday February 11th, 1838. With also the Resolutions of a Public or General Character adopted by the Legislative Council. By Authority. Tallahassee: S.S. Sibley, 1838.

88, v p. 22.5 cm.
Acts and resolutions relating to the Seminole War.

Macomb, Alexander

Head Quarters of the Army, Adjutant General's Office, Washington, D.C., April 10, 1838. General Orders No. 7. [Washington, 1838.]

Broadside. 20 cm.
An order assigning to the Cherokee country the troops freed by the collapse of Seminole resistance in Florida.

Message from the President of the United States transmitting a Report from the Secretary of War on the Claim of Econchatta Nico. [Washington, 1838.]*

15 p. 23 cm. Caption title.

Report from the Secretary of War with Statements of the Number of Troops employed in the war with the Seminole Indians. [Washington, 1838.]

12 p. 22.5 cm. Caption title.

Seminole and Cherokee Indians. Memorial of the Cherokee Mediators. [Washington, 1838.]

24 p. 22.5 cm. Caption title.

Seminole Indians—Prisoners of War. Letter from the Secretary of War, in reply to a resolution of the House of Representatives as to whether any Seminole Indians, coming in under a Flag of Truce, or brought in by Cherokee Indians, acting as Mediators, have been made Prisoners by General Jesup. [Washington, 1838.]

14 p. 22.5 cm. Caption title.

1839

Call, R. K.

Correspondence, &c. [Tallahassee, 1839.]

16 p. 19.5 cm. Caption title.
Correspondence between Governor Call and state militia officers on the conduct of the Seminole campaign. The only known copy.

CALL, R. K.

Correspondence, &c. [Tallahassee, 1839.]

16 p. 19.5 cm. Caption title.

Highly important correspondence between Governor Call and General Zachary Taylor on the prosecution of the Seminole War. The only known copy.

Document relating to the Bill "to Provide for the Armed Occupation and Settlement of that Part of Florida which is now Overrun and Infested by Marauding Bands of Hostile Indians." [Washington, 1839.]

3 p. 24.5 cm. Caption title.

1840

Acts and Resolutions of the Legislative Council of the Territory of Florida, passed at its Eighteenth Session, which commenced on the sixth day of January, and ended on the second day of March, 1840. By Authority. Tallahassee: B. F. Whitner, Jr., 1840.

76, 9 p. 21 cm.

Acts and resolutions regarding Seminole hostilities.

CALL, RICHARD K.

Memorial of Richard K. Call. [Washington, 1840.]*

15 p. 24.5 cm. Caption title.

General Orders No. 6. Head-quarters of the Army, Adjutant General's Army, Washington, Feb. 17th, 1840. [Washington, 1840.]

11 p. 19 cm. Caption title.

A review of the court martial convictions of Captain T. Dade and First Lieutenant W. Hardia on charges of misconduct and neglect of duty in the Seminole campaign.

Message from the President of the United States, communicating Copies of the Correspondence between the War Department and Governor Call concerning the War in Florida. [Washington:] Blair & Rives, [1840].

246 p. 25.5 cm. Caption title.

One of the foundation documents on the Seminole War.

1842

Appalachicola Indians. [Washington, 1842.]

7 p. 22.5 cm. Caption title.

Report of the Committee on Indian Affairs on the proposed payment of the Appalachicola Indians for improvements on lands in Florida surrendered to the United States.

Correspondence—Secretary of War and Commanding Officer in Florida. Letter from the Secretary of War, transmitting the Correspondence between the War Department and the Commanding Officer in Florida, since the 1st of January last. [Washington, 1842.]

46 p. 25 cm. Caption title. Folded table.

Important reports on the Seminole campaign.

1844

Journal of the Proceedings of the Senate of the Territory of Florida, at its Third Session. Tallahassee: C. E. Bartlett, 1844.*

150, lxxviii, 12 p.

1845

The Acts and Resolutions of the First General Assembly of the State of Florida, passed at its Adjourned Session, begun and held at the Capitol, in the City of Tallahassee, on Monday, November 17, 1845, and ended December 29, 1845. Tallahassee: Office of the Floridian, S. S. Sibley, 1845.

Pp. 4, [63]–158, xxii. 23 cm.

Important acts and resolutions relating to the Seminole Indians.

The Acts and Resolutions passed by the Legislative Council of the Territory of Florida, at its Twenty-third Session, begun and held in the City of Tallahassee on Monday, January 6, 1845. By Authority. Tallahassee: The Star of Florida, W. & C. J. Bartlett, 1845.

107, iv p. 22 cm.

Important resolutions relating to Creek and Seminole hostilities.

1846

Acts and Resolutions of the General Assembly of the State of Florida, passed at its Second Session, begun and held at the Capitol, in the City of Tallahassee, on Monday, November 23, 1846, and ended January 6, 1847. Published by Authority of Law. Tallahassee: Office of the Floridian, Samuel S. Sibley, 1846.

99, v p. 23 cm.

Important resolutions relating to the Seminole Indians.

[Reports on the claim of John J. Bulow Jr. N.p., 1846.]

21 p. 21 cm. Caption title.

Apparently a private reprint of reports and supporting documents relating to the Bulow claim for property destroyed on his Florida plantation by the Seminole Indians in 1836. The affidavits and depositions have considerable historical value.

1848

Sprague, John T.

The Origin, Progress, and Conclusion of the Florida War. New York: Appleton, 1848.

557 p. 23 cm. Map and 10 plates.

Field 1475.

A mint copy of this great authority.

1849

Brown, Thomas

Head Quarters, Florida Militia, Executive Department, Tallahassee, October 1st, 1849. General Orders No. 2. [Tallahassee, 1849.]

Broadside. 25.5 cm.

Mustering out of Florida state troops because of the arrival of a United States military force sufficient to prosecute the Seminole War unaided. Unrecorded, and no other copy traced.

HUTCHINS, G. W.

To the Inhabitants Occupying the Frontier of the Indian Country. [St. Augustine, 1849.]

Broadside. 26 cm.

Official account of a Seminole Indian outbreak and of the state militia's progress in suppressing it. Unrecorded.

1850

Message of the President of the United States, communicating Information relative to Hostilities committed by the Seminole Indians in Florida during the past year, their Removal, &c. [Washington, 1850.]

173 p. 25.5 cm. Caption title.

A fine copy, entirely uncut and unopened, of this important document.

1853

DUVAL, MARCELLUS

Copy of a Letter to Commissioner Indian Affairs, from M. Duval, late Seminole Agent, in reference to the Causes of his Removal. [Tahlequah? 1853.]

8 p. 25 cm.

Dated: Seminole Agency, April 8th, 1853.

The only known copy. DuVal was removed because of his questionable course in the capture and sale of runaway Creek slaves.

1855

HUMPHREYS, GAD

Petition of Gad Humphreys, of St. Augustine, Florida, praying Indemnity for Indian Depredations and Damages by United States Troops. Washington: Henry Polkinhorn, 1855.

12 p. 15 cm.

Important detail on the Seminole War.

1856

Journal of the Proceedings of the House of Representatives of the General Assembly of the State of Florida at its Eighth Session, begun and held at the Capitol, in the City of Tallahassee, on Monday, twenty-fourth November, 1856. Tallahassee: Office of the Floridian & Journal, Printed by James S. Jones, 1856.

264, 32, 136 p. 23 cm.

The final 136 pages are devoted to correspondence relating to Indian affairs, and contain vitally important information on the Seminole hostilities of 1855 and 1856.

A Journal of the Proceedings of the Senate of the General Assembly of the State of Florida. Eighth Session, begun and held at the Capitol in the City of Tallahassee, on Monday, November 24, 1856. Tallahassee: Office of the Florida Sentinel. Printed by Benjamin F. Allen, 1856.

216, 32, 136 p.

The final 136 pages are devoted to correspondence relating to Indian affairs.

1858

GIDDINGS, JOSHUA R.

The Exiles of Florida: or, the Crimes committed by our Government against the

Maroons, who fled from South Carolina and other Slave States, seeking Protection under Spanish Laws. Columbus, Ohio: Follett, Foster & Co., 1858.

338 p. 20 cm.

A fine copy of a book usually found in bad condition. The volume contains considerable information on the Seminole War and throws important light on the negotiation of early Creek treaties.

LOOMIS, GUSTAVUS

Proclamation. The Delegation of friendly Indians in charge of Col. Elias Rector, Superintendent of Indian Affairs, having succeeded in removing the hostile Chief Billy Bowlegs and most of his band, with some of the band of Sam Jones, leaving only about thirty warriors, all told, in the State of Florida, and those being very widely scattered upon the Islands, in the swamps of the country, and no trace of them having been discovered for some months back, no depredations having been committed, and no hostile gun fired by them, for some months, except in defence of their fastnesses, and hiding places. I now consider it unnecessary, and unwise in view of the rapid settlement of the country, to prosecute scouting the swamps and everglades, to hunt up the few remaining Indian Families. I therefore, hereby declare the Florida War closed, and the people can now return to their homes and usual avocations without fear of further molestation. [Fort Brooke, 1858.]

Broadside. 25 cm. Signed in autograph by Colonel Loomis.

Unrecorded, and the only known copy.

1859

BRINTON, DANIEL GARRISON

Notes on the Floridian Peninsula, its Literary History, Indian Tribes, and Antiquities. Philadelphia: Joseph Sabin, 1859.

viii, 202 p.

Field 189.

An authoritative study.

1864

JUMPER, JOHN

Speech delivered by Col. John Jumper to the Creeks and Seminoles comprising the 1st Seminole Reg't. July 6th, 1864. Government Printing Office, Ft. Towson, C.N., July 21st, 1864.

4 p. 19.5 cm.

No other copy is recorded.

1868

MCCALL, GEORGE A.

Letters from the Frontiers. Written during a Period of Thirty Years' Service in the Army of the United States. Philadelphia: J. B. Lippincott & Co., 1868.*

539 p. 21 cm.

A valuable source for the Seminole and Black Hawk Wars. A fine copy of a very scarce volume.

1871

Fairbanks, George R.

History of Florida from its Discovery by Ponce de Leon, in 1512, to the Close of the Florida War, in 1842. Philadelphia: Lippincott. Jacksonville: Drew, 1871.*

350 p. 19.5 cm.

A recognized authority.

1876

The Indian Key Massacre. This is the Newspaper Account, published at the Time of Our Escape, 1840. [Albany, N.Y.? 1876?].*

Broadside. 39.5 cm.

A vivid account of the Perrine massacre by the Seminole Indians at Indian Key, Florida, in 1840. The only known copy.

Perrine, Henry E.

Biscayne Bay, Dade Co., Florida, between the 25th and 26th Degrees of Latitude. A Complete Manual of Information concerning the Climate, Soil, Products, etc., of the Lands bordering on Biscayne Bay, in Florida. Albany, N.Y.: Weed, Parsons & Co., 1876.

18 p. 23 cm. Printed wrapper.

With a notice of the Perrine massacre by the Seminoles at Indian Key in 1840.

1881

Shipp, Bernard

The History of Hernando de Soto and Florida; or, Record of the Events of Fifty-six Years, from 1512 to 1568. Philadelphia: Collins, 1881.

689 p. 25 cm.

English translations of the earliest and most important narratives of discovery and exploration.

1882

Record of Officers and Soldiers killed in Battle and died in Service during the Florida War. Washington, 1882.

64 p. 23 cm. Folded plat.

Western Baptist Association

Minutes of the Fifty-fourth Annual Session of the Western Baptist Association, held with the Church at Ramah, Campbell County, Georgia, September 16th, 17th, and 18th, 1882. Newnan, Ga.: Herald Job Office, 1882.*

15, [1] p. 21.5 cm. Printed wrappers.

Contains an interesting report from John Jumper, the Seminole principal chief and Baptist missionary, on his missionary labors among the Wichita.

1888

Churchill, Franklin Hunter

Sketch of the Life of Bvt. Brig. Gen. Sylvester Churchill, Inspector General U.S. Army, with Notes and Appendices, by Franklin Hunter Churchill. New York: Willis McDonald & Co., 1888.*

vi, 201 p. 23 cm. 2 printed slips inserted at front.

The volume contains interesting and important extracts from Churchill's journals of the Seminole campaign in 1836 and 1837.

Message from the President of the United States transmitting a Letter of the Secretary of the Interior relative to Land upon which to Locate Seminole Indians. [Washington, 1888.]*

15 p. 23 cm. Caption title.

1890

FORD, WORTHINGTON CHAUNCEY

The United States and Spain in 1790. An Episode in Diplomacy described from hitherto unpublished sources. Brooklyn, 1890.*

109 p. 24.5 cm. Printed wrappers.

Negotiations dealing with Florida and Louisiana, with some attention to the Indians.

Message from the President of the United States, transmitting Letter of the Secretary of the Interior and Reports relative to the Proposed Purchase of Certain Lands by the Seminole Indians. [Washington, 1890.]

11 p. 22.5 cm. Caption title. Folded color map.

1891

WHITEHEAD, CHARLES E.

Camp-fires of the Everglades or Wild Sports in the South. Edinburgh: David Douglas, 1891.*

x, [2], 298 p. 24.5 cm.

There are chapters on the Seminoles.

1895

Experience of Rev. A. J. Holt when Missionary among the Indians. Atlanta, [1895].*

8 p. 8.5 cm.

Experiences among the Seminole, Comanche, and Arapahoe Indians. The author was once captured and robbed by a band of Arapahoes.

1896

MOORE-WILLSON, MINNIE

The Seminoles of Florida. American Printing House, Philadelphia, 1896.

[8], 126 p. 20 cm. Photographs.

Contains a valuable Seminole vocabulary.

1898

An Act to Ratify the Agreement between the Dawes Commission and the Seminole Nation of Indians. [Washington, 1898.]*

[4] p. 23.5 cm. Caption title.

CRAWFORD, SAMUEL J.

In Re Seminole National Government and Agreement with the United States. Brief and Argument. Washington: Gibson Bros., 1898.

16 p. 23.5 cm. Wrapper title.

1900

An Act to ratify an Agreement between the Dawes Commission and the Seminole Nation of Indians. [Washington, 1900.]

[4] p. 23.5 cm. Caption title.

1909

Prout, Iranaeus

The Mission to the Seminoles in the Everglades of Florida. Orlando, Florida: Sentinel Print, [1909].*

21 p. 22.5 cm. Wrapper title. Photographs.
Late, but a rare and valuable account.

1911

Everglades of Florida. Acts, Reports, and other Papers, State and National, relating to the Everglades of the State of Florida and their Reclamation. Washington, 1911.

208 p. 23.5 cm. Printed wrappers.
Incidental Seminole history of great value.

1915

Moore, J. Read

Moore's Seminole roll and land guide. [Wewoka, 1915.]

[4], 52, [2], 28 in double, [1] p. 17.5 cm. Folded color map.

1928

Bushnell, David I., Jr.

Drawing by Jacques LeMoyne de Morgues of Saturious, a Timucua Chief in Florida, 1564. Washington, 1928.*

9 p. 24.5 cm. Printed wrappers. Plate.

1932

Nash, Roy

Survey of the Seminole Indians of Florida. Washington, 1932.*

88, [1] p. 21.5 cm. Map.
Of great value.

1934

Read, William A.

Florida place-names of Indian origin and Seminole personal names. Baton Rouge: University Press, 1934.*

[10], v, 83 p. 23 cm.
A valuable monograph.

1936

A 17th Century Letter of Gabriel Diaz Vara Calderon, Bishop of Cuba, describing the Indians and Indian Missions of Florida. Transcribed and translated by Lucy L. Wenhold. Introduction by John R. Swanton. Washington, 1936.*

14 p. 24.5 cm. Printed wrappers. Plates.

1941

Coe, Charles H.

Debunking the so-called Spanish Mission near New Smyrna Beach, Volusia County, Florida. By Capt. Chas. H. Coe. [Daytona Beach], 1941.

29 p. 18 cm. Printed wrappers.

Recent but very scarce.

SENECA INDIANS

1811

Red Jacket and Farmer's Brother

Native Eloquence, being Public Speeches delivered by Two Distinguished Chiefs of the Seneca Tribe of Indians, known among the White People by the Names of Red Jacket and Farmer's Brother. Published under the Revision of the Public Interpreter. Canandaigua: J. D. Bemis, 1811.

24 p. 17.5 cm.

Excessively rare.

1824

Seaver, James E.

A Narrative of the Life of Mrs. Mary Jemison, who was taken by the Indians in the year 1755. Canandaigua: Printed by J. D. Bemis and Co., 1824. Republished by Random House, at New York, MCMXXIX.*

191, [1] p. 14 cm. Frontisp.

Number 84 of 950 numbered copies.

1830

Reservation—Seneca Tribe of Indians. Letter from the Secretary of War, transmitting Information in relation to the wishes of the Seneca Tribe of Indians to Sell a Reservation of Land, called the Seneca Reservation, in the State of Ohio. [Washington, 1830.]

3 p. 22 cm. Caption title.

1831

Brish, Henry C.

Indian's Sale. Will be Offered at Public Auction, on the 22nd, 23rd and 24th instant, at the following places, viz. at the House of Small Cloud Spicer, on the Sandusky, on the 22nd, at the Council House on the Sandusky, on the twenty third, and at the New Council House near Green Creek on the twenty fourth all the Live Stock, Farming Utensils and other Chattle Property which the Seneca Indians may not be able to take with them on their Removal, etc. Sandusky City, Ohio: E. & J. H. Brown, Printers, 1831.

Broadside. 27.5 cm.

Unrecorded, and the only known copy.

1838

Pierce, Marius B.

Address on the Present Condition and Prospects of the Aboriginal Inhabitants of

North America, with particular reference to the Seneca Nation. By M. B. Pierce, a Chief of the Seneca Nation, and a Member of Dartmouth College. [Buffalo:] Steele's Press, 1838.

16 p. 21.5 cm.

The original edition, which is very rare.

1839

Pierce, Marius B.

Address on the Present Condition and Prospects of the Aboriginal Inhabitants of North America, with particular reference to the Seneca Nation. Delivered at Buffalo, New York, by M. B. Pierce, a Chief of the Seneca Nation, and a Member of Dartmouth College. Philadelphia: J. Richards, 1839.

24 p. 18.5 cm. Plain wrappers.

1840

The Case of the Seneca Indians in the State of New York. Illustrated by Facts. Printed for the Information of the Society of Friends, by direction of the Joint Committee on Indian Affairs, of the Four Yearly Meetings of Friends of Genesee, New York, Philadelphia, and Baltimore. Philadelphia: Merrihew & Thompson, 1840.

256 p. 22.5 cm. Printed wrappers.

A valuable compilation of documents on Seneca affairs.

1841

A Further Illustration of the Case of the Seneca Indians in the State of New York, in a Review of a Pamphlet entitled "An Appeal to the Christian Community, &c. by Nathaniel T. Strong, a Chief of the Seneca Tribe." Philadelphia: Merrihew & Thompson, 1841.

84 p. 22 cm. Printed wrappers.

1842

Ne Jaguh'nigo'ages'gwathah. The Mental Elevator. Buffalo Creek Reservation and Cattaraugus Reservation. Nos. 3 to 19, inclusive. March 2, 1842–April 15, 1850. An almost complete file of this rare and valuable periodical.

1843

Report of the Proceedings of an Indian Council at Cattaraugus, in the State of New York; held 6 month, 1843. Baltimore: William Wooddy, 1843.

31 p. 21 cm.

1845

Declaration of the Seneca Nation of Indians in General Council assembled, with the Accompanying Documents. Also an Address to the Chiefs and People, of that Nation. Baltimore: Printed by Wm. Wooddy, 1845.

53 p. 21 cm. Printed wrappers.

A presentation copy, with inscription, from Philip E. Thomas, Seneca ambassador to the United States. [See page 348.]

1847

Proceedings of the Joint Committee appointed by the Society of Friends, constituting the Yearly Meetings of Genessee, New York, Philadelphia and Baltimore, for

DECLARATION

OF THE

SENECA NATION OF INDIANS

IN

GENERAL COUNCIL ASSEMBLED,

WITH THE ACCOMPANYING DOCUMENTS.

ALSO

AN ADDRESS

TO THE

CHIEFS AND PEOPLE,

OF THAT NATION.

BALTIMORE:
PRINTED BY WM. WOODDY,
Corner of Market and Calvert sts.
1845.

promoting the Civilization and Improving the Condition of the Seneca Nation of Indians. Baltimore: William Wooddy, printer, 1847.

189, [1] p. 21 cm. Printed wrappers.

1848

Constitution of the Seneca Nation of Indians. Baltimore: Printed by William Wooddy & Son, 1848.

15 p. 21 cm.

Report of the Secretary of War submitting a Communication from the Commissioner of Indian Affairs, with a Report from the Commissioner appointed to Investigate whether the Seneca Indians have Sustained Losses through a late Sub-Agent of the United States. [Washington, 1848.]

77 p. 22.5 cm. Caption title.

1849

Communication from the Governor, transmitting Certain Proceedings of the Seneca Nation of Indians. [Albany, N.Y.: 1849.]

30 p. 24.5 cm. Caption title.

Headed: State of New York. No. 108. In Assembly, Feb. 20, 1849.

Contains the important "Declaration of the Seneca Nation of Indians, Changing their Form of Government, and Adopting a Constitutional Charter," together with resolutions, letters and addresses.

1850

Further Proceedings of the Joint Committee appointed by the Society of Friends, constituting the yearly meetings of Genessee, New York, Philadelphia, and Baltimore. For Promoting the Civilization and Improving the Condition of the Seneca Nation of Indians, from the year 1847 to the year 1850. Baltimore: Wm. Wooddy & Son, 1850.

119 p. 21.5 cm. Printed wrappers.

1857

Documents and Official Reports illustrating the Causes which led to the Revolution in the Government of the Seneca Indians, in the year 1848, and to the Recognition of their Representative Republican Constitution, by the Authorities of the United States, and of the State of New York. Baltimore: Wm. Wooddy & Son, 1857.

92 p. 19 cm.

1864

Silverheels, Henry

Proclamation! Seneca Nation of New York Indians! Cattaraugus and Allegany Reservations, Executive Department, Nov. 3d, 1864. [Cattaraugus Reservation? 1864.]

Broadside. Folio.

Appointment of tribal officers. The only known copy.

1871

Sundown, Peter

Proclamation! [Allegany Reservation, New York, 1871.]

Broadside. 25.5 cm.

Call for a constitutional convention of the Seneca Nation. No other copy is known.

1875

[A Memorial of the Council of the Seneca Nation of New York relating to the leasing of lands on the Cattaraugus and Allegany Reservations. Salamanca, N.Y., 1875.]*

Broadside. 25.5 cm.

1877

A Brief Statement of the Rights of the Seneca Indians in the State of New York, to their Lands in that State, with Decisions relative thereto by the State and United States Courts, and Extracts from United States Laws, etc. Philadelphia: W. H. Pile, 1877.

32 p. 22 cm.

1878

TWOGUNS, NOAH

Seneca Nation of Indians. Executive Department, Cattaraugus Reservation. Whereas, on the first Tuesday in June, 1877, William Redeye was duly inaugurated President of the Seneca Nation of Indians for the term and period of one year, which term expired on the first Tuesday in June, 1878, etc. Salamanca, N.Y.: Salamanca Gazette Power Press Print, [1878].

Broadside. Folio.

A proclamation relating to election frauds and calling a session of the council. The only known copy.

1884

The New York Indians, being those Indians who were Parties to the Treaty concluded at Buffalo Creek, in the State of New York, on the 15th day of January, 1838, and George Barker, James B. Jenkins, Sayles J. Bowen, George R. Herrick, and the Legal Representatives of John T. Cochrane and Hiram T. Jenkins, deceased, vs. the United States. Original Petition. [N.p., 1884.]*

88 p. 23 cm. Wrapper title.

The exhibits throw much light on the history of the Cayuga, Oneida, Seneca, and Tuscarora Indians.

1893

Amended Constitution of the Seneca Nation of Indians, adopted January 13th, 1893. Printed by Order of the Council. Salamanca, N.Y.: Cattaraugus Republican Printing House, 1893.

6 p. 22 cm. Wrapper title.

The only known copy.

STATE OF SEQUOYAH

1905

An Address to the People of Indian Territory on the Question of Independent Statehood for Indian Territory, by the Campaign Committee of the Constitutional Convention. Authorized and Assembled August 21, 1905. [Muskogee: Phoenix Printing Co., 1905.]*

13 p. 22.5 cm. Caption title.

Very rare.

Constitution of the State of Sequoyah. [Muskogee, 1905.]

68 p. 25.5 cm. Caption title. Folded color map.

The only known copy of the first issue, which may be distinguished by the absence of imprint at the foot of the last page and by the fact that the last page is numbered. The second issue lacks the page number and has the imprint. [See page 352.]

A Memorial to the Congress of the United States on behalf of the State of Sequoyah. [Muskogee, 1905.]

70 p. 23 cm. Wrapper title.

Rare.

1906

Proposed State of Sequoyah. Mr. Foraker presented the following Memorial from Citizens of Indian Territory, praying for Admission into the Union upon an Equal Footing with the Original States, and also presenting the Form of a Constitution for the Proposed State, to be known as the State of Sequoyah. [Washington, 1906.]*

87 p. 23 cm. Caption title. Folded color map.

SHAWNEE INDIANS

1832

"Seat of War." [Galena, Illinois, 1832.]

Broadside. Folio.

A restrike from the "Galenian" of Wednesday, Aug. 8, 1832, of four columns of detailed dispatches on events of the Black Hawk War. The only known copy.

1842

LYKINS, JOHNSTON, tr.

The Gospel according to Saint Matthew, translated into the Shawanoe Language, by Johnston Lykins, Missionary of the Amer. Bap. Bd. of For. Missions, aided in revising and comparing with the Greek by James Andrew Chute, M.D. Shawanoe Baptist Mission Press, J. G. Pratt, printer. 1842.*

116 p. 16.5 cm.

Pilling, Algonquian Bibliography, p. 321.

McMurtrie-Allen locates only the New York Public Library and Library of Congress copies.

1846

Translation of John's Gospel from the Original Greek e editionibus Greenfield et Bloomfield. By Francis Barker, Missionary of the Amer. Ba. Bd. of Foreign Missions. Press of the Amer. Bap. Bd. of Foreign Missions, Stockbridge, Ind. Ter. 1846.*

90 p. 16 cm. Text in Shawnee.

Not in Pilling.

E. A. Hitchcock's copy, with his bookplate. McMurtrie-Allen locates only the Kansas Historical Society copy.

1848

Original and Select Hymns in the Shawanoe Language. By Missionaries of the

CONSTITUTION

OF THE

STATE OF SEQUOYAH

PREAMBLE.

Invoking the blessing of Almighty God and reposing faith in the Constitution and Treaty obligations of the United States, we, the people of the State of Sequoyah, do ordain and establish this Constitution.

Article I.

BILL OF RIGHTS.

SECTION 1. All political power is vested in and derived from the people; is founded upon their will, and is instituted for the good of the whole.

SEC. 2. The people of this State have the inherent and exclusive right to regulate the internal government and police thereof, and to alter and abolish their Constitution and form of government whenever they may deem it neccessary to their safety and happiness: Provided, Such change be not in conflict with the Constitution of the United States.

SEC. 3. All persons have an inherent right to life, liberty, the pursuit of happiness, and the enjoyment of the gains of their own industry. To give security to these things is the princinal office of government.

SEC. 4. All men have a natural and indefeasable right to worship God according to the dictates of their own consciences. No person shall, on account of his religious opinions, be rendered ineligible to any office of trust or profit under this State, or be disqualified from

American Baptist Missionary Union. Third Edition. Stockbridge, Ind. Ter.: Press of Am. Baptist Missionary Union, 1848.

48 p. 13 cm.

Not in Pilling.

The following penciled note appears on one of the endpapers: "I preached at the Shawanoe Mission. Charles Bluejacket, Head Chief, Interpreter, Octr. 7, 1855." Not in McMurtrie-Allen, and possibly the only known copy.

1854

The Great Indian Chief of the West: or, the Life and Adventures of Black Hawk. Cincinnati: Applegate & Company, 1854.

288 p. 18 cm. Port.

1855

HARVEY, HENRY

History of the Shawnee Indians, from the Year 1681 to 1854, inclusive. By Henry Harvey, a Member of the Religious Society of Friends. Cincinnati: Ephraim Morgan & Sons, 1855.

316 p. 17.5 cm. Frontisp. port.

Field 663.

1856

DRAKE, BENJAMIN

Life of Tecumseh, and of his Brother the Prophet; with a Historical Sketch of the Shawanoe Indians. By Benjamin Drake. Cincinnati: H. M. Rulison, 1856.

235 p. 18.5 cm. Illustrated.

1868

GUTHRIE, ABELARD

The Shawnee Indians. [N.p., 1868.]

11 p. 22.5 cm. Caption title.

A history of the tribe, and of its treaties, internal divisions, and present condition. Abelard Guthrie's writings, few in number, are excessively rare, and this is the rarest of all. No other copy can be traced.

1869

Agreement between the Shawnees and Cherokees, concluded June 7, 1869, approved by the President June 9, 1869. [Washington, 1869.]

Broadsheet. Folio.

1870

CLARKE, SIDNEY

Black Bob Indian Lands. Supplement to the Tribune. [Lawrence, Kansas], July 21, 1870.

Broadside. Folio.

The only known copy.

Memorial in behalf of the "Black Bob" Band of Shawnee Indians, in favor of the

Issuance of Patents to their Land in Severalty. Washington: Powell, Ginck & Co., 1870.

22 p. 21.5 cm. Wrapper title.

1877

Green, William M.

Life and papers of A. L. P. Green, D.D. By the Rev. Wm. M. Green. Edited by T. O. Summers, D.D. Nashville, Tenn.: Southern Methodist Publishing House. 1877.

viii, 592 p. 18 cm. Frontisp. port.

Contains a description of an Indian ball play and the legend of a Shawnee and Osage ball play.

1887

Argument of Charles W. Blair and Van H. Manning in support of the Application of Gov. Thos. Carney to the Secretary of the Interior for the Approval of certain Deeds executed to him by Members of the Black Bob Band of Shawnee Indians in Johnson County, Kansas. August, 1887. Washington: Gibson Bros., [1887].

20 p. 23 cm. Wrapper title.

1891

Johnson Blackfeather, Principal Chief of the Shawnee Tribe of Indians, vs. The United States and vs. The United States Government and the Cherokee Nation. Treaties of the United States with the Shawnee Indians; treaty of July 19, 1866, of the United States with the Cherokee Nation; Articles of Agreement with the Cherokee Nation and the Shawnee Indians of June 7, 1869; and Acts and Resolutions of Congress and Acts of the Cherokee National Councils, and Executive Documents, relating to Shawnee Affairs, alleged and referred to in the allegations and pleadings in the above entitled cases. [Washington, 1891.]

185 p. 22 cm. Wrapper title.

A valuable compilation.

1892

Johnson Blackfeather, the Principal Chief of the Shawnee Tribe of Indians, for the use and benefit of the Shawnee Indians, vs. The United States Government. Amended petition. Washington: Judd & Detweiler, [1892].

21 p. 22 cm. Wrapper title.

A claim brought by Blackfeather as principal chief for losses suffered by the tribe from depredations committed by the whites and for property lost during the war.

1894

Johnson Blackfeather, Principal Chief of the Shawnee Indians, v. The United States. Defendant's motion for an additional finding of fact, and brief thereon. [Washington, 1894.]

47 p. 22 cm. Wrapper title.

Contains a list of chiefs, warriors, and heads of families of the Shawnee tribe in 1844.

SIOUX INDIANS

1865

Laws, Memorials and Resolutions of the Territory of Dakota, passed at the Fifth Session of the Legislative Assembly. Yankton: G. W. Kingsbury, Union & Dakotian Office, 1865–66.

605 p. 21.5 cm.

Contains important acts, resolutions, and memorials on Indian affairs. An early example of Dakota printing.

Pope, John

Official Communications from General Pope, commanding Military Department of the Missouri, concerning Indian Affairs. St. Louis: Missouri Democrat, 1865.

30 p. 19 cm.

A valuable report on Indian hostilities in the West, with particular attention to the Sioux outbreak.

1867

[Instructions to the special commissioners sent to Fort Laramie to investigate the Sioux outbreak. Washington, 1867.]

3 p. 24 cm. Printed without title page or caption title.

No other copy can be traced.

Kelly, Fanny

[A petition for compensation for the injuries, losses, and other damages suffered in her captivity by the Sioux Indians in 1864. N.P., 1867.]

Broadside. Folio.

The memorial includes an excellent first person account of her captivity. Excessively rare, and a fine copy.

1870

Welsh, William

Report and Supplementary Report of a Visit to Spotted Tail's Tribe of Brule Sioux Indians, the Yankton and Santee Sioux, Ponkas and the Chippewas of Minnesota, October 1870. Philadelphia, 1870.

28 p. 21.5 cm. Wrapper title.

Welsh, William

Sioux and Ponca Indians. Reports to the Missionary Organizations of the Protestant Episcopal Church, and to the Secretary of the Interior, on Indian Civilization, by Wm. Welsh. Philadelphia: M'Calla & Stavely, 1870.

v, 27, 28 p. 21.5 cm. Printed wrappers.

1872

Welsh, William

Report of a Visit to the Sioux and Ponka Indians on the Missouri River, made by Wm. Welsh, July, 1872. Philadelphia: M'Calla & Stavely, 1872.

36 p. 21.5 cm.

1874

McCann, D. J.

Letter of a Western Man to the Commissioner of Indian Affairs. [N.p., 1874.]

4 p. 20 cm. Caption title.

Practical suggestions regarding the Indians of the Red Cloud and Whetstone agencies.

Report of the Commissioners appointed by the Secretary of the Interior to examine the Red Cloud and Whetstone Indian Agencies. The Commission consisted of Right Reverend Bishop W. H. Hare, Missionary Bishop of Niobrara; Reverend Samuel D. Hinman, Missionary to the Santee Sioux; Dr. J. D. Bevier, one of the five Indian Inspectors; and Francis H. Smith, Member of the Board of Indian Commissioners. Washington, 1874.

50 p. 23.5 cm. Printed wrappers.

1875

Sheridan, P. H.

[Report on events in the Military Division of the Missouri. Chicago, 1875.]

3 p. Folio.

Contains an important discussion of the gold rush to the Black Hills of the Dakota and a prediction of serious troubles there with the Sioux Indians; and a report on the successful campaign in Indian Territory against the Cheyennes, Kiowas, and Comanches. With the autograph signature of General Sheridan.

1890

Letter from the Secretary of War transmitting a Letter from the Major General commanding the Army relative to Implements of Warfare supposed to be in the possession of the Indians of certain States. [Washington, 1890.]

23 p. 23 cm. Caption title.

Sioux Indian troubles.

1942

Burdick, U. L., and Eugene D. Hart

Jacob Horner and the Indian Campaigns of 1876 and 1877 (the Sioux and the Nez Perce). Baltimore: Wirth Bros., 1942.*

30, [2] p. 23 cm. Printed wrappers.

SISSETON AND WAHPETON INDIANS

1903

Sisseton and Wahpeton Indians vs. The United States. Arguments of Geo. S. Chase and William H. Robeson on behalf of Plaintiffs. [Washington, 1903.]*

220 p. 23.5 cm. Wrapper title.

An encyclopedia of information about a tribe of which little has been published.

SIX NATIONS

1829

Petition and Appeal of the Six Nations, Oneida, Stockbridge, &c. to the Government of the United States. Sangerfield: Joseph Tenny, 1829.

32 p. 20.5 cm.

A protest against the government's action in forcibly depriving them of lands in Michigan purchased from the Menominee Indians. A fine copy of a volume printed at an obscure press and now of the very greatest rarity.

1848

CUSICK, DAVID

David Cusick's Sketches of Ancient History of the Six Nations, comprising First, A Tale of the Foundation of the Great Island (now North America), the Two Infants Born, and the Creation of the Universe. Second, A Real Account of the Early Settlers of North America, and their Dissensions. Third, Origin of the Kingdom of the Five Nations, which was called A Long House: the Wars, Fierce Animals, &c. Lockport, N.Y.: Turner & McCollum, 1848.

35 p. 22 cm. Printed wrappers. Plates.

1900

KIMM, S. C.

The Iroquois. A History of the Six Nations of New York. Middleburgh, N.Y.: Pierre W. Danforth, 1900.

122 p. 19.5 cm. Printed wrappers. Portrait.

1905

BEAUCHAMP, WILLIAM M.

A History of the New York Iroquois, now commonly called the Six Nations. Albany, 1905.*

461 p. 23 cm. Plates. Folded map.

STOCKBRIDGE INDIANS

1735

APPLETON, NATHANAEL

Gospel Ministers must be Fit for the Master's Use, and Prepared to every Good Work, if they would be Vessels unto Honour: Illustrated in a Sermon preached at Deerfield, August 31, 1735, at the Ordination of Mr. John Sargent, to the Evangelical Ministry, with a Special Reference to the Indians of Houssatonnoc, who have lately Manifested their Desires to Receive the Gospel. By Nathanael Appleton, M.A. Pastor of the Church of Christ in Cambridge. Boston: S. Kneeland & T. Green, 1735.

33 p. 19 cm.
Very rare.

1743

SERGEANT, JOHN

A Letter from the Revd. Mr. Sergeant of Stockbridge, to Dr. Colman of Boston; containing Mr. Sergeant's Proposal of a More Effectual Method for the Education of Indian Children; to Raise 'em if possible into a Civil and Industrious People; by Introducing the English Language among them; and thereby Instilling into their Minds and Hearts, with a More Lasting Impression, the Principles of Virtue and Piety. Made public by Dr. Colman at the Desire of Mr. Sergeant, with some General Account of what the Rev. Mr. Isaac Hollis of——has already done for the Sons of this Indian Tribe of Houssatannoc, now erected into a Township by the General Court, and called Stockbridge. Boston: Rogers and Fowle, 1743.

16 p. 19 cm.

Also a facsimile reprint on fine quality rag paper, issued at Lancaster, Pennsylvania, in 1929.

TABLES OF DISTANCES

1866

WILLIAMSON, R. S.

Table of Distances from Big Bend of Truckee River to Ruby City, Idaho. New Route Measured and Proposed by Brevet Lieutenant-Colonel R. S. Williamson, U.S. Engineers. [San Francisco? 1866.]

Broadside. 20 cm.

With remarks on the country. Unrecorded.

1868

EVANS, A. W.

Headquarters District of New Mexico, Santa Fe., N.M., July 16, 1868. Circular No. 8. [Santa Fe, 1868.]

Broadsheet. 19 cm.

Table of distances from Fort Union, New York to Fort Garland, Colorado Territory, via the Moreno Mines, with remarks on the country. Unrecorded.

EVANS, A. W.

Head Quarters District of New Mexico, Santa Fe, New Mexico, August 29, 1868. Circular No. 11. [Santa Fe, 1868.]

3 p. 20.5 cm. Caption title.

Table of distances from Camp Blummer, New Mexico (Fort Lowell), to Santa Fe, with valuable remarks on the country. Unrecorded.

Headquarters District of New Mexico, Santa Fe, New Mexico, June 12, 1868. Circular No. 6. [Santa Fe, 1868.]

Broadsheet. 19 cm. Caption title.

Table of distances from Fort Stanton to Fort Sumner via the Rio Hondo, with interesting remarks on the country. Unrecorded.

1869

JACKSON, HENRY

Table of Distances between Fort Harker, Kansas, and Fort Sill, I.T., and between Fort Harker, Kansas, and Fort Arbuckle, C.N., and between Fort Sill, I.T., and Fort Arbuckle, C.N.; also showing Distances between Camping Places. [Fort Leavenworth, Kansas, 1869.]

Broadside. 31 cm.

Dated Headquarters Department of the Missouri, Fort Leavenworth, Kansas, June 26, 1869.

The only known copy.

1870

Evans, A. W.

Headquarters District of New Mexico, Santa Fe, New Mexico, June 1, 1870. Circular No. 4. [Santa Fe, 1870.]

4 p. 20 cm. Caption title.

Table of distances from Fort Wingate, New Mexico, to Fort Whipple, Arizona, with valuable and detailed remarks on the country. Unrecorded.

Smith, Henry E.

Headquarters District of New Mexico, Santa Fe, New Mexico, October 11, 1870. Circular No. 8. (Santa Fe, 1870.)

Broadside. 20 cm.

Table of distances from Zuni to Camp Thomas, Arizona Territory, with remarks on the country. Unrecorded.

1872

Lists of Elevations and Distances in that Portion of the United States West of the Mississippi River. Collated and arranged by Prof. C. Thomas, Asst. U.S. Geol. Surv., under Dr. F. V. Hayden. Washington, 1872.

31 p. 18.5 cm. Printed wrappers.

1874

Van Vliet, Stewart

Table of Distances in the Department of the Missouri. Compiled under the direction of Brevet Major General Stewart Van Vliet. Fort Leavenworth, Kan., May 20, 1874. Washington, 1874.

20 p. 23.5 cm. Printed wrappers. 3 folded maps. 1 folded table.

Rare.

1880

Headquarters Department of Texas, San Antonio, Texas, December 14, 1880. Circular No. 28. [San Antonio, 1880.]

Broadside. 20.5 cm.

Overland distances between San Antonio and the various military posts in the Department of Texas. Unrecorded.

1881

Itineraries of Routes and Tables of Distances, with a List of Posts, their Location, Garrisons, and Commanding Officers; Posts which have been Occupied, with Dates of Establishment and Abandonment; Forage Agencies; Distances to Indian Agencies and Names of Agents, in the Department of the Columbia, Brevet Brig.-Gen. Frank Wheaton, Colonel, 2d Infantry, Commanding, Prepared by First Lieut. Thomas W. Symons, Corps of Engineers, Chief Engineer, Department of the Columbia. Vancouver Barracks, W.T., May 1, 1881.

60 p. 20 cm. Folded color map.

No other copy has been traced.

1886

Revised Edition of the Tables of Distances and Itineraries of Routes, in the Department of the Missouri. Fort Leavenworth, 1886.*

74 p. 20 cm.

No other copy has been traced.

1893

Tables of Distances and Itineraries of Routes in the Department of Texas. San Antonio, 1893.

24, [2] p. 21 cm. Printed wrappers.

No other copy has been traced.

TAENSA INDIANS

Undated

Calhoun, Robert Dabney. The Taensa Indians. The French Explorers and Catholic Missionaries in the Taensas Country. [New Orleans, n.d.]*

64 p. 25 cm. Wrapper title.

TEXAS INDIANS

1837

Examination and Review of a Pamphlet printed and secretly circulated by M. E. Gorostiza, late Envoy Extraordinary from Mexico; previous to his Departure from the United States, and by him entitled "Correspondence between the Legation Extraordinary of Mexico and the Department of State of the United States, respecting the Passage of the Sabine by the Troops under the command of General Gaines." Washington: Peter Force, 1837.

188 p. 24.5 cm. Plain wrappers.

Highly important information on the incursions of American Indians into Texas (at the time a part of Mexico), and on the resulting disturbances. A fine copy. Very rare; the Union Catalog locates only the Library of Congress and Houston Public Library copies.

1838

BONNELL, G. W.

Report of G. W. Bonnell, Commissioner of Indian Affairs. Third Congress—First Session. Published by Order of Congress. Houston, Texas, 1838.

15 p. 22.5 cm.

Perhaps the rarest and most desirable volume in the field of Texas Indian history. The report recites details of Tonkawa, Lipan, and Comanche hostilities, and describes other tribes as well. Only one other copy appears to be known. [See page 361.]

Laws of the Republic of Texas. In Two Volumes. Printed by Order of the Secretary of State. Volume 1 (and Vol. 2). Houston: Office of the Telegraph, 1838.

Vol. 1: 276, v p. Vol. 2: 122, v p. 20.5 cm.

The acts and resolutions of 1836 and 1837. Important acts relating to the protection of the frontiers against Indian depredations and hostilities.

REPORT

OF

G. W. BONNELL,

COMMISSIONER INDIAN AFFAIRS.

THIRD CONGRESS—FIRST SESSION.

Published by order of Congress.

HOUSTON:

1838.

Laws passed at the 2d Session of the 2d Congress of the Republic of Texas. April and May, 1838. [Houston? 1838.]

48, [2] p. 19.5 cm. Caption title.

Ordinances and Decrees of the Consultation, Provisional Government of Texas, and the Convention which assembled at Washington March 1, 1836. By Order of the Secretary of State. Houston: National Banner Office, 1838.

156, iii p. 20 cm.

Highly important acts on the negotiation of treaties with the Cherokees and the Comanches.

1839

Journal of the Proceedings of the General Council of the Republic of Texas, held at San Felipe de Austin, November 14th 1835. Houston: National Intelligencer Office, 1839.

363 p. 19 cm.

Excessively rare.

Laws of the Republic of Texas, passed the First Session of Third Congress, 1839. Houston: Intelligencer Office, 1839.

167, v p. 20.5 cm.

Important acts relating to hostilities with the Comanches and other Indians and to the employment of friendly Indians for service with the Texas militia.

Laws of the Republic of Texas, passed at the First Session of the Third Congress. In one volume. Houston: Telegraph Power Press, 1839.

145, v p. 19 cm.

Highly important acts relating to Indian hostilities, trade with the Indians, and protection of the frontiers against Indian depredations.

1841

Laws of the Republic of Texas, passed at the Session of the Fifth Congress. Printed by Order of the Secretary of State. Houston: Telegraph Power Press, 1841.

19 cm. [200], viii p.

Notices of Indian hostilities and provisions for protection of the frontier.

1842

Laws passed by the Sixth Congress of the Republic of Texas. Published by Authority. Austin: B. Whiting, 1842.

120, vii, viii p. 20 cm.

Important acts relating to the recovery of white citizens held in captivity by the Indians.

1843

Laws passed by the Seventh Congress of the Republic of Texas. Houston: Telegraph Office, 1843.

42, xxvi p. 19 cm.

Contains highly important acts for the establishment of peace and friendly trade with the Indians and for the protection of the frontiers from Indian depredations. The appendix is devoted to treaties between the Republic of Texas and Great Britain and the Netherlands.

1844

Proceedings of the Senate and Documents relative to Texas, from which the Injunction of Secrecy has been removed. [Washington, 1844.]*

119, 12, 1 p. 25.5 cm. Caption title.

Documents of the highest importance to the history of Texas, and hence, inferentially, to the history of her neighbors on the north.

SEDGWICK, WILLIAM E.

Thoughts on the Proposed Annexation of Texas to the United States. New York: D. Fanshaw, 1844.

55 p. 22 cm.

1845

HITCHCOCK, ETHAN ALLEN

Memorial to the Congress of the United States, from Officers of the United States Army, on the subject of Brevet and Staff Rank. Corpus Christi, December 12, 1845.

23 p. 20.5 cm. Plain wrappers.

Manuscript note, in the hand of E. A. Hitchcock, on front wrapper: "Corpus Christi. Decr. 1845. This Memorial on Brevet and Staff rank was written by myself. Pres. Polk re-established the regulation of 1829—as within." A rare imprint.

Proceedings of the Grand Royal Arch Chapter of the Republic of Texas, at their Annual Communications, in Washington, for Jan'y, A.L. 5844; R.A.M. 2374–'75; A.D. 1844–'45. National Vindicator Office, Washington, [Texas], 1845.

22 p. 20 cm. Printed wrappers.

A very rare Texas pamphlet.

1846

Articles of a Treaty made and concluded at Council Springs, in the County of Robinson, Texas, near the Brazos River, the 15th day of May, A.D. 1846, between P. M. Butler and M. G. Lewis, Commissioners on the part of the United States, of the one part, and the Chiefs, Counsellors, and Warriors of the Comanche, I-on-i, Ana-da-ca, Cadoe, Lepan, Long-wha, Keechy, Tah-wah-carro, Wichita, and Wacoe Tribes of Indians, and their Associate Bands, in behalf of their said Tribes, on the other part. [Washington, 1846.]*

15 p. 24 cm. Caption title. Uncut and unopened.

The excessively rare "confidential" printing, submitted to the Senate for ratification or rejection, which preceded the official folio edition of the ratified treaty. Two issues.

1847

CATLETT, H. G.

National Road to California. Public Meeting in Victoria. [Victoria, Texas, 1847.]*

8 p. 21.5 cm. Caption title.

Of the very highest degree of importance. The volume reports the proceedings of the meeting at Victoria which recommended the establishment of a road from the Gulf of Mexico to Chihuahua, to Passo del Norte, and to Santa Fe, and the immediate establishment of a permanent line of military posts from Fort Washita to Passo del Norte "as a present and perhaps permanent line of separation between the frontier of Texas and the Indian Territory," and contains a valuable communication by Captain Catlett in which the proposed routes are examined and discussed in detail. One of the rarest and most highly desirable items relating to Texas, to the Indians of the Southwest, and to the southern overland route to California. The volume is lacking from all the great Texas collections, public and private, and is not even mentioned by Wagner. But one other copy, that at Harvard College, is known to exist.

Darby, William

Notes in regard to my Survey of the Sabine River. [Washington, 1847.]*

Broadsheet. Folio.

Darby claims to have done much of the work in the Southwest for which Melish took credit. Very rare.

Texas Indians—Report of Messrs. Butler and Lewis. Letter from the Secretary of War transmitting a Report of Messrs. Butler and Lewis relative to the Indians of Texas and the Southwestern Prairies. [Washington, 1847.]

9 p. 22.5 cm. Caption title.

A highly important report.

1848

Communication from the Commissioner of Indian Affairs, and other Documents in relation to the Indians in Texas. [Washington, 1848.]

52 p. 22.5 cm. Caption title.

A vitally important document not noted by Raines or Field.

1850

Articles of a Treaty made and concluded on Spring Creek, near the River San Saba, in the Indian country of the State of Texas, this, the 10th day of December, A.D. 1850, between John H. Rollins, Special Agent of the United States for the Indians of Texas, acting for the United States on the one part, and the undersigned Chiefs, Warriors, Captains and Councillors, for themselves and for those under their control, and acknowledging their authority, on the other part . . . . [San Antonio, 1850.]*

[3] p. Folio.

A treaty, never ratified, between the United States and the Comanches, Caddoes, Lipans, Quapas, Tawacanoes, and Wacoes, and hence not elsewhere available. The text of the treaty is prefaced by Order No. 69, Head Quarters 8th Military Department, San Antonio, Dec. 25, 1850, pointing out that the treaty has not been sanctioned by the United States Government or by the State of Texas but urging officers of the army to carry out the spirit of its terms. A rarity of superlative importance. No other copy can be traced.

1853

Report of the Secretary of State, communicating Certain Correspondence relative to the Encroachments of the Indians of the United States upon the Territories of Mexico. [Washington, 1853.]*

135 p. 25 cm. Caption title.

A document of the highest interest and importance. A fine copy, uncut and unopened.

1856

YOAKUM, HENDERSON

History of Texas from its First Settlement in 1685 to its Annexation to the United States in 1846. New York: Redfield, 1856.

2 vols. 23 cm.

A very fine set.

1870

Headquarters Department of Texas, San Antonio, Texas, November 25, 1870. General Orders, No. 77. [San Antonio, 1870.]

10 p. 20.5 cm. Caption title.

Instructions and suggestions on frontier service, with specific attention to Indian warfare.

1871

COOPER, CALVIN

The following is a Description of a Little Son of Francis M. Whitlock, deceased, killed by the Indians on the 27th Dec., 1870, together with Whitlock's Entire Family, except the aforesaid Son, who, it is supposed, was Carried into Captivity at the time of the aforesaid Terrible Slaughter. [Burnett, Texas, 1871.]

Broadside. 28 cm.

Signed: Calvin Cooper, Grandfather of aforesaid Boy.

An appeal for assistance in recovering the child. Unrecorded, and the only known copy.

1872

Herald Extra!! Indians—Retaliation—Serious Results. [Kinney, Texas, 1872.]

Broadside. 20 cm.

A spirited account of a Mexican Indian raid into Texas and of a retaliatory excursion by Texans into Mexico. Unrecorded, and the only known copy.

1875

Adjutant General's Report. [Austin, Texas, 1875.]

15 p. 20.5 cm. Caption title.

An important record of Indian depredations, forays, and skirmishes.

Memorial. Committee Room, Austin, Nov. 24, 1875. To the Hon. E. B. Pickett, President of the Constitutional Convention of the State of Texas. [Austin, 1875.]

4 p. 22.5 cm. Caption title.

A plea to secure the southern borders of Texas from Mexico and the northern borders from Indian depredations.

Reports of the Committee of Investigation sent in 1873 by the Mexican Government to the Frontier of Texas. Translated from the Official Edition made in Mexico. New York: Baker & Godwin, 1875.*

viii, 443 p. 22.5 cm. Maps.

The committee was charged with the investigation of Indian raids and depredations.

1876

SHAFTER, W. R.

[Report of Operations against the Indians in Western Texas and New Mexico. Fort Duncan, 1876.]

13 p. 20.5 cm. Printed without title page or caption.

Colonel Shafter employed Seminole scouts.

1879

ORD, E. O. C.

Report relative to Certain Information connected with his Department, and the Security and Protection of the Texas Frontier. [San Antonio, 1879.]

28, [2] p. 19.5 cm. Folded table.

Headed: Headquarters Department of Texas, San Antonio, Texas, Dec. 1, 1879. Brigadier General E. O. C. Ord, Commanding.

A very fine copy. No other copy can be traced.

1880

ORD, E. O. C.

Annual Report for the year ending Sept. 30, 1880. [San Antonio, 1880.]

7, 19, 6, 16, [1], 4, 9, 10, 8, [2], 4, 3 p. 20 cm. Wrapper title.

Headed: Headquarters Department of Texas, San Antonio, Texas, October 1, 1880. E. O. C. Ord, Brevet Major General Commanding.

1884

Special Report of the Adjutant-General of the State of Texas. September, 1884. Austin: E. W. Swindells, State Printer, 1884.

51 p. 22.5 cm. Printed wrappers. Folded table.

An important report on depredations by the Indians and on military operations against them.

STANLEY, D. S.

Headquarters Department of Texas, San Antonio, Texas, September 30, 1884. D. S. Stanley, Brigadier General (Brevet Major General), commanding. Annual Report. [San Antonio, 1884.]

5, 2, 16, 4, [8], [1], 2, 4, 7, 10, [1], 6, [1], 2, 3, [1], [1] p. 20 cm. Folded table.

An exceptionally full and complete report on conditions in his department, with rosters and descriptions of posts, Indian reconnaissances, and diseases. No other copy can be traced.

1896

RAINES, C. W.

A Bibliography of Texas: being a Descriptive List of Books, Pamphlets, and Documents relating to Texas in print and manuscript since 1536, including a Complete Collection of the Laws; with an Introductory Essay on the Materials of Early Texas History. Austin, Texas: Gammel Book Co., 1896.

xvi, 268 p. 26 cm.

An indispensable bibliography.

1901

ADAMS, RICHARD C.

A Brief Sketch of the Sabine Land Cession in Texas, lying between the Angelina and Nethes Rivers and West and North of the Old San Antonio Road, made by the Republic of Texas, to the Cherokees, Delawares, Shawnees and Associated Bands, made by Treaty and signed by General Sam Houston and others, February 23, 1836, under authority of "The Consultation of Texas, in General Convention assembled," Nov. 13th, 1835, and under authority of the Resolutions of the General Council of the Provisional Government of Texas of December 22, 1835, and December 28, 1835. Washington: John Byrne & Co., [1901].*

78 p. 23 cm. Printed wrappers. Maps.

Adams was a Delaware Indian. A rare and important volume.

1903

WINKLER, ERNEST WILLIAM

The Cherokee Indians in Texas. [In The Quarterly of the Texas State Historical Association, Vol. 7, No. 2, October 1903.]*

1912

LOKER, WILLIAM

Alabama Indians of Texas. Report of William Loker and Letters to the Indian Department relative to the Alabama Indians of Texas. Washington, 1912.

18 p. 23 cm.

A brief but excellent survey. Included is a roll of the tribe.

1925

GILLETT, JAMES B.

Six years with the Texas Rangers, 1875–1881. By James B. Gillett. Edited, with an Introduction, by M. M. Quaife. New Haven: Yale University Press, 1925.*

xvi, 259 p. 23.5 cm. Plates.

A lively narrative.

TRAVEL AND DESCRIPTION

1650

RALEIGH, WALTER

Judicious and Select Essayes and Observations. By that Renowned and Learned Knight, Sir Walter Raleigh. Upon the First Invention of Shipping, the Misery of Invasive Warre, the Navy Royall and Sea-Service. With his Apologie for his Voyage to Guiana. London: T. W. and Humphrey Mosele, 1650.

[10], 42, [2], [64], [2], [46], [2], 69 p. 14 cm. Frontisp. port.

The rare first edition. [See page 368.]

JUDICIOUS
AND
Select Essayes
AND
OBSERVATIONS.

By that RENOWNED and
Learned KNIGHT.

Sir *WALTER RALEIGH*.

UPON

The first Invention of Shipping.
The Misery of Invasive Warre.
The Navy Royall and Sea-Service.

WITH HIS

Apologie for his voyage to Guiana.

Virtus recludens immeritis mori
Cælum, negatâ tentat iter viâ. Hor:

LONDON,
Printed by *T. W.* for *Humphrey Mosele*
and are to be Sold at the Princes Armes in
St. Pauls Church-yard. 1650.

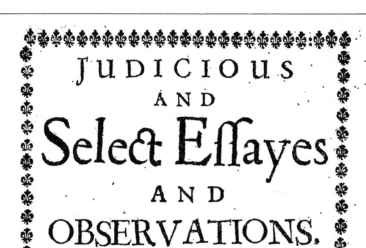

Tam Marti, Quam Mercurio.

The true and lively Portraiture of the Ho.ble and learned Knight S.r Walter Ralegh.

Ro: Vaughan. sculp:

1670

CLARKE, SAMUEL

A True, and Faithful Account of the Four Chiefest Plantations of the English in America. To wit, of Virginia, New-England, Bermudas, Barbados. With the Temperature of the Air: the Nature of the Soil; the Rivers, Mountains, Beasts, Fowls, Birds, Fishes, Trees, Plants, Fruits, &c. as also, of the Natives of Virginia, and New-England, their Religion, Customs, Fishing, Huntings, &c. Collected by Samuel Clarke, sometimes Pastor in Saint Bennett-Fink, London. London, Printed for Robert Clavel, Thomas Passenger, William Cadman, William Whitwood, Thomas Sawbridge, and William Birch. 1670.

85, 35 p. 30 cm.

The thirty-five pages at the end are often lacking. Very rare. [See page 371.]

1748

WALCOT, JAMES

The New Pilgrim's Progress: or, the Pious Indian Convert. Containing a Faithful Account of Hattain Gelashmin, a Heathen, who was Baptis'd into the Christian Faith by the name of George James, and by that means Brought from the Darkness of Paganism to the Light of the Gospel, of which he afterwards became an Able and Worthy Minister. Together with a Narrative of his Laborious and Dangerous Travels among the Savage Indians for their Conversion; his Many Sufferings and Miraculous Deliverances, and the Wonderful Things which he saw in a Vision. By James Walcot, A.M. London: M. Cooper. MDCCXLVIII.

[1], 316 p. 17 cm.

The rare first edition.

1767

MITCHELL, JOHN

The Present State of Great Britain and North America, with regard to Agriculture, Population, Trade, and Manufactures, impartially considered: containing a Particular Account of the Dearth and Scarcity of the Necessaries of Life in England; the Want of Staple Commodities in the Colonies; the Decline of their Trade; Increase of People; and Necessity of Manufactures, as well as of Trade in them hereafter. In which the Causes and Consequences of these Growing Evils, and Methods of Preventing them, are suggested; the Proper Regulations for the Colonies, and the Taxes Imposed upon them, are considered, and compared with their Condition and Circumstances. London: T. Becket, 1757.

[8], xvi, 363, [1] p. 20.5 cm.

Contains important notices of the Indians and of the Indian trade.

1768

BOSSU, M.

Nouveaux voyages aux Indes Occidentalles; contenant une relation differens peuples qui habitent les environs du grand Fleuve Saint-Louis, appelle vulgairement le Mississippi; leur religion; leur gouvernement; leurs maeurs; leurs guerres & leur commerce. Paris, 1768.

2 vols. in one. 17 cm. Plates.

A True, and Faithful

ACCOUNT

OF THE

FOUR CHIEFEST

PLANTATIONS

OF THE

English in America.

TO WIT,

Of { *VIRGINIA.*
NEW-ENGLAND.
BERMUDUS.
BARBADOS. }

With the temperature of the Air: The nature of the Soil: The Rivers, Mountains, Beasts, Fowls, Birds, Fishes, Trees, Plants, Fruits, *&c.*

AS ALSO,

Of the Natives of *Virginia*, and *New-England*, their Religion, Customs, Fishing, Huntings, *&c.*

COLLECTED
By *Samuel Clarke*, sometimes Pastor in Saint *Bennet-Fink*, London.

LONDON,
Printed for *Robert Clavel*, *Thomas Passenger*, *William Cadman*, *William Whitwood*, *Thomas Sawbridge*, and *William Birch*. 1670.

1770

BURKE, EDMUND

An Account of the European Settlements in America. The Fifth Edition, with Improvements. London: J. Dodsley, 1770.

2 vols. Maps.

A valuable account, with considerable attention to the Indians. A fine copy.

1775

ADAIR, JAMES

The History of the American Indians; particularly those Nations adjoining to the Mississippi, East and West Florida, Georgia, South and North Carolina, and Virginia: containing an Account of their Origin, Language, Manners, Religious and Civil Customs, Laws, Form of Government, Punishments, Conduct in War and Domestic Life, their Habits, Diet, Agriculture, Manufactures, Diseases and Method of Cure, and other Particulars, sufficient to render it a Complete Indian System. With Observations on former Historians, the Conduct of our Colony Governors, Superintendents, Missionaries, &c. Also an Appendix, containing a Description of the Floridas, and the Mississippi Lands, with their Productions—the Benefits of Colonising Georgiana, and Civilizing the Indians—and the way to make all the Colonies more valuable to the Mother Country. With a new Map of the Country referred to in the History. By James Adair, Esquire, a Trader with the Indians, and Resident in their Country for Forty Years. London: Printed for Edward and Charles Dilly, in the Poultry. MDCCLXXV.

[12], 464 p. 30 cm. Original boards. Map.

The large paper edition, which is very rare.

1784

BENEZET, ANTHONY

Some Observations on the Situation, Disposition, and Character of the Indian Natives of this Continent. Philadelphia: Joseph Crukshank, M DCC LXXXIV.*

59 p. 16 cm.

HUTCHINS, THOMAS

An Historical Narrative and Topographical Description of Louisiana and West-Florida, comprehending the River Mississippi, its Principal Branches and Settlements, and the Rivers Pearl, Pascagoula, Mobille, Perdido, Escambia, Chacta-Hatcha, &c. By Thomas Hutchins, Geographer to the United States. Philadelphia: Printed for the Author. M.DCC.LXXXIV.

94, [1] p. 20.5 cm.

A rare and valuable account of the southern Indians.

1807

PERRIN DU LAC

Travels through the Two Louisianas, and among the Savage Nations of the Missouri; also, in the United States, along the Ohio, and the Adjacent Provinces, in 1801, 1802, & 1803. With a Sketch of the Manners, Customs, Character, and the Civil and

Religious Ceremonies of the People of those Countries. By M. Perrin du Lac. Translated from the French. London: Richard Phillips, 1807.

106, [2] p. 21 cm.

Robin, C. C.

Voyages dans l'interieur de la Louisiane, de la Floride Occidentalle, et dans les isles de la Martinique, et de Saint-Domingue, pendant les annees 1802, 1803, 1804, 1805 et 1806. Paris, 1807.

3 vols.

The map is lacking.

1810

Cuming, F.

Sketches of a Tour to the Western Country, through the States of Ohio and Kentucky; a Voyage down the Ohio and Mississippi Rivers, and a Trip through the Mississippi Territory, and part of West Florida. Commenced at Philadelphia in the Winter of 1807, and concluded in 1809. By F. Cuming. With Notes and an Appendix, containing some Interesting Facts, together with a Notice of an Expedition through Louisiana. Pittsburg: Cramer, Spear & Eichbaum, 1810.

504 p. 17 cm.

A fine copy of a rare and important volume.

Pike, Zebulon

An Account of Expeditions to the Sources of the Mississippi, and through the Western Parts of Louisiana, to the Sources of the Arkansaw, Kans, La Platte, and Pierre Jaun Rivers; performed by Order of the Government of the United States during the years 1805, 1806, and 1807. And a Tour through the Interior Parts of New Spain, when conducted through these Provinces by Order of the Captain-General, in the year 1807. By Major Z. M. Pike. Philadelphia, C. & A. Conrad.

Complete, with all maps and charts. 23 cm.

Wagner-Camp 9. Field 1217.

1815

Melish, John

The Traveller's Directory through the United States: consisting of a Geographical Description of the United States, with Topographical Tables of the Counties, Towns, Population, &c. and a Description of the Roads, compiled from the most Authentic Materials. By John Melish. Philadelphia: Printed for the Author, 1815.

32, 82 p. 17.5 cm. Maps.

Shows distances in the Indian country of the South.

Mills, Samuel J., and Daniel Smith

Report of a Missionary Tour through that Part of the United States which lies West of the Allegany Mountains; performed under the Direction of the Massachusetts Missionary Society. Andover: Flagg & Gould, 1815.*

64 p. 21.5 cm.

Very scarce.

1822

The Connecticut Emigrant. A Dialogue between Henry, an Intended Emigrant; Mary, his Wife; Hezekiah, his Father; Hepzibah, his Mother; George, his Son. By a Descendant of the Connecticut Pilgrims. Hartford: Printed for the Purchasers. 1822.

12 p. 19 cm. Plain wrappers.

Life in the rude and uncivilized West unfavorably compared with the culture and security of life in New England. The volume is rare, and this is a fine copy.

MORSE, JEDEDIAH

A Report to the Secretary of War of the United States on Indian Affairs, comprising a Narrative of a Tour performed in the Summer of 1820 under a Commission from the President of the United States, for the Purpose of Ascertaining, for the Use of the Government, the Actual State of the Indian Tribes in our Country. New Haven: S. Converse, 1822.

400 p. 23.5 cm. Original printed boards.

In a protective case.

"The most complete and exhaustive report of the condition, numbers, names, territory, and general affairs of the Indians ever made."—Field 1098.

1824

HODGSON, ADAM

Letters from North America, written during a Tour in the United States and Canada. London: Hurst, Robinson & Co., 1824.

2 vols. 21.5 cm. Maps.

A fine copy, presented to William Scoresby, the Arctic explorer, with inscription by the author on dedication page, and with A. L. S. to Scoresby tipped in. The letters throw valuable light on the ethnology, social conditions, and political temper of the southern Indians.

1825

CHAPIN, WALTER

The Missionary Gazetteer, comprising a View of the Inhabitants, and a Geographical Description of the Countries and Places, where Protestant Missionaries have Labored. By Walter Chapin, Pastor of the Church in Woodstock, Vermont. Woodstock: David Watson, 1825.

[4], 420 p. 17 cm.

Field 279.

The volume contains many factual articles on missions to the American Indians.

WETMORE, ALPHONSO

Petition of Sundry Inhabitants of the State of Missouri upon the subject of a Communication between the said State and the Internal Provinces of Mexico, with a Letter from Alphonso Wetmore upon the same subject. Washington: Gales & Seaton, 1825.*

8 p. 22 cm.

Wetmore's letter is a highly important account of the Santa Fe trade.

1832

McCLUNG, JOHN A.

Sketches of Western Adventure: containing an Account of the Most Interesting

Incidents connected with the Settlement of the West, from 1755 to 1794: together with an Appendix. By John A. McClung. Philadelphia: Grigg & Elliot, 1832.

360 p. 20.5 cm.

Field 975.

A very fine, perhaps the very finest copy, of this well-known classic; uncut, and in original boards, with paper label. Laid in is an autograph letter of the author.

1835

FEATHERSTONHAUGH, G. W.

Geological Report of an Examination made in 1834, of the Elevated Country between the Missouri and Red Rivers. By G. W. Featherstonhaugh, U.S. Geologist. Washington: Gales & Seaton, 1835.

97 p. 23 cm. Plain wrappers. Folded colored profile.

IRVING, WASHINGTON

The Crayon Miscellany. By the Author of the Sketch Book. No. 1. Containing A Tour of the Prairies. Philadelphia: Carey, Lea & Blanchard. 1835.

274 p. 18 cm.

Langfeld, p. 33. Field 763. Wagner-Camp 56.

The first issue.

LATROBE, CHARLES JOSEPH

The Rambler in North America, MDCCCXXXII–MDCCCXXXIII. New York: Harper & Bros., 1835.

2 vols. 18.5 cm.

The author accompanied Washington Irving on his tour of the prairies, and a large part of each volume is devoted to personal observations of Indian life. The American edition of Wagner-Camp 57.

1836

HILDRETH, JAMES

Dragoon Campaigns to the Rocky Mountains: being a History of the Enlistment, Organization, and First Campaigns of the Regiment of United States Dragoons; together with Incidents of a Soldier's Life, and Sketches of Scenery and Indian Character. By a Dragoon. New York: Wiley & Long, 1836.

288 p. 19 cm.

Wagner-Camp 59. Field 692.

1841

DE SMET, PIERRE JEAN

The Indian Missions in the United States of America, under the care of the Missouri Province of the Society of Jesus. Philadelphia. King & Baird, 1841.

34 p. 18 cm.

An authoritative volume, which possesses the highest degree of rarity and importance. Not recorded in the Union Catalog, and no other copy traced.

1843

LANG, JOHN D., and SAMUEL TAYLOR

Report of a Visit to some of the Tribes of Indians located West of the Mississippi

River, by John D. Lang and Samuel Taylor, Jun. New York: M. Day & Co., 1843.

34 p. 21.5 cm. Printed wrappers.

See Wagner-Camp 96.

1844

GREGG, JOSIAH

Commerce of the Prairies: or the Journal of a Santa Fe Trader, during Eight Expeditions across the Great Western Prairies, and a Residence of nearly Nine Years in Northern Mexico. New York: Henry G. Langley, 1844.

2 vols.

Wagner-Camp 108. Field 625.

A fine copy, in a protective case.

HARRIS, N. SAYRE

Journal of a Tour in the "Indian Territory," performed by Order of the Domestic Committee of the Board of Missions of the Protestant Episcopal Church, in the Spring of 1844. By their Secretary and General Agent. New York, [1844].

74 p. 21.5 cm. Wrapper title. Color map.

The June, 1844, Extra Number of *The Spirit of Missions,* wholly devoted to the Harris journal. The first issue, not noted by Wagner-Camp.

HARRIS, N. SAYRE

Journal of a Tour in the "Indian Territory," performed by Order of the Domestic Committee of the Board of Missions of the Protestant Episcopal Church, in the Spring of 1844, by their Secretary and General Agent. New York: Daniel Dana Jr., 1844.*

74 p. 22 cm. Printed wrappers. 3 maps.

Wagner-Camp 109.

A fine copy.

KENDALL, GEORGE WILKINS

Narrative of the Texan Santa Fe Expedition, comprising a Description of a Tour through Texas, and across the Great Southwestern Prairies, the Camanche and Cayuga Hunting-Grounds, with an Account of the Sufferings from Want of Food, Losses from Hostile Indians, and Final Capture of the Texans, and their March, as Prisoners, to the City of Mexico. New York: Harper & Bros., 1844.

2 vols. 20 cm. Plates and map.

Field 818. Wagner-Camp 110.

1846

McKENNEY, THOMAS L.

Memoirs, Official and Personal; with Sketches of Travels among the Northern and Southern Indians; embracing a War Excursion, and Descriptions of Scenes along the Western Borders. Second Edition. New York: Paine and Burgess, 1846.

2 vols. in one. 340, 136 p. 23 cm. Plates, one, a portrait of Pocahontas, in color.

Field 993.

1848

WISLIZENUS, A.

Memoir of a Tour to Northern Mexico, connected with Col. Doniphan's Expedition. Washington: Tippin & Streeper, 1848.

141 p. 25 cm. Maps. Profile.

Wagner-Camp 159.

A fine copy, entirely uncut and unopened.

1850

SIMPSON, JAMES HERVEY

Route from Fort Smith to Santa Fe. Letter from the Secretary of War, transmitting a Report and Map of Lieutenant Simpson of the Route from Fort Smith to Santa Fe; also, a Report on the same subject from Captain R. B. Marcy, 5th Infantry. [Washington, 1850.]

89 p. 25 cm. Map. 2 plates.

This edition is not noted by Wagner-Camp.

SIMPSON, JAMES HERVEY

Report of the Secretary of War communicating the Report and Map of the Route from Fort Smith, Arkansas, to Santa Fe, New Mexico made by Lieutenant Simpson.

25 p. 24.5 cm. Caption title. 4 maps.

Wagner-Camp 192. An uncut and unopened copy.

1851

BAYLIES, FRANCIS

A Narrative of Major General Wool's Campaign in Mexico, in the Years 1846, 1847 & 1848. By Francis Baylies, Massachusetts. Albany, N.Y.: Little & Co., 1851.

78 p. 23 cm. Printed wrappers. Portrait.

A fine copy.

STEVENS, ISAAC I.

Campaigns of the Rio Grande and of Mexico. With Notices of the Recent Work of Major Ripley. Brevet-Major Isaac I. Stevens, U.S. Army. New York: D. Appleton & Co., 1851.*

108 p. 23.5 cm. Printed wrappers.

A fine copy.

WHIPPLE, AMIEL WEEKS

Report of the Secretary of War communicating the Report of Lieutenant Whipple's Expedition from San Diego to the Colorado. [Washington, 1851.]

28 p. 25 cm. Caption title. Uncut and unopened.

Not noted by Wagner-Camp.

1854

LOWRIE, JOHN C.

A Manual of Missions; or, Sketches of the Foreign Missions of the Presbyterian Church: with Maps, showing the Stations, and Statistics of Protestant Missions among Unevangelized Nations. By John C. Lowrie, one of the Secretaries of the Board of

Foreign Missions of the Presbyterian Church. New York: Anson D. F. Randolph, 1854.*

74 p. 19 cm. 6 color maps and 1 view.

The map opposite page (15) which shows the location of the various Indian tribes in the West is a valuable one.

Nebraska and Kansas. Report of the Committee of the Massachusetts Emigrant Aid Co., with the Act of Incorporation and other documents. Boston: Published for the Massachusetts Emigrant Aid Co. 1854.

32 p. 19.5 cm.

1855

Lowrie, John C.

A Manual of Missions: or, Sketches of the Foreign Missions of the Presbyterian Church, with Maps showing the Stations; and Statistics of Protestant Missions among Unevangelized Nations. Second edition. New York: Anson D. F. Randolph, 1855.

144 p. 18.5 cm. Maps.

Pages 26–47 contain an account of missions to the American Indians. At page 26 is a folded map showing, with considerable detail, the location of Indian tribes in the United States.

1858

Reid, John C.

Reid's Tramp: or, A Journal of the Incidents of Ten Months Travel through Texas, New Mexico, Arizona, Sonora, and California. Including Topography, Climate, Soil, Minerals, Metals, and Inhabitants; with a Notice of the Great Inter-oceanic Rail Road. By John C. Reid. Selma, Alabama. Printed at the Book and Job Office of John Hardy, 1858.

237 p. 21 cm.

Wagner-Camp 307.

A very fine copy of a prime rarity, in a protective case.

1859

Marcy, Randolph B.

The Prairie Traveler. A Hand-book for Overland Expeditions. With Maps, Illustrations, and Itineraries of the Principal Routes between the Mississippi and the Pacific. By Randolph B. Marcy, Captain U.S. Army. New York: Harper & Bros., 1859.

340 p. 16.5 cm. Folded map. Illustrations. Frontisp. view of Fort Smith.

Wagner-Camp 335.

1860

Beale, Edward Fitzgerald

Wagon Road—Fort Smith to Colorado River. Letter of the Secretary of War transmitting the Report of Mr. Beale relating to the Construction of a Wagon Road from Fort Smith to the Colorado River. [Washington, 1860.]

91 p. 25 cm. Caption title. Folded map. Uncut and unopened.

Wagner-Camp 350.

CARLETON, JAMES HENRY

Report on the Subject of the Massacre at the Mountain Meadows, in Utah Territory, in September, 1857, of One Hundred and Twenty Men, Women, and Children, who were from Arkansas. By Brevet Major James Henry Carleton, U.S. Army. And Report of the Hon. William C. Mitchell, relative to the Seventeen Surviving Children who were brought back by the Authorities of the U.S. after their parents and others, with whom they were Emigrating, had been Murdered. Little Rock: True Democrat Steam Press, 1860.

32 p. 23 cm.

A classic rarity of the West, and one of the most valuable and highly desirable volumes in this entire collection. Wagner-Camp 354 locates only two copies.

The Central Overland California and Pike's Peak Express Company. Pony Express to San Francisco in Ten Days. Passenger Express to Denver City and Pike's Peak Gold Regions in Five Days. New York: R. C. Root, Anthony & Co., [1860].

4 p. 19 cm. Printed in red and blue.

The first page has a cut showing a horse and rider of the Pony Express.

Accompanied by a card, printed at Leavenworth City, Kansas, and dated Sept. 8, 1860, announcing a reduction of postage from Leavenworth City and St. Joseph to Denver City.

Neither item is recorded, and each may be the only copy known.

1869

Military Division of the Missouri, comprising the Department of the Missouri, Department of the Platte, Department of Dakota, commanded by Lieutenant General P. H. Sheridan, Headquarters, Chicago, Illinois. Troops: Cavalry. 2d, 3d, 5th, 7th and 10th. Artillery. 1st, Battery "K"; 2d, Battery "A"; 3d, Battery "C"; 4th, Battery "B". Infantry. 3d, 4th, 5th, 7th, 9th, 15th, 20th and 22d. September 30, 1869. [Chicago, 1869.]*

[15] p. 20.5 cm.

Virtually a directory of Indian fighters in a large section of the West.

1871

Brief Description of the Public Lands of the United States of America. Prepared by the Commissioner of the General Land Office for the Information of Foreigners Seeking a Home in the United States. Washington, 1871.*

16 p. 23 cm. Folded map, with German legend.

1873

BEADLE, J. H.

The Undeveloped West; or, Five Years in the Territories. Philadelphia: National Printing Company, [1873].

823 p. 21 cm.

Brief Description of the Public Lands of the United States of America. Prepared by the Commissioner of the General Land-Office for the Information of Foreigners Seeking a Home in the United States. Washington, 1873.*

16 p. 23 cm. Folded map.

Roster of Troops serving in the Department of the Platte, commanded by Brigadier General E. O. C. Ord. Omaha, Nebraska, 1873.

15 p. 20.5 cm.

1874

GLISAN, R.

Journal of Army Life. By R. Glisan. San Francisco: Bancroft, 1874.*

xi, 511 p. 22 cm. Folded table. Plates.

A valuable and highly readable narrative of life at various Indian frontier posts in the Southwest and of participation in Indian wars in the Far West.

POWELL, J. W.

Report of Explorations in 1873 of the Colorado of the West and its Tributaries, by Professor J. W. Powell. Washington, 1874.*

36 p. 23.5 cm. Printed wrappers.

1875

MARGRY, PIERRE

Decouvertes et etablissements des Francais dans l'ouest et dans le sud de l'Amerique Septentrionale (1614–1754). Memoires et documents originaux. Paris, 1875–1886.

6 vols. Original wrappers.

A fine set. A primary source of incomparable richness and value.

1876

COUES, ELLIOTT

An Account of the Various Publications relating to the Travels of Lewis and Clarke, with a Commentary on the Zoological Results of their Expedition. [Washington, 1876.]

Pp. 417–99. 22 cm. Printed wrappers.

An indispensable guide.

1877

PUMPHREY, STANLEY

Indian Civilization: a Lecture by Stanley Pumphrey of England. With an Introduction by John G. Whittier. Philadelphia, 1877.

52 p. 23.4 cm. Printed wrappers. Large folded color map of Indian Territory.

1880

RITTENHOUSE, RUFUS

Boyhood Life in Iowa Forty Years Ago, as found in the Memoirs of Rufus Rittenhouse. Dubuque: Chas. B. Dorr, 1880.

23 p. 19.5 cm. Printed wrappers.

Very scarce.

1882

SHERIDAN, PHILIP H.

Report of Lieut. General P. H. Sheridan, dated September 20, 1881, on his

Expedition through the Big Horn Mountains, Yellowstone National Park, etc., together with Reports of Lieut. Col. J. F. Gregory, A.D.C., Surgeon W. H. Forwood, and Capt. S. C. Kellogg, Fifth Cavalry. Washington, 1882.

39 p. 23 cm. 2 folded maps.

1884

ARMSTRONG, S. C.

Report of a Trip made in behalf of the Indian Rights Association to some Indian Reservations of the Southwest. Philadelphia, 1884.*

30 p. 22 cm. Printed wrappers.

1887

BRISTOL, S.

The Pioneer Preacher. Incidents of Interest, and Experiences in the Author's Life. Revival Labors in the Frontier Settlements. A Perilous Trip across the Plains in time of Indian wars, and before the Railroads. Three Years in the Mining Camps of California and Idaho. Twenty-one Years' Residence in Southern California, etc. By Rev. S. Bristol, San Buena Ventura, Cal. Illustrated by Isabelle Bloof. Chicago and New York, [1887].

330 p. 19 cm.

1890

A Business Outing in Texas. A Visit of the Commercial Club of Kansas City to Northern Texas, Indian Territory, Oklahoma, and Kansas. Kansas City, [1890].*

58, [5] p. 24.5 cm. Illus.

1892

FREEMAN, G. D.

Midnight and Noonday or the Incidental History of Southern Kansas and the Indian Territory, giving Twenty Years Experience on the Frontier; also the Murder of Pat. Hennesey, and the Hanging of Tom. Smith, at Ryland's Ford, and Facts concerning the Talbot Raid on Caldwell. Also the Death Dealing Career of McCarty and Incidents happening in and around Caldwell, Kansas, from 1871 until 1890. By G. D. Freeman, Caldwell, Kansas 1892. [Caldwell, 1892.]

406 p. 19.5 cm. Frontisp. port. and illus.

1893

BARNUM, FRANCIS

Life on the Alaska Mission with an Account of the Foundation of the Mission and the Work Performed. By the Rev. Francis Barnum, S.J. For Private Circulation Only. Woodstock (Md.) College Press, 1893.*

39 p. 23 cm.

An important narrative of a residence among the Eskimo. The Woodstock Papers, printed in extremely small numbers for private circulation, are virtually unobtainable.

1897

Government Lands. The Comanche, Kiowa and Apache Lands soon to be Opened to Settlement. A Tract of Land rich in Mineral, with Fine Timber and Good

Water; a Tract of Land beautiful in Scenery and rich for Agricultural Purposes. [Perry, 1897.]*

4 p. 15 cm. Caption title.

The only known copy.

INMAN, HENRY

The Old Santa Fe Trail. The Story of a Great Highway. New York: Macmillan, 1897.*

xvi, [1], 493 p. 22 cm. Map. Port., and illus.

LEUPP, FRANCIS E.

Notes of a Summer Tour among the Indians of the Southwest. Philadelphia, 1897.

26 p. 23 cm. Printed wrappers.

1898

FOWLER, JACOB

The Journal of Jacob Fowler narrating an Adventure from Arkansas through the Indian Territory, Oklahoma, Kansas, Colorado, and New Mexico, to the Sources of the Rio Grande del Norte, 1821–22. Edited, with Notes, by Elliott Coues. New York: Francis P. Harper, 1898.

xxiv, 183 p. 23 cm.

1899

PEARNE, THOMAS HALL

Sixty-one Years of Itinerant Christian Life in Church and State. Cincinnati and New York, 1899.*

506 p. 19.5 cm.

1902

CARLETON, J. H.

Special Report of the Mountain Meadow Massacre. By J. H. Carleton, Brevet Major, United States Army, First Dragoons. Washington, 1902.*

17 p. 23 cm. Wrapper title.

1905

DODGE, GRENVILLE M.

Biographical Sketch of James Bridger, Mountaineer, Trapper, and Guide. New York: Unz & Co., 1905.

27 p. 23 cm. Folded view. Photographs.

1907

STANLEY, E. J.

Life of Rev. L. B. Stateler, or Sixty-five Years on the Frontier. Containing Incidents, Anecdotes, and Sketches of Methodist History in the West and Northwest. Nashville, 1907.

xvii, 356 p. 19 cm.

A scarce and valuable account. Stateler spent many years among the Indians in Kansas and Indian Territory. The latter portion of the volume narrates his experiences in Montana.

1909

Carrington, Henry B.

The Indian Question. An Address, by General Henry B. Carrington, U.S.A. Boston: DeWolfe & Fiske, [1909].*

32 p. 22.5 cm. Printed wrappers. Map.

With supplemental matter on the Fort Phil Kearney Massacre and the 1866 expedition to open the wagon road to Montana.

1914

Callison, J. J.

Bill Jones of Paradise Valley, Oklahoma. His Life and Adventures for over Forty Years in the Great Southwest. He was a Pioneer in the Days of the Buffalo, the Wild Indian, the Oklahoma Boomer, the Cowboy and the Outlaw. By John J. Callison, Kingfisher, Oklahoma. [Chicago, 1914.]

328 p. 19 cm. Illustrated.

Hughes, John T.

Doniphan's Expedition. Account of the Conquest of New Mexico. General Kearney's Overland Expedition to California; Doniphan's Campaign against the Navajos; his Unparalleled March upon Chihuahua and Durango; and the Operations of General Price at Santa Fe. Washington, 1914.*

202 p. 23 cm. Printed wrappers.

A reprint of the Cincinnati 1847 edition.

1915

Young, Harry (Sam)

Hard Knocks: a Life of the Vanishing Past. Chicago: Laid & Lee, [1915].*

242, [1] p. 18.5 cm. Illus.

1916

James, Thomas

Three Years among the Indians and Mexicans. By General Thomas James, of Monroe County, Illinois. Edited, with Notes and Biographical Sketches, by Walter B. Douglas. Saint Louis: Missouri Historical Society, 1916.

316 p. 21.5 cm. Portraits.

The original edition of 1846 is unobtainable and this reprint is itself now hard to come by. See Wagner-Camp 121.

Schiller, Rudolf

The Ordaz and Dortal Expeditions in Search of El-Dorado, as described on Sixteenth Century Maps. Washington, 1916.*

15 p. 24.5 cm. Printed wrappers. Plates.

1917

Pelzer, Louis

Marches of the Dragoons in the Mississippi Valley. An Account of Marches and

Activities of the First Regiment United States Dragoons in the Mississippi Valley between the years 1833 and 1850. Iowa City, 1917.

x, 282 p. 22.5 cm.

1919

Akin, James, Jr.

The Journal of James Akin Jr. Edited by Edward Everett Dale. Norman, Oklahoma, 1919.*

32 p. 21.5 cm. Wrapper title. Map. With autograph inscription by the editor.

The annotated journal of a trip from Iowa to Oregon in 1852.

1923

Twitchell, Ralph Emerson

Dr. Josiah Gregg, Historian of the Santa Fe Trail. By Ralph Emerson Twitchell. Santa Fe: New Mexican Publishing Corp., [1923?].*

45 p. 23 cm. Printed wrappers. Port.

1925

Bond, Fred G.

Flatboating on the Yellowstone, 1877. New York, 1925.*

22 p. 25.5 cm. Printed wrappers. Frontisp. port.

1927

Drawings by A. DeBats in Louisiana, 1732–1735. Washington, 1927.*

8 p. 24 cm. Printed wrappers. Plates.

1936

Reed, Nathaniel

The Life of Texas Jack. Eight Years a Criminal—41 Years Trusting in God. [Tulsa, 1936.]*

55 p. 23 cm. Printed wrappers.

1939

Swanton, John R., and others

Final Report of the United States De Soto Expedition Commission. Washington, 1939.

xvi, 400 p. 23.5 cm. Maps.

A masterful presentation of all the available evidence on De Soto's probable itinerary through the southern states. The document is now out of print and unavailable.

1940

Bushnell, David I., Jr.

Sketches by Paul Kane in the Indian Country, 1845–1848. Washington, 1940.

25 p. 24.5 cm. Printed wrappers. Plates.

Colt, Katherine Gideon

The Letters of Peter Wilson, Soldier, Explorer and Indian Agent West of the Mississippi River. Baltimore: Wirth Bros., 1940.*

39 p. 25.5 cm. Printed wrappers. Photographs.

Undated

LOCKLEY, FRED., ed.

Captain Sol Tetherow, Wagon Train Master. Personal Narrative of his Son, Sam. Tetherow, who Crossed the Plains to Oregon, in 1845, and Personal Narrative of Jack McNemee, who was born in Portland, Oregon, in 1848, and whose Father built the Fourth House in Portland. Portland, [N.d.]*

27 p. 23 cm. Printed wrappers.
Inscribed by the editor.

Story of Fort Union and its Traders. [Williston, North Dakota, n.d.]*

48 p. 23 cm. Wrapper title. Illustrated.

TULSA

1889

Minutes of the First Session of the Indian Mission Conference of the Methodist Episcopal Church, held at Tulsa, Creek Nation, Indian Territory, March 21–25, 1889. Ottawa, Kansas: Ottawa Printing Co., [1889].*

20 p. 21.5 cm. Printed wrappers.
Rare.

1903

DICKERSON, PHILIP

History of Tulsa, I.T. Her Natural Advantages of Location, Climate, Fertile Soil, etc. A Railroad Centre of the Creek, Cherokee, and Osage Nations. [Tulsa, 1903.]

36 p. 19 cm. Wrapper title.
Rare.

1907

HOFFKINE, D. C., and B. C. HOFFKINE

Tulsa City Directory, 1907. Tulsa: Tulsa OK Press, [1907].

240 p. 24 cm.
Not recorded in Foreman.

UTAH INDIANS

1853

Acts and Resolutions passed at the Second Annual Session of the Legislative Assembly of the Territory of Utah, begun and held on the second Monday of December, 1852, at Great Salt Lake City. Also the Constitution of the State of Deseret and the Ordinances of said State now in force in the Territory of Utah. Published by Authority of the Legislative Assembly. Great Salt Lake City: George Hales, 1853.

168, [1] p. 20 cm.
Important resolutions relating to Indian affairs. This and the five volumes which immediately follow are among the very rarest of the early Utah laws.

1857

Acts and Resolutions passed at the Legislative Assembly of the Territory of Utah, during the Sixth Annual Session, 1856–7: together with the Laws of the United States applicable to Territories. Great Salt Lake City: James McKnight, 1857.

35, xi, 211 p. 19 cm.

Contains laws relating to the Indians.

1859

Acts and Resolutions of the Legislative Assembly of the Territory of Utah. Eighth Annual Session, for the years 1858–9. Also Memorials to Congress. Great Salt Lake City, Utah Territory: J. McKnight, 1859.

39, ii p. 18 cm.

Contains memorials on Indian affairs.

1860

Acts, Resolutions and Memorials passed by the Legislative Assembly of the Territory of Utah during the Ninth Annual Session, for the years 1859–60. Great Salt Lake City: John S. Davis, at the Mountaineer Office, 1860.

iv, 44 p. 17.5 cm.

1861

Acts, Resolutions and Memorials passed by the Legislative Assembly of the Territory of Utah, during the Tenth Annual Session, for the years 1860–61. Great Salt Lake City: Elias Smith, 1861.

[2], 50 p. 17.5 cm.

Contains a valuable memorial urging the removal of the Indians and the purchase of their lands for the whites.

1864

Acts, Resolutions and Memorials passed by the Legislative Assembly of the Territory of Utah, during the Thirteenth Annual Session, for the years 1863–64. Great Salt Lake City: Henry McEwan, 1864.

52 p. 18 cm.

Important memorials relating to Indian hostilities and Indian lands.

UTE INDIANS

1872

General Laws, Private Acts, Joint Resolutions, and Memorials, passed at the Ninth Session of the Legislative Assembly of the Territory of Colorado, convened at Denver, on the First Day of January, A.D. 1872, together with the Declaration of Independence, the Constitution of the United States, and the Organic Act of the Territory, with the Amendments thereto. Published by Authority. Central City: D. C. Collier, 1872.

245, [1] p. 22.5 cm. Printed wrappers.

Contains memorials and resolutions on Indian affairs. Rare.

1879

Annual Message of the President of the United States, to the Two Houses of Congress at the commencement of the Second Session of the Forty-sixth Congress. Washington, 1879.*

29 p. 23 cm. Printed wrappers.

The message contains notices of the White River Ute outbreak, the Mescalero atrocities, and illegal intrusions into Indian Territory.

1890

A Memorial to Congress asking No Change to be made in the Reservation of the Southern Ute Indians of Colorado such as shall Involve their Transfer to the Territory of Utah. Approved January 30, 1890. [Salt Lake City:] Geo. E. Lambert, [1890].*

3 p. 23 cm. Wrapper title.

1892

Kane, Francis Fisher, and Frank M. Riter

A Further Report to the Indian Rights Association on the Proposed Removal of the Southern Utes. [Philadelphia, 1892.]

32 p. 23 cm. Wrapper title.

1895

Leupp, Francis E.

The Latest Phase of the Southern Ute Question. Philadelphia, 1895.

39 p. 22.5 cm. Wrapper title. Map.

VIRGINIA INDIANS

1819–23

Hening, William Waller, ed.

The Statutes at Large; being a Collection of all the Laws of Virginia, from the First Session of the Legislature, in the Year 1619. New York, Philadelphia, and Richmond, 1819–1823.

13 vols.

For the period (1619–1792) covered by this work, Virginia embraced an immense portion of the present eastern and middle United States, and the hundreds of acts here included, many of them the earliest relating to the Indians of this vast area, easily rank as one of the most important original sources of information on the American aborigines. With its wealth of historical data, nowhere else available, the collection must forever remain one of the final authorities on the American Indians of the seventeenth and eighteenth centuries.

1883

Dinwiddie, Robert

The Official Records of Robert Dinwiddie, Lieutenant-Governor of the Colony of Virginia, 1751–1758, now First Printed from the Manuscript. R. A. Brock, ed. Richmond, Va., 1883.*

2 vols. Map. Portraits.

Of great value for its documents on the Indians, particularly the Cherokees.

1894

Pollard, John Garland

The Pamunkey Indians of Virginia, by John Garland Pollard. Washington, 1894.*

19 p. 24.5 cm. Printed wrappers.

With the autograph on the front wrapper of James Mooney, the Cherokee scholar. The principal source of information about this small tribe.

1930

Bushnell, David I., Jr.

The Five Monacan Towns in Virginia, 1607. Washington, 1930.

38 p. 24.5 cm. 14 plates.

1935

Bushnell, David I., Jr.

The Manahoac Tribes in Virginia, 1608. Washington, 1935.*

56 p. 24.5 cm. Printed wrappers. Plates.

Pollard, John G.

The Pamunkey Indians of Virginia. By John Garland Pollard, Governor of Virginia, 1930–1934. [Richmond, 1935.]*

12 p. 18 cm. Wrapper title.

A rare little volume, printed privately in a very small edition for the membership of the Pamunkey Tribe of Real Indians, a social organization. It contains a history of the tribe and the important "Laws of the Pamunkey Indian Town" adopted at the Pamunkey state reservation in 1887.

WAPPINGER INDIANS

1768

A Geographic, Historical Summary; or Narrative of the Present Controversy between the Wappinger Tribe of Indians, and the Claimants, under the Original Patentee of a Large Tract of Land in Philipse's Upper Patent, so called. Containing a Brief, but Faithful Account of the Proceedings thereon, from the First Rise of the Dispute, until the 12th day of March, Anno Domini, 1767. Hartford: Printed by Green & Watson, Opposite the Court-House. M,DCC,LXVIII.

56 p. 17.7 cm. Plain wrappers. Small engraved map.

A superlative rarity, and apparently the only copy known with the map, which is titled "Philips's Upper Patent," and which shows "The Lands in Controversy, and Indian Wigwams."

WASHINGTON TERRITORY INDIANS

1855

Acts of the Legislative Assembly of the Territory of Washington, passed at the Second Regular Session begun and held at Olympia December 4, 1854. Olympia: J. W. Wiley, 1855.

75 p. 20 cm.

Acts and resolutions relating to Indian affairs.

Statutes of the Territory of Washington: being the Code passed by the Legislative Assembly at their First Session begun and held at Olympia February 28th, 1854. Also, containing the Declaration of Independence, the Constitution of the United

States, the Organic Act of Washington Territory, the Donation Laws, &c., &c. Published by Authority. Olympia: Geo. B. Goudy, 1855.

488, [1], viii, lxviii p. 22 cm.

Contains provisions regarding the Indians. These are the first Washington territorial laws. This and the following seven volumes of laws and assembly journals are very rare.

1856

Acts of the Legislative Assembly of the Territory of Washington, passed at the Third Regular Session begun and held at Olympia December 3, 1855. Olympia: Geo. B. Goudy, 1856.

79 p. 20 cm.

Resolutions and memorials relating to Indian affairs and to Indian hostilities.

Journal of the House of Representatives of the Territory of Washington: together with the Memorials and Joint Resolutions of the Third Session of the Legislative Assembly, begun and held at Olympia, December 4th, 1855, and of the Independence of the United States, the eightieth, Olympia: Geo. B. Goudy, 1856.

255 p. 22 cm. Printed wrappers.

Important matter on Washington and Oregon Indian hostilities. Early Washington printing, and a rare volume.

1857

Journal of the House of Representatives of the Territory of Washington: Fourth Session of the Legislative Assembly, begun and held at Olympia, the Seat of Government, upon the first Monday of December, to-wit: the first day of December, Anno Domini, 1856. Olympia: Edward Furste, Public Printer, 1857.

163, cxxxiii p. 22.5 cm. Printed wrappers.

Laws of the Territory of Washington. Containing also the Joint Resolutions and Memorials passed at the Fourth Annual Session, begun and held at Olympia, December 1, 1856; and of the Independence of the United States the Eighty-second. Published by Authority. Olympia: Edward Fursts, Public Printer, 1857.

32, 95 p. 22 cm. Printed wrappers.

Resolutions and memorials relating to Indian hostilities.

1858

Acts of the Legislative Assembly of the Territory of Washington: passed at the Fifth Regular Session begun and held at Olympia December 7th, 1857. Olympia: Edward Furste, 1858.

106 p. 20 cm.

Important resolutions and memorials relating to Indian affairs.

1859

Acts of the Legislative Assembly of the Territory of Washington: passed at the Sixth Regular Session, begun and held at Olympia December 6th, 1858. Olympia: Edward Furste, 1859.

104 p. 20.5 cm.

Important resolutions and memorials relating to Indian affairs and to military roads through the Indian country.

1879

Howard, O. O.

Report of Brigadier General O. O. Howard, Brevet Major General, U.S. Army, commanding Department of the Columbia. September 10, 1879. Vancouver Barracks, W.T., 1879.

25, [1] p. 20 cm. Printed wrappers.

A fine copy. Rare.

1880

Howard, O. O.

Headquarters Department of the Columbia. In the Field, Spokan Falls, W.T., September 3, 1880. Special Field Orders No. 8. [Spokan Falls: Army Field Press, 1880.]

Broadside. 26.7 cm.

Provision for protection of the Spokan Indians from squatters. Unrecorded, and the only known copy.

1881

Miles, Nelson A.

Report of Brigadier General Nelson A. Miles, Brevet Major General, U.S. Army, commanding Department of the Columbia. 1881. Vancouver Barracks, Washington Territory, 1881.

[2], 4 p. 20 cm. Printed wrappers.

Rare.

1882

Miles, Nelson A.

Report of Brigadier General N. A. Miles, Brevet Major General, U.S. Army, commanding Department of the Columbia. 1882. Vancouver Barracks, Washington Territory, 1882.

7 p. 20.5 cm.

Rare.

1884

Miles, Nelson A.

Report of Brig. General N. A. Miles (Brevet Major General, U.S.A.) commanding the Department of the Columbia, 1884. Vancouver Barracks, Washington Territory, 1884.

8 p. 20 cm. Printed wrappers.

A fine copy. Rare.

1906

Lewis, Albert Buell

Tribes of the Columbia Valley and the Coast of Washington and Oregon. Lancaster, Pa., 1906.*

Pp. 147–209. 24.5 cm. Printed wrappers.

WEA INDIANS

1837

The Wea Primer, Wev mus nv kv ne, to Teach the Wea Language. Cherokee Nation: Mission Press: John F. Wheeler, Printer. 1837.

16 p. 11 cm.

The first sixteen pages only of the first and only book in the Wea Language and one of the rarest examples of printing in Indian Territory. The only known complete copy, which is in the Newberry Library at Chicago, extends to forty-eight pages. No other fragment, even, is known. [See page 392.]

1866

Yellow Beaver et al., representing the Wea Indians residing in Kansas, vs. The Board of Commissioners of the County of Miami, State of Kansas. In error to the Supreme Court of the State of Kansas. Opinion (of the United States Supreme Court.) [Washington, 1866.]*

2 p. 32 cm. Caption title.

The decision upheld the contention of the Wea Indians that their holdings were not taxable by the state of Kansas.

WICHITA INDIANS

1873

Agreement with Wichitas and other Indians. Letter from the Acting Secretary of the Interior, inclosing Articles of Agreement with the Wichitas and other Affiliated Tribes, granting them a Home in the Indian Territory, concluded in this City October 19, 1872. [Washington, 1873.]

3 p. 24.5 cm. Caption title.

WINNEBAGO INDIANS

1833

Mazzuchelli, Samuel Charles

Ocanagra aramee wawakakara (or Winnebago Prayer Book). Waiastanoeca, 1833. Geo. L. Whitney, Printer. Detroit, 1833.*

A fragment of four leaves, including the title page. The complete copy, of which only the Boston Athenaeum and New York Public Library examples are known, extends to eighteen pages. The first book in the Winnebago language, and the first book printed in any of the Siouan languages.

1839

Execution of Treaty with the Winnebagoes. Letter from the Secretary of War, transmitting Information in relation to the Execution of the Treaty of 1st November, 1837, with the Winnebago Indians. [Washington, 1839.]

112 p. 24.5 cm. Caption title.

A valuable document which sets forth an episode unusually scandalous even for the history of the frauds practiced upon the American Indians.

Hitchcock, Ethan Allen

Letter to the Hon. James Buchannan, of the Senate of the United States, on the Subject of the Document No. 229, Printed by Order of the House of Representatives, Feb. 1839, on the Execution of the Winnebago Treaty of 1837. By Maj. E. A. Hitchcock, United States Army. St. Louis: C. Keemle, 1839.

15 p. 23.5 cm.

One of only two known copies, the other being at the Newberry Library.

1840

Gaines, Edmund P.

Hd. Qr. Western Division, St. Louis, August 28th, 1840. Division Orders No. 4 [St. Louis, 1840.]

Broadside. 25.5 cm.

Deals largely with the troubles with the Winnebagoes brought about by the illegal smuggling of liquor to that tribe. Unrecorded, and the only known copy.

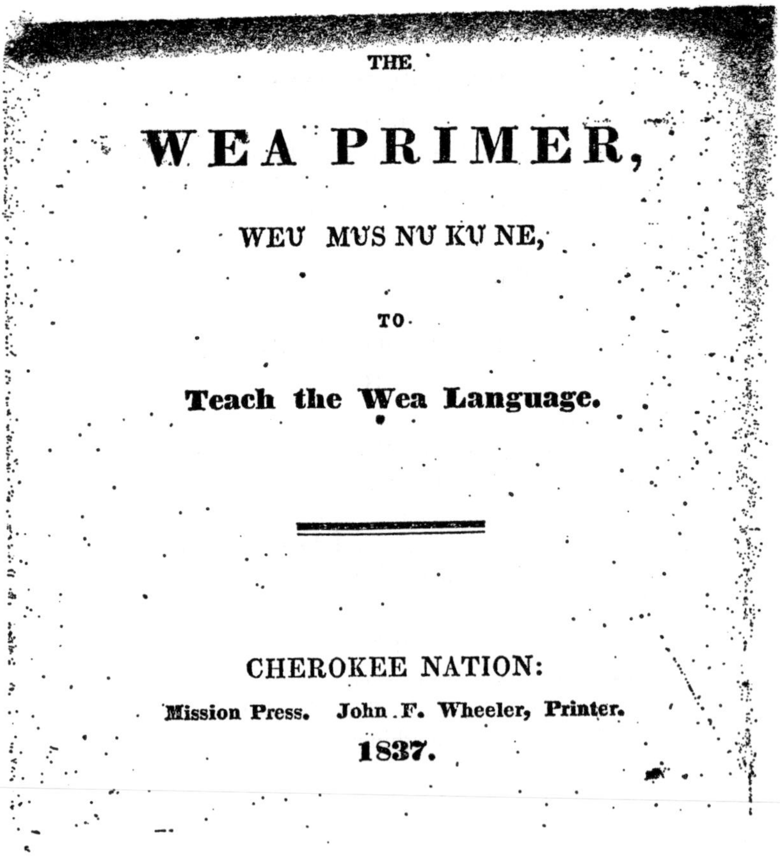
THE

WEA PRIMER,

WEU MUS NU KU NE,

TO

Teach the Wea Language.

CHEROKEE NATION:

Mission Press. John F. Wheeler, Printer.

1837.

1855

Weidman, John

Rejoinder to the Defence published by Simon Cameron, February 6th, 1855, to the Charges made against him as Commissioner to carry into effect the Treaty with the Half-breed Winnebago Indians; also, Public Document, No. 229, of House of Representatives of U.S., 25th Congress,—3d Session. To the Members of the Senate and House of Representatives of Pennsylvania, and all others whom it may concern. [N.p., 1855.]

xvi, 72 p. 22.5 cm. Printed wrappers.

A rare pamphlet not noted by Field.

1868

Laws and Regulations adopted by the Winnebago Tribe of Indians, in Council held at the Winnebago Agency, Nebraska, July 21st, A.D. 1868. Omaha: Daily Herald Book and Job Printing Establishment, 1868.

6 p. 21 cm.

One of but two known copies of the only printed laws of the Winnebago Indians. A volume of superlative importance.

1884

Lee, H. W.

The Winnebago Indians of Wisconsin. Application for Relief. [Stevens Point, Wiscon., 1884.]

Broadside. Folio.

A presentation of Winnebago grievances. No other copy can be traced.

WYANDOT INDIANS

1815

Message from the President of the United States transmitting Copies of Two Ratified Treaties entered into on the part of the United States; one on the twenty-second of July, 1814, with the several Tribes of Indians called Wyandots, Delawares, Shawnees, Senekas, and Miamis; the other on the ninth of August, 1814, with the Creek Nation of Indians. Washington: A. & G. Way, 1815.

12 p. 23 cm.

Important, and very rare.

WYOMING INDIANS

1870

General Laws, Memorials and Resolutions of the Territory of Wyoming, passed at the First Session of the Legislative Assembly, convened at Cheyenne, October 12th, 1869, and adjourned sine die December 11th, 1869, to which are prefixed the Declaration of Independence, Constitution of the United States, and the Act Organizing the Territory, together with Executive Proclamations. Published by Authority. Cheyenne, W.T.: S. Allan Bristol, 1870.

xvi, 784 p. 22.5 cm.

Contains highly important memorials and resolutions relating to Indian affairs, and an early description of the Territory. These are the first Wyoming laws. The volume is very rare.

1886

The Chinese Massacre at Rock Springs, Wyoming Territory, September 2, 1885. Boston: Franklin Press: Rand, Avery & Co., 1886.

92 p. 23 cm. Printed wrappers.

INDEX

The paper on which this book is printed bears the watermark of the University of Oklahoma Press and has an effective life of at least three hundred years.